D0744543

Bettina Brentano-von Arnim

Kritik:
German Literary Theory and
Cultural Studies

Liliane Weissberg, Editor

*A complete listing of the books
in this series
can be found at the
back of this volume.*

Bettina Brentano-von Arnim

GENDER AND POLITICS

Edited by
Elke P. Frederiksen and
Katherine R. Goodman

Wayne State University   Detroit

Copyright © 1995 by Wayne State University Press,
Detroit, Michigan 48201. All rights are reserved.
No part of this book may be reproduced without formal
permission.
Manufactured in the United States of America.
99 98 97 96 95   5 4 3 2 1

Library of Congress Cataloging-in-Publication Data

Bettina Brentano-von Arnim : gender and politics / edited by Elke P.
   Frederiksen and Katherine R. Goodman.
      p. cm.—(Kritik)
   Includes bibliographical references and index.
   ISBN 0-8143-2516-5
   1. Arnim, Bettina, 1785–1859—Political and social views.
   2. Arnim, Bettina, 1785–1859—Knowledge—Language and languages.
   I. Frederiksen, Elke. II. Goodman, Katherine, 1945–   .
   III. Series.
   PT1808.A4B38   1995
   838'.709—dc20   94-22975

Designer: Mary Primeau

Special Acknowledgment: "Your Next Life Begins Today: A
Letter about Bettine" from THE AUTHOR'S
DIMENSION: SELECTED ESSAYS by Christa Wolf,
translated by Jan Van Heurck. Reprinted by permission of
Farrar, Straus & Giroux, Inc.

To Christa Wolf

CONTENTS

ACKNOWLEDGMENTS

The idea for this volume dates back to an MLA conference session entitled "Bettina von Arnim in Social, Historical, and Literary Contexts" which Elke Frederiksen co-chaired in 1985 with Ruth Ellen Boetcher Joeres (University of Minnesota). Both editors would like to thank Professor Joeres for her advice in the initial stages of the book. We gratefully acknowledge the assistance of the following libraries in obtaining illustrations and documentary materials: Freies Deutsches Hochstift, Frankfurt/Main; Märkisches Museum, Berlin; The Pierpont Morgan Library, New York; Bildarchiv Preußischer Kulturbesitz, Berlin; Stiftung Weimarer Klassik, Weimar. We are grateful to Farrar, Straus and Giroux, Inc. for permission to reprint Christa Wolf's essay. Our special thanks go to Liliane Weissberg, University of Pennsylvania, and editor of the "Kritik: German Literary Theory and Cultural Studies" series for her many helpful suggestions, and to Arthur Evans for his friendly, patient advice in guiding the manuscript through the various stages of publication.

I

Introduction

"Locating"[1] Bettina Brentano-von Arnim, A Nineteenth Century German Woman Writer

Elke P. Frederiksen and Katherine R. Goodman

Today Bettina Brentano-von Arnim[2] (1785–1859) is undoubtedly one of the best-known women writers in German literature. This has not always been so. She came to public attention through her first literary work, the autobiographical epistolary novel *Goethe's Correspondence with a Child* (Goethes Briefwechsel mit einem Kinde) in 1835. She was fifty years old when she published this book and, until then, had been known among her family and within elite intellectual circles only as the sister of one Romantic poet (Clemens Brentano, 1778–1842) and the wife of another (Achim von Arnim, 1781–1831). The controversy that greeted her first literary endeavor did not subside with her later works. She was never a comfortable author, and at best she was known as an emotional and naive admirer of Goethe's genius.

In the main it has been German feminists today who have revived interest in Bettina Brentano-von Arnim. For about a decade now her works have been eagerly re-discovered, re-read, and re-interpreted. New editions have appeared, in Munich and in Weimar. Several books about her have recently been published in Germany,[3] and dissertations are appearing in both Germany and the United States. German feminists are celebrating a vibrant and provocative Bettina Brentano-von Arnim. In the process the critical focus has shifted, and the image of an emotional and naive admirer of Goethe has given way

13

to one of a politically and socially aware poetic talent, an author who developed narrative strategies anticipating much of our feminist thinking today.

English-speaking readers have not had access to this brilliant and colorful personality. Nineteenth-century English translations of two of her books are usually buried deep in dusty library stacks. There have been a few new translations of excerpts and shorter texts, but no new translations of her books, and there is only one monograph on Bettina Brentano-von Arnim in English.[4]

This volume is an introduction to the complexities and multifaceted character of this unusual author. It is the first collection of critical essays in English, which presents new readings of better known texts by Brentano-von Arnim, such as *Goethe's Correspondence with a Child* (Goethes Briefwechsel mit einem Kinde) (1835), *Günderode* (Die Günderode) (1840), and *Clemens Brentano's Spring Wreath* (Clemens Brentanos Frühlingskranz) (1844). More importantly, our volume also concentrates on the author's later writings (e.g., *Conversations with Demons* [Gespräche mit Dämonen] [1852]; the *Poor Book* [Armenbuch] [1844?; published in 1962]) which have been neglected by most critics up to now, and which present her as a female author deeply engaged in the political and social events of her time. Bettina Brentano-von Arnim raises a multitude of issues concerning gender, anti-semitism, social inequity, female bonding, women and traditional literary genres, women and language, women and music, women and religion, women and nature, and women and utopia. Contemporary readers are quite familiar with these issues, but they will probably be surprised at the provocative and modernist treatments she gives them.

1. Biographical Background

Bettina Brentano was born in Frankfurt am Main on April 4, 1785, as the seventh child of the upper middle-class merchant family Brentano. She lost her mother Maximiliane von La Roche, daughter of the well-known writer Sophie von La Roche (1730–1807) and a close friend of Goethe, when she was eight. The four years she subsequently spent in the Ursuline Convent near Fritzlar left many pleasant memories, which found entry into her literary texts (part 3 of her *Goethe Book*, *Günderode*, *The Spring Wreath*, and *Gritta* [Das Leben der Hochgräfin

Gritta von Rattenzuhausbeiuns]). In 1797, after her father's death, she had to leave the convent and moved back to Frankfurt to live with her older half-brother and his wife and then with her grandmother La Roche in Offenbach. It was here that she met famous literary and political figures of the time and, above all, was exposed to the ideas of the French Revolution. In particular, she was fascinated by the writings of the French revolutionary Comte de Mirabeau (1749–1791), which she read and discussed with her grandmother.

And it was also here that she came much closer to her older brother Clemens, who returned home between semesters at the University of Halle in 1797. He opened new horizons for his young sister, who knew little about developments in the literature of the time. He introduced her to Goethe's writing by reading her his novel *Wilhelm Meister's Apprenticeship* (Wilhelm Meisters Lehrjahre) (1795/96). Their ensuing correspondence from 1801 to 1803 portrays a close, if problematic, relationship between brother and sister. Many years later, after her brother's death, Brentano-von Arnim wove this, the earliest of her actual correspondences, into the third and last of her autobiographical epistolary novels, *The Spring Wreath* (1844).

Of equal importance for the young Bettina Brentano was her friendship with the poet Karoline von Günderrode[5] (1780–1806), which lasted from 1802 until 1806. Günderrode lived a quiet life in a Protestant convent for impoverished women of noble birth in Frankfurt, and she welcomed the close friendship with the younger, livelier Bettina Brentano and her family. The few existing letters of their actual correspondence provide insight into the intense intellectual exchange between the two women. Günderrode, in particular, suffered from the restrictions placed on her as a woman and a female writer in early nineteenth-century German society. Using the pseudonym Tian, Günderrode published two volumes consisting mostly of poetry during the years of her friendship with Bettina Brentano. The frustrations of trying to reach the ultimate in her writings and in her personal life (she had fallen in love with a married man) eventually destroyed this gifted writer when she was only 26 years old. She committed suicide in July 1806. Many years later, Bettina Brentano-von Arnim immortalized her friend in the epistolary novel *Günderode* (1840), again integrating actual correspondence into her second text of fictionalized letters.

In April of 1806, after her friendship with Günderrode had become strained, the twenty-one-year-old Bettina Brentano turned to Frau Rat Goethe, Goethe's seventy-five-year-old mother, who lived

Karoline von Günderrode (1780–1806). (From: Karoline von Günderode, *Gesammelte Dichtungen*, Mannheim, 1857. Photo by Ursula Edelmann.)

in Frankfurt. Her reasons appear to have been twofold. She had found her grandmother La Roche's correspondence with the young Goethe and was fascinated. Goethe's frequent admiring references to her mother Maximiliane were—at least in Bettina Brentano's eyes— signs of a "love relationship" which made the famous poet and "genius" a friend of her family. The second reason was loneliness and disappointment because Günderrode had broken off their friendship a month before she took her own life. During her frequent visits to Frau Rat, Bettina Brentano listened carefully and then wrote down the story of Goethe's mother and her famous son. Goethe himself later used parts of these notes for his own autobiography. Brentano-von Arnim immortalized Frau Rat in her novel *Dies Buch gehört dem König* (The King's Book) (1843) portraying her as a character with political initiative who is not afraid to express and defend her progressive ideas.

Her friendship with Frau Rat Goethe was to be important for Bettina Brentano in yet another unexpected way, for it led to her correspondence with the mother's famous son during the years 1807 to 1811. These letters would form the core of Bettina Brentano-von Arnim's first (and to date most famous) autobiographical epistolary novel, the so-called *Goethe Book* (Goethes Briefwechsel mit einem Kinde) (1835). But she did not write the book until after her husband Achim von Arnim died in 1831.

Bettina Brentano had first met her brother's friend, Achim von Arnim (1781–1831), in 1802. Like Clemens Brentano, he was a poet, and the two young Romantics collaborated on a collection of modified German folksongs, *Des Knaben Wunderhorn* (1805 and 1808). Achim von Arnim and the as yet unliterary Bettina Brentano were married in 1811. She bore seven children who consumed much of her time during her married life. Even so, she spent a large part of those years in Berlin, the most lively cultural center in Germany at the time, while Achim von Arnim spent much of his time alone on his Wiepersdorf estate in rural Brandenburg. She had been quite unhappy there and much preferred living in Berlin, where her salon eventually became a cultural institution and she something of a celebrity. Even though husband and wife did not see each other that often and Bettina Brentano-von Arnim essentially raised the children by herself, their marriage seems to have been a loving one. Interestingly enough she never dedicated a book to her husband; instead we have an extensive correspondence between Bettina and Achim von Arnim which was not published until 1961. This correspondence, ranging from March 11, 1811, (the morning of their wedding) to January 18, 1831, (three days before Arnim died), is testimony to a complex, and at times strained, yet close love relationship.

Four years after her husband's death Bettina Brentano-von Arnim scandalized the literary world with her publication of the *Goethe Book*.

Bettina Brentano-von Arnim's apartment, Berlin, In den Zelten.
Watercolor by M. Hoffmann. (Märkisches Museum, Berlin.)

It was undoubtedly her famous subject (Goethe had been dead for only
two years) that ensured the book's success. This text is based on her
actual correspondence with Goethe from 1807 to 1811. Until recently,
critics were concerned primarily with the "inaccuracy" of the Goethe
letters in the novel, not realizing that the deviation from the original
correspondence is intentional and very much part of Brentano-von
Arnim's aesthetic concept. A comparison with the actual correspondence shows that her text has indeed little in common with it; the book
is almost ten times longer, and her rewritten letters are much more
passionate than the originals. Bettine (the fictional character in the
book) is obviously seeking Goethe's admiration and affection; she
wants to be his muse, his prophetess, and she seeks a spiritual union

with him, but at the same time, he becomes *her* muse. It is as much a book about Bettina Brentano-von Arnim herself as it is about Goethe. The two other epistolary novels, *Günderode* and *The Spring Wreath*, followed in 1840 and 1844, respectively. Brentano-von Arnim had created these works in a similar fashion, and they, too, are as much about her own persona as about the correspondents portrayed. In the turbulent mid-1840s, after the publication of these three auto-biographical epistolary novels, the author turned increasingly to the political and social issues of her day. Her conversational novels, *The King's Book* (Dies Buch gehört dem König) and *Conversations with Demons* (Gespräche mit Dämonen. Des Königsbuch zweiter Band) were published in 1843 and 1852. Much less known than her first publication, these later novels give evidence of her versatility as a writer. *The King's Book* in particular shows her as a politically and socially involved author who is deeply concerned about the poor and the politically persecuted, and who strongly criticizes the social conditions of her time, for which she blames the state. The author addresses this book to the king, Friedrich Wilhelm IV, who was a disappointment to her and many of her contemporaries because he did not fulfill their hopes for political and social reforms when he became king in 1840. Brentano-von Arnim wants him to be the *Volkskönig* (King of the People) who will live up to his promises. Interestingly enough, a woman (the fictional creation of Goethe's mother Frau Rat) takes the political initiative by expressing and defending her progressive ideas in discussions with the mayor and a minister. The author focuses on a multitude of contemporary issues: German unity, censorship and intellectual imprisonment, the educational system, the oppression of minorities (in particular the Jews), and economic problems amidst increasing industrialization.

Of note in this context is also Brentano-von Arnim's attempt to document the miserable living conditions of the working class (e.g., the weavers in Silesia). She had collected interviews and lists of the poor, describing their plight, which she intended to publish but never did. (We shall discuss the reasons later.) The text appeared in 1962 under the title *Poor Book* (Das Armenbuch) and is nevertheless, in its present fragmentary form, an important collection of essays and documents providing information about socio-historical developments in Prussia and Germany. It contains pre-revolutionary ideas and suggestions for social reform which go far beyond its time. The book differs from most works of the period that describe the suffering of the poor in its realistic, practical approach. It includes statistics on workers, listing their income, their living expenses, the taxes they had to pay, and the illnesses they suffered to provide a most moving story of the misery of the poor.

The second of the *King's Books*, (Conversations with Demons), appeared four years after the failed 1848 revolution, which shattered Germany's hope for a democracy. The author could not hide her resignation in this text, although her fundamental beliefs remained the same. This last of Brentano-von Arnim's major works is the most complex and least understood of all. The author, as Demon, seeks the ear of the "sleeping king," still trying to enlighten him, to press him for reforms, to open his thoughts to democratic ideals and the family of nations. Jews and Muslims, Poles and Hungarians, German political prisoners: all become the concern and cause of Brentano-von Arnim's rhapsodies. This complex, untimely book found little resonance in 1852.

In 1853 Brentano-von Arnim began the edition of her collected works that filled eleven volumes. She lived the remaining years of her life in declining health, largely in family circles, but still with enough energy, grace, and mobility of expression to impress people she met for the first time. Bettina Brentano-von Arnim died in the night of January 19/20, 1859. She was buried in the family cemetery in Wiepersdorf.

2. Cultural Affinities

The first of our contemporaries to "re-discover" Bettina Brentano-von Arnim was the West German author Ingeborg Drewitz, whose 1969 biography cleared the way of much misinformation.[6] But it was the well-known contemporary East German writer Christa Wolf's (b.1929)[7] essay "Your Next Life Begins Today: A Letter about Bettine" ("Nun ja! Das nächste Leben geht aber heute an. Ein Brief über die Bettine," 1979), the afterword to the reissue of Bettina Brentano-von Arnim's epistolary novel *Günderode* (Die Günderode), which clearly established the two poles of our current theme, gender and politics. In Wolf's reading of Brentano- von Arnim's life gender plays a prominent role as the locus of political struggle. She writes of the difference between men and women and "of the way the experience and perspective of women have been systematically and fallaciously assimilated into the generic masculine, and of the need to correct this error."[8] In the case of both writers the politics of repressive societies, including censorship, affected their ability to publish. Of necessity Wolf's allusions to her own situation are anything but explicit. But for Wolf, as well as for Brentano-von Arnim, writing and reading were part of the political struggle—a vital component of interpreting the world in order to change it.[9]

Since Christa Wolf's essay on Bettina Brentano-von Arnim is also a subtle and sensitive biographical representation of the forgotten author, intended as an introduction for Wolf's contemporaries in East and West Germany today, it is quite fitting that we open with it. It will provide American readers as well with the necessary context for a better understanding of Bettina Brentano-von Arnim's life and the complexities of her writings.

Wolf's intricate text offers multilayered reflections of the author, Christa Wolf, on densely interwoven biographical and literary aspects of the life and works of Bettina Brentano-von Arnim. Wolf considers the relationship between Brentano-von Arnim and Karoline von Günderrode; she discusses the form of the epistolary novel; and she explores the inner (emotional) and outer (political-historical) situation of Brentano-von Arnim in the 1830s. From her vantage point (in a late-industrial, socialist society in the 1970s), Wolf relates episodes in the lives of both authors from the early phases of industrialized society in the nineteenth century. She both *locates* Brentano-von Arnim in the historical context of the rebellious movements of the 1830s and 1840s (Young Germany and *Vormärz*, respectively) and *constructs* a personal and political affinity between Brentano-von Arnim, Günderrode, and herself: as women, as citizens, as authors. For Christa Wolf, biography, authorship, literary text, history, and politics can only be understood in their mutual connections.

The political message of this essay on Bettina Brentano-von Arnim is strong. We know that Wolf wrote this epistolary afterword in December, 1979, barely one month after she had begun the story *What Remains* (Was bleibt), revised and published only in the summer of 1990, shortly before the unification of the two Germanies. *What Remains* relates the story of Wolf's surveillance by the Security Service of the German Democratic Republic (which existed from 1949 to 1990).[10] No doubt, this surveillance was occasioned in part by her semi-fictive autobiographical book *Patterns of Childhood* (Kindheitsmuster, 1979) in which certain fascist sentiments in her own society become visible.

The form of *Patterns of Childhood*—the intermingling of time frames, the overlay of personalities, the blurring of reality and fiction—as well as Wolf's own situation in an authoritarian society (the German Democratic Republic) all evoke the writing and life of Bettina Brentano-von Arnim in an early-nineteenth-century patriarchal Prussian society. Indeed, reading Wolf's essay on Brentano-von Arnim is also an exercise in reading about writing in the former German Democratic Republic, reading about politics and gender. In a sense, this is the kind of reading one learns by reading Bettina Brentano-von Arnim: the reader constructs more than one story as he or she reads. The affinity apparent in Wolf's reception of Brentano-von Arnim has several dimensions, some of which bring us to the most immediate past. While an exploration of the controversy surrounding the story *What Remains* belongs elsewhere,[11] it may still be possible to note that, at a time when one patriarchy is succeeding another and when it is not at all clear that women in the former German Democratic Republic have not lost things in the exchange, it is quite appropriate to recall this tradition of political struggle by women who have reflected profoundly on the experience of multiple oppressions.

3. Gender and Politics/Politics and Gender

Whereas Christa Wolf's essay provides the introduction to Bettina Brentano-von Arnim's complex life and texts within the context of gender and politics as the theme of our book, the second and third parts of this volume discuss Bettina Brentano-von Arnim's gendered and political responses to her society in more detail. For an author like Brentano-von Arnim these terms cannot be isolated. Therefore, while chapters in the second part place emphasis on issues of gender, and those in the third part accentuate issues of politics, all address the complex issues around these two terms.

If, despite affinities, we needed to be reminded of the differences in historical situations, then Lorely French begins by placing Brentano-von Arnim squarely in the context of mid-nineteenth-century women activists such as Louise Aston (1814-1871), Mathilde Franziska Anneke (1817–1884), Emma Herwegh (1817–1904), and Fanny Lewald (1811–1889). The gender constructions under which they labored provoked political responses in epistolary form. The epistolary structure of many of Brentano-von Arnim's works has been linked to the long

Wilhelm and Jacob Grimm. (Freies Deutsches Hochstift. Photo by Ursula Edelmann.)

tradition of women's epistolary writing, in Germany and in other countries.[12] Such a tradition included actual correspondence, epistolary novels, and epistolary autobiography. But French shows us that women used this epistolary tradition to engage in political discourse, and she examines Brentano-von Arnim's strategy of epistolary intervention at various political junctures. Her efforts on behalf of the Grimm brothers are but one example.

Even as she participated in epistolary politics, Brentano-von Arnim was engaged in constructing epistolary relationships in her published literary works. But Brentano-von Arnim's technique in this genre remains unique. As mentioned previously in this introduction, she re-*created* physically existing correspondence she had maintained with various people as much as 30 years earlier (e.g., Goethe, Karoline von Günderrode, Clemens Brentano). These correspondences are to be taken as true only on the subjective level, and this has given scholars much difficulty. The roles in which Brentano-von Arnim placed her correspondents were ones that were necessary for her own development. She portrays her individual coming-to-herself relationally. Examining the Psyche myth in Bettina Brentano-von Arnim's works, Monika Shafi studies the subtle ways in which the author was able to draw on these "correspondences" for her own growth, and ultimately for her own interactions with the world.

All of Brentano-von Arnim's works are thus subjective in the extreme, but in a manner radically different from our usual understanding. They are subjective in a way that binds her inextricably to the objective world around her, to her "correspondents" and to physical reality. The growth of portions of her identity are bound to the discovery of persons who permit her to evolve in those directions. The limitations of social constructions therefore place limits on her own subjectivity. But she is also able to echo or mirror (two favorite words) undeveloped aspects of her "correspondents"—indeed, if she herself is to develop, she is bound to. The dependence of any individual subject for its evolution on the social conglomerate makes us all responsible in a way that is at once concrete and immediate. Words and actions always exist in a social context, even when it is claimed they do not. In this case, awareness of subjective dependence on social constructions does not imply fatalism or determinism. It induces rather a dynamic and active response to "reality."

Brentano-von Arnim's acute insights into the "reality" of social constructions necessarily have ramifications for her views on gender. Here, as Katherine R. Goodman demonstrates, Brentano-von Arnim revolts against any a priori limitations on particular biological entities and seeks to dismantle the very categories on which notions of gender rest. Unlike those of her contemporaries such as Goethe, Schiller, and Friedrich and August Wilhelm Schlegel, Brentano-von Arnim's views on gender do not rely on Romantic understandings of the complemental nature of gender or on the idealization or re-valuation of virtues thought to be "feminine." Rather, she dismantles dichotomistic definitions of reality. To be sure, as Lorely French has shown us, the awareness of the force of these social constructions does not free her from the ambivalence of wrestling as a woman with the real social pressures inspired by those constructions, but Brentano-von Arnim's understanding of her own more complex identity obliges her to engage in activities traditionally thought to be the prerogative of men. That they are thought to be masculine, however, is shown to be the perspective of her culture and not her own. Moreover, while she manipulated certain conventions to her advantage, there is no evidence that *she* considered the form in which she engaged in politics to be a priori "feminine."

What emerges as the author's dynamically pantheistic view of the world is one aspect of her work that stirred the most controversy in her own time, at least among pastors. It is also that quality of her work which drew her into political debates of her day and to which the rebellious Young Hegelians in particular were drawn. Heinz Härtl elaborates these long neglected connections. Brentano-von Arnim not only felt herself to be engaged in political activity, her contemporaries clearly understood her that way, too. She was admired and acclaimed, privately and publicly, by the Young Hegelians and denounced by conservative theologians. The reasons were clear. For instance, in her vision of a connected social context she formulated the thought that the state was the cause of criminal activity. Indeed, this connection may be telling. For, as repeatedly becomes clear, Brentano-von Arnim associated herself with no identifiable feminist and/or political movement. In attempting to label the form of her political activities we encounter linguistic barriers. Her activities might be called individualistic, were it not for the extremely unindividualistic way in which she formulated notions of identity. In any case they might be said to be twofold: on the one hand her published works, on the other her personal, epistolary interventions of the sort identified by French. Only her work on the unpublished *Poor Book* (Armenbuch) seems to fall outside these forms.

However, it is not only the form of her political engagement, it is also the content that falls outside what have become traditional categories. The ways in which her approach to issues of class and race differ from "classical" political movements are just as unconventional as her approach to gender. Her primary concern does not seem to have been integration into a political system. She does not plead for political rights, either passive or active ones (namely the rights to vote or to hold office). Nor is it a simple matter of economic welfare for her. It is a different kind of integration for which she seems to strive, one which we are tempted to say is more fundamental, since it appears to be more inclusive. It might be called social integration.

Given the traditions of political thought in Western culture, today such seemingly vague and abstract views might not be regarded as very progressive, or even realistic. Nevertheless, it must be clear that the textual examples of political activity Bettina Brentano-von Arnim gives us are not abstract. They are immediate, direct, and concrete. They entail and require the most personal kind of intervention and engagement, and they represent a constant challenge to daily thought and action. Examples involving class and race are appropriate.

The text concerning class (*The Lucky Purse* [Erzählung vom Heckebeutel]) that is included in our discussion here derives from a larger project intended to represent the plight of the poor to the authorities. In May 1844 Brentano-von Arnim had placed an advertisement in the newspaper requesting reports from all over the German states on the situation of the poor. She had collected newspaper articles and lists of the poor describing their particular circumstances. Her plan, so it seems, was to publish the lists with an afterword. In June the Silesian weavers rioted. One weaver, with whom she had spoken, was shot. According to reports Brentano-von Arnim was beside herself. She proposed that the funds for a new cathedral in Berlin be used to construct housing for the weavers. She dropped plans for her book, which would not have passed the censor. But because her plan had been so public and information had been collected, she was also accused of inspiring the riots.

Among the papers pertaining to this event the story of *The Lucky Purse* was found. It probably dates from 1845, but it was published in 1962. It is not only Brentano-von Arnim's political views, but also her literary style that establish her direct connection to the revolutionary writers of the German Vormärz (pre-1848) like Heinrich Heine (1797–1856). Birgit Ebert shows us that even in this text, which is not epistolary and which on the surface bears so much resemblance to one of her brother's Romantic texts,[13] Brentano-von Arnim's distinctive treatment of similar motifs results in a more dialogic and action-oriented text. The open-ended story allows the traditional figure of the old woman of the people her own dignity and integrity. Unlike Clemens Brentano's text in which narration is completed with death, Bettina Brentano-von Arnim's old woman continues her efforts to sustain life. The text illustrates Brentano-von Arnim's tendency not to write *on* or *about* anything or anyone, without writing herself into the relationship. This is less an egoistic trait than a sign of moral responsibility, since it does not objectify the subject or establish a distance between subject and author. From her perspective, it might be more appropriate to say: she does not write herself out of the relationship. In this sense it is not a text that disengages—and disobliges—the author. It is not academic; Bettina Brentano-von Arnim always writes in media res.

The treatment of the so-called Jewish question in a late Brentano-von Arnim text makes it clear that her experience of political questions borders on the inexpressible. As with the issues of gender and class we are once again thrown into the midst of one of the most controversial topics of her day; again we see her take a thoroughly unique position, one which even puts her at odds with those Young Hegelians, like Bruno Bauer, with whom she sympathized on other issues. It is, as Claire Baldwin shows us, Brentano-von Arnim's pantheistic understanding of nature and her relationship to it that organizes her political perceptions. This non-dualistic philosophy had also enabled her to distance herself from the usually gendered conceptions of society. The author's refusal to accept normal boundaries and definitions and simplistic dichotomies—traditional cultural constructions—is precisely what renders her "speechless" in the ordinary sense of the word. As Baldwin illustrates, Brentano von-Arnim is forced to rely on both her own poetic talents and a non-linguistic form of expression (music) in order to do justice to reality. In this context Brentano-von Arnim's theorizing about the origins of language and music exhibits its political significance.

4. Translating Experience

Theorizing about language and music are so fundamental to Brentano von-Arnim's literary and political actions that we devoted the fourth part of this book to her understanding of the translation of experience.

Contemporary feminist debates, here and in Germany, tend to polarize around post-structural theory on the one hand and political theory on the other. One position appears to emphasize cultural constructions of reality, the other the reality of cultural constructions. Is gender exclusively a social construct, and is it therefore impossible to say that we experience reality, but rather only articulate cultural conceptualizations of it? Or is it possible that the very real experience of sexual domination builds resistence to social constructions of gender in some women, who then work to undermine them? With the appropriation of our culture do we all possess and exercize the oppressive power of that culture? Or is there a direction to social oppression? In

truth, of course, the lines are not so clearly drawn and few con-
structivists or realists claim the concerns of the others are irrelevant
to their own.[14]

At the core of the dispute lies the validity of terms like subjective
experience and historical agency. If human beings are not fully defined by social constructions, how and where does one begin to locate
what eludes those constructions? Is there human experience prior to
social constructions of it, experience which can form the core of
alternative visions and the motivation for alternative action? What
might the nature of such experience be?

These questions of enormous import have not been invented exclusively in our time, and we hope to inject the writings and the life of our
nineteenth-century author into the contemporary discussion of them.
Brentano-von Arnim's rhapsodic prose will surely not resolve these
questions to any contemporary philosopher's satisfaction. At least
three reasons come to mind. In the first place, it is not clear that
theoretical issues ever get "resolved." In the second place, Brentano-
von Arnim lived in a far different time and place and responded to the
problems she encountered with historical specificity. Nineteenth-
century Prussia was an agrarian-based monarchy consisting of hun-
dreds of separate political entities. The "German nation" existed in
theory only. This period also witnessed the rapid ascendency of bourgeois culture and industrialization. Bettina Brentano-von Arnim was a
near contemporary of Karl Marx (1818–1883) and, like him, was both
heir to the idealist Romantic philosophy at the beginning of the nineteenth century and active participant in *realizing* the critical impulses
of that philosophy. Although she shared certain cultural critiques with
Marx, she formed her own gender-related responses. Her responses,
because of their "eccentric" forms, have not yet been fully appreciated
in their political depth. Thus, despite affinities between her situation
and ours today, her responses remain rooted in nineteenth-century
thinking.

In the third place, Bettina Brentano-von Arnim refused to be an
analytical, rational writer; in fact, she explicitly eschewed this kind of
thinking (whether in philosophy or history). The analytical consis-
tency implicit in her writing, however, may throw a different light on
current debates, challenging us to rethink our categories of subjectivity and experience—precisely those categories of central concern in
our theoretical difficulties. These are key to any theoretical approach
to the social interaction of gender and politics.

Brentano-von Arnim's rhapsodies on poetry and music occur

throughout her works, and the pantheistic perspective organizes her thoughts on these twin vehicles for the translation of experience. Patricia Anne Simpson examines Brentano-von Arnim's speculation about language, poetry, and nature in a work that precedes the author's first explicitly political foray, *Günderode*. In this work, more than any other, Brentano-von Arnim grapples with the relationship of epistemology and rhetoric, thought and expression. For the poet Karoline von Günderrode no thought for which there is not already poetic expression should be thought; for Brentano-von Arnim thought precedes expression. As a Romantic the latter understand poetry as an originary act of creation in imitation of the divinity, and nature as the inimitable model of divine expression.

That Brentano-von Arnim's views on language seem to rest on some originary notion of experience might seem to contradict our understanding of her incisive awareness of the constructedness of social relationships. It need not, or at least the answer is not as clear as it may seem. In this respect the English language itself is missing a term. In German there are two words for "experience" (*Erlebnis* and *Erfahrung*), and the distinction merits our consideration. It is one that is actively upheld, even today. In a recent interview Christa Wolf made the distinction as clearly as it can be made. When Wolf was asked what was biographical in her texts, Bettina Brentano-von Arnim might well have provided the same response. Wolf differentiated between "the material that life brings you, often forces on you" ("den Stoff, den das Leben einem zugeführt, oft aufgezwungen hat") and "that mysterious process, which cannot be marveled at enough, which makes an 'Erlebnis' into an 'Erfahrung.' " ("jenen geheimnisvollen, nicht genug zu bestaunenden Vorgang, der aus einem Erlebnis erst eine Erfahrung macht.")[15] In connection with her book *Patterns of Childhood* Wolf then noted: "In the meantime my childhood has changed within me, it is becoming more complicated, also more powerful and more definite; I don't even know if I would be capable of describing it today." ("Meine Kindheit hat sich in mir inzwischen weiter verändert, sie wird komplizierter, auch mächtiger und bestimmender, ich weiß gar nicht, ob ich der Aufgabe, sie zu beschreiben, heute noch gewachsen wäre.")[16] In this sense the originary experience (Erlebnis) may remain the same, but its interpretation or translation into experience (Erfahrung) varies. It is the second that may be historically or culturally structured. If we uphold this linguistic distinction in the case of Bettina Brentano-von Arnim, then the apparent contradiction need not be a real one.

Immediately prior to the publication of the book most concerned with poetry, *Günderode*, Brentano-von Arnim had been working on an English translation of *Goethe's Correspondence with a Child*. Although the text of the *Goethe Book* makes it clear that she was already interested in poetry as a means for expressing the inexpressible, her work on the translation provides important insights into her thoughts on language. Marjanne Goozé situates these thoughts in the context of German Romantic theories of language and translation. Since the act of translation illuminates the structures of language as language, this process becomes an arena for working out Brentano-von Arnim's speculations. All language is seen as a translation. Her goal, as a non-versifying poet, is to imitate the creative power of the language of the divinity. It is not the semantic content of a sentence that carries meaning, but its melody and rhythm. Certainly her experiments with English are nothing if not original.

Once again we are confronted with the importance of the expressive power of music for Brentano-von Arnim, for musical analogies to poetry pervade her writing. Once again we are pushed to the limits of linguistic expression, and music acquires central significance in her understanding of epistemology. In and of itself this is not an unusual component of German Romantic thought, but the details of Brentano-von Arnim's perspective are unique and challenge the traditional form of music. Ann Willison surveys not only the author's views on music, but some of her efforts at composition. Brentano-von Arnim had studied composition for several years in her youth and published some of her songs in her husband's works. Willison describes how Brentano-von Arnim's initial frustration with a *Generalbass,* or harmony, yielded to a conviction that this cultural convention also inhibited the production of music. In particular she favored the composition of writing *Lieder*. The musical support for the melody of the words suggests the ways in which she understood this art form to be an extension of language beyond its natural limitations. Baldwin and Goozé have suggested this, but it only becomes absolutely clear when we are confronted with her compositions.

As abstract as Brentano-von Arnim's theories of language and music may seem, these compositions were also sometimes placed in the service of concrete political or social goals of some personal immediacy: the dedication of the songbook to the prisoner Spontini, or the composition of songs for the benefit of widows and orphans in the Greek war for independence. The essential connectedness of all human enterprises is not only a theme in Brentano-von Arnim's books. When she wrote of *Lebensmelodien* (life's melodies) and meant everyday events, she created a metaphor for this sense of pantheistic wholeness. Her philosophical concerns with the restrictions of cultural constructions did not conflict with her immediate concerns for those around her. Rather, they were an integral part of her daily functioning as a political being.

5. Defying the Canon: Cultural Incompatibilities

In the final part of this book Marjanne Goozé returns to the question of why this remarkable author has not been canonized. She details the history of misunderstandings, misprisions, and misconstructions, which often reveal more about the readers and critics than the author. In this review of the problematic reception of Brentano-von Arnim's writings, Goozé shows clearly that the long, but sparse tradition of scholarship on Bettina Brentano-von Arnim has been plagued by its desire—and inability —to distinguish between "reality" and "fiction," for instance in her treatment of the various correspondences. Some have been incensed by her refusal to uphold normal distinctions, others have (too) easily taken her fiction for reality. But if there is anything Bettina Brentano-von Arnim knew, it was the *reality* of the spirit/mind (*Geist*). By taking this essentially Romantic concept more literally than any of its other exponents, she made herself virtually uncanonizable. In particular, until recently that scholarly confusion has obfuscated her political understanding. Reality (language, social conventions, and social categories) structures our subjectivity, but conversely, reality, including the structure of gender, is constructed by minds—and can be changed by them.

Notes

1. The title of our introduction was inspired by the introduction in *Responses to Christa Wolf. Critical Essays,* ed. Marilyn Sibley Fries (Detroit: Wayne State University Press, 1989).

2. Throughout our book we use the name Bettina Brentano-von Arnim in reference to the author. We use her maiden and married names "Brentano-von Arnim" to preserve her independence as writer/artist. Neither "Bettina" (the intimate first name) nor "Arnim" (her husband's name) reflects this identity. Furthermore, we use the spelling Bettina Brentano-von Arnim instead of Bettine Brentano-von Arnim as she is frequently referred to in more recent scholarship. We consider it important to distinguish between Bettina, the author, and Bettine, the fictional character in her literary texts.

3. Helmut Hirsch, *Bettine von Arnim* (Reinbek bei Hamburg: Rowohlt, 1987); Ursula Lieberts-Grün, *Ordnung im Chaos: Studien zur Poetik der Bettine Brentano-von Arnim* (Heidelberg: Carl Winter Universitätsverlag, 1989).

4. Shorter texts and excerpts from her books have appeared: "The Queen's Son" and "Report on Günderode's Suicide" in *Bitter Healing: German Women Writers 1700–1830,* eds. Jeannine Blackwell and Susanne Zantop (Lincoln/London: University of Nebraska Press, 1990) 443–472. Also "The Butterfly and the Kiss" in *Women in German Yearbook* 7, eds. Jeanette Clausen and Sara Friedrichsmeyer (Lincoln/London: University of Nebraska Press, 1991) 69–78. For a complete listing of English translations see *Women Writers of Germany, Austria, and Switzerland: An Annotated Bio-Bibliographical Guide,* ed. Elke Frederiksen (New York/Westport/London, 1989) 13–14. The English-language monograph is Edith Waldstein's *Bettine von Arnim and the Politics of Romantic Conversation* (Columbia, S.C.: Camden House, 1988).

5. According to family documents the poet's name was spelled with a double "r" (Günderrode). Bettina Brentano-von Arnim entitled her novel *Die Günderode* using only one "r."

6. Ingeborg Drewitz, *Bettine von Arnim: Romantik-Revolution-Utopie* (Munich: Heyne, 1969).

7. For more detailed information about Christa Wolf see the excellent collection of recent studies: *Responses to Christa Wolf. Critical Essays*, ed. Marilyn Sibley Fries (Detroit: Wayne State University Press, 1989).

8. The quote is taken from Patrocinio P. Schweickart's essay "Toward a Feminist Theory of Reading," *Gender and Reading. Essays on Readers, Texts, and Contexts*, eds. Elizabeth A. Flynn and Patrocinio P. Schweickart (Baltimore and London: The Johns Hopkins University Press, 1986) 39. We are applying it to our reading of Christa Wolf's essay.

9. See Schweickart 39.

10. Christa Wolf, *Was bleibt* (Frankfurt a.M.: Luchterhand, 1990). The fact that Wolf did not publish this book until now stirred an intense controversy in the West German press. Wolf was accused (unjustifiably in our

opinion) of cowardess and opportunism. See the debates in *Die Zeit* 8
June 1990; *Der Spiegel* 16 July 1990; *Die Zeit* 7 July 1990.

11. For a lucid analysis of the recent controversy surrounding Christa Wolf,
    see Gertrude Postl's "The Silencing of a Voice: Christa Wolf, Cassandra,
    and the German Reunification," *differences* 5.2 (1993):92–115.

12. For further discussion of Bettina Brentano-von Arnim and the epistolary
    tradition see Christa Wolf, "Nun ja! Das nächste Leben geht aber heute
    an. Ein Brief über die Bettine." In this volume. See also Elke Fred-
    eriksen, "Die Frau als Autorin zur Zeit der Romantik: Anfänge einer
    weiblichen literarischen Tradition," *Gestaltet und gestaltend: Frauen in
    der deutschen Literatur*, ed. Marianne Burkhard, Amsterdamer Beiträge
    zur Germanistik 10 (Amsterdam: Rodopi, 1980) 83–108; Katherine
    Goodman, *Dis/Closures: Women's Autobiographies in Germany between
    1790 and 1914* (New York, Berne, and Frankfurt a.M.: Peter Lang, 1986)
    78–120; Lorely Elsa French, "Bettine von Arnim: Toward a Women's
    Epistolary Aesthetics and Poetics," diss., U of California at Los Angeles,
    1986; and Edith Waldstein, *Bettine von Arnim and the Politics of Roman-
    tic Conversation*, Studies in German Literature, Linguistics, and Culture
    (Columbia, SC: Camden House, 1988).

13. Bettina Brentano-von Arnim's story seems to resemble on the surface
    her brother's novella *The Story of Honest Caspar and Fair Annie*
    (Geschichte vom braven Kasperl und dem schönen Annerl).

14. See, for example, the exchange between Linda Gordon and Joan Scott in
    Signs Summer 1990: 848–860.

15. Christa Wolf, *Im Dialog* (Frankfurt a.m.: Luchterhand, 1990) 25.

16. Christa Wolf, *Im Dialog* 25.

Works Cited

Blackwell, Jeannine, and Susanne Zantop, eds. "The Queen's Son" and "Report on Günderode's Suicide," *Bitter Healing: German Women Writers
1700–1830*. Lincoln/London: University of Nebraska Press, 1991. 443–472.

Clausen, Jeanette, and Sara Friedrichsmeyer, eds. "The Butterfly and the
Kiss," *Women in German Yearbook*. Lincoln/London: University of Nebraska Press, 1991. 69–78.

Drewitz, Ingeborg. *Bettine von Arnim: Romantik-Revolution-Utopie*. Munich: Heyne, 1969.

Frederiksen, Elke. "Die Frau als Autorin zur Zeit der Romantik: Anfänge einer weiblichen literarischen Tradition," *Gestaltet und gestaltend: Frauen in der deutschen Literatur*, ed. Marianne Burkhard. Amsterdamer Beiträge zur Germanistik 10. Amsterdam: Rodopi, 1980. 83–108.

Frederiksen, Elke, ed. *Women Writers of Germany, Austria, and Switzerland: An Annotated Bio-Bibliographical Guide*. New York/Westport/London, 1989.

French, Lorely Elsa. "Bettine von Arnim: Toward a Women's Epistolary Aesthetics and Poetics." diss., University of California at Los Angeles, 1986.

Fries, Marilyn Sibley, ed. *Responses to Christa Wolf. Critical Essays*. Detroit: Wayne State University Press, 1989.

Goodman, Katherine. *Dis/Closures: Women's Autobiographies in Germany between 1790 and 1914*. New York, Berne, and Frankfurt a.M.: Peter Lang, 1986.

Hirsch, Helmut. *Bettine von Arnim*. Reinbek bei Hamburg: Rowohlt, 1987.

Lieberts-Grün, Ursula. *Ordnung im Chaos: Studien zur Poetik der Bettine Brentano-von Arnim*. Heidelberg: Carl Winter Universitätsverlag, 1989.

Schweickart, Patrocinio P. "Toward a Feminist Theory of Reading," *Gender and Reading. Essays on Readers, Texts, and Contexts*, eds. Elizabeth A. Flynn and Patrocinio P. Schweickart. Baltimore and London: The Johns Hopkins University Press, 1986. 31–62.

Waldstein, Edith. *Bettine von Arnim and the Politics of Romantic Conversation*. Studies in German Literature, Linguistics, and Culture. Columbia, S.C.: Camden House, 1988.

Wolf, Christa. *Im Dialog*. Frankfurt a.M.: Luchterhand, 1990.

Your Next Life Begins Today:
A Letter about Bettine[1]

Christa Wolf

> There is a lot of work to be done in the world. To me at least, it
> seems that nothing is how it ought to be.
>
> —Bettina von Arnim

Dear D.:

Instead of the letter which you are expecting, I want to write to you
about Bettine. Maybe this will help us both. I will escape the normal
rules for writing an afterword to a book. You will learn something
about an ancestor with whom you are not yet acquainted. We will
both be able to continue working on the basic themes of our dialogue-
in-letters, as we rediscover the same themes in Bettina von Arnim's
letter-novel *Die Günderode*; and the historical distance between her
time and ours will give us the advantage of perspective. In fact,
Bettine herself made use of this kind of historical gap. The letters on
which she based her book in 1839 were actually written back in 1804
and 1806, which for her was not merely a different era but amounted
to a different lifetime. Bettine was not yet twenty when she met
Karoline von Günderrode (whose family wrote their name with a
double *r*, by the way, although we have only reverted to this spelling
since the 1960s). The two met at the home of Bettine's grandmother,
the famous writer Sophie La Roche. Bettine immediately attached
herself to Günderrode, who was five years older; visited her daily in
her room at the convent in Frankfurt am Main, read aloud to her,

35

jotted down her poems, made long trips with her on paper, and shared everything with her, because otherwise she felt alone and estranged in the midst of her large family and in the fashionable world to which the wealthy Brentanos belonged, and was driven to make all sorts of wry faces. "Dear Arnim," her brother Clemens wrote to Achim von Arnim in 1802, informing his friend about his sister: "This girl is very unhappy, she is very ingenious and does not know it; she is thoroughly abused by her family, and endures it by quietly eating away at herself."

But Bettine, a plucky person behind all her masquerades, promised herself that she would never consider herself unhappy and, if the ideal form of life proved unavailable, would accept the life she was offered and make it her own as far as possible. In this respect she differed from Günderrode, who not only felt subject to the bourgeois code of life, as a woman, but made herself subject to the bourgeois code of art, as a poet; who was under compulsion both from sensitive moral feelings and from a sensitive artistic conscience; and who was driven to the point where the things she needed in order to live her life became incompatible. A woman and an artist of her kind does not take her life because the man on whom she has staked everything abandons her. The question one must ask is: Why did she stake everything on him?

It was that same man, the classical scholar Friedrich Creuzer, who some while before Günderrode's suicide persuaded her to stop seeing Bettine. But first she appears to have returned Bettine's letters, as Bettine requested. In these letters you can read that Bettine was able to defend herself against the reproaches of her family, who were concerned about how the twenty-year-old girl would find a husband when she refused to adapt to domestic virtues and instead was learning Hebrew from "an old black Jew." "A man is repelled by that sort of thing," her oldest brother wrote her—"dear good angel-Franz," who acted as head of the household because both their parents had died young. "I wrote him that . . . there was no longer time enough left for me to change; and that the time with the Jew was just something I had worked into my daily schedule to protect myself from being eaten up by the moths of domesticity; and I had noticed that people who are happy in their domestic life always spend their Sundays counting the roof tiles on their neighbor's roof, which I find so terribly tedious that I prefer not to marry."

Bettine's dread of philistine life stayed with her all her days. But

Bettina, Self Portrait (drawing). (Stiftung Weimarer Klassik. From: Fritz Böttger, *Bettina von Arnim. Ein Leben zwischen Tag und Traum.* Berlin, Verlag der Nation, 1986).

she had an equally strong fear of being useless ("better dead than unneeded"). In 1811 she married Achim von Arnim, the friend of her beloved brother Clemens, and at his side she began to live a radically different life in Berlin, Prussia's capital, which was at that time occupied by Napoleon, and put herself through the school of self-denial with scarcely a word of complaint. Twenty years of marriage, seven pregnancies, seven births, the care and education of seven children, exhausting moves from one place to another, financial worries, household annoyances of every sort; and not least, a relationship with her husband which was not "simple" or untroubled—the natures and needs of the pair were too different for harmony—but which she sincerely did all she could to live up to. Arnim was a patriot who, disappointed by developments in Prussia, withdrew in resignation to Wiepersdorf, his country estate, where he was plagued with problems of management. But Bettine never stopped seeing the poet in him, and persistently urged him to bring out that part of himself, to become what, in her inner vision of him, he "really" was. The evidence of her first life meanwhile rested, unheeded and forgotten, in some drawer: the letters from her friend, Günderrode, along with the letters from Goethe's mother, from Goethe himself, from Beethoven; the wooing, often effusive letters from her brother Clemens; and the rather pedagogical letters from her brother-in-law Savigny, whom she met again in Berlin when he entered government service in Prussia. Locked and barricaded in a drawer or a cabinet lay the spirit of her youth, preserved intact, waiting to revive in the work of a fifty-year-old woman: a rebirth which can never astonish us enough.

Her book, this book of letters which I am recommending to you, bridges a span of thirty-five years in Bettine's life. No one who knew Bettine as an ecstatic child, as a wild young girl, would have thought her capable of metamorphosing into a housewife and mother who subordinated all her exuberant fantasies and wishes to the demands of her large family. Thus it is remarkable that she should have been the one, in the circle of the Romantics, who resurfaced in the 1830s with her Romantic principles intact, and who—no easy achievement in the stultifying atmosphere of Prussia in the period between the downfall of Napoleon in 1815 and the March revolution of 1848—earned the title of herald of the revolution for later generations. Who readopted the positive, provocatively naïve attitudes of her childhood and early youth, because only a child can get away with saying what everyone knows: "The Emperor has no clothes." Who—and this is one reason why I recommend her to you—did not accept the false alternatives which were imposed on all their lives; who did not consent to be an ineffective outsider on the one hand, or a well-adjusted philistine on the other. Those alternatives had exhausted her generation, the descendants of intellectual revolutionaries. Clemens Brentano had described the choices this way at the turn of the century: "In today's world, one can only choose between two things. One can either become a human being or a bourgeois, and all one sees is what ought to be avoided, but not what ought to be embraced. The bourgeois have occupied the whole of temporal existence and the human beings have nothing but themselves."

That is the radical voice of the early Jena school of Romanticism, whose spirit Bettine preserved faithfully. Her letters to Günderrode (who was not one of the Romantics but was linked to them by friendships and intellectual exchange) are a remarkable reflection of Bettine's seemingly playful involvement with the Romantic motifs of longing for another, better life—at a time when practical reality had taken a totally different turn.

She knew the aura that surrounded her, and she knew the fear of having the aura stripped away, of being freed from her magic spell and turned into one of those terrifying human automatons who made their debut in literature during her lifetime. To Goethe, the greatest of her imaginary lovers, she confessed her insights, her fears, and her suspicions about herself. On June 29, 1807, she wrote to him—when Günderrode had been dead for a year:

> These magic charms, the power to cast spells are my white dress . . . but, sir, I cannot deny the presentiment that the white dress will be stripped from me, too, and that I will go around in the common garb of everyday life, and that this world, in which my senses are alive, is going to perish; that what I ought to shield and protect, I will betray; that where I ought to patiently submit, I will take revenge; and when childlike wisdom artlessly beckons, I will act defiant and claim I know it all. But the saddest thing is that I will label with the curse of sin what is not sin, just as they all do. And I will be justly punished for it.

Everything that she tried to keep from happening to her—everything that she succeeded by her spells in warding off—actually did happen, before her very eyes, to the friends of her youth, both famous and unknown, as hope—animator of souls—drained away from them. Some died young, like Novalis; others committed suicide, like Kleist and Günderrode; while others wandered throughout Europe searching for someplace where they felt at home, like August Wilhelm Schlegel; became political reactionaries, at least for a time, like Friedrich Schlegel; or drowned in Catholic mysticism like Clemens Brentano.

Bettine saw friendships break down under pressure from reactionary political forces, she experienced painful separations and estrangements—from Günderrode, from Clemens, from Savigny, from Goethe; saw how their need to earn a living forced the men to adapt. Joseph Görres, for instance, who moved by a series of steps from being a revolutionary to joining the clerical reaction, said in 1822: "Of the whole generation who saw the [French] Revolution . . . who went through all the honor and disgrace, not one [would] behold the promised land of freedom and peace."

The land of Utopia, the supposed abode of liberty, equality, and fraternity, yielded to the reality of the Holy Alliance and the Carlsbad Decrees within the German petty principalities, especially in Prussia.[2] It was smashed by reactionary politics on the public scene, and by Biedermeier tastes in private life. It drowned in persecution, censorship, and spies; was lost in a social order which clung tenaciously to the idea that middle-class production methods could be combined with a monarchical regime, and which refused to acknowledge its own internal contradictions. And finally, it was carried abroad by its most radical literary adherents—Heine, Börne, Büchner—when they were forced to emigrate, and was preserved only in their melancholy, painfully questioning, ironic, lonely, and rebellious songs, plays, and essays. Social conditions in Germany, which the young Karl Marx described as "below the plane of history," isolated those who had the qualities to serve as spokesmen of a historical movement. Meanwhile, Bettina von Arnim, who had withdrawn into marriage and spent her days with her children "like a cat with her kittens"; who kept silent, wrote letters, and drew sketches—was perceptively described by Joseph Görres (the same Görres who fell prey to reactionary Catholicism in later life) in the 1820s, when he saw one of Bettina's drawings: "It's not classical, and not Romantic either. It's Bettinical, her own charming genre somewhere in between."

The unclassifiable Bettinical, which did not fit into any frame or into any of the movements with which she came in contact in the course of her long lifetime; the fact that she lived "in the order of her own nature" is what had made Bettine's work survive. At the same time, it made her a unique case, easily underrated by posterity. She cannot readily be used to demonstrate any thesis. Later generations clung to the magical image of the young Bettine, projecting their own unfulfillable longings and wishes onto this impish, untamable, seemingly ageless being; this youthful enthusiast; this ingenious, somewhat shocking, immature child, a second Mignon: androgynous, enigmatic, dusky, fey. Bettine, fully aware of the temptation to immerse herself, and if possible to transform herself, into this artistically manufactured figure, brought off the difficult trick of destroying her own myth, the deceptively finished image of herself as she was in her youth, and allowed herself to be caught up in an "ordinary," everyday life. Who would be surprised to learn that she was often overwhelmed by feelings of misery? "I have spent the twelve years of my marriage on the rack, physically and spiritually, and my claims to consideration are not being met," she wrote from Wiepersdorf to her sister Gunda von Savigny in Berlin, at New Year's, 1823. "What I always endured patiently because I felt I was strong enough I now endure with impatience because I am weak enough. What I see ahead is the end of everything."

The importance of such isolated remarks must not be exaggerated. All the same, it is impossible to exaggerate the degree to which Bettine was ensnared in everyday drudgery and cut off from the dreams of her youth. This picture of her as a woman groaning under the burden of self-denial and monotony did not last. But to show how complete her desperation could be, I will quote you a few more lines from the same letter:

One loses the ability to write here where all day long, all year long, one's whole life long, nothing happens which would make a person bother to stir a leg or an arm. I know of no task which saps the mind more than doing and experiencing nothing. In every thought one struggles to escape one's situation. One flies up and soars far above the present, exerting one's strength, only to fall all the deeper and more dangerously back to earth, feeling as if one has smashed every bone. So it is with me. I keep candles lit all night, I wake up every hour, I compare what I think to what I dream, and only too often I am forced to realize that both alike drag me down into the emptiness of my daily surroundings. Nothing so weakens the mind as not to be called on to perform those operations which uniquely correspond to its nature . . .

Oh, how my demands on life have lowered. And the less I demand, the more life makes me agree to give up, and will grant me nothing except to turn into a rogue or a scoundrel.

The embers glowing under the ashes. The same fear of the one sin, giving up her true self, that she had expressed sixteen years earlier in her letter to Goethe. But hard-pressed as she may often have been by the "earthly guest," it did not succeed in driving out the "heavenly guest" from her completely, in the twenty years of her marriage. In her letters to Arnim, the affectionate tones became less frequent, and the irritated, self-defensive tones more so, when his extremely sober and spartan habits challenged her unselfish devotion as a mother and wife. Even so, her pain at Arnim's early death in 1831 was deep and genuine. Bettine was forty-six and did not marry again. Never, as far as I can tell, did she express any regrets or changes of heart about her marriage, once it was over. Her character was noble, like Arnim's. Although she could be capricious and cranky, she was not self-pitying, hostile, and bitter. In the first letters she wrote to friends on the day that Arnim died, we can see her burning the earthly dross from her husband's image and resurrecting him as a new and saintlike person whom she could venerate. But besides this emotional Bettine, there was another Bettine inside her, a levelheaded person who never lost sight of life's day-to-day demands. She administered her husband's estate for her children. She arranged for the publication of the first collected edition of Arnim's works, and contributed substantially to preparing it. And to everyone's surprise, and the displeasure of her family in Frankfurt, she became a productive author after her husband's death, publishing six books in seventeen years and leaving behind an unpublished manuscript, letters enough to fill volumes, and scores of notes and outlines. Bettine began her third life.

"I am very happy. Is there anything more blissful, than from the simple spent years of the past, as from the fire's center, to burst into newly awakened flames? . . . Last night I could not sleep because a thought rooted in my childhood was putting forth so many blossoms." She wrote this to Prince Pückler[3] in 1835. Is it important to know to whom she expressed her feelings and who disappointed her by rejecting them? Is it important that she sometimes used the wrong approach? With a sure instinct, she took what she needed to stoke up her desire to create. The incubation period was over, the virus which had lain dormant for so long awoke and incited its host to feverish activity. Frau von Arnim began to be active—of all things—in the most petrified decade of the nineteenth century. She made her home in the heart of the Prussian capital, at 21 Unter den Linden, turning it into a meeting place for independent spirits. With complete disdain for mail censorship, surveillance, and government spies, she welcomed visits from travelers and admirers, and received so many letters each day that she could hardly cope with them all. She tended people sick with cholera, as well as the poor in the "custodial land" outside the Hamburger Gate. And she wrote.

In 1839 she produced her second letter-novel, the book on Günderrode. (The first was *Goethe's Correspondence with a Child*.) That same year represented the nadir of the political trough through which Germany was passing: the exact midpoint between the revolutions of 1830 and 1848. But people at the time could not know that an upswing lay ahead. There was no talk of any "springtime of nationalist liberation." Twilight reigned, a mood of gloom and doom. The liberal Berlin journalist Adolf Glassbrenner commented that every Prussian seemingly was born into the world equipped with an "inner gendarme." Yet in that setting, hard as it is to imagine, the students of Berlin actually held a torch parade in Bettine's honor, right after her Günderrode book was published in 1840. It seems certain that they had read no more of it than the dedication—it was dedicated to them—and had interpreted it exactly as it was meant: politically. "You who first sprouted again like golden flowers on the trodden-down field!" An effusive speech, no doubt, but above all a daring message. For it dared to mention the banned students' associations (there is a reference to "the student anthems"), expressed confidence that "the times will change," and wished the young men that "a gentle star may shine protectively upon you." Such language is understood by those who know that in December 1836 the Prussian High Court in Berlin had sentenced first to death, and then to thirty years' fortress confinement, forty-one students from Greifswald who were members of student associations; that in 1832 Prussia's response to the participation of student associations in the "Hambacher Fest"[4] was to saddle them with another tyrannical law "for the maintenance of public peace and lawful order"; that the peace of the graveyard ruled in the states of the German Bund, and especially in Prussia, after a few isolated democratic-republican protest actions were defeated in the 1830s; that the senseless assault on the Frankfurt guardhouse in April

1833 was followed by the relentless persecution of the participants, mostly students; that the *Hessische Landbote* was confiscated in 1834, its revolutionary co-author Friedrich Weidig arrested, and Georg Büchner forced into flight and emigration; that the writings of "Young Germany" were banned throughout the confederation.[5] A well-organized government and security operation stifled every free impulse in German society. And as always when political discussion is suppressed in public, the differing parties and opinions waged their struggle in the form of literature instead. In the 1830s (although you will find it hard to believe), Goethe and the unpublished works he left behind at his death were an explosive topic. And Bettine's first book, *Goethe's Correspondence with a Child,* was in all innocence addressed to this now controversial figure. The *Correspondence,* published in 1835 under the magic seal of the motto "This book is for the good people, not for the bad," went virtually unscathed by the debate and created a sensation. Its author became famous overnight and was regarded by her contemporaries as a prodigy or an apparition. For the second time—the first was in her adolescence—people treated her as a figure outside history.

"Our political parties evidently have gotten mixed up over this mysterious child," wrote a Young Germany newspaper. "Those who ought to be for her are against her, and those who ought to be against her are for her"—a sign (as we have cause to know) that the political parties are at the end of their tether. Bettine, called "the sibyl of the Romantic era in literature," was dubbed, by the followers of Young Germany, an "inspired, romantic, mystical, prophetic, impish will-o'-the-wisp." The ardent democrat Ludwig Börne termed her an "avenging fury" and, from his vantage point in Paris, reinterpreted her volume of homage to Goethe so as to turn it into an attack on Goethe instead; and the historian Leopold Ranke stated: "The woman has the instinct of a pythia." If all the contradictory traits which were attributed to her could be joined into a single person, they would produce a kind of monster. It seems to me that this tells us less about Bettine's character, temperament, and aspect than it does about the need of people in her time for a figure who stood outside and above history, who alone might appear capable of introducing some ferment into the stagnant swamp of German society, especially in Prussia.

Prussia was a state where every chair was occupied, every post filled: from the Minister of Culture to the board of Supreme Censors, from the Privy Councilor to the secret government deputy at the university, from the Minister of the Interior to the Postmaster General (whose name at that time was Nagler, by the way, and who showed such a commendable interest in the letters of authors under surveillance that he often insisted on reading them personally). The spectrum of intellectual workers ranged from the official state poet to the popular leader locked up in the dreaded town jail, the "tin box"; and all the roles in the opposition seemed to have been handed out, too. With the benefit of hindsight, we could say that only one role remained to be filled: a woman in a high-ranking position, barred from holding any official post and not a member of any existing faction, but a critical thinker, educated and fearless, committed and empathetic, clairvoyant and a skilled dreamer. This sounds like the description of a chimera, and it fits Bettine.

Do you feel the proper amazement at how subtly outward circumstances can coordinate with a person's innermost needs? Bettine deserves credit for having accepted the role assigned to her and filled the gap, apparently without asking what the consequences might be. One cannot help but feel a secret satisfaction at the skill with which she used the advantage which sometimes is hidden in the disadvantage of being a woman in a male-run society—provided that the woman can tolerate being considered slightly crazy. Bettine began early to practice this skill, as you will see by reading her letters to Günderrode. She often referred to herself as a "simpleton." In serious times, it can be a protection not to be taken absolutely seriously. Writer Karl Gutzkow's deep sigh when he read Bettine's *King's Book* testifies to this: "Sad indeed that only a woman is permitted to say what any man would have been locked up for saying." Who would lock up a sibyl, an imp, a pythia?

But was there ever really any danger of her being locked up? Actually, we are still on the subject of how she dedicated her Günderrode book to the students, remember? But before we go back to the book, we need to forge ahead into Bettine's later life, to look at this question of whether she was really in danger of imprisonment. I will quote to you a passage from a surveillance report written in 1847:

> Social questions were discussed even at tea parties. The political leaning at these tea parties is socialist, in that members of the gathering prefer to talk and debate how the substance and form of life could be improved. The female sex especially long for liberation from the bonds

of tradition, fashion, convention. Among all the women of this type in
Berlin who enjoy a public reputation, Bettina von Arnim is indisput-
ably the chief and most prominent. It is generally known, even to the
court, that her soirées have the character I just described. She is left in
peace because she is held in universally high regard here, and no fault
can rightly be found in her.

This report was written by one of those trustworthy confidential
agents who worked for the Central Information Bureau in Mainz,
which Prince Metternich himself had urged should be established, not
least because of the unruly student population ("The struggle of eternal justice against the principle of revolution is imminent and unavoidable"). The Central Information Bureau was one of the very few
institutions which transcended the borders between the individual
German states. By the end of the 1830s, the Bureau's confidential
agents reported, the spirit which now reigned at German universities
was very different from what it had been in the previous decades:
students engaged only in drinking bouts. But even though the Mainz
Bureau, and other spy organizations, no longer felt that the student
population posed a threat, they continued to show a marked hostility
toward the intelligentsia. Wittgenstein, the Prussian Minister of
State, merely said out loud what others were thinking when he declared that "bookworms and hairsplitting scribblers" were a blot on
human society, and that he would gladly contribute to fighting them.
And a leading post in the "central committee," which processed instructions and reports from the Mainz central bureau, was held by an
unspeakably vile privy councilor named Tschoppe, who died in a
severe state of mental illness. Tschoppe loved dramatic effects. One
morning when the banned author Karl Gutzkow came to ask that the
ban on all his writings be lifted, Tschoppe—who was still shaving—
greeted him by saying, "You were at the theater yesterday!" He enjoyed posing as a powerful man who knew everything. Triumphantly
he showed the dismayed writer a list of all those who, the evening
before, had claimed free passes at the Royal Theater in Berlin.
    The Prussian capital teemed with political anecdotes and witicisms.
Frau von Arnim no doubt was familiar with most of them, for people
thronged to her democratic salon. Of course, she was only too aware
that the decision by the police and censors to let her carry on her
activities in peace, owing to the wide respect in which she was held,
could not be relied on. Moreover, she had not been *given* this right

but had won it, and expanded it, by her own bold and sometimes reckless efforts. People were not certain how to interpret her. Was she naïve? Or only pretending to be naïve? Was she cunning? Or did her habit of acting as she saw fit simply not match any of the categories available to people bred to self-censorship and subservience?

When Bettine dedicated her *King's Book* (1845) to the King—"This Book Belongs to the King" was simultaneously the title and the dedication—one high-ranking censorship bureau was determined to believe that this was a subtle ploy on the part of the now famous author to escape the ban which ought to have been placed on the work. "Born of the vineyard country, baptized by sunshine!" So the flattered King addressed the startled Bettine in his letter of reply, although in fact he had only leafed through her book. Not so his Minister of the Interior, who gave it a thorough reading and afterward felt compelled to address a letter to the monarch, Friedrich Wilhelm IV. He tucked its central idea into an involved bureaucratic argument which is worth quoting here:

> If the book were not written in a tone of prophetic ecstasy aimed at a small readership but instead in the form of simple logic and prudent reflection which would make it accessible to the public at large; and if the author (whose identity is well known if not expressly named) did not by her quixotic nature render doubtful the practical accuracy and applicability of the doctrines the book contains, it would, according to the prescriptions of law, have to be declared among the writings which are hazardous to society, owing to the irreligion which it expresses and defends, and owing to the utter radicalism which it preaches.

The man was in the right job.

Besides, time verified what he had said. Two rather shorter works were written as a follow-up to Bettine's book, and their authors translated her "prophetic ecstasy" into the plain political German of the time. One work, ironic in tone and printed anonymously in Bern four years before *The Communist Manifesto*, called Communism a "specter" and linked it to the author of the *King's Book*. ("So now the devil stands before us unmasked, in all his hideousness, and the name of this darkly threatening specter is: Communism.") The second work, which condensed the "putative meaning and content" of the *King's Book* into a fifty-six-page pamphlet, was published in Hamburg, whereupon the King promptly confiscated it on political grounds and it was banned by the supreme censorship tribunal. ("Nineteen pages are dangerous, but with twenty you're in the clear," people mocked: books of twenty pages or more, with the author's name on them—Bettine had always refused to have her name on the title page—were not subject to censorship.) This was a lesson for Bettine. In times when a lack of public political forums forces literature to fill the gap and become the conscience of society—which was the case now, for Berlin's three daily newspapers were subject to censorhip, so that Bettine did not even read them—literature will be prey to increasingly severe sanctions, the more intelligibly it communicates to the public. Bettine wrote in 1844: "What else is one to publish in Prussia today but religious pamphlets, reading primers, and fairy tales!"

But when she dedicated her book to the King, was that really a deliberate hoax? Clearly, Bettine was safeguarded not only by her popularity but by her illusions as well. When Friedrich Wilhelm IV ascended the throne in June 1840, many advocates of democracy hoped to see him support their cause. Bettine believed that he had the will and energy to bring about fundamental changes. "No, the disgrace of mental enslavement does not emanate from him!" Her devotion to the idea of a populist monarchy had an element of fantasy in it. "We must save the King!" But only six months after the coronation, in December 1840, Varnhagen von Ense recorded this about her: "She is beside herself about the state of affairs that is developing here, she distrusts all the King's intimates and favorites, she wants a constitution, freedom of the press, air and light." But in her *King's Book* she suggested to the King in all seriousness—or was she less serious than she seemed?—that he might bypass his courtiers and ministers, that "circle of heraldic beasts," and with the aid of the people he might "throw the old machinery of the state onto the scrap-heap," replace intellectual slavery with "freedom of thought," and rule jointly with the popular leaders who so far had been persecuted.

Was that naïve? shrewd? deluded? In any case, the surest way to lose one's illusions was (and still is) to try them out. Nine years later, in Volume II of her *King's Book* (called *Conversations with Demons,* 1852), she wrote this sardonic description of a utopian state: "I do not mean any state where the censors can cross out my views, I mean a different state altogether, located beyond the Himalayas, which is the reflected image of the state I could be thinking of. But if the censors should try to erase that one, too, well then, that is not the one I have in mind either. I do not have in mind anything which could be crossed out."

In the interval between the first and second volumes of the *King's Book* lay the period before the March revolution of 1848 and the failure of that revolution. In the interval, too, lay Bettine's persistent clashes with the censors, which forced her to found her own publishing house, the Arnim Verlag, and the new troubles which it brought her. In the same period, increasingly grave accusations piled up against her, including the charge that she was a Communist. (Gutzkow: "If the most ardent, intense love of humanity is Communism, then we may logically expect that Communism will attract many followers.")

In 1843, by the way, Bettine reportedly met with Karl Marx and his fiancée, Jenny von Westphalen, in Bad Kreuznach and, to Jenny's annoyance, took long, solitary walks with the young doctor of philosophy.

Once—this event, too, fell in the interval between the two volumes of the *King's Book*—Bettine broke off work on one of her books because she could not have gotten it printed. The Prussian Minister of the Interior, in a typically ministerial confusion of cause and effect, accused her, in 1844, of having made the weavers of Silesia "rebellious." "Merely wishing to help the poor is now described as preaching revolution," a friend wrote to her in warning. Then Bettine stopped writing her *Book of the Poor*, a sort of first attempt at a sociological study of the living conditions of the Fourth Estate, using many examples from the huts of the Silesian weavers. She must have realized that this incident marked a clearly defined boundary which she could not cross with impunity—the point at which social conflicts, and the impossibility of resolving the conflicts under the present regime, were most sharply in evidence. The energy to revolutionize society had not been developed, the times were not ripe for anything more than an ineffectual willingness for self-sacrifice. What alternative was left? To write to the King again, saying that instead of the cathedral in Berlin, he ought rather to build a thousand peasant huts in Silesia. The fate of the Silesians (she said) is more tragic than Sophocles'.—Don't you agree that this is a significant aesthetic statement, even if, as often happens in the history of German literature, aesthetic statements take the place of the action which the case really demanded? The statement is significant, because Bettine regards the rules of tragedy, which derived from the conflicts of the ruling elite and from a "high" art form, as applicable to this situation of the

"lower" classes. But, as you will see, the roots of this attitude go back
to the letters she exchanged with Günderrode.

"Bettina allows her humanity to lead her astray. She always believes that the oppressed are in the right," remarked Gunda von
Savigny, Bettine's sister, in a tone of mild reproof. Undoubtedly, her
view of the matter was correct. It made Gunda—the wife of the
Prussian Minister for Legislative Review—uncomfortable to see
where her sister's radical humanism could lead; namely, to a disregard for any official authority which Bettine did not consider morally
justified. In 1847, when a Berlin magistrate forcibly accused her of
tax evasion in opening her publishing firm, because she had neglected
to obtain Prussian citizenship first, she responded with a withering
counter-attack. She was sentenced first to three months' imprisonment, and then, after a review, to two months—the maximum penalty for persons of rank. Influential people, chiefly her brother-in-law
Savigny, managed to stop the sentence from being carried out. But
Bettine realized that a technical mistake on her part had been used as
a pretext to show her what was in store for her if she did not watch her
step. A witness reported what Bettine said about the matter later, at a
social gathering, that the charges against her had been trumped up by
government ministers who wanted to get her out of Berlin because
"His Romantic Majesty's female court jester was causing them noticeable inconvenience."

So, you see, at least once she really was in danger of being locked
up. But, as a rule, material threats drive a person even further beyond
the mental limits which seemingly are set by his background and
mode of life, if he is the sort of person who does not depend on the
approval of the establishment; that is, who cannot be bribed and who
is radicalized in his views and principles. This is what happened with
Bettine. Her court hearing enabled her to pass an impartial sentence
on the structure of her society, and to determine what developments
would be necessary in the future. As evidence of what I am claiming,
I will quote to you several paragraphs from the letter of defense
which she wrote to the Berlin magistrate who heard her case:

> As for your last remark, that there was no reason to extend Prussian
> citizenship to me as a mark of esteem, I do admit this, especially
> because I value the right of citizenship more highly than noble
> rank . . . By the same token, I value even more highly the class of the
> proletariat . . . The treasure of the poor consists in the inherent wealth

of nature; the merit of the bougeois lies in using and exploiting this wealth, which by means of his professional skills, and for his own advantage, he bestows upon that class of humans whose arrogance, pampered nature, and poorly educated minds devour everything, precisely because they have no productive energy of their own.—Thus, the reason why I attribute the highest value to the proletarian is that he is exempt from the baseness of profiting from the condition of society: for the proletarian gives everything and in return he consumes no more than he needs in order to revive his energy, so that others may profit . . . And If I . . . therefore prefer the crown of citizen to a medal of honor, yet rather than that crown I would prefer to have the approval of the people, whose renunciations are heroic and whose sacrifices are the least self-seeking.

Now back to literature, back to the year 1839, when Bettine wrote her Günderrode book. I would like to convince you not only that this comparatively quiet year brought Bettine experiences which prepared her for the directly political conflicts of the 1840s but also that her very preoccupation with the ideas and feelings she had known at the start of the century gave her a deeper insight into contemporary patterns. Her actions and writings in midlife show that she remained loyal to basic themes of her youth, and continued to develop them, before broaching them in the Günderrode book. At the same time, this book in many respects reflects the emotional upheavals she went through in 1839 and 1840: the drama of her last romance, and her passionate defense of the unjustly punished brothers Grimm.

While Bettine assembled key pieces of her correspondence with Günderrode and elaborated them into a novel in letter form, a second letter-novel was born in that same year, made up of her current correspondence with a young student, Julius Döring from Wolmirstedt near Magdeburg, who began to write to her at the beginning of 1839 to express his admiration of her Goethe book. It disturbed Döring that she had dedicated the book to Prince Pückler, and he called on her to dedicate her next book to the students. She responded enthusiastically to his suggestion: "It is time for the young men to bloom from my mind with joy, for I am a tree that bears young-man blossoms. The buds are just about to open, and how should I not live on into the future, since it is being born from the marrow of my mind?" And she wrote to another young male admirer, with whom she shared a more intellectual and less erotic fascination: "I am nothing, but such an air blows around me that I believe the young people must snort it like mettlesome horses into their wide-open nostrils!"

It is apparent that she intended, with her Günderrode book, to pass on the legacy of her own youth to her grandchildren's generation. Emotionally stirred, she yielded to visions from her early life which at times approached the intensity of supernatural visitations. She kept Döring informed about the progress of her work, and in November 1839 she wrote to him from Wiepersdorf:

> I am so buried in work that I can no longer make room for sleep. At 1 a.m. I go to bed where, too excited by the work to sleep, I often read a play or some other material. And scarcely is the room heated again than I am at my desk, and work continuously without getting up from it, sparing barely four minutes for a midday meal, so that I can build you all a monument wherein refined minds can perceive everything which I have not said to you and to others, or which you all have misunderstood. In four weeks I hope to have reached the point that I can begin printing [the book] in Berlin.

She was mistaken about that. The printing did not begin until the spring of 1840, mainly because amid the most intensive work on the manuscript, she pushed it aside and began her great confrontation with her brother-in-law Savigny on behalf of the Grimms. So in January 1840 we find her saying—still referring to the Günderrode book—in another letter to Döring:

> I have worked very hard up to now and, strangely enough, during this work I have needed more sleep than usual . . . but on the other hand, the past has become so vivid to me that I could not say like Thomas, "Let me put my fingers in your wound so that I may believe it is really you."—Günderrode stands before me, and she often calls me away from my place when the light burns in the evening. [She stands] there in the corner where the tall green pines have stood since Christmas, reaching to the ceiling in front of my sofa, and then I wrap myself in my coat because I cannot resist going to meet her in my thoughts, and then sleep overcomes me . . . just as if Günderrode were sleeping, and so now I must sleep, too, because I have come close to her again through my awakened memory. —But in the daytime I feel so close to everything in the past that I am absolutely convinced of the enduring presence of everything which we have truly experienced.

The deeper meaning of this vision, which she describes in a biblical metaphor and links to the calling-up of spirits, is the desire to win love; and the same secret impulse lies behind her work. "Whoever reads this book of mine and does not love me has never had youth in his heart." I will say it: she compensated for giving up the possibility of consummating her real-life love by transferring her desire into other areas over which she could exercise control. She must have found a peculiar gratification in connecting her last love to her first by a thousand well-considered threads. This woman, now in her fifties, offered an overflowing erotic devotion to an average young man who believed he had to be a poet. ("Sensuality in the brain," old Count Pückler had woundingly labeled it.) She poeticized Döring, turning him into her lover, and revealed to him her emotional secrets ("I have not felt a breath of life in poetry since the sun set for me back then, when Goethe rejected me"). Soaring to biblical language, she dedicated this young man to poetry, to become the new Goethe ("And I will give you that, Be thou a poet!"). She played the role of a priestess out of whom "the spirit" speaks, and pined for a repetition, in mid-life, of that "painfully sweet" surrender, that traumatizing scene which she claimed to have experienced with Goethe, when she lay down on the ground in front of him and would not "be still until he placed his foot on my breast so that I could feel the weight of him."

Blissful with self-induced illusion, she revealed the intellectual-sexual proclivities which had marked her at the age of twenty-two, practiced a fetishistic cult with the plaster cast of a young man's foot on her bed, and, inspired by this current source of stimulation, became receptive to the "spirit's breath" of her early life. Not some speculative act of will or thought-out policy but this compelling inspiration was what moved her to open herself up to visionary memories of the life she had shared with the friend of her youth, Günderrode. "For long years I was cut off from any such power as had called up my love in earlier years . . . Ah, I was far too alone."

She experienced feelings of rejuvenation, a pedagogical eroticism that continued to glow even after the brief rush of intense emotion for Döring had yielded to sobriety: "But I do not trust you, you are no genuine somnambulist, and reality is firmly imprisoned in your heart. You press your thumb into reality's eye, it dares not budge, then you slide home the bolt and mock it for being your prisoner." Why am I quoting that to you? Must we intrude into Bettine's late adventures of the heart? Must we summon again the painfully insecure tone of the questions in a letter she wrote in the middle of the year, a letter in which she sounds as if she were waking up from a dream: "I will not give you up— You don't mean to vanish from right under my nose, do you? —You cannot be merely a figment of my imagination: you really are live, aren't you? —Everything has stolen away from me. —How strange, if you, too, should prove an illusion." On the other hand, I think it is a good idea for us to listen to these most personal sounds, because I feel sure that these same sounds went into forming the Günderrode book as we know it today. Because—with the illogic of emotional events—when Bettine relived her separation from her first love, Karoline, that made it easier for her to renounce her last love, and love in general. Because she could not and would not disassociate the person she was in 1839 from the feelings and fantasies she had known in 1805; and because it is the book's connection to her life which gives it its luster and attraction, its rich treatment of time. For it is not all of a piece but is built up of layers atop or intersecting each other, of intercalations whose edges are not smoothed over but left rough. It contains inaccurate transitions, discrepancies, cracks. And that very fact reveals the indissoluble contradication and secret sorrow of her life.

But first—I hope that you are not getting impatient—we have not yet looked at the case of the brothers Jakob and Wilhelm Grimm, which occupied so much of Bettine's attention in the year 1839 that, as I said, she set aside her Günderrode manuscript and postponed the printing in order to tackle it. On November 1, 1839, she wrote to Döring from Bärwalde-Wiepersdorf: "I have just written an epistle to Savigny on behalf of the Grimms—and said all manner of things. It is eight pages long. I would be so interested to have you read it—in fact, it would certainly be useful to you your whole life long—for you to see how far one can and should express the truth openly."

The case of the Göttingen Seven—seven professors among whom were the two Grimm brothers—is brought up frequently, although few people know its fascinating details. I must describe it to you, at least in its general outlines, because Bettine followed it closely and cared deeply about it. In October 1839, she had visited Jakob and Wilhelm Grimm in Kassel, where they had taken refuge after their banishment. Some time earlier, she had read Jakob's little treatise *On My Dismissal.* Savigny, of all people, had given her a copy, because he himself felt convinced by the sincerity of Jakob's statement: "If things are as he describes them, then indeed I must concede that he is right," he allegedly said to her. "Why didn't you tell the King, the Crown Prince, the people what you thought?" Bettine asked her brother-in-law, in her eight-page letter to him, which later became famous.

I would like to see Jakob's treatise put into the curriculum of our secondary schools, as a thrilling example of how strength of character and loyalty to convictions have the power to shape a person's writing style. "The lightning which struck my quiet home is stirring hearts in every walk of life," it begins. And I must keep a grip on myself, so as not to start quoting long passages from the treatise, and from Bettine's epistle, for my fierce pleasure and yours. —Here, briefly, are the details of how the conflict unfolded between the University of Göttingen and its overlord, the newly crowned sovereign, King Ernst August of Hanover: In the summer of 1837, the King, on his own authority, abruptly revoked the comparatively progressive constitution of 1833 and released all his civil servants—who included the university professors at Göttingen—from their oaths of allegiance to basic constitutional law. After waiting patiently for some time, several members of the university lodged a "most humble complaint," dated November 18, 1837, stating that they could not in good conscience stand by silently while the nation's constitution, which was in their opinion still valid, was destroyed "solely on the grounds [that the King] had the power to do so." Instead, they said, they had to consider themselves "permanently bound by their oath." Moreover (they asked him almost ingenuously), how could the King take seriously any future vow of fidelity and fealty he might ask them to make if it came from men who a short time earlier had sacrilegiously violated their oaths?

In a powerful passage, Jakob Grimm explained without anger or heated emotion why, in the end, only seven professors signed their names to this petition: Dahlmann, Albrecht, J. and W. Grimm, Gervinus, Ewald, Weber. Jakob told of the many ways in which the others, with the same or similar views, withheld or retracted their support; and how many, as a last resort, anchored their cowardice to the most specious but most convincing "argument" of all: that by abandoning the legal constitution without a struggle they were saving the university. "People's characters began to shed their leaves like the trees of autumn in an overnight frost," Jakob remarked tersely. Business as usual. Jakob Grimm then described, "leniently" but "freely and with-out constraint," how this conflict of loyalties swelled to incredible proportions, intruding into the personal and civic life of all, owing to the stubbornness of authority, which did not wish to examine objections but to coerce confessions of guilt and enforce submission; and how—because there was no way that a royal university trustee board could debate a case whose salient feature was the King's violation of the law—they were driven to inflict absurd accusations and punishments. "The truth is the only thing that lasts," Jakob Grimm asserted, and the disarming fact is that he believed it. Just as Bettine believed it. It is not hard to imagine her enthusiasm for the dignified, courageous language of this man who thought as she did. "Men still exist who show conscience, even when confronted by force."

Jakob's treatise is a model from the first line to the last. The seven professors were dismissed from their posts, and several were banished from the state of Hanover. ("I never invite the attention of power, until it compels me to carry away my hearthfire and light it in a new place"—Jakob Grimm.) Was it for insubordination that they were banished? No, not in this age of absolute monarchy, post-Enlightenment-style. The university tribunal which immediately summoned the seven to try their case addressed only one issue: How could news of the "most humble complaint" have leaked out so quickly to an English newspaper—a matter about which none of the seven knew anything? "In the feeling that other causes were lacking [Grimm wrote], they attempted to interpret the rapid publication of that statement [the professors' "complaint"] as something culpable . . . Are we to blame if a correspondent from an English or French newspaper, someone we have never met, heard of our intention and reported it? . . . And even if we really had to confess that we were directly responsible for its immediate publication, would that act merit banishment, or indeed any kind of punishment, if all we did was to convey a statement to the authorities?"

Indeed, not what they wrote to the King, but the fact that they might have mentioned him to a third party was the cited reason for banishing the Grimms. Bettine, trembling with outrage, reproached Savigny for not following his initial urge to do all he could to assist the brothers, two of the finest scholars in Germany, to immediately obtain material support for their work from the Berlin Academy; and for instead hurting them even more by trying to "excuse" them to the authorities on the grounds that they had been led astray by others.

"When I had to leave a home that is full of innocence, where God's blessing spreads serenity and peace, I thought of you, and how truly miserable it is that you, in the prime of your life enjoyed their noble companionship, should now be separated from them." It is glorious to see how she tells off Savigny, by now the Prussian Minister of Justice as well as the guardian of her children, and at last gives free rein to the anger which she has held in for so long. She reminds him of the role he played in her own youth, when he "shielded her freedom of thought"—a freedom to which she has stayed loyal, unlike Savigny himself. She appeals to the scholar in him to show solidarity with two outstanding members of his profession. "But no, you will leave me in the lurch and not help me. For ever since you cut off your long hair, your strength has gone from you, and I say to you not what was said to Samson: The Philistines will rule over you, but rather: You will dwell among the Philistines, as one of themselves!"

Incidentally, when the Crown Prince succeeded to the Prussian throne one year later (1840), the Grimms were in fact called to work at the Berlin Academy. But in the meantime Bettine's efforts to defend their rights gave her a deep insight into the way that kings, politicians, and their administrations thought and operated. All of a sudden she realized the whole perverted separation between the morality of government and the morality of everyday life (an observation which would bear fruit in her later books).

> One sees that false politics do not create mental discernment. Look how Metternich said to the deputies from Hanover: We admit that morally you are in the right, only our policy is such that we must oppose you. —And Prussia is based on this kind of attitude, which makes the state no more enduring than a mayfly . . . I know that you would not talk this way to the King. For to tell a monarch about the mistakes in his government, or to show him a higher point of view, would violate the policy of respect which bids you treat sovereigns like automatons. Indeed, you do not trust yourselves to think, and you hide from the truth as if from a creditor whom you cannot pay. You tell sovereigns only the things they expect to hear, so that they can reply without waking up.

Do you want to know the link between these political views and Bettine's book on Günderrode—not just chronologically but thematically? If so, then read what Bettine claims an older friend told her when she was young, about those who serve princes: "The more they are weighed down by the demands which their times place on them, the more they believe they must shelter behind philistinism, and seek support in old, worm-eaten, burdensome prejudices, and create advisory bodies of every kind, both secret and public, which neither secretly nor publicly are anything but wrong—because genuine truth is so incredibly simple that, for that very reason, it never comes to the fore." I would be surprised if, when an older Bettine was reviewing Günderrode's papers, sentences like these did not remind her of the case of Savigny and the brothers Grimm.

But Bettine's political views are not what I am asking you to explore; or at least not the only thing. When I think how I recommended the publication of a new edition of Bettina von Arnim's *Correspondence with Günderrode* and wonder how I am to justify it, apart from the tired formula that we need to "preserve the Tradition"; when I reread her writings, more dubious than confident that today's readers, accustomed to thinking soberly and objectively, will be able to tolerate the dithyrambic language, the often effusive tone, the intemperance; when I consider whether readers will be able to get beyond feeling disconcerted by the relationship between the two women, and locate the contemporary features in their dialogue— then I think of you, your unappeasable curiosity about history and your earnest efforts, through liberated language, to rub off the layers of unlived life which segregate your mind, your consciousness, your feelings, and your body from each other. And I think about the connection between the layers of our history which were left unfinished, the productive beginnings which were mowed down by an "iron" tread, or merely by the crush of busy feet, and our own alienation. We should change our lives. But we are not.

I see how irredeemably naïve this remark is, and how disputable. And yet, as the letters of Bettine and Günderrode prove, men and women have never spoken such sentences without facing dispute from others. Nevertheless, I feel bound to confess that something in me contracts with envy and grief when I read and picture the innocent way (that is not to say the casual and carefree way) that two young German women were able to treat each other. For poetry, the truly human, flourishes only in the innocent; and they had poetry. We have poems, but poetry as a form of human intercourse is barred to us. No doubt, people of a different culture miss that quality in us. And we would seem to have gotten over the loss, except that many of us appear to suffer from a sort of phantom pain which makes us visibly eager to escape into phrases, activities, and actions remote from our emotions. I cannot help thinking: Am I perhaps recommending this book as a way to keep the phantom pain alive? But no, our ancestors cannot relieve us of anything. They can only add something to us.

The most striking thing about this book is the easiest thing to overlook, because it is not explicitly formulated: the statement made by the book's structure; namely, its refusal to abide by any aesthetic canon. I cannot help smiling at the cunning of our [German] language, which makes "literature" and "aesthetics"—both of them authorities to which we submit secretly—into words of feminine gender, although women's share in these fields is slight, and (as you yourself know by painful experience) a woman who takes on the task of creating her own individuality cannot move within their magnificent systems of rules without feelings of constraint. For one achievement of this aesthetics, which was developed and established by classicism during the lifetime of the Romantics, was the method of separating the "work" from its creator and allowing it to soar away into another sphere, the sphere of art, once it was freed from the life circumstances out of which it first arose. The letters which Bettine and Karoline exchanged do not lay claim to being "art," and gathered into a book, their very formlessness gave a suitable form in which to transmit experiences without having to de-form them. Of the then existing literary genres, not one—not the epistolary novel à la *Werther,* and certainly not the bourgeois novel—would have adequately allowed this. But when, toward the middle of the nineteenth century, Bettine remembered the forms proposed by the Romantics (which had since been forgotten), she did not simply reproduce literally the letters which she and Karoline had exchanged. The form that she felt compelled to adopt was a hybrid, a form which had the flexibility to follow the motions which the two women experienced with and through each other, and to show the person whole, incommensurable and contradictory; whereas the closed form of the novel would have been forced to reduce, to judge, to classify, and to regulate. This tells you something about the resistance to the domination of a certain canon of form: a canon to which they both submitted all the same, as a standard for their work. Günderrode, especially, tried to meet that standard, because to be a "significant" poet meant to serve the canon. But was it equally applicable to a woman poet? Bettine invited her friend to enter her School for Insignificance, offered her relief from day-in day-out austerity, from the immoderate demands which taxed Günderrode's strength. We should not be deceived by the lighthearted tone of Bettine's offer. After all, we know what it means and always has meant to refuse the one-sided training of the abilities which make a person "significant" in the world. Almost hesitantly, Günderrode accepted the role of Bettine's disciple in insignificance: "The same way that you regarded yourself as my pupil when I wanted to mold you into a powerful mind. Now that I am headed backward, you must become my teacher."

Backward? The word is startling. It betrays her, and no doubt sprang unconsciously from a feeling of relaxation after too much tension. Günderrode's choice of this term reveals her idea of what it meant to move "forward." But Bettine, despite her convent education, felt less compelled to submit to the norm and was quite unselfconscious about expressing her pleasure: "I am so happy that I am insignificant. That means I don't have to dish up clever thoughts anymore. When I write to you, all I have to do is tell a story." After all, she says, she has no "head for philosophy."

What does she mean? That she is not capable of thought? On the contrary, no matter how people badgered her on that account, Bettine insisted on using her head. No, what she means is that she believes that the way "philosophers" think is wrong; that is, unnatural. "But a philosopher seems to me no philosopher if he lies on the bosom [of nature] and is intimately devoted to her with all his strength. —Instead, I think that he is bent on plunder. Whatever he can swindle out of her he messes up in his secret factory, and there he has all he can do to keep it all running, as here a wheel jams, there a weight: one machine meshes with the next." The soulless, mechanistic approach which derived from the rise of industrial machinery and was then transferred into social relations and applied to man was a horror to Bettine. And she was flooded with premonitory insights into the possible pitfalls of our dependency on human reason: insights for which science had not yet invented any system or even a name. Just read the description she sent to Günderrode, of the philosopher who cobbles together "his whole edifice of thought," not "to understand himself," but merely "to display the hocus-pocus of his Superlative Machine." But the only one to be "imprisoned" by this machine, she says, is the "futile man" who is "out of touch with his own feelings." Today's psychologists would say the "frustrated" man, although the new nomenclature does not improve much on the old.

The views which Bettine and Günderrode exchanged on this

subject—whether to think in the way prescribed by philosophers, which Günderrode tentatively recommended to Bettine because Günderrode herself was susceptible to "rational" intellectual structures—make up the inner plot of their "novel," as exciting and worth telling as any plot there is. Must or can a person leave himself out of the account in philosophy, history, and art? Are thinking and writing to be used as a *means* to create oneself; or as an *end,* an object one manufactures—a work, a system—which ultimately turns against its producer? Bettine, who was often scolded for laziness and whom Günderrode assigned to study history ("Where will you get a grip on yourself if you have no ground to stand on?"), complained that her "teacher" had driven her into a "desert of history." "Meanwhile, I am all fired up about the present, I would like to apply myself to that, without first laying myself down on the anvil of the past and there letting myself be hammered flat." But she voluntarily studied the twelve emperors of Rome in order to compare them with Napoleon in his threatening rise to power and in order to rediscover in every tyrant "the same monster of mediocrity." And don't you agree that that is an astonishing insight, given that she did not have access to the data on dictators which our century so abundantly provides?

"I feel moved to accept your feelings and your actions as valid, without raising any objection," Bettine says, gently winning Günderrode over to side with her counterproposal, her woman's philosophy, her "floating religion," which, if it had only had a slight chance of being realized, would not have been driven to the brink of self-annihilation by the male culture of aggression. The two women philosophized in unison about a religion of *joie de vivre,* of sensory pleasure and humane attitudes, and developed "thoughts about government," ideas of how they would "revolutionize the world while they laughed out loud." And along with that, they formed a bond of love—one of the very few examples in our literature (perhaps the only one?) of an alternative to male bonding, and to the teacher-pupil relationships which are so prevalent.

> I cannot write poetry like you Günderrode, but I can talk with nature when I am alone with her . . . And when I come back . . . we put our beds side by side and chat away together all night long . . . and we two philosophers engage in . . . great profound speculations which make the old world creak on its rusty hinges, if it does not positively turn upside down as a result. —Do you know what? You are Plato, and you

are exiled to the fortress there, and I am your dearest friend and pupil Dion. We love each other tenderly and would be willing to die for each other if necessary, and even if it only *might* be necessary: for there is nothing I would rather do than risk my life for you . . . Yes, that's what I will call you in future: Plato!—and I want to give you a pet name, I will call you Swan, which is what Socrates called you, and you call me Dion . . . Good night, my Swan, go to sleep there on the altar of Eros.

Thinking together, out of love and for love's sake. Using love, using longing as a means of knowledge; not having to leave oneself out of the account in order to think and know; making each other's "temples burn" with "ardent zeal for the future." Giving each other names, playing roles which did not tally with everyday reality and which nevertheless allowed them to step outside themselves, to go beyond themselves. Playing with language, inventing new words and calling them out to each other: "spirit's-eye," "day-nature," "web-of-art," "reality's sensing-nerves." —You will discover all this, and much more, for yourself. You, and many others, I believe, will understand this language, as if you had dreamed of it. You will understand that this book describes an experiment which two women agreed to carry out, supporting each other, strengthening each other, learning from each other. A utopian experiment, certainly. It ended with them. But why have we let the word "utopia" deteriorate into a term of abuse?

I know why. Who has more cause than we to shut the door on irrationalism in all its forms? But, reading Bettine's book, you find a form of thinking which tries to unite in one person a heightened rationality with an intensified ability to feel; which fears the one-sidedness of instrumental, objective thinking (a *different* kind of irrationalism!)—and we are the first people who are really able to judge how justified that fear is; which sets up a personal way of approaching nature—including human nature—that differs from the soulless, mechanistic attitudes of "spirit-killing philosophy." An alternative, yes. An alternative which was conceived and proposed at the very moment when the society switched irreversibly onto the track of the exploitation of nature, the twisting of ends into means, and the oppression of every "feminine" element in the new civilization. The melancholy note in Bettine's questions shows that she felt all this; Günderrode's suicide proves her despair.

Naturally, Bettine knew Goethe's *Faust,* or as much of it as had been printed at the time—including the vain struggle of Faust the scientist to force the Earth Spirit to serve him. How differently Bettine addresses nature.

> I have very often had this feeling as if nature were lamenting in a melancholy voice, begging me for something, so that it tore my heart not to understand what she was asking for . . . Then I stood still for a while, the roaring seemed just like a sigh to me, which sounded as if it came from a child; and I spoke to her as if she were a child. "Sweetheart!—what's wrong?" and when I had said that, a shudder came over me and I felt ashamed, as if I had addressed someone who is far above me, and then I suddenly lay down and hid my face in the grass . . . and then, lying on the earth with my face hidden, I felt tender.

What a different scene from Faust's confrontation with the Earth Spirit! Not a declaration of war to the death, not the unconditional subjugation of nature, not the hybris of the "Faustian" man who, casting aside Faust's doubts, gains knowledge by putting nature on the rack, forcing confessions out of it with screws and irons. Hers is a different kind of progress. A different kind of magic from the diabolic sort for which Faust sells his soul, and which destroys him, a man become a stranger to himself. How different an adversary was created by God the Father when he made Mephisto to incite man to ambivalent creation than was bred by Mother Nature when she made her army of witches, nymphs, and sprites—those beings who now, in the Faustian age, were repressed, accursed, and labeled taboo, and whose ranks Bettine, their latter-day descendant, joined trembling with emotion. What a counterdesign we find at the roots of this culture going astray! What boldness in the dialogue of the two women!

> Here on this globe, where people slide apart as if it were covered with a sheet of ice; where they have not the power to hold on to each other for the space of a breath and yet are forever dizzy with passion. If love were real, it would show itself not as a ghost in the form of passions but would be our native element, and then of course there would be no need to talk about restraining oneself. Look! Am I not right in not asking to be loved?—since a person can do nothing to oblige himself, not to mention someone else. I do not love, but everything I do is to oblige others . . . My ideal is this *irony in love,* which smiles at not achieving its end, but does not "lament" at its forlornness.

I know of no more apt explanation of what is called "romantic irony," which, psychologically speaking, consists in bravely concealing a wound. The theme of love denied permeates Bettine's entire life, taking the form of a painful knowledge, of paradox, of contradiction, of an "innermost secret." The passage I just quoted to you is from her last letter-novel, *Ilius Pamphilius und die Ambrosia* (1848), which became a vehicle for her experiences with Julius Döring. And remarkably, this "painful knowledge" of hers was linked, from the outset, to a conviction that she was as much barred from writing poetry as from loving. When Günderrode sent Bettine her *Apocalyptic Fragment*, Bettine wrote back: "The fire of jealousy rages inside me when you do not stay down on the ground, where I am . . . I cannot write any fragments, I can only write to you . . . Nor can I change the fact that my senses are focused exclusively on you . . . That is how it is for someone who is consumed by fire and yet cannot endure that any water should put it out . . . I know how it will be for me my whole life long, I know it well." And then she went on to struggle nonstop—how could she help it?—to repeal this sentence.

An obscure but meaningful link exists between these evidences of a forcible renunciation of love and Bettine's refusal to write poetry. She resisted Clemens's importunings. Irresponsible as the young Bettine may have seemed, she observed herself closely, and self-knowledge forbade her to exploit her talents as a poet. She expressed it with astonishing clarity to Günderrode: "It would be sacrilege for me to write poetry, because I drink wine and feel the god while I am intoxicated, because the mind's urge to make divinities passes through me, making me tremble . . . I myself will not create love, no more than I will create a poem, that is what I feel. And also there is a secret contradiction in me: I do not want to be disturbed, in the inner workshop of my spirit, by having my love returned."

Not being disturbed also means: not being destroyed. Unconditional surrender makes a person defenseless. Thus, being unable may be equivalent to not wanting to. The two women, each in her own way, are rigorous thinkers who think things out to the end even if they must oppose their own interests, and this kind of courage is where they understand and touch each other most intimately, sometimes without words. You will find much that is unspoken, deliberately held back, carried along on the river of the spoken.

Bettine sensed that the aesthetic structures she knew must in some way be linked to the hierarchical structures of society, whatever the

form in which these were mediated. An insoluble paradox of literature is that it is dependent on the very rules which it must continually
overstep in order to become literature. Bettine tried to get around
this trap. She surrendered herself neither to love nor to art. Günderrode did not have this strategy at her command. Her letters are tuned
to a more earnest note. She could only surrender herself completely,
or refuse herself completely. She wanted to be both a lover and a
poet. So she placed herself within a system of laws based on the
masculine concepts of "artwork" and "genius," which demanded of
her what she could not achieve: to separate her work from herself as a
person; to create art at life's expense; to create in herself the detachment and coolness which produces "the work" but which kills the
direct relationship with other people because it turns them into objects. I wonder, and I ask you: Couldn't the frequently (and sometimes hypocritically) lamented scarcity of women artistic "geniuses"
relate not only to women's social condition but also to their unfitness
to adapt to an image of the genius which is modeled on a man?

Didn't Günderrode herself intuit something of the sort? It is evident that in her poetry, too, she saw herself captive between irrecon-
cilables. She never forgot that, in poetry, "nothing is more essential
than that its germ spring directly from the inner self." At the same
time, she complained of the strictness of convention, which made it so
hard for the laws of nature to operate successfully. "If only the playing field where energies now exercise by traditional rules were to be
deregulated, to make it easier for nature to change its laws . . . I have
controlled myself, too, and learned to obey."

Couldn't it be that the thing in her which she had to suppress in
order "to obey" one day rebelled against her, self-destructively? That
she exhausted herself in the struggle to attain those "simple forms"
which "at the same time assist creation, in a feeling of inner harmony," and which, as she said, characterized only the "supreme master in poetry"? No doubt of it, she toiled over the aesthetics of the
masterpieces which she could not hope to produce herself. (Have you
ever heard the term "mistresspieces"?) She renounced those masterworks for the truth's sake, but felt inferior as she did it.

I myself often could not help but recognize the poverty of the images in
which I couched my poetic moods. I sometimes thought that lusher
forms, more beautiful vestures lay close by, ready for use, and that
more significant subject matter was easily available to me; only it did

not originate as a primary mood in the soul, and so I have always rejected it and have stuck to what deviated least from my real feelings. This was also why I dared to have [my poems] printed. They had that value for me, the sacred value of graven truth. I regard all the little fragments as poetry, in that sense.

We are indeed witnessing the attempt at a new aesthetics, and the fragments of it merit our collecting them. We will hear Georg Büchner say very similar things. The experience of being unable to actualize herself, either in love or in art, led to Günderrode's death. She envied Bettine her greater degree of inner freedom. "I myself often do not know which wind to steer by, and let myself be driven by all. Have patience with me, since you know me, and keep in mind that it is not one voice alone that I have to oppose but a general voice which, like the Lernaean serpent, continually produces new heads."

I will close with this image. The "general voice" which imposed on Günderrode a standard that was not her own is what killed her. You know the lines in which she said goodbye to the world: "Earth, my mother, and you, air, who nourish me . . ." Those same lines would have fit into Bettine's book, into her dialogue with Bettine, in which the underlying tone of earnestness is made all the more apparent by the gay and playful arabesques in which the two women bravely engage. You know what happened to Bettine later in her life. You know she could not stop proposing a different way of being in the world, a way that would not kill. This book is a beautiful document, a moving voice from a time that is long gone.

You know how the general voice speaks to us today, and what it is speaking about.

December 1979

Notes

1. The variable spelling of Bettine's name, which was sometimes written with an *a* at the end and sometimes with an *e*, has been retained by Christa Wolf.

2. The Holy Alliance (1815) was an agreement between the rulers of Russia, Austria, and Prussia, later joined by others, confirming the political
system that was restored after the fall of Napoleon. This was followed in
the German states by the Carlsbad Decrees of 1819, which enacted further repressive measures, such as government censorship and surveillance, and strict controls on university life. After the revolution of July
1830, the persecution of democratic thinking was stepped up yet again.

3. Prince Hermann Pückler (1785–1871), German writer.

4. A democratic protest demonstration held at Castle Hambach in May
1832. Protesters called for democratic freedoms, for German unity in a
federated German republic, and for an alliance of democratic forces in
various nations such as Poland, France, Italy, and Greece. The German
Bund, a loose federation of German states, replied with more reactionary policies.

5. The *Hessische Landbote* [Hessian Courier] was a revolutionary pamphlet
published by Georg Büchner in 1834. In 1835 and 1836 Büchner had to
flee to Strassburg and then to Switzerland to escape persecution. "Young
Germany," *c.* 1830–50, was a literary movement with radical political
leanings which included a number of authors viewed as "enemies of the
state," such as Karl Gutzkow and Heinrich Heine.

II

Gender and Politics

Strategies of Female Persuasion: The Political Letters of Bettina Brentano-von Arnim

Lorely French

And exactly out of the conviction I was given that a woman was incapable of such business, and that her voice did not matter, I dared to write these pages, for if they prevent a stricter view or at least should mitigate one, this does not stem from human wisdom, which has no voice in a woman, but rather from divine inspiration, to which the magnanimity of the King is allowed to acquiesce itself undauntedly.

Und grade auf die überzeugung hin, die man mir gab, daß eine Frau untüchtig zu solchem Geschäft, und daß ihre Stimme nicht gelte, wagte ich es [sic] diese Blätter zu schreiben, denn, wenn sie einer strengeren Ansicht zuvorkommen oder sie doch wenigstens mildern sollten, so rührt dies nicht von menschlicher Weisheit her, die in einer Frau keine Stimme hat, sondern von göttlicher Eingebung, der sich die Großmut der Könige unverzagt ergeben darf.

—Bettina Brentano-von Arnim[1]

With these mixed feelings of female incompetence on the one hand, and unabashed, divine inspiration on the other, Bettina Brentano-von Arnim explains to Crown Prince Friedrich Wilhelm why she feels justified to advise him in letters. Problematic about Brentano-von Arnim's assertion is how ambivalently she discloses an awareness of her position as a woman writing from the margins of a male-dominated political sphere while attempting to manipulate that position and strengthen her argument.

To accept Brentano-von Arnim's belief in her incompetence risks devaluing her epistles as a form of political expression directed not by intellect and knowledge, but by innate feelings and emotions—a dichotomizing view that has led to marginalization of her political writings in secondary literature.[2] But to ignore her awareness of traditional concepts of femininity neglects the complex role that mid-nineteenth-century gender ideology plays in her political letters. This neglect has often caused scholars to isolate Brentano-von Arnim's activism from that other women, who, during the 1830s and 1840s, seem to critique gender constraints more directly and acutely.[3] Such isolation is partially valid, for Brentano-von Arnim did not actively participate in or align herself with any women's groups who were publicly demanding sexual equality and democracy in rebellion against patriarchal domination. An understanding of how she handled restrictive feminine norms, however, as in the above quote, requires a more comparative perspective that will also lend an important cohesion to German women's culture and history, especially in the nineteenth century.[4]

The following analysis considers the equivocal messages in Brentano-von Arnim's epistles in the context of similar examples from the writings of her politically active contemporaries, including Mathilde Franziska Anneke (1817–1884), Louise Aston (1814–1871), Emma Herwegh (1817–1904), and Fanny Lewald (1811–1889). There are existing feminist literary studies that offer models to help understand the tradition in which Brentano-von Arnim's conflicting subservience to and subversion of male norms are rooted. For example, Sandra Gilbert and Susan Gubar's *The Madwoman in the Attic* (1979) and Sigrid Weigel's "Double Focus: On the History of Women's Writing" (1983) recognize the tensions evolved from women writers' struggles with androcentric literary conventions.[5] Although these two studies offer useful paradigms by which to interpret the ambivalent sentiments in Brentano-von Arnim's epistles, my discussion assumes a somewhat different approach. Instead of concentrating on the role that fictional metaphors play in women's struggle against patriarchal literary authority, my investigation focuses first on the women's conflict with a powerful gender ideology that determined epistemological conceptions of the political and the personal, and the roles of each sex in these spheres. Second, I address how the letter form offered these nineteenth-century women what they saw as a non-fictive means to subvert gender ideology by disguising political action and challenging the public/private dichotomy. A study of the ambivalences found in the epistolary writings of Brentano-von Arnim, Anneke, Aston, Herwegh, and Lewald will help understand their attempts to reconcile their desires for political expression with conventional feminine roles. Moreover, by examining how carefully constructed such ambivalences appear, we can identify their effectiveness as strategies whereby the women exercise their political voice by manipulating the patriarchal powers-that-be.

Bettina Brentano-von Arnim's political consciousness surfaces in her first work, *Goethe's Correspondence With A Child* (Goethes Briefwechsel mit einem Kinde) (1835), as she challenges Goethe's resignation to occurrences such as the Tyrolean struggle for independence. In the diary part of the work, she displays a concern for the poor, oppressed, or disabled.

In the 1840s, her works and deeds assume a more obvious political stance, which caused the officials to take restrictive action, including filing secret reports on her political activities in 1843 and 1847 and creating difficulties with her publishing her two later works, *Clemens Brentano's Spring Wreath* (Clemens Brentanos Frühlingskranz) (1844) and *Ilius Pamphilius and the Ambrosia* (Ilius Pamphilius und die Ambrosia) (1848). In her conversational work, *This Book Belongs to the King* (Dies Buch gehört dem König) (1843) she advises the king on political issues, criticizing him for following the advice of his inept advisors and for his lack of humaneness and justice in such areas as censorship, restricted religious freedoms, and the death penalty. Her unfinished compilation of data on Silesian weavers, published first in 1962 as *Das Armenbuch* (Poor Book), includes empirical evidence of the misery of the working poor and Brentano-von Arnim's personal commentary on the urgent need for change. In her volunteer work with the poor during the 1831 Berlin cholera epidemic and her notoriously liberal salon in the late 1840s, she displayed a continued concern for the socially underprivileged. Her political involvement remained consistently personal and interactive, in that her publications and activities show a dialogic narrative form that demands an important subjective viewpoint when discussing public concerns.

Consonant with this personal, conversational approach to public issues are the numerous letters that Brentano-von Arnim wrote to influential people on behalf of political activists whom she felt officials had treated injustly. Her letters to the king and the Berlin magistrate contain her harshest critiques of the political system and her clearest proposals of alternatives to that system, based on the individual cases she defends.[6] Between 1838 and 1852 Brentano-von Arnim wrote her strongest political epistles to Crown Prince, later King Friedrich Wilhelm IV, on behalf of acquaintances who had been indicted or dismissed for their subversive actions. From 1838 to 1840 she pleaded the case of Jakob and Wilhelm Grimm, who as members of the dismissed "Göttingen Seven" had to seek new positions; in 1845 she defended Friedrich Wilhelm Schlöffel, from whom she had received lists of poor workers for her *Poor Book*, against accusations that he was a communist; in 1846 and 1847 she wrote on behalf of Ludwig von Mieroslawski who was sentenced to death in 1847 for his involvement in Poland's independence struggle; in 1849 she pleaded against the death sentence of the former Storkow mayor Tschech who had attempted to assassinate the king in 1844; in 1849 she tried to persuade the king to acquit the theologian and art historian Gottfried Kinkel, who was sentenced to life imprisonment for his participation in the 1848 Revolution. From 1846 to 1847 Brentano-von Arnim engaged in an involved correspondence with the Berlin magistrate to defend her actions in publishing Achim von Arnim's work and her own material privately. The magistrate had ordered her to purchase her citizenship, which she needed to continue the private publishing business she had begun in 1846. She stated that she would not pay for the honor of citizenship, but would accept it, if conferred upon her. The magistrate was insulted by her remark and brought suit against her.

Male reactions to Brentano-von Arnim's political epistles constantly reminded her that she was overstepping the boundaries of the traditionally female private sphere and impinging upon the male-centered public domain.[7] In responses to her, for example, Friedrich Wilhelm IV characterized her method of defending the Polish independence fighters as typically "feminine" for its lack of objective evaluation, ignorance on political issues, and emotionalism (*Bettine von Arnim und Friedrich Wilhelm IV* 99–101). His advice to Brentano-von Arnim when she asks him to allow Xavière Mazurkiewicz to visit her brother, the Polish insurgent Ludwig von Mieroslawski, in prison demonstrates the passive, subservient attitude that men expected women to have toward politics: "Advise Frau von Mazurkiewicz to yield to *the order not to make or incite any sensation*. This is genuinely feminine advice in such an unfeminine time as the present time" (Rathen Sie Frau von Mazurkiewicz, sich *der Ordnung zufügen, kein Aufsehen zu machen oder zu veranlassen*. Dies ist ein echt weiblicher Rath in so unweiblicher Zeit als die Jetztzeit) (*Bettine von Arnim und Friedrich Wilhelm IV* 100–101). The king's attempt to suppress women's participation reflects an epistemological dichotomy that views political expression as intellectual, systematic, and thus masculine, whereas personal concerns are emotional, unsystematic, and feminine. In this male-dominated dichotomy, privacy becomes defined only in opposition to the public and political, that is, as that which the public and the political have the right to suppress and censor.[8] The king demands submission and silence under the auspices of "feminine advice," using his power as a public man to exclude the private emotions of a woman.

The "unfeminine time" of social and political unrest in the mid-nineteenth century was characterized not only by open protests and battles, which were traditionally men's activities, but also by the formidable control that men possessed to restrict women's public participation. Legally, women had no voting rights, and thus no official say in any policy-making decisions.[9] Moreover, cultural stereotypes of women as mothers, virgins, and housewives psychologically censored them from participating in any activities that defied those roles.[10] If a woman did engage in political action, she was not supposed to display any self-initiative or desire to participate for the sake of making herself a public figure. Women could legitimize their actions by stressing that loyalty to be at their husbands' sides, an altruistic desire to help others, or the need to enhance familial or cultural life had drawn them into political service.

Despite these restrictions, several women, including Bettina Brentano-von Arnim and the four others discussed in this essay, did become politically outspoken in the 1830s and 1840s, using their evolutionary call for democratic representation in government and for elimination of all human oppression to defend their own equal political rights.[11] Mathilde Anneke became involved in the social-democratic/republican cause after marrying her second husband, Fritz Anneke. When he was imprisoned, she became editor of the *New Cologne Newspaper*, which she renamed the *Women's Newspaper* to avoid censorship. The couple's participation in the Baden-Pfalz battle in 1849 led to their exile in Switzerland and eventually the United States. She relates her revolutionary experiences in *Memoirs of a Woman in the Baden-Pfalz Campaign* (Memoiren einer Frau aus dem badisch-pfälzischen Feldzuge 1848/49) (1853). In the United States she became an active member of the American women's movement, founding a *German Women's Newspaper*, traveling widely to present speeches at national conventions, and establishing a girls' school in Milwaukee.[12]

Novelist, editor, and insurgent Louise Aston, in an attempt to prove women's equality with men, often assumed attire and mannerisms that resembled those of George Sand. Aston wore pants, smoked cigars, expounded on religious and sexual freedoms in public, and frequented local taverns alone. Her unconventional behavior led to her eventual banishment from Berlin, an experience she related in her book *My Emancipation, Banishment, and Vindication* (Meine Emancipation, Verweisung und Rechtfertigung) (1846). Subsequently, she joined the democratic rebellion, became the editor of a short-lived newspaper called *The Insurgent* (Der Freischärler) (1848), and wrote two novels, *Lydia* (1848) and *Revolution and Contrerevolution* (1849), which tell about events of 1848 from the perspective of a politically engaged woman.[13] After marrying in 1850, Aston retreated from public, political life. Instead, she followed her husband Dr. Daniel Eduard Meier around Germany, Russia, Hungary, and the Ukraine in connection with his medical work, although the reputation she had established in her earlier years as a rebel lived on.

Emma Herwegh supported the revolution alongside her husband, the writer Georg Herwegh. When both were expelled from Prussia in 1842, they spent their exile in Zurich and Paris. Emma Herwegh accompanied her husband's armed troops in their effort to support the 1848 Revolution in Germany from Switzerland. In exile, she contributed to his history of the battle and to translated works by Italian and French activists, including Garibaldi.

Fanny Lewald was a prolific writer of novels, travel literature and short stories. Her early writings criticized women's restricted social situation, especially in marriages of convenience, and advocated less stringent divorce laws. Lewald, too, was an enthusiastic supporter of the 1848 Revolution and traveled around, writing reports and letters on its progress. In *Recollections From the Year 1848* (Erinnerungen aus dem Jahre 1848) (1850), she presents her observations on the Revolution while in Paris. She later became a monarchist, a complex turn that can be considered from several viewpoints—the influence of her conservative husband, the general Jewish political discussion, and the dialectics of bourgeois rationality that both encouraged and restricted Utopian thinking.[14] Lewald's subsequent writings, *Easter Letters for Women* (Osterbriefe für die Frauen) (1863) and *For and*

Against Women [Für und wider die Frauen] (1870), however, still promote equal opportunity for women in education and employment.

Born at least twenty-five years before any of these four women, Brentano-von Arnim did not participate with them in causes or publicly defend their works or actions. Age differences, however, do not adequately explain what one might regard as an absence of women's solidarity and should not deter a comparative study of their writings. Brentano-von Arnim began her career late; the form and dates of her political epistles coincide with those of the other women.[15] Fanny Lewald's *Recollections from the Year 1848* includes, as she states in the introduction, letters to her friend Therese (von Struve) von Lützow, to whom the book is also dedicated. Louise Aston incorporates her letters to the king into *My Emancipation, Banishment, and Vindication* to defend her free, liberated actions after her 1846 expulsion from Berlin. Mathilde Anneke's and Emma Herwegh's autobiographical accounts of their activism converge with the epistle in an introductory, dedicatory address to a reader and a direct invocation of a specific reader throughout the work. Anneke addresses *Memoirs of a Woman from the Baden-Pfalz Campaign* to "You women at home" (9). Herwegh directs *On the History of the German Democratic Legion from Paris. By a Traitor* (Zur Geschichte der deutschen demokratischen Legion aus Paris. Von einer Hochverräterin) (1849) to the prisoners taken captive during the uprising in Baden. She corrects what she believes were false accounts of her escape with Georg Herwegh at the conclusion of the battle.

To be sure, these works differ in subject matter and political intent. Aston's vindication has as its sole political agenda her bitter defense, and thus represents the most rebellious perspective on women's individual freedoms of the four. Both Anneke and Herwegh portray frontline revolutionary action from their personal perspectives as participants; Anneke recognizes herself as a focal point of developments in her memoir, whereas Herwegh seeks a more documentary account that centers on the whole troop's actions. In contrast, Lewald, as an observer of events, produces a report more typical of journalistic travel literature than the others. Brentano-von Arnim, unlike the other women, did not publish her letters, and thus her pleas to high officials on behalf of her acquaintances appear more personal. As various passages in her letters during the magistrate's process indicate, however, she did consider publishing the correspondence, or parts of it (*Magistratsprozess* 103, 111, 132, 154). Moreover, in personal letters, Brentano-von Arnim eventually expands her defense to critique official restrictive public policies on basic human rights and addresses her letters to public officials, just as the other women write for public audiences.

Despite their differences, these texts, in their appropriation of the letter, still depict women's repeated return to the epistolary form to become involved in public events. Widespread use of the letter form seems to be a direct consequence of the previously discussed paradox between a gender ideology that limited women's access to the public sphere and revolutionary demands that tolerated women's call for equality as part of the general protest against oppression. The letter, often penned from inside the writer's own personal space, and yet assuming the presence of an outside addressee, offered women a viable link between the public and private spheres. As an act that did not appear self-initiated, and thus evoked no air of ambition or fame, but rather responded to an issue or concern coming from another person or outside source, letter writing enabled women to feign subordination to norms of the feminine while voicing their opinions. In letter writing, women could adopt various strategies whereby they could internalize patterns of normative behavior while satisfying their needs for political expression.

Virginia Woolf best explains the significance of the letter's double-edged quality for women, writing: "The art of letter writing is often the art of essay-writing in disguise. But such as it was, it was an art that a woman could practice without unsexing herself. . . . without exciting comment, anonymously as it were, and often with the pretense that it served some useful purpose" (52). Besides allowing women to interject subversive comments into what might be perceived as harmless, private texts, the disguise of the letters also permitted them to challenge the hegemonic system of formal discourse and gender norms. Recently, the scholar Anne Hermann, in her study of epistolary essays by Virginia Woolf and Christa Wolf, points out how the letter form has allowed women to stress their historical exclusion from full participation in society and their isolation from more canonized forms of rhetoric in the male-dominated literary world. Women letter-writers, working within a traditional form of female rhetoric outside more conventional forms of patriarchal discourse, are still able, under the letter's pretense, to criticize authoritarian power structures.

As disguised protests then, letters often reveal ambivalence and hesitation, demonstrating women writing as gendered subjects as they reformulate the authoritarian political system that has excluded them. In an effort to deny political motivations that are not fitting for a woman, Bettina Brentano-von Arnim, especially in letters to the king, continually stresses her own unfamiliarity with politics. She insists that her advice and requests are based on her own personal connections, and not on any larger ideology (Köln 5: 349; *Bettine von Arnim und Friedrich Wilhelm IV* 5). When defending Schlöffel, Mieroslawski, and Kinkel, she emphasizes not the public loss, but the private grief that each man's incarceration would cause his family. The death of her own son, she contends, has driven her to empathize with the hardships of these men (*Bettine von Arnim und Friedrich Wilhelm IV* 95). She underscores her personal involvement and political isolation by asserting that she does not read newspapers (*Bettine von Arnim und Friedrich Wilhelm IV* 105, 161). In the following passage, she undermines her influential powers over the king, doubting her informal speech and proclaiming a lack of ambition.

> How do I come to hold such confidential conversations arising out of the depth of the heart in front of Your Majesty? Considering that one finds it permissible to speak only in a stilted manner in front of sovereigns, and also only the stiltedness is recognized as rational. It is not ambition, I have by nature no ambition— no none at all!—I have never striven for relations that guaranteed me distinction, my relations to humanity were much more private, much more intimate in their connections.

> Wie komme ich dazu, so vertrauliche Reden vor Euer Majestät zu führen, die aus der Mitte des Herzens hervorkeimen? Da man vor Fürsten doch nur auf hölzerne Weise zu sprechen erlaubt findet, und auch nur das Hölzerne als vernunftgemäß anerkennt! Es ist nicht Ambition, ich habe von Natur keine Ambition—nein gar keine!—ich habe nie nach Verhältnissen getrachtet, die mir Glanz gewährten, meine Verhältnisse zur Menschheit waren viel heimlicher, viel inniger in ihren Beziehungen. (Köln 5: 366)

One might initially accept Bettina von Arnim's arguments that she had no ambition and that her interests were not public and political, but personal. For years readers including the scholar Ludwig Geiger (*Bettine von Arnim und Friedrich Wilhelm IV* 75) believed her assertion that she did not read newspapers. This assertion, however, is doubtful. She often acknowledged the power of the press, especially during the trial by the magistrate (*Magistratsprozess* 158–171), and availed herself of the press, as in the French newspaper *Voix des Femmes* on 22 March 1848 in which she published parts of her book, *The King's Book*. In view of the discrepancy between her words and actions, questioning her public ambition and stressing her personal contacts became ways for her to undermine the threat her pleas may have caused.

Moreover, another reading reveals how claims to political naiveté and questions about the purpose and style of her letters become tactics designed to contrast her more personal form of discourse with the formal styles used in the king's circles. In the above example, she criticizes a world in which ambition means adopting a stilted discourse that alienates rather than cultivates more personal forms of speech. Her critique comes specifically from someone who has decided not to adopt an impersonal form of discourse and, in a letter, a form that supports that claim. In the context of her political critique, her statements represent direct attacks on the king's ministers who have advised the king poorly and in a manner that leaves no room for human compassion. At other points in her letters, she raises questions about the king's powers of reasoning (*Bettine von Arnim und Friedrich Wilhelm IV* 143) and admonishes the king for listening too uncritically to his ministers and for accepting false advice (129). The boldness of her recommendations and her later admission that she deems it her "occupation to exchange thoughts with the King" (167) belie her claims to innocence.

To comply with the androcentric dichotomy assigning women to the private sphere, the other women also often refute any implications that their political writings and deeds might be publicly oriented. In the introduction to *Recollections From the Year 1848*, Fanny Lewald stresses that friends have cajoled her to publish her letters, even though she doubts the public worth of her personal views (Lewald I: vii–viii). Louise Aston opens her defense of her unconventional appearance and way of life in a letter that expresses her disapproval of women who publish merely for the sake of self-exposure, accusing them of vanity. Instead, the most legitimate reason why women should publicize their private lives is out of self-defense, i.e., as response to a situation inflicted from an outside source. Her own work reflects the latter motive.

A woman who brings her private affairs in front of the general public forum must either be immensely vain or have been forced to make this step by the *most extreme necessity,* a necessity against which it would be, because of a false sense of shame, both cowardly and dishonorable to struggle. In this latter case I find myself.

Eine Frau, die ihre Privatangelegenheiten vor das Forum der Öffentlichkeit bringt, muß entweder grenzenlos eitel sein oder von der *äussersten Notwendigkeit* zu diesem Schritte gezwungen werden, einer Notwendigkeit, gegen welche sich aus falschem Schamgefühl zu sträuben, ebenso feig als ehrlos wäre. In diesem letztem Falle befinde ich mich. (*Meine Emancipation, Verweisung und Rechtfertigung* 5)

In a similar manner, Emma Herwegh cautions readers directly against interpreting her history as the work of a professional author, for she would never want to increase "the number of literary women (called by the technical term *bluestockings*)" (die Zahl der schriftstellerischen Frauen [mit dem technischen Ausdruck *bas-bleus* genannt]) (Herwegh 130). Instead, she denies any ambition or talent in her work. In addition to renunciations of self-interest, Herwegh states that she has fought for the democratic cause not to seek her own fame, but to accompany her husband (153).

Likewise, Mathilde Franziska Anneke, in the introduction to her memoir, pleads belief in the revolution along with loyalty to her husband to justify her fighting in Baden and the Palatinate. She advises her female readers to understand her actions.

Be gentle, you women, I appeal to your most beautiful virtue, be gentle and do not judge; know that not war, but love, called me—but I assure you—also hate, the burning hate produced in the struggle of life, hate against the tyrants and oppressors of the sacred human rights. With love I followed the man of my heart, whose mighty arm is devoted to the struggle of vengeance against these tyrants.

Seid milde, Ihr Frauen, ich appelire an Eure schönste Tugend, seid milde und richtet nicht; wisset, nicht der Krieg hat mich gerufen, sondern die Liebe,—aber ich gestehe es Euch—auch der Hass, der glühende, im Kampf des Lebens erzeugte Hass gegen die Tyrannen und Unterdrücker der heiligen Menschenrechte. Mit der Liebe bin ich dem Manne meines Herzens gefolgt, dessen kräftiger Arm dem Kampf der Rache gegen diese Tyrannen geweiht ist. (Anneke 10)

As in the case of Bettina von Arnim's assertions, one might be inclined to believe these women's modest claims to political innocence and question how we may consider these strategies of political persuasion. Remarkable in each case, however, is the incongruence between the initial justifications and the rest of the text, between, as with Bettina Brentano-von Arnim, the word and the action.

While Lewald may have originally written about the 1848 revolution in letters to her friend as spontaneously as she claims she did, the final, published collection is so highly stylized and well-organized that the reader cannot help but surmise that she edited the letters carefully before publication. Her letters seem to be well-planned, conscious attempts to temper politically motivated events—such as her visits to Heinrich Heine and Georg Herwegh and to political clubs in Paris, and her reports on the Parliament sessions and the assassination of Prince Lichnowsky in Frankfurt—with less controversial cultural affairs, such as visits to museums, the opera, and fancy restaurants.

Similarly, Aston outlines in her preface only two options available for women who wish to publish, neither of which allow for independently motivated self-expression. Yet Aston's own career is a poor model for her observations. As the author of numerous critical poems, articles, and novels, many with autobiographical tendencies, Aston relied often on the public arena to voice her personal opinions on female emancipation and the revolution. Anneke and Herwegh, too, in their introductions, contend that they did not partake in political activities independently from their husbands. They use the autobiographical form, however, to display the many activities that they did undertake and to state their views on a wide variety of contemporary issues. Neither woman was submissive or passive. Herwegh acted many times as a messenger between the German Legion in Paris and their leaders in Baden, as the former waited for orders to cross the Rhine. Anneke, too, was a messenger for the troops during the Baden-Pfalz battles. Both women also comment freely on the state of the revolution, criticizing problems of disorder among the rebels and pointing out conflicts between the people and the revolutionaries.

Each woman initially negates any political motivation behind writing her political epistle, but then publishes (Anneke, Aston, Herwegh, and Lewald) or sends (Bettina Brentano-von Arnim) the epistle anyway. The letter serves as a shield between the self and the public in that each writer refutes any demands for attention but receives the attention anyway. The text represents the subversive activity of writing that the author alleges she would never attempt and actually offers a pretext for assertions. Moreover, the letter form directly addressing a reader personalizes the statements and thus leads the reader to believe claims of naivete. Under this veil of intimacy, the women can adeptly assert their opinions or portray their rebellious actions.

While self-effacement reveals Brentano-von Arnim's anxiety about political authority, it also remains a pretense for speaking openly. Through self-deprecation she concurrently advances her opinions on free expression. She voices innate fears about writing to the king, declaring that her words and deeds are meaningless compared to his great feats (Köln 5:349). Yet she counters her low self-worth with an expressed need to articulate her opinions (Köln 5:340, 371). She insists on her lack of ambition, but statements referring to her letter writing as her occupation belie her assertion: "There I had thoughts that delighted me, and premonitions of fate from which I thought, it was my occupation to exchange thoughts with the King" (Da hatte ich Gedanken, die mich ergötzen, und Schicksalsahnungen, von denen dachte ich, es sei mein Beruf, Gedanken auszutauschen mit dem König) (*Bettine von Arnim und Friedrich Wilhelm IV* 167). Behind the familiarity of the letter, however, her ambition comes across as nonthreatening to the male reader.

In Brentano-von Arnim's letters and in the four other women's appropriations of the letter form for political causes, the reader can assume two specific tactics—conscious conformity to the norm that women should not be involved in politics and deviation from it. Such ambivalent expressions enable the women activists to interpret the restrictive political system and to assert their views within accepted boundaries of female discourse. Their interpretation becomes most interesting when they write, as Virginia Woolf states, "without unsexing themselves," that is, by calling particular attention to their gender and thus allowing readers to view the controversial intersection between the sexual and the political. For example, in the quote from Bettina Brentano-von Arnim's letter that began this essay, the author affirms presumed feminine traits in her political motives, thereby showing conformity to a norm that views women as incompetent for such actions. But she also exploits this acknowledged feminine position as a rhetorical excuse for, and not against, writing to the king. Again, undermining the quality of her deeds, she attempts to adopt norms of female passivity to avoid threatening him as a male reader.

In such instances, Brentano-von Arnim couches subversive messages in statements that affirm her femininity, a strategy other women use to clarify their motives. Anneke, for example, was a large, muscular woman who rode horseback to deliver messages and to fight in battle. Men opposed her actions by satirizing her masculine dress. In her memoir, Anneke argues that a newspaper portrayal of her wearing men's clothes is a lie: "A powerful sledge-sabre, a hunting knife, muskets and men's clothing are the requirements that it [the Cologne Newpaper] also held ready for me out of its cupboard of lies and with which it armed me in this opportune time" (Ein wuchtiger Schleppsäbel, ein Hirschfänger, Muskete und Männerkleidung sind die Requisiten, die sie [die Kölnische Zeitung] aus ihrem Lügenschrein auch für mich in Bereitschaft gehalten, und womit sie mich, zu dieser gelegenen Zeit, ausgerüstet hat) (Anneke 47–48). She counters these accusations of masculinity by describing how she stood instead: "unarmed and in my usual women's costume that was only made into a riding costume by linen trousers, participating in the campaign on the side of my husband" (unbewaffnet und in meiner gewöhnlichen Frauentracht die nur durch ein leinenes Beinkleid zu einem Reitanzuge complettirt wurde, den Feldzug an der Seite meines Gatten mitgemacht habe) (Anneke 48). Anneke asserts her femininity by clarifying that she only conveniently wore trousers underneath woman's clothing, and by emphasizing once again how she was not fighting independently of her husband. Behind Anneke's justification, however, lurks a harsh criticism of how male reporters had concentrated more on her masculine clothing than on her rebellious intents.

Even Louise Aston, one of the most adamant defenders of women's rights to untrammeled action and speech, uses a letter to the king, which she includes in her published defense, to stress her feminine nature. Unlike Anneke, however, who espouses feminine traits to clarify and validate her actions, Aston does not apologize for her behavior per se. Instead, she tries to take advantage of her presumed disadvantaged situation as a woman to convince the king merely to allow her to stay in Berlin. She turns to the king as a "helpless" woman, "without protection and refuge" (Aston 32), pleading: "A man finds himself quickly in a new situation totally different than his earlier one, or has the power to shape his new relations himself according to his needs; for a woman that becomes infinitely difficult" (Ein Mann findet sich schnell in eine neue, von seiner frühern ganz verschiedene Lage, oder hat die Kraft seine neuen Verhältnisse selbst

seinen Bedürfnissen gemäß zu gestalten; einem Weib wird das unendlich schwer—) (Aston 32).

In like manner, Brentano-von Arnim, in arguments to the Berlin
magistrate, relies on her position as a woman writing from outside the
dominant discourse to explain how male officials have misunderstood
her individual use of the language. Her humor and irony, she claims,
have been misinterpreted as insults; her lack of experience in official,
governmental language caused her unintentional solecisms. In pleading her case, Brentano-von Arnim exploits her reputation as a woman
writer whose previous works demonstrate that she can express herself
only in an emotional, unstructured way, as opposed to the formal,
bureaucratic *Kanzleistil*.

> We thus ask: how should a woman here, where persecution without
> reason does not need to justify itself, who lets herself be guided by her
> feelings, unaccustomed to senseless forms of the letter style meant for
> the Magistrate, obtain the right to be allowed to demand, does not
> consider, because she is unable to write differently than she talks and
> thinks, but also, because she was attacked by the Magistrate in an
> insulting way, that, in order to spare him from serious accusations, she
> explains his injustice to him only in the disguise of a joke—O noble
> woman, that was your mistake!

> Wir fragen also: wie soll sich hier, wo Verfolgung ohne allen Fug sich
> nicht zu rechtfertigen braucht—eine Frau Recht verschaffen, die durch
> ihr Gefühl sich leiten läßt, sinnloser Formen ungewohnt, des Briefstyls,
> den der Magistrat gemeint ist, fordern zu dürfen, nicht achtet, weil sie
> unfähig ist, anders zu schreiben als sie spricht und denkt, sondern auch,
> weil sie vom Magistrat auf eine so ehrenberührende Weise ist ange-
> gangen worden, daß, um ernstere Vorwürfe ihm zu ersparen, sie nach-
> sichtsvoll nur im Gewand des Scherzes ihm sein Unrecht darlegt!—O
> edle Frau, das war gefehlt von Ihnen! (*Magistratsprozess* 161)

Behind the excuses for not being able to write in the formal style
required in letters to high officials and calls for sympathy for her
"mistakes," however, exist strong attempts to reformulate authoritarian structures of discourse. She critiques the magistrate for misunderstanding her style that relies on emotions and not on formalized
rhetoric. Her final statement draws attention to her position as a
woman, but with its ironic overtones her self-admonishment comes
across as a patronizing attempt to excuse and not defend her mistakes. In another letter, Brentano-von Arnim molds similar apologies

for not being able to write in formal language into protests against restrictive laws, inflexible conventions, and political intolerance (45). Her insistence that she is offering political advice solely for personal and private reasons is weakened by her assertions to friends that letters between her and the Berlin officials represent a sequel to her published *Königsbuch* (154) and that she intends to publish the correspondence eventually (103, 111, 132).

By promoting the "feminine," personal quality of their political intents, Brentano-von Arnim and the other women echo the patriarchal view that female-instigated political action is harmless.[16] However, women might gain from presenting their political requests in this manner. Christa Wolf observes that marginalization can also work in women's favor: "In serious times it can be a protection not to be taken seriously," (In ernsten Zeiten kann es ein Schutz sein, nicht ernst genommen zu werden.) (556). In fact, nineteenth-century women's writings were often regarded as hysterical outpourings of the weaker sex and were therefore allowed more poetic license than men's works. Fanny Lewald concurs in her *Recollections From the Year 1849*, stating that her early provocative stories might have been published because she was a woman, and therefore considered to be "extravagant" and unthreatening to the male order (348–349).

In the cases of Aston and Brentano-von Arnim, however, women could not always elude the male persecutors by affirming their femininity. The helplessness that Aston promotes in her letters to the king is severely undermined by emphatic demands throughout the rest of the pamphlet for free speech and action for women. Aston's reputation as a woman of strong, independent beliefs eclipsed her perceived defenselessness, for she was eventually banned from Berlin. Similarly, Brentano-von Arnim's assertions of incompetence and inferiority are sharply undercut by her professional accomplishments, a fact that the Berlin magistrate must have realized when he sentenced her to two months in prison.

If women could not conceal their determination by conforming to standards of femininity, they opted instead to disengage their own individual political activities from those of other women. In such instances, the private, solitary act of writing letters reinforces the harmless picture of isolation that the women try to paint. The wish for separatism is apparent, in Aston's defense, when she denies accusations that she is an "emancipated woman" because she smokes, wears men's clothes, frequents local taverns, and talks publicly about politics and religion (Aston 39–40). Women also try to transcend their sex, attempting to locate their endeavors in a gender-neutral realm. In her letter to her readers, Herwegh contends that her history of the Democratic Legion in Paris is only the work of a person whose "emotional nerves extend somewhat beyond the circle of one's private relations" (Gefühlsnerven etwas über den Kreis seiner Privatverhältnisse hinausreichen) (Herwegh 129). Wary that readers might attribute sex-linked traits to this characterization, however, she states: "This attribute, it seems to me, is neither exclusively a masculine or feminine one—it belongs to both sexes, in so far as they have emancipated themselves to *humans* even with adherence to their own particular way of perceiving things" (Diese Eigenschaft dünkt mich, ist weder eine ausschließlich männliche noch weibliche—sie gehört beiden Geschlechtern an, soweit sie sich eben mit Beibehaltung der ihnen eigentümlichen Auffassungsweise zu *Menschen* emanzipiert haben) (129).

Bettina Brentano-von Arnim's letter to the king written on behalf of the Polish insurgent Mieroslawski displays her efforts to transcend gender norms. In this letter, she overtly expresses her desire for the king to allow Mieroslawski's sister to visit her brother in prison, while covertly pleading with the king to dismiss Mieroslawski's death sentence. Referring to the king's previous characterization of her own politics as both ignorant and cunning, she retorts:

> What the dubious character of femininity demands, I know nothing to say about that! I know nothing about that! . . . I do not know, is that a bad fault?
>
> I know nothing about me! Am I feminine or not? Proud I am, but retired into myself, not turned toward the world!—My pride has insulted nobody yet. . . .
>
> Your Majesty, gently strew a little dust onto this scattering pride, so that the King has nothing more to excuse a deeply ashamed woman who signs her name in timid flight.

> Was nun den bezweifelten Charakter der Weiblichkeit verlangt, so weiß ich nichts davon zu sagen! ich weiß nichts über sie! . . . Ich weiß nicht, ist dies ein böser Fehl?
>
> Ich weiß nichts von mir! Bin ich weiblich oder nicht? Stolz bin ich, aber in mich gekehrt, nicht der Welt zugewendet!— Mein Stolz hat noch Niemand beleidigt. . . .
>
> Streuen Euer Majestät milde ein wenig Staub auf diesen verwehenden

Stolz, damit der König nichts mehr zu verzeihen habe einer tief-
beschämten Frau, die in schüchterner Flucht sich unterzeichnet.
(*Bettine von Arnim und Friedrich Wilhelm IV* 106)

Although Brentano-von Arnim demonstrates boldness and conviction in her opinions and advice, qualities that grow stronger the more
she writes, she does not explicitly promote female solidarity in any of
her letters. Thus, as one scholar has observed, it is doubtful that
Brentano-von Arnim's statement here represents an ironic critique of
inhibiting gender roles, a critique that would align her demands with
those of equal rights activists (Goozé 321–322). Instead, she is more
likely, as in the above quote, to portray herself as standing beyond
gender constrictions in a way that could help her escape sexual stereotypes and thus mitigate her questionable actions. In characterizing
herself as a deeply ashamed and timid woman whose interests are
purely private, she once again uses the standards of the prevalent
gender ideology to hold the attention of her male listener. Within the
context of a personal letter, those characteristics may have been credible. Her other writings and deeds, however, make her self-portrayal
in this passage dubious.

To interpret Brentano-von Arnim's persuasion tactics as either embracing feminine norms to her own advantage or rejecting her female
nature at the expense of women's solidarity would be too simple.
Along with her efforts to transcend her gender, she shared with other
politically conscious women of her time an awareness of the influence
that confining norms of femininity exerted on her political expression.
In ambivalent sentiments toward their sex, Brentano-von Arnim,
Aston, Anneke, Herwegh, and Lewald realize that the reception of
their political works is based more on the fact that they are women than
on their actual political beliefs or innate powers of reasoning. Apologies for writing, denial of ambition or legitimate claims to authority,
stress on the personal connections that led them to political activism,
and disavowal of any relations with organized women's movements
contrast with their strong desire to assert themselves and indicate how
they interpreted their precarious positions as politically active females.

Such contradictions signal viable strategies to deal with a world
markedly divided along the lines of public/private, male/female do-
mains. By appropriating the letter form to claim a public role for what
they define as their private concerns, the women question the right of
men to force certain issues into privacy. In using this private means to

deal with public concerns, Brentano-von Arnim and the other women reformulate politics as a field that demands personal interaction. They also question the innate strength of the dichotomy established and maintained by men. By developing the essay-letter genre, they open a third sphere of discourse, one that challenges the divisions between public/private, political/personal, male/female, even as it acknowledges the boundaries that safeguard and define the dichotomies. Most of all, by showing an awareness of the boundaries limiting women's political involvement, they ask for tolerance of gender.

Notes

I would like to thank the Deutscher Akademischer Austauschdienst (DAAD) and The American Council of Learned Societies (ACLS) for grants to conduct research for this essay. I also wish to thank Diane Young for her editorial comments.

1. This passage is in a draft of a letter, most likely to Crown Prince Friedrich Wilhelm, in which Brentano-von Arnim defends the theologian Friedrich Schleiermacher, whose liberal ideas had caused him political difficulties since 1823. The Bettine von Arnim exhibition catalogue of Das Freie Deutsche Hochstift postulates that this letter was probably written around 1828 and initiated Arnim's subsequent lengthy and involved correspondence with Friedrich Wilhelm (*Herzhaft in die Dornen der Zeit zu greifen* . . . 102–103). The complete passage is in Brentano-von Arnim's *Werke und Briefe*, 5:377.

2. Püschel describes sexist reactions to Brentano-von Arnim's political works (63–74). Ludwig Geiger, for example, who first published Brentano-von Arnim's letters to the king, categorizes her politics as "unpolitische Politik" (Bettina Brentano-von Arnim, *Bettina von Arnim und Friedrich Wilhelm IV* 75). Tanneberger views Brentano-von Arnim's work with the poor and her advice to the king as "womanly compassion" performed "out of purely feminine impulses"(74). Even Drewitz states that Bettina Brentano-von Arnim "was no political mind par excellence" and that she was ruled by emotional empathy instead of objective knowledge of the political reality (146). Classifying Brentano-von Arnim's political activities as "femininely" emotional undermines the seriousness of her intentions and the impact of her writings. As Waldstein observes, this view also

presumes that politics is not a compassionate field, but rather one requiring a set standard of objectivity and intellect (64–65). In contrast to older studies, studies by scholars in the former German Democratic Republic (Püschel; Meyer-Hepner in: *Magistratsprozess*; Härtl's article in this volume) and recent feminists (Goozé and Waldstein) have given Bettina Brentano-von Arnim's political works and deeds serious, scholarly attention. In addition, recent collections of primary literature have thoroughly considered Brentano-von Arnim's political engagement, namely the correspondence between her and the Grimm brothers (Schultz in: *Der Briefwechsel Bettine von Arnims mit den Brüdern Grimm 1838–1841*) and the 1985 exhibition catalogue (*Herzhaft in die Dornen der Zeit greifen . . .*).

As a point of clarification, my use of the term "political" in this essay is based on a definition by Iris Marion Young: "Expression and discussion are political when they raise and address issues of the moral value or human desirability of an institution or practice whose decisions affect a large number of people" (73).

3. Most studies of Brentano-von Arnim's political ideas and writings conduct an individual, and not comparative, analysis (Hahn, 1959), categorize her writings with those of the Romantic women in the first three decades of the century (Tanneberger, 1928), or compare her ideas only with those of men (Wyss, 1935). These studies offer interesting observations on Brentano-von Arnim's social and political thoughts, but they do not consider her ambivalent statements regarding the complex relationship between gender and political activism. Recent feminists have observed her equivocal thoughts on gender, but they have not looked closely at similar complexities in other women's political writings of the time, suggesting that Brentano-von Arnim's ambivalence may have been anomalous (Goozé, 316–356; Waldstein, 105–162).

4. Some scholars have shown such a cohesion in women's letters during Romanticism (Frederiksen) and in women's autobiographies from 1790 to 1914 (Goodman).

5. Gilbert and Gubar posit the existence of a nineteenth-century female literary tradition with cohesive metaphors and images by which women conveyed "submerged meanings, meanings hidden within or behind the more accessible 'public' content of their works" (72). By creating "palimpsestic" literary works (73) with subversive metaphors of madness, confinement, and doubling, women fiction writers direct their anger against patriarchal oppression and ultimately escape male texts and norms. Weigel views the tendency of women both to accommodate and to protest norms as a necessary step toward finding a "female language of experience" (92). In order to overcome existing limitations on female creativity while formulating new expressive means the woman writer "must learn to voice the contradictions, to see them, to comprehend

them, to live in and with them, and also learn to gain strength from the rebellion against yesterday and from the anticipation of tomorrow" (73).

6. My sources for these letters are Ludwig Geiger's *Bettine von Arnim und Friedrich Wilhelm IV* (quoted as *Bettine von Arnim und Friedrich Wilhelm IV*), volume 5 of Bettina von Arnim's *Werke und Briefe* (quoted as Köln), and Meyer-Hepner's *Der Magistratsprozess der Bettina von Arnim* (quoted as: *Magistratsprozess*).

7. Püschel describes the responses of Karl Lachmann and Jakob Grimm to Brentano-von Arnim's pleas on behalf of the Grimm brothers (80, note 3). Also, see letters by Brentano-von Arnim's brother-in-law, Friedrich Karl von Savigny, and by the Berlin attorney, Otto Lewald, who worked toward having Bettina Brentano-von Arnim acquitted after the Berlin magistrate sentenced her to two years in prison. These two men, afraid that Brentano-von Arnim's tendencies toward over-emotionality could have created further difficulties, insisted on writing her letter of apology to the magistrate for her. (122–123).

8. See Young's article for a feminist critique of the normative definitions of male-dominated Western political thought.

9. See Gerhard for a discussion of women's legal limits in nineteenth-century Germany (154–189; Document 17:396–442).

10. See Lipp's articles "Bräute, Mütter, Gefährtinnen," and "Frauen und Öffentlichkeit." In the latter article, Lipp points out that certain logistical factors could also deter women's engagement, including impractical clothing, transportation, and inconvenient meeting times and places (289).

11. Other women besides the four I discuss here were actively writing and speaking for the democratic cause around 1848. See Secci's article for an examination of women's published works around the 1848 Revolution and for a good bibliography of primary and secondary literature. See Kuby's article on women's political organizations.

12. See Wagner's book for Anneke's biography.

13. See Goetzinger's book for Aston's biography.

14. For interpretations of ambivalences in Lewald's fictional works and her later turn to more conservative political attitudes see articles by Bäumer, Venske, and Weigel.

15. For Anneke, Aston, Herwegh, and Lewald, I am looking only at published works in the epistolary form. Concerning unpublished personal letters, they are not the only women writing political epistles at the time. Other noteworthy personal letters include those of Clotilde Koch-Gontard to her liberal friends to describe the Parliament meetings in Frankfurt and political discussions at her salon. Carola Lipp, in her study of women's limited public options during the revolution, cites the letters of Emilie Ritter as examples of political commentary from the private sphere (285-288).

16. The Democrat Johannes Scherr, for example, attacked activists for defying their traditional roles, claiming that public women's groups were comprised "aushäßlichen und hysterischen alten Jungfern" or "saloppen Hausfrauen und pflichtvergessenen Müttern" (188–189) (of ugly and hysterical old spinsters [or] slovenly housewives and negligent mothers.)

Works Cited

Anneke, Mathilde Franziska. *Memoiren einer Frau aus dem badisch-pfälzischen Feldzuge 1848/49.* 1853. Münster: tende, 1982.

Arnim, Bettina von. *Der Magistratsprozess der Bettina von Arnim.* Ed. Gertrud Meyer-Hepner. Weimar: Arion Verlag, 1960.

———. *Werke und Briefe.* Ed. Gustav Konrad. 4 vols. Frechen/Köln: Bartmann Verlag, 1958–1963. Vol. 5. Ed. Johannes Müller. Frechen/Köln: Bartmann Verlag, 1961.

Arnim, Bettina von, and Friedrich Wilhelm IV. *Bettine von Arnim und Friedrich Wilhelm IV: Ungedruckte Briefe und Aktenstücke.* Ed. Ludwig Geiger. Frankfurt a. M.: Rütten und Loening, 1902.

Arnim, Bettine von, and Jakob and Wilhelm Grimm. *Der Briefwechsel Bettine von Arnims mit den Brüdern Grimm 1838-1841.* Ed. Hartwig Schultz. Frankfurt am Main: Insel, 1985.

Aston, Louise. *Meine Emancipation, Verweisung und Rechtfertigung.* Brüssel: C. G. Vogler, 1846.

Bäumer, Konstanze. "Reisen als Moment der Erinnerung: Fanny Lewalds (1811–1889) 'Lehr- und Wanderjahre'." In *Out of Line/Ausgefallen: The Paradox of Marginality in the Writings of Nineteenth-Century German Women.* Ed. Ruth Ellen Boetcher Joeres and Marianne Burchard. Amsterdamer Beiträge zur neueren Germanistik 28. Amsterdam: Rodopi, 1980.

Drewitz, Ingeborg. *Bettine von Arnim: Romantik, Revolution, Utopie.* Düsseldorf/Köln: Eugen Diederichs Verlag, 1969.

Frederiksen, Elke. "Die Frau als Autorin zur Zeit der Romantik: Anfänge einer weiblichen literarischen Tradition." In *Gestaltet und Gestaltend: Frauen in der deutschen Literatur.* Ed. Marianne Burkhard. Amsterdamer Beiträge zur Germanistik 10. Amsterdam: Rodopi, 1980.

Gerhard, Ute. *Verhältnisse und Verhinderungen: Frauenarbeit, Familie und Rechte der Frauen im 19. Jahrhundert: Mit Dokumenten.* Frankfurt a. M.: Suhrkamp, 1978.

Gilbert, Sandra M., and Susan Gubar. *The Madwoman in the Attic. The Woman Writer and the Nineteenth-Century Literary Imagination.* New Haven: Yale University Press, 1979.

Goetzinger, Germanine. *Für die Selbstverwirklichung der Frau: Louise Aston.* Frankfurt a.m.: Fischer,1983.

Goodman, Katherine. *Dis/Closures: Women's Autobiography in Germany Between 1790 and 1914.* New York University Ottendorfer Series Neue Folge 24. New York: Peter Lang, 1986.

Goozé, Marjanne Elaine. "Bettine von Arnim, the Writer." Diss. University of California, Berkeley, 1984.

Hahn, Karl-Heinz. *Bettina von Arnim in ihrem Verhältnis zu Staat und Politik: mit einem Anhang ungedruckter Briefe.* Weimar: Herman Böhlaus Nachfolger, 1959.

Hermann, Anne. "Epistolary Essays by Virginia Woolf and Christa Wolf." *New German Critique* 38 (1986):161–180.

Herwegh, Emma. "Zur Geschichte der deutschen demokratischen Legion aus Paris. Von einer Hochverräterin." 1849. In *1848: Briefe von und an Georg Herwegh.* Ed. Marcel Herwegh. 2nd ed. Munich: Albert Langen's Verlag, 1898. 127–214.

Herzhaft in die Dornen der Zeit greifen . . . : Bettine von Arnim 1785–1859. Ausstellung 1985. Ed. Christoph Perels. Frankfurt am Main: Freies Deutsches Hochstift-Frankfurter Goethe Museum, 1985.

Koch-Gontard, Clotilde. *Clotilde Koch-Gontard an ihre Freunde: Briefe und Erinnerungen aus der Zeit der deutschen Einheitsbewegung 1843–1869.* Frankfurter Lebensbilder 16. Ed. Wolfgang Klötzer. Frankfurt a. M.: Waldemar Kramar, 1969.

Kuby, Eva. "Politische Frauenvereine und ihre Aktivitäten 1848 bis 1850." In *Schimpfende Weiber und patriotrische Jungfrauen. Frauen im Vormärz und in der Revolution 1848.* Ed. Carola Lipp. Bühl-Moos: Elster Verlag, 1985. 248–269.

Lewald, Fanny. *Erinnerungen aus dem Jahre 1848.* 2 vols. Braunschweig: Friedrich Vieweg und Sohn, 1850.

Lipp, Carola. "Frauen und Öffentlichkeit. Möglichkeiten und Grenzen politischer Partizipation im Vormärz und in der Revolution 1848." In *Schimpfende Weiber und patriotische Jungfrauen. Frauen im Vormärz und in der Revolution 1848.* Ed. Carola Lipp. Bühl-Moos: Elster Verlag, 1985. 270–301.

———. "Bräute, Mütter, Gefährtinnen. Frauen und politische Öffentlichkeit in der Revolution 1848." *Grenzgängerinnen: Revolutionäre Frauen im 18. und 19. Jahrhundert.* Ed. Helga Grubitzsch, Hannelore Cyrus, and Elke Haarbusch. Düsseldorf: Schwann, 1985. 71–92.

Püschel, Ursula. "Weibliches und Unweibliches der Bettina von Arnim." 1964. *Mit allen Sinnen: Frauen in der Literatur.* Halle-Leipzig: Mitteldeutscher Verlag, 1980. 51–86.

Scherr, Johannes. *Von Achtundvierzig bis Einundfünfzig. Eine Komödie der Weltgeschichte.* Leipzig, 1868.

Secci, Lia. "German Women Writers and the Revolution of 1848." *German Women in the Nineteenth Century: A Social History.* Ed. John C. Fout. N.Y.: Holmes & Meier, 1984.

Tanneberger, Irmgard. *Die Frauen der Romantik und das soziale Problem.* Oldenburg: Schulzesche Hofbuchdruckerei und Verlagsbuchhandlung, 1928.

Venske, Regula. "Discipline and Daydreaming in the Works of a Nineteenth-Century Woman Author: Fanny Lewald." In *German Women in the Eighteenth and Nineteenth Centuries: A Social and Literary History.* Ed. Ruth-Ellen B. Joeres and Mary Jo Maynes. Bloomington: Indiana University Press, 1986. 175–192.

Wagner, Maria. *Mathilde Franziska Anneke in Selbstzeugnissen und Dokumenten.* Frankfurt a. M.: Fischer 1980.

Waldstein, Edith. *Bettine von Arnim and the Politics of Romantic Conversation.* Studies in German Literature, Linguistics, and Culture 33. Columbia, S. C.: Camden House, 1988.

Weigel, Sigrid. "Double Focus: On the History of Women's Writing." In *Feminist Aesthetics.* Ed. Gisela Ecker. Trans. Harriet Anderson. Boston: Beacon Press, 1985. 59–80. (The English version was abridged from the original German version: "Der schielende Blick: Thesen zur Geschichte weiblicher Schreibpraxis." *Die verborgene Frau: Sechs Beiträge zu einer feministischen Literaturwissenschaft.* Ed. Inge Stephan and Sigrid Weigel. Argument Sonderband 96. Berlin: Argument Verlag, 1983. 83–137.)

Wolf, Christa. "Nun ja! Das nächste Leben geht aber heute an. Ein Brief über Bettine." In *Die Günderode* by Bettine von Arnim. Frankfurt a. M.: Insel, 1983. 545–584.

Woolf, Virginia. "Dorothy Osborne's Letters." *The Second Common Reader.* New York: Harcourt Brace Jovanovich, 1960. 50-57.

Wyss, Hilde. *Bettina von Arnims Stellung zwischen der Romantik und dem jungen Deutschland.* Bern: Paul Haupt, 1935.

Young, Iris Marion. "Impartiality and the Civic Public: Some Implications of Feminist Critiques of Moral and Political Theory." In *Feminism as Critique.* Ed. Seyla Benhabib and Drucilla Cornell. Minneapolis: University of Minnesota Press, 1987. 57–76.

The Myth of Psyche as Developmental Paradigm in Bettina Brentano-von Arnim's Epistolary Novels

Monika Shafi

> That we are never able to acknowledge love as an accomplishment
> in life? And probably it is the only thing that counts.
>
> —Luise Rinser 49[1]

Bettina Brentano-von Arnim's life and works are characterized by contradictions. The simultaneity of reality-transcendent enthusiasm for the arts and down-to-earth pragmatism, of traditional female existence and progressive literary and political commitments cannot be explained by just the three stages in Bettina Brentano-von Arnim's life: ingenious youth, restrictive wife/mother role, and intensive literary production in her old age. These factors characterize—albeit to varying degrees—all phases of her life. Thus, Bettina Brentano-von Arnim's biography corresponds neither to conventional nor to critical gender patterns, and her texts spurn any attempt to classify them rigorously according to genre, style, or literary epoch.

Bettina Brentano-von Arnim's contradictions—which have been referred to as her "double life" (*Herzhaft* 70) or "dual voice" (Kaiser 211)—are understood in this analysis as the matrix of a process that reflects how she dealt with the working and living conditions of a woman writer in the first half of the nineteenth century. Her position can be understood as a kind of creative strategy, its individuality and boldness rendering it absolutely unique in German literary history. The case of Bettina Brentano-von Arnim challenges us to explain the

Brentano-von Arnim's draft design for a Goethe monument.
(Verwaltung der Staatlichen Schlösser und Gärten Hessen, Bad
Homburg v.d.H. Photo by Ursula Edelmann.)

"paradoxically productive aspects of patriarchal ideology," that is to say "that some women manage to counter patriarchal strategies despite the odds stacked against them" (Moi 64).

Existing research has drawn upon individual biographical factors as well as literary and social-historical elements to explain the phenomenon of Bettina Brentano-von Arnim (among others, Dischner, Drewitz, Frederiksen, and Wolf). Brentano-von Arnim's upper class background, intellectual-literary socialization, and romantic aesthetics, as well as the treatment of her experiences in life and literature in the Romantic and *Vormärz* periods, can all be seen as decisive influences on her work and biography. My interpretation draws on these analyses to investigate Bettina Brentano-von Arnim's treatment of the myth of Psyche in the epistolary novels *Goethe's Correspondence with a Child* (Goethes Briefwechsel mit einem Kinde) (1835), *Günderode* (Die Günderode) (1840), and *The Spring Wreath* (Clemens Brentanos Frühlingskranz) (1844) as an example of her appropriation of reality and her own identity formation.[2]

Understanding Brentano-von Arnim's development within the mythical image in these works is justified first by the author's own identification with the figure of Psyche. She expressed this identification primarily in her outlines for the Goethe monument. This monument, which she worked to realize over decades with unfailing patience and perseverance, was conceived as an apotheosis of the poet, in which Bettine was to be present as the figure of the winged Psyche (Bäumer 104–118). Second, the subject of Amor and Psyche is repeated in Brentano-von Arnim's drawings and sketches. This identification with the figure of Psyche is also supplemented by numerous allusions to Psyche and her attributes (butterfly, soul) in the epistolary novels.

In *Goethe's Correspondence* Bettina Brentano-von Arnim explains in great detail her first encounter with the character of Psyche. She meets Johann Gottfried Herder in the home of her grandmother Sophie von La Roche. The famous author, highly regarded by La Roche, wants to kiss the young girl. She undergoes this sexual initiation with both astonishment and rejection, but when Herder characterizes her as "Psyche," the name helps to reconcile her with this experience (513–514). This event can thus be seen as a passive adoption of a configuration that the male gaze projected onto her, and it seems fitting to understand the myth of Psyche as a kind of development and identity model, a "cipher of her self" (*Herzhaft* 210).

Moreover, the myth of Psyche is considered to be a general paradigm for the process of identity formation, and the development of her self is again at the center of Brentano-von Arnim's epistolary novels. The author's own experiences can therefore be interpreted as corresponding to the main structures of the myth. However, as I will show, the mythical features undergo a decisive change in Brentano-von Arnim's adaptation.

To analyze the fictional figure through the manifestation of the myth not only allows us to understand an extraordinary biography in its main components, but in the transformation of and divergence from the mythic prototype it also enables us to recognize the specific problems of writing and living as a woman author in the nineteenth century.

The myth of Amor and Psyche was told for the first time by the Latin author Apuleius in his work *The Golden Ass* in the second century after Christ. Psyche is the youngest of three daughters of a king. Because of her extraordinary beauty and grace people neglect to worship Venus and instead pay homage to Psyche. Amor, Venus's son, is supposed to punish Psyche for such undue admiration but instead he falls in love with her and becomes her husband. Provoked by her jealous and curious sisters, Psyche violates Amor's rule never to seek the secret of his identity. Consequently, Amor abandons her. Psyche searches desperately for her lost lover but the gods, fearful of Venus, refuse to support her efforts. Finally, Venus herself sets four trials for Psyche. With the help of plants and animals Psyche manages three of the virtually unsolvable tasks. The fourth challenge takes her into Hades, where she violates one of the essential rules of conduct and falls into a deep sleep. Amor then breaks his mother's injunction and saves Psyche. The birth of a daughter terminates all disputes and Venus grants the child immortality (Apuleius 100–179).

The cultural importance of this myth, which focuses simultaneously on the conflict-ridden development of an individual as well as of a couple, has been compared to the *Odyssey*, because this text too outlines an archetypal, heroic developmental paradigm (Ferguson 229). According to Lee Edwards the importance of the Psyche myth lies in the fact that a female outsider acquires the heroic qualities that enable society to adopt a new understanding of love, one founded on reciprocity: "The tale suggests . . . that heroism depends on the transforming and transcendent qualities that link social change to love and individuation for both men and women" ("Labors" 45). In her extended book-length study of the Psyche myth, Edwards investigates among other topics the gender-specific context of the Psyche figure. To the extent that Psyche's love story demonstrates a detachment from patriarchal power structures, it can be seen as specific for the female outsider, who—and herein lies the essential element of the myth—experiences and practices heroic power and love as a unity: "Heroic power is inseparable from the love the hero expresses and inspires" (*Psyche as Hero* 13).

Psyche's developmental process comprises fundamental life experiences that I designate as love/sexuality, death, and work. Work is to be understood here in the sense of praxis and refers to Psyche's probation in the tasks set by Venus. Love, work, and death can be seen, however, as the main structural devices of any developmental process, and Brentano-von Arnim's epistolary novels reveal how she comes to terms with these fundamental experiences. These three categories thus provide useful analytic tools for understanding Brentano-von Arnim's creation of self. For this very reason they function as the conceptual framework for the following text analysis, which begins with a brief explanation of the particular conditions of text production with which Bettina Brentano-von Arnim worked.

The complexity of Brentano-von Arnim's epistolary novels results among other things from the inherent circumstances of their origin. The author reworked her original correspondence with Goethe, with her friend Günderrode, and with her brother Clemens Brentano more than thirty years after the original letters were written. These texts contain the political and emotional experiences of a fifty-year-old woman who is also responding to the social and political conflicts of her contemporary situation. This retrospective stance, however, is not addressed as such. On the contrary, the author goes to great pains to retain in the letters the original tone of direct communication and reflection.

Brentano-von Arnim's works assimilate elements of biography, autobiography, and the developmental and epistolary novel without tying themselves unequivocally to any one of these genres (Goodman 90–96; Bäumer 42–44). The formal features of these texts function as much to lay traces as to conceal traces of a developmental process in which the complex relationship between reality and idealization also raises issues having to do with writing itself. This shows that certain strategies of female writing reflect women's double stance in the patriarchal order: the coexistence of participation in and exclusion from the dominant cultural order. As Sigrid Weigel has convincingly argued, narrative structures do reveal among other things how women come to terms with male conceptions of femininity (85–87).

Katherine Goodman has interpreted Brentano-von Arnim's epistolary novels as "radical autobiography" (91), in which the I reflects itself through a partner and tries to construct its identity through this interaction with the Other: "Bettine von Arnim's character emerges with and in contrast to others; it defines itself and evolves because of their influence and in opposition to them" (106). Goodman points out that Brentano-von Arnim intended to create and project an idealized image of herself which she also understood as part of her true self. The emphasis given to her inner spiritual development reveals, on the one hand, pietistic influences, and on the other, the dominant paradigm for the developmental and autobiographical novel as shaped by Goethe (Bäumer 206–209; Goodman 77). Both *Wilhelm Meister* as well as *Poetry and Truth* (Dichtung und Wahrheit) do follow a teleologically oriented process of maturity. The contradictions resulting from the imitation of a life pattern fundamentally opposed to female biography lead to the numerous breaks and distortions in the depiction of the fictional as well as Brentano-von Arnim's self which Bäumer has identified specifically in *Goethe's Correspondence* (190–216). The depiction of the inner world, not only reflects, however, Goethe's overpowering influence and the pietistic tradition, but also refers to the limits of the female sphere both in life and literature.

Marianne Hirsch, in her analysis of heroines in English novels of the nineteenth century, has argued that the dominant ideology of gender, particularly for creative women, offered no alternative to developing their inner lives. Excluded from any public activity, trapped in the monotony of domestic privacy, introspection was the only productive mode of development. In most cases, however, this form of productivity turned out to be self-destructive, as the overwhelming number of images dealing with death, illness, and insanity convincingly testifies. According to Hirsch the story of the female *Bildung* of the inner self is "the story of the potential artist who fails to make it" (28). In concentrating on the realm of feelings and fantasies, Bettina Brentano-von Arnim responds also to the gender-specific constraints imposed on her. But the question is, how does she nevertheless manage to avoid the deadly peril connected with them and thus transform a potentially regressive, self-destructive pattern into a productive strategy, that is, to constitute herself as a self and as a writer? In the context of this article one can reformulate this question: What does the developmental model depicted in the myth of Psyche disclose about Brentano-von Arnim's way of dealing with love, death, and work, and how are these experiences related to her conception of herself as a writer?

Bettina Brentano-von Arnim's epistolary novels have been characterized as "love stories" because love is the decisive medium that transforms the concrete life into a poetic and therefore into a more suitable, truer form for Brentano-von Arnim (Bürger 317). Bäumer, too, has extensively investigated Brentano-von Arnim's concept of love. She interprets it as her principle of education: understood as a liberating force, it aids the fictional Bettine's self-discovery (145–155). Of course, playing with different roles and identity patterns always revolves around Bettine's self and her (inner) world.

Similarly, in her correspondence with Clemens, Karoline von Günderrode, and Max Prokop von Freyberg, the self-centered nature of her conception of love has been noted. Bettine's personality is always the focal point, and for that reason the person she addresses functions primarily as mirror and medium for the enthusiasm she expresses about herself and about love. She sees her love for her various partners in absolute terms and deprives both herself and the others of any concrete individuality, since her prime aim is the creation of her own self (Drewitz 152; Bürger 324).

Brentano-von Arnim's epistolary novels certainly evince this conception of self and love, but these texts are not exhausted by mere introspection and self-conceit. One can find many references that emphasize a loving interaction and appreciation of self and partner. In this context Brentano-von Arnim intends a kind of reciprocal exchange, in which love and knowledge (of self) finally merge so that a synthesis of "you" and "I", "I" and "you" become possible. She uses love as a way of obtaining knowledge, but in so doing she does not negate the identity of the other, but instead evokes a kind of ecstasy of love and knowledge into which she integrates the partner.

> The spirit wants to unite with the idea: I want to be loved or to be understood, that is the same.[3]

> Der Geist will sich vermählen mit dem Begriff: ich will geliebt oder ich will begriffen sein, das ist eins. (*Briefwechsel*, Weimar 1: 449)

I feel with certainty, my life wakes only when you call, and it will perish
if it cannot continue to grow in you . . . Yes, my life is insecure, without your love in which it is planted, it will never come to blossom.[4]

ich fühl's recht, mein Leben ist bloß aufgewacht, weil Du mir riefst,
und wird sterben müssen, wenn es nicht in Dir kann fortgedeihen . . .
Ja mein Leben ist unsicher; ohne deine Liebe, in die es eingepflanzt ist,
wird's gewiß nicht aufblühen. (*Die Günderode*, Weimar 2: 10)

Yes you want me to love you always as you love me. And if you would
be very close to me and I could clasp you to my breast in return for
what I find in you and what I looked for in vain in others, a conversation where the soul stands in the doorway resting but so inclined to its
neighbor, as to tempt him ever so gently to express himself, too.

Ja, Du willst, daß ich Dich immer so liebe, wie Du mich liebst. Und
wärst Du doch ganz nah bei mir und könnt Dich ans Herz drücken
dafür, daß ich in Dir finde, was ich vergebens in anderen suchte, ein
Gespräch wo die Seele in der Pforte, steht in ruhender Stellung zwar,
aber so hingebeugt zum Nachbar, so sanft lockend, daß der auch sich
ausspreche. (*Frühlingskranz*, Weimar 2: 482–483)

To understand removes this limit; two who understand each other, are
within each other unbounded. (*Goethe's Correspondence* 2: 162)

Verstehn hebt die Grenze auf; zwei, die einander verstehen, sind
ineinander unendlich. (Weimar 1: 433)

Here her desire does not aim at the creation of her self but at an
apprehension of self and love in which both partner and self can
participate. Neither in the concrete reality of her various encounters
nor in their poetically idealized transformation has Brentano-von
Arnim experienced the kind of intensive devotion which she herself
would like to pour out.

Clemens loved and admired the ingeniously poetic nature of his
sister, but she was to be his muse, the reflection of his own personality, and at the same time conform to the role-specific demands of their
family. According to his advice, knitting socks and a sense of duty
were to guide her out of the dreamworld in which she had sunk
(*Clemens Brentanos Frühlingskranz*, Weimar 2:627). Moreover, his
suggestions and ideas concerning her literary production misjudge the
true nature of his sister. Brentano-von Arnim realizes the double
nature of Clemens's letters, which actually concede no space for her

own experiences and development whether in the poetic or in the real world. She knows that despite their close bonds, Clemens can neither accept nor understand her true character.

The exchange with the famous Goethe could not reasonably entail the claim for a reciprocal exchange, although Bettina Brentano-von Arnim wished for it and stimulated it.

She experienced a decisive disappointment, however, in her relationship with Günderrode. Günderrode's abrupt termination of their friendship and her suicide shortly thereafter left a crucial mark on Brentano-von Arnim and influenced her future attitude towards love and friendship. To Achim von Arnim she reports the following about the death of her friend:

> I will not attach myself so easily to an individual, I will probably not attach myself to anything any more, and I will have to struggle with this in pain and sorrow.
>
> ich werd mich nicht so leicht mehr an den einzeln fesseln, ich werd mich wohl an nichts mehr fesseln, und um dieses werd ich oft mit Schmerz und Trauer zu ringen haben. (*Bettine und Arnim 73*)

Her relationships with Goethe, Clemens, and Karoline Günderrode reveal to the fictional Bettine in varying degrees her lack of a like-minded congenial partner. Only in a very limited way does she experience the same readiness to love that she is able to offer. This contrasts significantly with Psyche's experience. At the decisive moment, Psyche received Amor's support which also demonstrated his rebellion against the personal and social order of his mother.

Brentano-von Arnim's great demands are frustrated by the social and individual limits of her various partners. Even the fictionalization of her letters cannot hide the distance their recipients maintained, either consciously or subconsciously. It seems to me that the self-centeredness expressed in the epistolary novels also reflected this fundamental lack of a "resonance" (Widerhall) (Weimar 2: 125), which the author nevertheless transformed into an even greater attention to her self. Her texts are not dominated by sorrow at her inability to fulfill her ardent desire for mutual appreciation and exchange, but rather by the endeavor to create her own self and that of the other at least through writing and thereby enable herself to overcome her disappointments. Bettine does not acquiesce, she abjures neither love nor the lover, and above all, she neither searches for guilt nor blames anyone.

In this context the portraits and miniatures worked into the various epistolary novels are very illuminating. Many of these stories describe amorous encounters through which Brentano-von Arnim deals with her own and other people's experiences. Renunciation, loneliness, abandonment, and brave endurance are woven into these tales. The story of the young French noblewoman whose love remained unfulfilled and who therefore took the veil (Weimar 1: 469–471), the idyll of the deserted mother who remains faithful to her distant lover (Weimar 1: 525), as well as Bettine's own adventure with a gardener who expresses his love for her through flowers (Weimar 2: 214)—these are all examples of highly ambivalent love stories. The melancholy mood prevailing in these episodes, although softened through the poetic charm of Brentano-von Arnim's style, is not totally diffused. One can understand these images as reflections of Brentano-von Arnim's own emotional destiny, in particular because all these figures, despite their unfulfilled desire, try to assert themselves and do not succumb.

With regard to the sexual domain, Brentano-von Arnim's play with gender roles and attributes is very revealing. An erotic tone, manifest in the third part of *Goethe's Correspondence*, a diary entitled "Book of Love" (Buch der Liebe), and also evident in her relationships with her correspondents, permeates these epistolary novels. However, Brentano-von Arnim does not restrict herself to a fixed sexual identity. In her correspondence with Günderrode, for example, she plays various male roles (revolutionary, founder of a religion, student, goblin) but they are not linked to a superior, dominant position. Rather, these androgynous fantasies suggest a fear of being tied down by society's restrictive gender roles which she evades through this role-play. To be sure she thus liberates herself from female stereotypes, which she replaces in the *Correspondence*, for example, with literary and mythological substitutes. However, these images are shaped by the very same patriarchal ideology from which Brentano-von Arnim in the end cannot escape. The contradiction in her conception of love lies in the fact that she both uses as escape and free space a mythical world that was highly influential in restricting women, *and* wants to re-design this concept of love as a liberating force. Thus she remains inevitably bound to an idea of self that is tied to the inner realm.

Philosophical concepts are also part of Brentano-von Arnim's understanding of love. She assimilates into it, among other things, neo-

Platonic and Christian elements, and thus integrates love into an identity triad of spirit, nature, and love, reciprocally complementing and stimulating each other. Goethe, she sees as the perfection and ideal representation of this unity. Consequently, love also involves a recognition of the divine power of creation, which in turn allows her to comprehend the universe, nature, and ultimately, one's own and another's self. This attitude helps her overcome the very real disappointment about the objects of her love. For example, she gives the following advice to Günderrode:

> is not our whole life love?—and you seek for something to love besides? Do then love in return the life by which you are penetrated. (*Correspondence of Fräulein Günderode* 303)
>
> ist das ganze Leben nicht lieben?—und Du suchst, was Du lieben kannst?—so lieb doch das Leben wieder, was Dich durchdringt. (Weimar 2: 424)

The biographical experiences of both women, as well as Brentano-von Arnim's philosophical comprehension of love as a mode of life, converge in this withdrawal from a partner-oriented love.

Her attitude towards death shows a similar cosmic-holistic approach. She refuses to grant death any power over life and thus postulates a death-transcending and continuing vital energy. At the same time she handles the concrete experience of death, which she had encountered as a child, with an increased attention to everyday life. Her way of conquering death reveals a form of active 'work of mourning' in which she does not succumb to pain and grief, but consciously turns towards and embraces life. After the death of his newborn son, she writes to her brother-in-law Savigny:

> That death has so cunningly deceived you, that is sad, quite sad, death is wrong; . . . that's why one must not be in contact with death, nothing but living—and that is why neither of you should give yourselves up to pain, for this is death.
>
> Daß Dich der Tod hinterlistig hintergangen hat, das ist traurig, recht traurig, er ist falsch der Tod; . . . drum muß man auf keine Weise in Verbindung mit ihm treten, nichts als leben—und eben darum sollt Ihr beide Euch auch nicht dem Schmerz überlassen, denn das ist Tod. (*Andacht* 49)

The same attitude characterizes her response to the death of Günder-rode. She turns increasingly to Goethe and his mother and decides "boldly . . . to raise myself above grief" (*Goethe's Correspondence* 1: 76) (sich kühn . . . über den Jammer hinauszuschwingen) (Weimar 1: 80) to overcome this encounter with death.

However, neither Brentano-von Arnim's attidude toward death nor her ambivalent notion of love suffice to explain her active resistance to every image of death. After all, this writer, too, vehemently deplores the lack of social options and the repressive gender-ideology that con-tributed substantially to the female longing for death in nineteenth century literature. In a letter to Achim von Arnim she explains:

> You won't believe how much I longed *to do* something . . . the exuber-ance, mischievousness, indignation, pain . . . was nothing other than lack of activity.

> Du glaubst nicht, wie groß oft die Sehnsucht in mir ist, *zu tun* . . . so war manche Ausgelassenheit, Mutwille, Unwille, Schmerz . . . nichts anders als Mangel an Tun. (*Bettine und Arnim 164*)

She longs to be freed "from this banishing of reality" (aus dieser Verbannung des Wirklichen), because her love would then be "not a longing desire but an active strength" (nicht ein sehnendes Ver-langen, sondern eine wirkende Macht) (Weimar 2:595).

This desire for activity and work—how should Bettine have at-tained it? She hates the gender-specific female domesticity for which the family members want to train her, even though she had to suc-cumb to this narrow world in her later life. At the same time she refuses a certain kind of creative productivity, she refuses to follow Clemens's suggestion to describe her childhood years and her time spent in a convent: "I cannot break the blossoming branches off the tree which is myself . . . For nothing is an object, it is me" (ich kann aber nicht die Blütenäste vom Baum abbrechen, der ich selbst bin . . . Denn alles ist mir ja nicht ein Gegenstand, ich bin es selber) (Weimar 2: 542). Not only would writing require her submission to coercive institutionalized aesthetics (Wolf 316–317), it would also demand as a first step that she give up her autonomy. Brentano-von Arnim certainly felt insecure about being a writer but her opposition to literary production also reflected her rejection of artistic norms (such as genre rules). Most importantly, however, she refused to succumb to the alienation she associated with literature, that is, the transition from the subconscious to the conscious, from this feeling of self to a perception of self objectified in writing. After all, this unlimited, undisturbed subjectivity is her sole sphere of being and any attempt to describe, to specify it would render her vulnerable to the limits and dangers of female authorship. She deliberates extensively on these problems in her dialogue with Günderrode. She lets her friend, who as an author has a certain professional competence, judge Bettine's poetic nature:

> You cannot compose because you are what poets call "poetical." Matter does not form itself, but is formed. (*Correspondence of Fräulein Günderode* 109)

> Du kannst nicht dichten, weil Du das bist, was die Dichter poetisch nennen, der Stoff bildet sich nicht selber, er wird gebildet. (Weimar 2: 153)

But one does not do justice to this attitude, if one understands Bettine only as the ingenious romantic muse, although she did play this role to some extent. Rather, a certain poetic self-creation is characteristic of her, serving to mediate and stimulate, although its core is a poetic self-perception which constantly transcends every particular articulation.

Neither female nor poetic praxis offered the young Bettina Brentano-von Arnim a congenial space for development. In addition, she was completely excluded from any political activity, for which she yearned even as a young girl. Her complaints about the lack of meaningful options are often directed to public activity. To be precise, she wished for a heroic role: "It is an immeasurable happiness to be called to great heroic deeds (*Correspondence of Fräulein Günderode* 25)." (Es ist ein Glück—ein unermeßliches, zu großen heroischen Taten aufgefordert sein) (Weimar 2: 43). Her political interests revealed themselves mainly in her enthusiasm, indeed identification with heroic or heroically interpreted figures and events (her grandfather La Roche, Count Stadion, the Tyrolean uprising, war and battle scenarios). She sees these heroic situations as corresponding to her personality and therefore as appropriate spheres of activity for her. Yet, Brentano-von Arnim was quite aware that these desires were impossible to realize. Even in her old age she confirms this heroic role in a letter to her sister Gunda, to whose worries about the contemporary political situation she responds with the following advice:

and do not grieve about the problems of the world because you are
unable to do anything about them; I should be the one to worry because I was actually born to turn the world upside down.

und gräme Dich nicht über das Weltunheil, weil Du unfähig bist, es zu
ändern; ich kann mir eher Sorge machen, weil ich eigentlich zum
Weltumwälzer geboren bin. (*Andacht* 338)

It seems to me that the pedagogical eros that she displays in the
correspondence with Max Prokop von Freyberg, and by which she
idealizes Prokop in a heroic role which he cannot fulfill, discloses the
frustrated desires of Brentano-von Arnim's youth, for which she tries
to compensate by the heroic education of others.

If one compares Bettina Brentano-von Arnim's situation with the
Psyche paradigm, it becomes clear that Brentano-von Arnim had no
public realm available for testing her concept of love within a social-
political context. This lack of a meaningful public sphere of influence
re-directs her once more to the development of her inner world and
self. However, development and depiction of her autonomy are not
entirely restricted to introspection but rather continuously tested in an
exchange with nature, as the only non-domestic reality available to
her. The dangerous adventures she undertook as a child during her
convent years become her way of actively dealing with her environment. This kind of exchange helps her to feel her "strength of self"
(Eigenmacht) (Weimar 2: 532). I therefore suggest that these self-
imposed perils, often undertaken in nature, can be regarded as the
only remaining type of work or praxis congenial to Bettine.

Christa Bürger, however, regards Bettine's refusal to work as the
reason for the failure of her friendship with Karoline von Günderrode
and for Brentano-von Arnim's alienation in general: "The process of
education is mediated by work; Bettine, however, is unable to concentrate on a specific piece of work" (322). This inability does not so much
reflect Brentano-von Arnim's personal idiosyncrasy as the structural
pattern of her female role. Forced between the Scylla of domestic work
and the Charybdis of a certain kind of poetic productivity, both of
which spell alienation from her self, Brentano-von Arnim tried to
establish her subjectivity in an exchange with various friends and with
nature. This communication with nature, also mentioned by Bürger
(328), preceded poetic creativity and represents Bettine's successful
mediation between self and environment. Like Psyche through her
trials, Bettine achieves self-perception and individuality through her

exchange with nature. "Speaking with nature" (Sprechen mit der Natur) (Weimar 2: 43) is meant not just metaphorically but indeed literally:

> All that I look upon, I suddenly perceive;—just as though I were Nature itself, or rather everything she produces, blades of grass . . . all flowers and all buds I feel differently. (*Correspondence of Fräulein Günderode* 185)

> Alles, was ich anseh—ja, das empfind ich plötzlich ganz—grad, als wär ich die Natur selber oder vielmehr alles, was sie erzeugt, Grashalme . . . und alle Blumen und alle Knospen, alles fühl ich verschieden. (Weimar 2: 248)

Through direct communication with nature she tries to find her identity and make it legitimate by using a value system different from the general social order. At the same time Brentano-von Arnim confers upon her self-perception a model character in which the alienation caused by society is confronted with a new mode of dealing with people and nature.

Bettine's subjectivity lives, however, in constant tension with her social environment. The strategy she developed in this context is mainly responsible for her successful self-assertion.

Numerous allusions and descriptions of the philistine manners in contemporary society can be found in all of Bettina Brentano-von Arnim's correspondences. In German literary history the origins of the critique of the philistine bourgeois originated in the *Sturm und Drang* (Storm and Stress) movement and were further developed during the Romantic period. While Brentano-von Arnim's epistolary novels reflect the main elements of this historically known critique, they also enable her to resist and challenge gendered life patterns, at least on an intellectual plane. She gains this latitude indirectly by her attacks on the philistine's nature and manner. By stigmatizing the entire social praxis as philistine, Brentano-von Arnim refuses to acknowledge this order as meaningful and binding on her actions. She gains the necessary freedom from these norms, which she then substitutes with the conviction of living in a much more meaningful and better world:

> for it is bright day(time)in my innermost self, whereas the world which you believe light, seems quite dark to me and this light is the only one

which the Philistines permit to let shine; a nasty, ugly tallow light of use
only to idlers, for whose advantage life is always calculated.—Thus I
do belong to a different community which embraces: children, heroes,
old men, figures of spring, lovers, spirits.

denn im Allerinnersten ist es Tag bei mir, dagegen mir die Welt sehr
dunkel vorkommt, in der Ihr glaubt Licht zu haben, und dies Licht ist
aber nur das, welches die Philister scheinen lassen; ein garstiges, schmut-
ziges Talglicht zum Nutzen und Besten der Bärenhäuter, zu deren
Nutzen immer das ganze Leben berechnet ist.—So gehöre ich denn in
einen anderen Kreis der Allgemeinheit, wo sich fassen möchten:
Kinder, Helden, Greise, Frühlingsgestalten, Liebende, Geister. (Weimar 2: 692–693)

Brentano-von Arnim exposes here the exclusively economic character of bourgeois reality, which subsumes life to a business-minded
profitability and which is therefore entangled in the wrong mode of
existence. She elevates the people at the margin of this society—their
marginality after all being due to their lack of productivity—to a new
community of which she wants to be considered an integral part. With
this subversive strategy she elevates her own outsider role to a desirable position that drives her not into isolation but to a new and better
community. While remaining within her social class, with the aid of
this idea she is able to create intellectual space for herself. At the
same time she actively supports and helps some outsiders (one example is the Jewish embroiderer, Veilchen) and thereby exposes herself
to the very harsh criticism of her family.

This "disloyalty to civilisation" (Meese 83) is characteristic of
Bettine's mode of thinking and behaving. Her active mediation between self and society revealed once again her quest for a meaningful
and congenial praxis. This kind of "work" of course does not fit any
of the pursuits friends and siblings had suggested to her, but this
concrete support of others helps her to better comprehend both herself as well as her society. Her independent thinking is supported
above all by Goethe's mother. But Brentano-von Arnim's autonomy,
however, is evident in her choosing this adviser herself without succumbing to her authority.

In her epistolary novels, then, Bettina Brentano-von Arnim describes developmental experiences in which she tries to carve out an
independent personality, one which is governed only by her own voice.

Bettina Brentano-von Arnim: Double Group: Venus and Amor. (Freies
Deutsches Hochstift. Photo by Ursula Edelmann.)

The happy reunion with Amor, symbolized in the birth of a daughter, concludes Psyche's destiny. Especially in the correspondence with
Clemens and Goethe, Brentano-von Arnim assumes the role of a
child, but she does not bear a child; rather through the process of
writing she gives birth or creates her own self. Psyche's maturity ends
in a more conscious loving relationship, in which she redefines herself
as lover and mother. Bettine's educational process is also mediated
through love but it is not fulfilled through a relationship. She creates
her self, not just as a loving woman but also as hero and as author.
While she thus succeeds in both loving *and* writing, she pays a hefty
price: the other, the lover, remains far away and does not recognize
her. Through writing she transcends this dualism of longing for love
and refusing love, this incompatability of an inner, ideal world and
the external, concrete reality. This dualism can also be seen in the fact
that she does not rework her correspondence with her husband
Achim von Arnim (Goodman 116). Only in her texts can she realize
the utopian potential of love, that non-authoritarian mode of dealing
with human beings and nature.[5]

Notes

I would like to express my gratitude to Marion Faber for a critical reading of the translated manuscript.

1. All translations are my own unless otherwise indicated.
2. Konstanze Bäumer has analyzed the role of the myth of Psyche in *Briefwechsel* and interpreted it in the context of Brentano-von Arnim's complex relationship with Goethe. I owe many useful ideas to Bäumer's work. My own interpretation of the Psyche motive, however, goes beyond Bäumer's, because I use it as a developmental paradigm for the three epistolary novels.
3. All translations of *Briefwechsel* are from: *Goethe's Correspondence with a Child*. 2 vols. Lowell: Bixby, 1841.
4. All translations of *Günderode* are from: *Correspondence of Fräulein Günderode and Bettine von Arnim*. Boston: T.O.H.P. Burnham, 1861. I have only modernized the forms of address.
5. For the role of the utopian imagination in *Günderode*, see: Bürger (327–328), Frederiksen/Shafi and Shafi (177–226).

Works Cited

Apuleius. *Der goldene Esel*. Frankfurt: Insel Verlag, 1975.

Arnim, Bettina von. *Werke 1. Goethes Briefwechsel mit einem Kinde*. Ed. Heinz Härtl. Berlin and Weimar: Aufbau Verlag, 1986. (Quoted as Weimar 1.)

———. *Werke 2. Die Günderode. Clemens Brentanos Frühlingskranz*. Ed. Heinz Härtl. Berlin and Weimar: Aufbau Verlag, 1989. (Quoted as Weimar 2.)

———. *Goethe's Correspondence with a Child*. Trans. von Arnim and Mrs. Austin. 2. vols. Lowell: Bixby, 1841.

———. *Correspondence of Fräulein Günderode and Bettina von Arnim*. Partially translated by Margaret Fuller Ossoli as *Günderode* (Boston: Peabody, 1842); translation completed by Minna Wesselhoeft. Boston: Burnham, 1861.

Bäumer, Konstanze. *Bettine, Psyche, Mignon: Bettina von Arnim und Goethe*. Stuttgarter Arbeiten zur Germanistik 139. Stuttgart: Akademischer Verlag, 1986.

Bettine Brentano: Die Andacht zum Menschenbild. Unbekannte Briefe. Ed. Wilhelm Schellberg and Friedrich Fuchs. Jena 1942. Rpt. Bern: Herbert Lang, 1970.

Bettine und Arnim: Briefe der Freundschaft und der Liebe. Ed. Otto Betz and Veronika Straub. Bd.1. 1806–1808. Frankfurt a. Main: Josef Knecht, 1986.

Der Briefwechsel zwischen Bettine und Max Prokop von Freyberg. Ed. Sibylle von Steinsdorff. Berlin: de Gruyter, 1972.

Bürger, Christa. Nachwort. "Der Hunger nach dem Ich." *Bettina von Arnim: Ein Lesebuch.* Ed. Christa Bürger and Birgit Diefenbach. Stuttgart: Reclam, 1987. 317–347.

Dischner, Gisela. *Bettina: Eine weibliche Sozialbiographie aus der Zeit der Romantik.* Berlin: Wagenbach, 1977.

Drewitz, Ingeborg. *Bettine von Arnim: Romantik—Revolution—Utopie.* München: Heyne, 1982.

Edwards, Lee R. *Psyche As Hero: Female Heroism and Fictional Form.* Middletown, Connecticut: Wesleyan UP, 1984.

————."The Labors of Psyche: Towards a Theory of Female Heroes." *Critical Inquiry* 6 (Autumn 1979): 33–49.

Ferguson, Mary Anne. "The Female Novel of Development and the Myth of Psyche." In *The Voyage in Fictions of Female Development.* Ed. Elisabeth Abel, Marianne Hirsch, and Elisabeth Langland. Hanover and London: University Press of New England, 1983. 228–243.

Frederiksen, Elke. "Die Frau als Autorin zur Zeit der Romantik. Anfänge einer weiblichen literarischen Tradition." In *Gestaltend und Gestaltet.* Ed. Marianne Burkhard. Amsterdam: Rodopi, 1980. 83–108.

Frederiksen, Elke und Monika Shafi. "'Sich im Unbekannten suchen gehen.' Bettina von Arnims *Die Günderode* als weibliche Utopie." In *Frauensprache—Frauenliteratur. Für und Wider einer Psychoanalyse literarischer Werke.* Ed. Inge Stephan und Carl Pietzker. Bd. 6. Akten des VII. Internationalen Germanisten-Kongresses. 11 Bde. Tübingen: Niemeyer, 1986. 54–62.

Goodman, Katherine. *Dis/Closures: Women's Autobiography in Germany between 1790 and 1914.* New York University Ottendorfer Series. Neue Folge 24. New York: Lang, 1986.

Herzhaft in die Dornen der Zeit gegriffen . . . Bettine von Arnim 1785–1859. Ed. Christoph Perels. Austellungskatalog des Freien Deutschen Hochstifts. Frankfurt am Main: Freies Deutsches Hochstift, 1985.

Hirsch, Marianne. "Spiritual Bildung: The Beautiful Soul as Paradigm." In *The Voyage in Fictions of Female Development.* Ed. Elisabeth Abel, Marianne Hirsch and Elisabeth Langland. Hanover and London: University Press of New England, 1983. 23–48.

Kaiser, Nancy. "A Dual Voice: Mary Shelley and Bettina von Arnim." *Identity and Ethos: A Festschrift for Sol Liptzin on the occasion of his 85th Birthday.* Ed. Mark H.Gelber. New York: Lang, 1986. 211–233.

Meese, Elisabeth A. *Crossing the Double Cross: The Practice Of Feminist Criticism.* Chapel Hill and London: UP of North Carolina, 1986.

Moi, Toril. *Sexual/Textual Politics: Feminist Literary Theory.* London and New York: Methuen, 1985.

Rinser, Luise. *Grenzübergänge: Tagebuch-Notizen.* Frankfurt a.Main: Fischer, 1982.

Shafi, Monika. *Utopische Entwürfe in der Literatur von Frauen.* Utah Studies in Literature and Linguistics. Vol. 30. Bern: Peter Lang, 1990.

Weigel, Sigrid. "Der schielende Blick: Thesen zur Geschichte weiblicher Schreibpraxis." In *Die verborgene Frau: Sechs Beiträge zu einer feministischen Literaturwissenschaft.* Ed. Inge Stephan und Sigrid Weigel. Berlin: Argument, 1983. 83–138.

Wolf, Christa. "Nun ja! Das nächste Leben geht aber heute an. Ein Brief über die Bettine. In *Lesen und Schreiben: Neue Sammlung. Essays, Aufsätze, Reden.* Darmstadt und Neuwied: Luchterhand, 1980. 284–318.

Through a Different Lens: Bettina Brentano-von Arnim's Views on Gender

Katherine R. Goodman

A round 1800 polarized gender characterizations found permutations in a wide variety of literary, philosophical, anthropological, and political speculations. Binary terms, explicitly or implicitly evocative of gender, began to dominate fundamental philosophical positions. In German culture this period is marked by the engendered conceptualization of life by authors like Novalis, Friedrich Schlegel, Friedrich Schiller, Wilhelm von Humboldt, and Immanuel Kant (Hausen, Hoffmann). Polarized terms ranged from life/death, dignity/grace, and sublime/beautiful to Europeans/native Americans; and each pair evoked connotations of male/female. Even Schlegel's supposedly radical combination of gender traits actually revealed his essentially dualistic assumptions (Friedrichsmeyer, Hoffmann). The binary opposition of gender traits, whether used to propound the polarity of the sexes or to envision their dichotomistic union in one individual, was thus a formative component of modern, industrialized society and its ideology.

It is therefore an item of particular interest when an author wrestles with the limitations of such a restrictive, dualistic vision and appreciates multiplicity or diversity. Bettina Brentano-von Arnim was such an author. However, despite the recent popularity of this nineteenth-century eccentric in German-speaking countries, the radicality of her views on gender has still not received the attention it deserves. No doubt this is due, in part, both to Brentano-von Arnim's failure to address directly the women's organizations of her time, as well as to the subtlety and indirect manner with which she addressed the issues themselves.

1.

Although she was born in 1785 Bettina Brentano-von Arnim lived to see the beginnings of the organized women's movement in Germany in the 1840s. (She died in 1859 at the venerable age of seventy-four.) Far from facing a decline in her talents in the 1840s, this heroine of the German women's movement of the 1970s and 1980s was just reaching her prime. Modern feminists may then wonder at her seeming distance from any of the initial stirrings of feminist activity undertaken by younger women like Louise Aston, Louise Otto-Peters, Fanny Lewald, Mathilde Anneke, or others (Waldstein 72, 85ff). This apparent distance seems all the more remarkable for the fact that she was well-attuned to the stirrings of revolt in the younger generation. For instance, she dedicated her book *Die Günderode* (1840) to German students, who were just then beginning the political rebellions that would culminate in the revolutions of 1848. The students recognized the distinction by honoring the fifty-five-year-old widow with a torchlight parade.

Günderode has most attracted the interest of modern feminists. In it Brentano-von Arnim articulates a radical aesthetic and political position which has been called feminist, pre-feminist, or female—depending on individual convictions (Frederiksen, "Die Frau"). To be sure, Brentano-von Arnim articulates there an aesthetics of conversation, illogicality, and dailiness; and she writes with fantasy, spriteliness, and poetry. But, while her works represent a conscious ideological departure from those of the dominant culture, it is debatable whether Brentano-von Arnim would have applied any of these labels. Her distaste for categories of gender was so strong that she almost surely would have objected to terms like "feminine" or "female," especially with reference to her writing.

Four years after *Günderode*, in 1844, Brentano-von Arnim published *The Spring Wreath*. As in the United States the history of gender debates is not often part of the self-understanding of Germans, and the significance of this date has all but gone unnoticed. Even the few years that had elapsed since the appearance of *Günderode* had witnessed a significant development in the discussion of gender issues in Germany. Signs of deep division of public sentiment had become visible, and the appearance of *The Spring Wreath* actually coincided with the reemergence of stormy public debates on women's role in society and *the* moment of ferment for the modern women's movement.

In 1842 the Prussian king Friedrich Wilhelm IV had commissioned Bettina Brentano-von Arnim's brother-in-law, Friedrich Karl von Savigny, minister for legislation (Gesetzgebung), with the draft of a new marriage law which was to have made divorce more difficult (*Zur Rolle* 10). The broad public discussion that followed included an article opposing it by Karl Marx ("Der Ehescheidungsgesetzentwurf," *Die Rheinische Zeitung* 19.XII.1842) (*Zur Rolle* 10) and the novel *Eine Lebensfrage* (1845) by Fanny Lewald. In 1843 the French socialist Flora Tristan demanded the right to work for both men and women (*Zur Rolle* 11). In the same year novelist Fanny Lewald demanded improved education for women ("Einige Gedanken über Mädchenerziehung," *Archiv für vaterländische Interessen oder Preußische Provinzial-Blätter* 1843) (*Zur Rolle* 11). And, anticipating a parliamentary democracy in Germany, the German socialist Robert Blum asked:

> If all people are called to participate in the community and the state, in which particular way shall women express their participation?—If we ask the question this way, we reject, from the very beginning, the older view that women are totally excluded from participation in the life of the state.

> Wenn alle Menschen zur Teilnahme an der Gemeinde, dem Staate usw. berufen sind, in welcher besonderen Weise werden dann die Frauen ihre Teilnahme zu äußern haben?—Indem wir die Frage so stellen, sprechen wir damit von vornherein uns gegen die frühere Ansicht der gänzlichen Ausschließung der weiblichen Welt von der Teilnahme am Staatsleben aus. (*Zur Rolle* 11)

To that Louise Otto-Peters answered, in the same paper, that it was not a right, but a duty for women (who were naturally patriotric, due to their love for the home) to take an interest in the affairs of state

(*Zur Rolle* 11). Because of this response (and, no doubt, also because
Otto-Peters went on to establish a feminist newspaper (*Frauenzeitung*
1849) and the *Allgemeiner deutscher Frauenverein* (1865)), Margrit
Twellmann dates the beginning of the modern German women's
movement in 1843 (Boetcher Joeres 58). In that year Bettina
Brentano-von Arnim published a lengthy conversational novel criticizing the government of the Prussian king, *The King's Book*, thereby
actually demonstrating one woman's profound interest in affairs of
state. In the controversy surrounding that novel, Arnim was (inappro-
priately) labeled a communist and an atheist (Waldstein 7ff, 77ff).

In 1844, the year in which *The Spring Wreath* appeared, Louise
Otto-Peters demanded the right for more education for women as
well as the right for women to live freer lives and to experience more
of the world (*Sächsische Vaterlands-Blätter* 15 February 1844) (*Zur
Rolle* 12). Just at this time Countess Ida Hahn-Hahn began publishing
a series of novels critical of the rule of men: *The Right One, Countess
Faustine*, and *Two Women* (Der Rechte, Gräfin Faustine, Zwei
Frauen), and Marx and Engels published *The Holy Family, or the
Critique of critical Critique* (Die heilige Familie oder Kritik der
kritischen Kritik). In 1846 Louise Aston was banished from Berlin for
her alleged interests in free love and women's emancipation. The
next year Mathilde Franziska Anneke publicly defended Aston in her
own work *Woman in Conflict with Social Relations* (Das Weib im
Konflikt mit den socialen Verhältnissen). In 1847 Louise Otto-Peters
condemned earlier calls for freedom on the grounds that they only
meant freedom for men (Lied eines deutschen Mädchens).

Definitions of gender roles were therefore high on the public
agenda by the mid 1840s. Surely a reader of newspapers as well as
other publications, Bettina Brentano-von Arnim was hardly unaware
of these definitions. It is, therefore, no accident that the author's
views on gender find their clearest and most deliberate elaboration in
the 1844 re-creation of her 1800–1803 correspondence with her older
brother, the romantic poet Clemens Brentano. During the years of
the actual early correspondence, the ideal of androgyny seemed progressive to young intellectuals of the Romantic movement like her
brother. However, despite Brentano-von Arnim's general affinity
with Romantic thought from those years, her treatment of these issues bears the imprint of the 1840s. This (perhaps anachronistic)
difference of opinion produces contention between the siblings in *The
Spring Wreath*.[1]

2.

Like her other volumes of epistolary prose the amorphous nature of *The Spring Wreath* makes it difficult to discern anything like a story. Although heavily reworked, this correspondence, like the others, has no plot with a well-delineated beginning, middle, and end. The lack of a clear structure retains the vague, lifelike shape of an authentic correspondence.

Nevertheless, there is a story to Brentano-von Arnim's early relationship to her brother, a relationship which changes in the course of the correspondence because of their differing views on gender roles. Since these documented changes are not immediately transparent, however, my reading of the text necessarily involves constructing the plot of that relationship. Brentano-von Arnim was surely no fan of novelistic plots, and such a construction of meaning would probably have been an anathema to her. Nevertheless, since her statements on gender issues and on the subtle exchanges which constitute events in relationships are so well balanced and consistent, it is difficult to believe that she herself had not already constructed something like a story here.

The Spring Wreath, then, tells the story of her relationship to her brother, with whom she had not been raised. Early in the correspondence Brentano-von Arnim (the author) allows Bettine (her character) to recall the siblings' first meeting since infancy, an event that occurred shortly before the correspondence begins. Bettine (the character) records finding with Clemens (the character) what she sought in vain with others: "a conversation in which the soul stands in the doorway, in a restful position to be sure, but so inclined toward its neighbor, so gently beckoning, that it also expresses itself" (ein Gespräch, wo die Seele in der Pforte steht, in ruhender Stellung zwar, aber so hingebeugt zum Nachbar, so sanft lockend, daß der auch sich ausspreche) (Weimar 2: 483). The character Clemens encourages his younger sister to follow the soundings of her own soul:

> Whatever you sense in yourself that exceeds the normal "being good," for that this poor world does not yet have an orderly place. You must evolve that quietly within yourself and answer to God for it and be thankful for it with the whole harmony of your feelings.

> Was Du mehr in Dir fühlst als das gewöhnliche *Bravsein*, dafür hat die arme Welt ja doch keine Ordnung, das mußt Du still in Dir bilden und

Gott selbst dafür Rechnung stehen und mit der ganzen Harmonie der
Gefühle dafür dankbar sein. (Weimar 2: 481)

The affinity of their souls in their shared rejection of the status quo
initially emerges as the basis for the sibling's intimate correspondence.
Gradually, however, the relationship loses its harmonious intimacy
and brother and sister become estranged. Brentano-von Arnim ends
the volume when the character Clemens marries Sophie Mereau.
While Brentano-von Arnim, as author, does not represent this as the
end of Bettine's love for her brother, it is clear that Clemens cannot or
will not listen to parts of Bettine's soul and that she no longer expresses
them to him. These points of discord or lack of resonance demonstrate
Bettine's revolt against social constraints on her behavior.

One of the first instances of this discord occurs when Bettine aids a
young Jewish seamstress. The girl, Veilchen, was supporting her
grandfather and two orphaned cousins with her handiwork. In the
process of helping her, Bettine had swept her front stoop and, having
been observed by an acquaintance, was chastized by her aunt for
unbecoming behavior. Clemens finds Bettine's act quite natural, but
warns her not to visit Veilchen again, for she might be seen by still
more people (Weimar 2: 494). For Bettine, however, this simple act
had had profound significance.

And I wanted there to weave a small, innocent thread in the fabric of
the world, a single little thread, and—no, I'm supposed to tear it out
because it's not seemly. Ah! where shall I attach my thread in the
eventful world if the most simple deed offends propriety!

Und ich wollte da ein kleines unschuldiges Fädchen anspinnen ins
Gewebe der Welt, ein einzig klein Fädchen, und—nein, ich soll's
abreißen, weil sich's nicht schickt. Ach! wo soll ich in der ereignisvollen
Welt meinen Faden anknüpfen, wenn das Einfachste gegen den Anstand
ist! (Weimar 2: 490)

With this incident Brentano-von Arnim opens themes reiterated
throughout the correspondence: Bettine's actions flaunting conventions and her interest in changing the world. For, as insignificant as
it may appear, this spontaneous act of kindness is actually portrayed
as a response to the French Revolution. Immediately following her
narration of this incident she reports that she and her grandmother
(the famous novelist Sophie von la Roche) had been discussing the

French Revolution and admiring the Girondist Mirabeau. The author, Brentano-von Arnim, continues the metaphor of weaving the history of the world—in order to change it—when she writes that the authors of the revolutionary pamphlets they read "[weave] with great earnestness on the fate of the world" ([weben] mit großem Ernst am Weltgeschick) (Weimar 2: 490). Both women were distressed by the excesses of the revolution, so their choice of the moderate Mirabeau is appropriate. Mirabeau had supported a constitutional monarchy with veto power for the monarch, but had also argued eloquently against the king's demand that the National Assembly be dismissed in 1789. Bettine's befriending of the Jewish seamstress demonstrates a similar desire to find a third path. She acts in a simple, but concrete and immediate way and avoids high-flying, abstract rhetoric.[2]

To Bettine's interest in revolution Clemens responds: "I never suspected that of you. But, child, isn't it a presumption on your part, or vanity?" (Das hab ich nicht von Dir geahnt. Aber Kind, ist es nicht etwas Einbildung oder Eitelkeit von Dir?) (Weimar 2: 492). Clemens had imagined Bettine's soul as a clear lake in which her fish-thoughts swam bravely in all directions. "And it was my only happiness, and now it looks different" (Und war mein einzig Glück, und nun klingt's anders) (Weimar 2: 492). At one point he warns her: "Don't babble about . . . Mirabeau, etc." (fasle nicht mit . . . Mirabeau, etc.) (Weimar 2: 509). But Bettine merely rhasodizes further about how Mirabeau speaks the fate of his people and ignites and fans it with his breath as he speaks (Weimar 2: 495f.). About herself she responds:

To see little fishes playing in the clear waters of my soul, that makes you happy?—Well, so look! How they dart here and there like lightning, they dash against the banks of the well-known fatal boredom, they bash their heads in; and I'm not supposed to light the craggy bottom to find a way out of this mud-hole—-into the world's ocean?— Where else?—Don't think that I will let myself get caught in some pleasant domestic circle.

Auf meiner Seele klarem Grund die Fischchen herumspielen sehen, das freut Dich?—Nun, so guck! Wie sie da fahren wie der Blitz hin und her, sie prallen ans Ufer der allbekannten todbringenden Langenweile, sie stoßen sich den Kopf ein; und soll ich keine Leuchte anzünden, zwischen diesem klippigten Grund einen Ausweg zu finden aus der

Pfütze—ins Weltenmeer?—Wohin sonst?—Glaub nicht, daß ich im
angenehmen häuslichen Kreis mich gefangen geben. (Weimar 2: 496)

Brentano-von Arnim thus argues with wit not only on behalf of her
political beliefs, but on behalf of her own interest in public affairs.
The latter contrasts with the boredom of domesticity and illuminates
her own escape from it. In the process, wittingly or not, Brentano-
von Arnim joins the mounting public sentiment of the 1840s for a
woman's right (and duty) to concern herself with public affairs.

Later in the volume Clemens fears Bettine has become too sentimental (Weimar 2: 628). She had gone to see the gardener. He had
become her best companion, for everything he said was so connected
to the present (Weimar 2: 619). After the visit she imagines flowers to
be the love-thoughts of nature, by whom nature is loved in return.
Flowers love all creatures, "And roses, they are the answer, which
transforms itself by teasing into a kiss and bears unhampered witness
through their own beauty to the fact that 'Love has conquered nature" (Und die Rosen, sie sind die Antwort, die im Necken schon sich
in einen Kuß verwandelt und ohne Widerstand durch ihre eigne
Schönheit Zeugnis gibt: 'Die Liebe hat die Natur besiegt') (Weimar 2:
623). So moved by the roses was she that she embraced them. For this
excess Clemens had scolded her. Now he wishes she were still interested in the French Revolution, and he recommends she help Agnes
in the kitchen instead of embracing rose bushes, or read Goethe, or
read Müller's history of Switzerland. Finally he asks her to knit him
six pairs of socks (Weimar 2: 627).

She did not know how to respond, so Bettine showed this letter to
her friend Günderode. Now she writes Clemens that she had continued discussing the revolution with her friend Günderode, but had not
told him about it because he had so strongly disapproved (Weimar 2:
629). In other words, a profound concern of hers could not be discussed in their correspondence. His more conventional views about
the proper interests of young women had undermined the discourse,
which had seemed so open and intimate at the beginning.

The character Bettine cannot restrain her sarcasm: "and then, you
say I'm sentimental and give me as an antidote to cure me an order
for a half dozen pair of linen boot stockings which I'm supposed to
knit around on for a half dozen years" (und dann, ich wär sentimental, und dann mir Heilmittel eingibt, ein halb Dutzend Paar leinerne
Stiefelstrümpf, an denen ich ein halb Dutzend Jahre knottlen soll, um

mich zu kurieren) (Weimar 2: 628). She sees clearly that Clemens is moved to this by a sense of duty: "When I look around for what is my duty, then I'm quite happy that she [duty] makes tracks away from me, because if I caught her I'd break her neck!" (Seh ich mich um nach meiner Pflicht, so freut mich's recht sehr, daß sie sich aus dem Staub macht vor mir, denn erwischte ich sie, ich würde ihr den Hals herumdrehen!) (Weimar 2: 630). Bettine rejects her "feminine" duty and continues in her ironic tone:

> I will set myself down with my duty-stocking and knit some duty-stitches, out of a sense of duty for my education I will read in the Swiss history that the Teutonic man, when he was free, never wore boot-stockings. And so out of a sense of duty I will lay my duty-stocking on the altar of the goddess Freia and swear her an oath, never again to knit boot-stockings, which shackle the free German spirit!

> Ich werde mich da mit meinem Pflichtstrickstrumpf hinsetzen und etliche Pflichtmaschen stricken, ich werde aus Pflicht gegen meine Bildung in der alten 'Schweizergeschichte' lesen, daß der Teutone keine Stiefelstrümpfe trug, als er noch ein freier Mann war, ich werde also aus Pflichtgefühl am Altar der Freia mein Strickzeug niederlegen und das Gelöbnis ihr tun, nie wieder Stiefelstrümpfe zu stricken, die dem freien deutschen Charakter Fesseln anlegen! (Weimar 2: 631)

The ironic tone assaults the nationalistic sentiments (including Clemens's) current at the beginning of the century, and in the general context of German freedom, Bettine asserts her "female" freedom by appealing to the ancient Germanic mother of the gods, Freia. From this passage we infer: neither free Germans nor the Germanic tradition demand the slavery of women. Thus, like Lewald, Otto-Peters, and others in the mid-1840s, Brentano-von Arnim assumes the rights of women to a broader range of activity.

Still later, Clemens regrets that they both lack life companions and imagines the domestic harmony of their future idyll. He thinks she should go to Frankfurt and learn to be more sociable. A woman should not and may not avoid the company of people. She should accommodate herself: "It would be the most beautiful enterprise to exert yourself (but so that it is not noticeable) and to work to make the sociability and friendliness of our home blossom under your secret protection" (Es wäre selbst das schönste Unternehmen, mit Mühe daran zu arbeiten [ohne doch deswegen es merken zu lassen], die Geselligkeit und Freundlichkeit unseres Hauses unter Deinem heimlichen Schutzrecht gedeihen zu machen) (Weimar 2: 672). With the key word "sociability" Clemens's image summons up the romantic ideal of domestic bliss, radical around 1800. According to it, the ideal woman does not merely perform household duties and remain unseen and unheard. Rather her "feminine" nature expresses itself in her ability to promote sociable discourse and unite disparate family members and friends in harmonious interchange. The character, Clemens, thus represents ideals formulated by a generation older than the one seeking new freedoms in the 1840s.

In Frankfurt Bettine would learn, according to Clemens, to suppress her more unconventional behavior, for that only leads to vexation, and while vexation in itself is not bad, "[it] is often unbecoming of a woman and often stands in the way of her efforts to do good" ([es] steht oft und bei dem Weib fast immer im Wege, Gutes zu wirken) (Weimar 2: 672). Previously Clemens had expressed the opinion that convention was a prison, but now the language of convention is a universal. No one should be entombed in it from childhood, but neither should one be made unfit for it. It is beautiful, Clemens now maintains, when a person chooses convention freely. He hopes Bettine will learn to make herself loved by all. If that were not enough, he persists: "The life of woman is firmer and less mobile than that of man, women touch people more closely and must spread their benevolence over their environment" (Das Leben des Weibes ist fester und unbeweglicher als das Leben des Mannes, das Weib berührt die Menschen näher und muß Segen über ihre Umgebung verbreiten) (Weimar 2: 673). In Brentano-von Arnim's work, Clemens represents the development, contradictions, and limitations of the ideals of his generation and sex.

Bettine claims this letter did not vex her, it isolated her (from him). She calls it an inquisition of her selfhood (Weimar 2: 676). She is amazed at the lack of understanding:

> Ah, were it possible that one foreign language could so express another with its sounds and diction that someone could write a novel in one and someone else could read it in the original and think it was a novel written in the other?—And got a story from it, of which no part had ever been imagined or intended. That's the way it is with you, and I must shatter all of your hopes that I will try *to become charming and loved by all.*

Ach, wär es möglich, daß eine fremde Sprache eine andre fremde
Sprache mit ihren Klängen und Wortarten so ganz decke, daß einer
einen Roman in der einen schrieb, der andre in der Meinung, es sei die
andre Sprache, in ihr diesen in der ersten geschriebnen Roman läse?—
Und kriegte da eine Geschichte heraus, von der keine Spur je geahnt
oder gemeint war. So ist's mit Dir und ich muß Deine Hoffnungen alle
niederschmettern, daß ich mich bemühen würde, "allgemein liebens-
würdig und geliebt zu werden." (Weimar 2: 677)

Two years after the appearance of *The Spring Wreath* Louise Otto-
Peters condemned earlier calls for freedom on the grounds that they
had only meant freedom for men. But she only touched the tip of the
iceberg of linguistic misunderstandings between the sexes represented by the character Bettine in this volume of correspondence.

Bettine later apologizes for this response, calling it the gesture of
an ill-mannered child; but when Clemens continues in the same vein,
she pleads with him to give up sighing about the dear husband he
dreams of for her:

You are concerned about me, dear Clemens, but believe me, I don't
need any support in life and I don't wish to be the victim of such foolish
prejudices. I know what I need!—I need to keep my freedom. For
what?—To undertake and complete the dictates of my inner voice.

Es ist Vorsorge, geliebter Clemens, aber glaube, daß ich keiner Stütze
im Leben bedarf, und daß ich nicht das Opfer werden mag von solchen
närrischen Vorurteilen. Ich weiß, was ich bedarf!—ich bedarf, daß ich
meine Freiheit behalte. Zu was?—dazu, daß ich das ausrichte und
vollende, was eine innere Stimme mir aufgibt zu tun. (Weimar 2: 692)

Clemens continues to preach that "a superior woman is something
quite other than a good man" (ein vortreffliches Weib etwas ganz
anderes ist als ein braver Mann) (Weimar 2: 695). Now she responds
pointedly:

Your illusions hop around in your letter like grasshoppers. I don't know
which I should catch first.—The most tedious grasshopper for me is
where you want to force on me the great difference between a "superior woman" and a good man. May these two find each other on some
happy star! I only request one thing of you, that you don't tell me about
it. Once and for all, I want to be totally excluded from this sacred state!

Deine Illusionen hüpfen wie Heuschrecken in Deinem Brief herum;
ich weiß nicht welche ich zuerst erwischen soll. —Die allerledernste
Heuschrecke ist mir die, wo Du mich mit Gewalt willst auf den
großen Unterschied hinweisen zwischen einem *vortrefflichen Weib* und
einem braven Manne. Mögen diese zwei beiden zusammenfinden auf
irgendeinem glücklichen Stern, nur das einzige bitte ich mir aus, daß
Du es mir nicht zu wissen tust; und ein für allemal will ich von diesem
Heiligtum gänzlich ausgeschlossen sein! (Weimar 2: 696)

Thus the character, Bettine, rejects the romantic ideal that she would
require an opposite gender for completion of her selfhood. The notion that marriage was not a socially responsible act to fulfill the
wishes of one's parents or society but rather something holy and a
foretaste of cosmic wholeness was a specifically romantic one. In fact,
later Clemens asserts that while convention and marriage are no
longer divine, because they are hollow, still they are honorable, because they suggest hope for something better (Weimar 2: 765).
Bettine is scornful and rejects the discussions of gender that assert
that both men and women require completion of their natures in a
heterosexual union.

After Bettine explains her desire to perform bold, public acts,
Clemens expresses the wish that she would dedicate herself to art and
poetry. This too is a perpetuation of the romantic ideal of women
(expounded, for instance, in Schlegel's *Lucinde*, 1799), which emphasized the importance of women exercizing their artistic or literary
skills, even though these were to be practiced only for the benefit of
the larger family circle and not for the public. Indeed, in reality, the
author Clemens Brentano's marriage to author Sophie Mereau virtually ended her publishing career. In *The Spring Wreath* Bettine's
friend Günderode suggests that Clemens has made Bettine into an
ideal through the rebirth of his intellect, but Bettine is horrified at
that thought and urges him not to idealize her (Weimar 2: 659f.). She
clearly wants to be regarded as a human being and not as a metaphor
or symbol for an abstract concept.

Even toward the end of the book Clemens persists in envisioning a
domestic idyll, when he shall have married Sophie Mereau and
Bettine a worthy man (Weimar 2: 735). Bettine no longer responds to
statements like these, but for someone to whom convention represented a form of slavery that made her stupid (Weimar 2: 488), she
surely had reason to feel that their souls were no longer in resonance.

That Clemens's marriage appears to end the correspondence only masks the fact that it had already ended.

Clearly Bettine rejects Clemens's "great difference" between an ideal man and an ideal woman, the polarity of the sexes. But her rejection implies more than a rejection of a simple dichotomy of gender characteristics. She explicitly rejects the affirmation of the connective and sociable role for women in the domestic sphere as too restrictive. This had been the allegedly progressive romantic ideal at the beginning of the nineteenth century. So it is not only against a traditional domestic role for women that Bettine revolts, it is also against the so-called liberated role for women articulated by the romantic poets—which both her brother and her husband had been. She rejects their idealization of feminine qualities. She stresses her desire to move world history and to act immediately. Throughout the volume Bettine objects to any restrictions placed on the thoughts and actions of girls as "police for girls" (Polizei für Mädchen) or "the restriction of labels" (Klausur der Etikette).

3.

But what should or could a woman be? Other potential models are presented in the volume. One is her grandmother, the author Sophie von La Roche, with whom Brentano-von Arnim had lived during most of the period portrayed in the fictive correspondence. La Roche, of course, had been the first significant woman author in modern Germany. Her epistolary novel *The History of Lady Sophia Sternheim* (Die Geschichte des Fräulein von Sternheims) (1771) had earned her broad acclaim. While it demonstrated the strong influence of Samuel Richardson, her heroine was more resourceful and resilient than any of his. She was a cultivated heroine, carefully educated by her parents; and she was a practical heroine, undertaking educational projects for underprivileged women. Sophie von Sternheim was dignified and principled, a woman who promoted the "active virtue" of charity for women.

Brentano-von Arnim, in the incident with the young Jewish woman (as well as in others), had shown the importance which she, too, attached to the principle of "active virtue." It is likely that Sophie von La Roche had at least some influence with her grandaughter. At first glance, however, it may appear that the grandmother was

an antagonist for the protagonist, Bettine. For instance, she inter-
cepted Clemens's first letter to Bettine and intended to withhold it
from her. (Bettine found it by chance.) Thus in the beginning she
seems one of those guardians of the abhorred "Polizei für Mädchen."
But this unusual grandmother would also have Bettine learn Latin.
Even in the 1840s this was an unconventional (and progressive) endeavor for a girl, and in the correspondence it may be said to represent the idea of increased schooling for girls, so that their education
would more closely resemble that of boys. At the time of the publication of *The Spring Wreath*, Fanny Lewald, Louise Otto-Peters, and
others were proclaiming the rights of girls to just such an education.
But even though Clemens provisionally supports his grandmother,
Bettine wants nothing to do with Latin, thereby rejecting particular
ideas of enlightenment. Bettine's perspective on education, like those
of the Romantics, is scornful of rote, book learning (even though
Romantics were well-educated and well-read), and in this regard (to
the extent that Bettine expressed Brentano-von Arnim's views) the
author differed, quite simply, with the emerging women's movement,
as well as with her grandmother.

In what would appear to be a contradiction, however, Bettine
admires the domesticity of her grandmother, claiming it had its own
poetic shimmer (Weimar 2: 660). Nothing is neglected, and the grandmother delights in the simplest effects of nature on her garden.

> There is no more noble woman than my grandmother!—Who can
> mistake the wonderful glance of her eye when she stands pensively
> sometimes in the middle of her garden, searching on all sides, and then
> suddenly walks over to give a branch more freedom, or to support a
> vine—and then leaves the garden in the evening as satisfied as if she
> had blessed everything with the conviction that it would flourish.

> es gibt doch keine edlere Frau wie die Großmutter! — Wer den
> wunderschönen Blitz ihres Auges verkennt, wenn sie manchmal sinnend
> mitten im Garten steht und späht nach allen Seiten und geht dann
> plötzlich hin, um einem Zweig mehr Freiheit zu geben, um eine Ranke
> zu stützen! — und dann so befriedigt in der Dämmerung den Garten
> verläßt, als habe sie mit der Überzeugung alles gesegnet, daß es fruchten
> werde. (Weimar 2: 660)

The loving cultivation of her immediate environment is a virtue
Bettine may have learned to appreciate in herself by watching her

grandmother. But this domestic idyll, with its overtones of Biedermeier tranquility, is not ultimately the vision Bettine carries for herself.

And yet, it is with this very grandmother that Bettine pours over pamphlets of the French Revolution. These ignite her imagination and compassion. Both women admire Mirabeau (although La Roche apparently finds Grandison an even more ideal hero and tries to moderate Bettine's revolutionary enthusiasm) (Weimar 2: 492,498). Still, Clemens opines that Bettine inherited her concern for freedom from her grandmother. Indeed, reading old books with her grandmother, Bettine becomes inspired to imagine herself in the "grandest roles" (höchsten Rollen) and plays out, in her fantasy, her "projects for humanity" (Menschheitsprojekte) (Weimar 2: 691). Moreover, although La Roche may be taken aback when Bettine tells her she wants to become a "cloud-swimmer" (Wolkenschwimmer), she gives her fantasies free reign (Weimar 2: 589). Bettine's desire to cultivate human life may resemble her grandmother's, but it exceeds the boundaries of domestic idylls as it ultimately exceeds the imagination of her grandmother.

If Bettine rejects earlier definitions of femininity and feminine roles, as well as expanded romantic affirmations of "the feminine," she remains unwilling to accept an androgynous model for her own development—although she is mightily attracted to one. Early in the correspondence Clemens writes Bettine about Madame de Gachet, a Frenchwoman and scholar spending time in Jena carrying out scientific experiments, a physicist on a par with the best in Europe, he writes.[3] This woman, whom he has sent to Bettine with a letter of introduction, is described as a Germanic heroine:

> a totally fearless soul, whose daring worked wonders during the Reign of Terror . . . she is supposed to be as beautiful, as perfectly formed as a woman from the *Nibelungenlied*, she rides the wildest horse.

> eine ganz unerschrockne Seele, die in der Terroristenzeit durch ihre Kühnheit Unendliches gewirkt hat . . . sie soll so schön sein, so vollkommen wohlgebildet wie ein Weib aus den Nibelungen, sie reitet das wildeste Pferd. (Weimar 2: 524f.)

Against the background of Bettine's interest in the revolution, such a strong, capable heroine acting a historical role and helping ordinary people was bound to inflame her fantasy. Indeed Clemens quickly writes again confessing to acting hastily and warning his sister about the scars the revolution had left on de Gachet. In particular he warns her "to overlook the masculine wildness of de Gachet's being and her intellect" (das männliche Wilde ihres Seins und Verstandes [zu] übersehen) (Weimar 2: 528). He wants her to remain his and God's.

When de Gachet arrives in male attire, riding like a man, Bettine in fact mistakes her for one. De Gachet talks politics like a man, too, "as though she had been present at all the battles" (als wär sie bei allen Schlachten mitgewesen) (Weimar 2: 532). When she leaves, Bettine cannot find peace: "I have to shout for joy over an uncertain something" (ich muß jauchzen vor Vergnügen über ein unbestimmtes Etwas) (Weimar 2: 532). Bettine cannot explain this something. Perhaps it was that this one encounter had made her own unconventional desires seem acceptable, as though she were not alone. In the same letter she writes Clemens: "But my soul is a passionate dancer, it leaps around to an inner dance music that only I hear and the others don't. Everyone is yelling for me to be quiet, and you do too, but because of my desire to dance, my soul doesn't listen to you" (Aber meine Seele ist eine leidenschaftliche Tänzerin, sie springt herum nach einer innern Tanzmusik, die nur ich höre und die andern nicht. Alle schreien, ich soll ruhig werden, und Du auch, aber vor Tanzlust hört meine Seele nicht auf Euch) (Weimar 2: 532).

Clemens had first hoped de Gachet would become an intimate, a "Du," for Bettine, but then feared she would unsettle her. And of course she did. On one excursion Madame de Gachet

swung herself onto her horse with complacent grace, greeted me as if to say: come, swing yourself on a horse, leave everything behind which restricts you, trust me, I want to give you a hand.—And away she went; and I ran into the garden and climbed the poplar, where should I have gone, so full of longing into the distance. . . . and if I had been able, I would find my entire happiness in that.

schwang sich mit selbstgefälliger Anmut aufs Pferd, sie grüßte mich, als wolle sie mir sagen: schwing dich auch aufs Roß, aus allem heraus, was dich beengt, komm, vertrau mir, ich will dir die Hand reichen.—Und fort war sie; und ich lief in den Garten und stieg auf die Pappel, wo hätt ich hingesollt, so sehnsüchtig in die Weite. . . . und hätt ich das gekonnt, mein ganz Glück würd ich darin finden. (Weimar 2: 539)

Clemens had reason to worry.

Strangely enough it seems to be the world of the grandmother that plays a role in holding Bettine back. Other Frenchmen come, and they spoil the carefully cultivated garden of the grandmother with their joyous apple fight. The grandmother interrupts by asking Bettine to pick some flowers. Later, when Bettine is seated on de Gachet's lap listening to her tell about the attraction of planets, Bettine nearly succumbs (to what is not clear, although perhaps it is to de Gachet's orbit)—but again her grandmother comes in unexpectedly (Weimar 2: 546). The cultivated grandmother functions as another planet.

The greatest resistance to de Gachet, however, comes from Bettine's own self. De Gachet indeed appears as a great planet capable of holding Bettine in her orbit; but Bettine pulls herself away as if to establish her own. If she were already what she is to become she could be de Gachet's friend, she writes, but she knows she must pull away now to remain fully herself (Weimar 2: 534). Although she longs to travel, she rejects de Gachet's invitation to go to Spain as something foreign to her nature. Bettine claims she would rather stay in her own garden, with her family, even though she aches with longing (Weimar 2: 557f.).

Bettine's rejection of de Gachet needs to be examined more carefully. Although she refuses to take an androgynous creature, like de Gachet, as a model for her own self, it is not androgynous creatures per se that Bettine rejects. On one occasion an androgynous chicken, with the name "Manwoman" (Männewei), was about to be slaughtered at her grandmother's. Bettine rushed the farm maid from behind, rescued the chicken, and left it with the gardener for protection. Later Bettine vows always to interfere when she sees a human life in danger, even if the knife is already on its neck:

> If I had reflected, for even a second, "Manwoman" would no longer be alive!—And it's a peculiar thing with such a creature, you don't know if it has a hereafter, and yet it likes to live and has more affinity with nature than we do. Yes, it's worth the trouble to save a life, no matter whose. Ah! The swans come to mind, now, who had to bathe their snow-white feathers in their own blood, like the heroes of the Gironde!

> Hätt ich nur einen Augenblick mich besonnen, so lebte jetzt kein Männewei mehr!—Und mit so einem Tier ist's eine besondere Sache, man weiß nicht, ob es ein Jenseits hat, doch lebt es gern, doch hat es mehr mit der Natur zu schaffen wie wir, doch gehört ihm die Welt, jeden Augenblick es drauf verweilt, ja es ist der Mühe wert, ein Leben

zu retten, sei es welches es wolle. Ach, die Schwäne fallen mir hier ein,
die ihr schneeweiß Gefieder im eignen Blute mußten baden, die
Helden der Gironde! (Weimar 2: 662)

At the end, then, the image of the knife at the neck provides the
connection between the slaughter of this androgynous life and that of
revolutionary heroes like Mirabeau.[4] The French Revolution had created such androgynous types. Madame de Gachet is but one example.
The revolutions of 1848 would create still more. Even if Bettine does
not choose this path for herself, she clearly values it, and respects and
protects its difference.

In all, Bettine protects the natural rights of anyone, regardless of
gender or type. What is of ultimate significance is not that Bettine
rejects androgynous characters as models for herself, but that she
seeks to rid herself of all foreign impositions of gender constructions,
all labels, in the evolution of her own native character. This becomes
clear in one final exchange with de Gachet. In the end de Gachet buys
an estate in Germany (near Mainz) and learns to guide the plow
herself. This de Gachet is more appealing to Bettine than the one
who rides off on a wild horse to foreign countries. When Bettine visits
her, the two talk of the revolution. De Gachet opines: "You must use
only the most holy means to achieve great ends. Wherever unholy
means are used for the most noble goal, it is lost and creates only
evil" (Das Große zu bewirken kann man immer nur die heiligsten
Mittel ergreifen, wo aber zum edelsten Zweck ein unheilig Mittel
dient, da ist er verloren und erzeugt nur Uebel) (Weimar 2: 599). Had
the French king had the greatness to encompass all things, had he
been a real king

> who merely collected his power through that genius which is always
> holy.—who could have resisted him! . . . But to take refuge in foreign
> means is unholy, and no matter how noble and grand the goal, it will
> never be honored, it will be buried in its own ruins.
>
> der nur seine Kraft sammelte durch das Genie, das immer heilig ist.—
> wer konnte ihm widerstehen! . . . Die Zuflucht aber zu fremden Mitteln
> ist unheilig, und sei der Zweck auch noch so edel und groß, er wird nie
> verehrt, er wird unter den eignen Trümmern begraben. (Weimar 2: 599)

Before Bettine leaves, de Gachet applies this specifically to any person's character. Bettine should never forget

that every person has the right to be the greatest, and that the entire education of the soul is founded in this . . . but the fates are the temple of all greatness and her own destiny proves that she had only one thought in mind: to be great in her own destiny.

daß jeder Mensch das Recht habe, der größte zu werden, und daß darin die ganze Erziehung der Seele begründet sei . . . aber die Geschicke, die seien der Tempel aller Größe und ihr eignes Geschick beweise es, daß sie diesen Gedanken immer vor Augen gehabt, sie wolle groß werden in ihrem Schicksal. (Weimar 2: 599f.)

So moved is Bettine that she cannot answer, she can only run away, wave goodbye to her from a distance, and then fall to the ground and let her heart beat itself out.

This is the kernel of Bettine's thoughts on character (and what is gender theory if not part of a theory of character?): to strive to become great in the exercise of one's specific character and circumstance, and not to reach for anything foreign (non-indigenous means or non-innate qualities) that may seem attractive in someone else. This is advice for nations and for personalities.

To modern readers this may seem the height of traditional humanistic subjectivity, and the analogy of individual and national identity may seem predictable. However, two aspects of her conceptualization elude contemporary critiques of humanistic subjectivity. The first is that, for Bettina Brentano-von Arnim, one's individual character can never be elaborated in isolation. It requires open and supportive exchange with other individuals to become all that it already *is*. Only with the help of others can we become ourselves, but they must not restrict, they must nourish. Brentano-von Arnim projects the social basis and historical complexity of this project in the depiction of Bettine's relationships with Clemens, her grandmother, and de Gachet, among others. The second distinction to be made between Brentano-von Arnim's view of subjectivity and the critique of humanistic subjectivity is that for her the process never ends. This is why her "epistolary" or "conversational" novels have no beginning, middle, or end. There is no resolution, no real story. Everything is always and continually in flux.

4.

This portrait of Brentano-von Arnim's views on character reveals her general indebtedness to German romantic thought. The organic view of human individuality and of political structures was held by romantic thinkers like Ernst Moritz Arndt and Friedrich Schelling. However, since her views on gender do not conform to theirs, one would naturally like to know if there was any further context in which one might understand her apparently quirky but strong opinions. After all, Bettine rejected for herself both the romantic domestic ideal, including strong notions of difference, as well as the romantic androgynous ideal, in favor of a notion of character in which gender polarities (whether between two people or within one person) became irrelevant or, to be more precise, in which gender labels both inhibited the evolution of character and endangered the very lives of those who were different. Were there predecessors or contemporaries with whom she shared her views? Or did they emerge idiosyncratically?

There are several possible sources of support for a theoretical view of gender that was nevertheless, to my knowledge, unique. Despite the tendency of the age to polarize concepts in binary terms, or perhaps precisely because of it, some thinkers resisted. A significant role in this resistance was played by a Dutch philosopher, now relatively unknown, but at the time extremely influential: Frans Hemsterhuis (1721–1790). We can be sure that Bettina Brentano-von Arnim knew his works, but not who the mediator may have been. The familiarity may have derived from her friendship with Friedrich Heinrich Jacobi (1743–1819) in Munich in 1808, but it almost surely predated that year. Hemsterhuis's works were among the favorites of Karoline von Günderrode (1780–1806), whose friendship Brentano-von Arnim had re-created in *Günderode* in 1840. The philosopher's name appears several times in that work, on some occasions in the context of Bettine reading Hemsterhuis with her grandmother, Sophie von La Roche (perhaps, if the incidents are true, around 1805 or 1806). It is virtually certain that Sophie von La Roche was familiar with Hemsterhuis's philosophy as she was in correspondence with members of the Münster Circle. Most likely the edition with which Brentano-von Arnim was familiar was the 1782/1792 German translation from the original French. L.S.P. Meyboom's standard French edition appeared beginning only in 1846, two years after the appearance of *The Spring Wreath*.

Hemsterhuis's perception of the polymorphous nature (Vielgestaltigkeit) of life was at the core of his philosophical and aesthetic views. The concept of multiplicity in unity grounded his hopes for the "coexistence," or "making coexistent," of the most numerous and widely diverging ideas and beings. Human interaction with nature was a primary theme of his. If something is capable of evoking a reaction, according to Hemsterhuis, it is active. Individuals may thus recognize and activate the otherness of nature, as they may recognize and activate the otherness of each individual. The recognition or "making coexistent" of otherness could extend to other areas, for example, to recognition of a variety of religious expression. The state and its laws restricted coexistence and made criminals. Diversity in unity is a goal of art, of character, of the state.

Only an active being (être activ), one who elicits a reaction and thereby realizes its activity, can become a guiding force in the creation of this world concept. Such beings render other beings coexistent, activate them. Beings become active insofar as they determine themselves through their own will (velléité), rather than that of another.

A genderized concept of society does not seem to have existed for this philosopher. Hemsterhuis rejected marriage since it forced two beings to take a common path. "Shame" enters relationships when one person becomes the "property" of another, as happens in the institution of marriage. The reification of human beings in marriage destroys the potential for them to become active, self-determining beings (Hammacher, 141). Progress in history is made only when each individual unit achieves its own particular culmination. Restraining the potential of any being by a priori definitions retards history.

If we want to look beyond Hemsterhuis for contemporary philosophical support for Brentano-von Arnim's non-dualistic views on character, we will probably also want to consider Spinoza. However, while we can say with some certainty that Brentano-von Arnim was familiar with the works of Hemsterhuis, the same cannot be said about the earlier Dutch philosopher Spinoza (1632–1677). Nevertheless, evidence points strongly in that direction. Certainly this philospher was well known in the circles Bettine Brentano-von Arnim frequented, and she was not likely to fail to read at least about him. Her friend Jacobi had become embroiled in a public debate about Spinoza, Goethe was fascinated by him, and her friend in later years, the theologian Friedrich Schleiermacher, was an admirer of his works. Even Hemsterhuis's philosophy may have been tinged by Spinoza's. While one recent scholar disputes this, many earlier ones (including Gotthold Ephraim Lessing) considered Hemsterhuis "spinozistic" (Hammacher, 114).

Spinoza's concept of substance, as the unity of thought and matter, was widely influential, and could well have inspired Bettina Brentano-vonArnim. However, for our purposes, it seems most fruitful to focus on Spinoza's concept of attributes. In Aristotelian logic objects are defined by their differences. Since humans differ from animals by use of reason, their essence is rational. In this way woman becomes defined by her womb. By contrast, nothing is defined for Spinoza until *all* of its attributes have been described. For him, as for Schleiermacher, this was an infinite task. No final definition would be possible, much less one a priori. In the richness of Schleiermacher's thought, this concept can be related to the evolution of the (already extant) wholeness of the self. For Bettina Brentano-von Arnim this could only mean that whatever actions or thoughts emerged fully and surely from the truth of her character were not out of character. No external definitions were applicable, no foreign influence was to be appropriated unless *she* determined it was in harmony with the totality of her own particular character, *itself* infinitely determined by circumstance. For us it also means that the definition of woman is not complete when one has determined her biological difference from man. It is always the whole which must be considered. A woman not only possesses a womb, she is also a human and capable of reason. And humans, men and women alike, are not only rational, they also possess bodies and are animal.

For Brentano-von Arnim, it was not the divisions of nature, but rather its totality that manifested itself in individuals. Spinoza's unity of substance shimmers through many of her statements: "Things, which we *have* to decide, do not exist. We observe the only god in us; he races through our limbs like electricity, that is decision" (Dinge, zu denen wir uns entschließen *müssen*, die sind nicht. Wir schauen den einzigen Gott an in uns; er durchführt elektrisch uns die Glieder; das ist Entschluß) (Weimar 2: 571). Explaining her final refusal to become caught in de Gachet's orbit, she wrote: "It seems like a crime to me to yield to a leadership, which might mislead what is original in me" (Es kommt mir wie Frevel vor, daß ich mich einer Leitung hingebe, die vielleicht das Ursprüngliche in mir verleitet) (Weimar 2: 587). "I shall become my own, this is the will of my "I", for otherwise I would be for naught. This one thing that makes me unique in the entire creation, this is the nobility of free will in me" (Ich soll doch mein eigen werden, dies ist doch der Wille meines Ichs, denn sonst wär ich umsonst; dies eine, was mich eingentümlich aus dem Gesamtsein heraus bildet, das ist der Adel des freien Willens in mir)(Weimar 2: 588). Why she rejects domesticity becomes crystal clear when she writes: "To be yourself is to be a hero; that's what I want to be. Whoever is himself must move the world; that is what I want" (Selbstsein ist Held sein; das will ich sein. Wer selbst ist, der muß die Welt bewegen, das will ich) (Weimar 2: 588). Her self is not separate from the world, from history. But if the world is part of her self, she can move it—as Mirabeau had.

Even Clemens had a vision of this when he wrote her:

> every individual power can only take root in the general, can only learn in it to understand itself, and can only test itself *on it*. That's why the history of things is the true element of the intellects, and that's why de Gachet has such an electric effect on people.

> jede individuelle Kraft kann nur durch und in der Allgemeinheit Wurzel fassen, kann nur in ihr sich selbst verstehen lernen; und kann nur *an ihr* sich erproben. Drum ist die Geschichte der Dinge das wahre Element der Geister, und darum hat diese de Gachet eine elektrische Wirkung auf die Menschen. (Weimar 2: 536)

Unfortunately he neglected to include his sister in this thought about the individual power only testing itself on the general (society). Bettine's response to Clemens's "inquisition" includes the thought that she wants to call everything hers, "because everything to which I speak is mine, and everything which arouses me" (weil alles mein ist was ich anrede, was mich erregt) (Weimar 2: 676f.). There are no limits to her self. She suggests Clemens go to sea "where nothing has a firm shape, everything comes and goes! It is better that everything dissolve, than that something take shape which is not total generosity and freedom!" ("wo nichts noch feste Gestalt hat, wie gewonnen, so zerronnen! besser, daß alles zerfließe, als daß Gestalt gewinne, was nicht ganz Großmut und Freiheit wäre!") (Weimar 2: 721). In the face of such a theory of personality the attempt to delimit gender characteristics appears tyrannical in the extreme. That the attempt to define anyone by gender is ultimately not only futile, but personally destructive, was precisely Bettina Brentano-von Arnim's point.

If Brentano-von Arnim's thoughts are compared with those of the leaders of the incipient women's movement, points of similarity can easily be found. She believed that women were political creatures, that something had to be done immediately to alleviate the conditions of the working poor, that women required freedom from constraints. Her views on education may seem elitist and her suggestions for political action possibly naive (compared to Otto-Peters, who also worked to aid the conditions of seamstresses), but on the issue of gender definition and theory of character she surpassed them all. No one, not even today, has so completely transcended the restrictions of gender definitions. As a judgment about character, the a priori category of gender, like Kant's a priori categories of time and space, remains ultimately and absolutely unaffirmable. It severely limits our vision of the world and inhibits our personal evolution. Like the daily usage of the categories of time and space, that of the category gender is far too simplistic an assumption. In Bettina Brentano-von Arnim, the feminist argument favors the elimination of all dualistic gender constructs as definitive categories.

Notes

1. Virtually all of the original correspondence is presumed lost or accidentally burned. The auction catalogue of 1929 (when the correspondence was still intact) stated that Brentano-von Arnim had made many changes, but that she had been faithful to the content (Weimar 2: 952). To judge by the letter in which Brentano actually chastized his sister for becoming too sentimental and recommended instead that she knit him socks and read Goethe and Swiss history, Brentano-von Arnim may have kept much, yet subtly shifted the emphasis (Weimar 2: 957–961).
2. Clemens had sent Bettine Friedrich Schiller's *Briefe über die ästhetische Erziehung des Menschen* in which Schiller also attempts to find an alternative to either the violence of oppression or the violence of revolution. Schiller's solution is to educate the aesthetic faculties of human beings. Bettine writes Clemens that she has not (and will not) read Schiller. She has nothing in common with his "cloud ghost" (Wolkengespenst) or "silhouette of sublimities" (Schattenriß der Erhabenheiten) (Weimar 2: 66). In opposition to Schiller's Idealism, Bettine chooses a more practical and earthly "third" route.
3. Louise de Gachet resided in Weimar and Jena around 1800. Clemens Brentano met her in Offenbach in 1801. He described her to his brother-in-law Savigny in November, 1801: "a woman as large as Ritter in innocent intellect, as charming as Pompadour and as commanding as Catherine and inspired as Joan of Arc, not Schiller's, and sweeter than [Sophie] Mereau, . . . grander than German *Bildung*, philosophy itself

returned, Bettine shall become her friend" (ein Weib so groß wie Ritter an unschuldigem Geist, so reizend wie Pompadour und herrschend wie Katharina und begeistert wie Jeanne d'Arc, nicht die von Schiller, und lieblicher als [Sophie] Mereau, . . . höher als die deutsche Bildung, die zurückgekehrte Philosophie, Bettine soll ihre Freundin werden) (Weimar 2: 980, ft. 524).

4. In real life some thought Brentano-von Arnim looked somewhat masculine (Waldstein, 69). In *The Spring Wreath* Bettine sometimes seems a little proud of a masculine edge to her personality and her intellect—when she writes Clemens that Günderode considers her her only "male" companionship (Weimar 2: 159)—or when someone else imagines her a Joan of Arc for freedom and human rights (Weimar 2: 160). Bettine composes music for hymns to the androgynous mythological figures of Diana and Dionysos (Weimar 2: 116).

Works Cited

Arnim, Bettina von. *Werke.* Ed. Heinz Härtl. 2 Vols. Berlin and Weimar: Aufbau, 1986 and 1989. Vol. 1 *Goethes Briefwechsel mit einem Kinde* (1986); Vol. 2 *Die Günderode* and *Clemens Brentanos Frühlingskranz* (1989). (Referred to as Weimar.)

Bäumer, Konstanze. *"Bettine, Psyche, Mignon" Bettina Brentano-von Arnim und Goethe.* Stuttgart: Verlag Hans-Dieter Heinz, 1986.

Becker-Cantarino, Barbara. "Priesterin und Lichtbringerin. Zur Ideologie des weiblichen Charakters in der Frühromantik." *Die Frau als Heldin und Autorin. Neue kritische Ansätze zur deutschen Literatur.* Ed. Wolfgang Paulsen. Bern: Francke, 1979. 111–124.

Blackwell, Albert L. *Schleiermacher's Early Philosophy of Life. Determinism, Freedom, and Phantasy.* Chico, CA.: Scholars Press, 1982.

Boetcher Joeres, Ruth-Ellen. *Die Anfänge der deutschen Frauenbewegung. Louise Otto-Peters.* Frankfurt/M.:Fischer, 1983.

———. " 'That girl is an entirely different character!' Yes, but is she a feminist?" *German Women in the Eighteenth and Nineteenth Centuries. A Social and Literary History.* Ed. Ruth-Ellen B. Joeres and Mary Jo Maynes. Bloomington: Indiana University Press, 1983. 137–156.

Frederiksen, Elke. "Die Frau als Autorin zur Zeit der Romantik: Anfänge einer weiblichen literarischen Tradition." *Gestaltet und Gestaltend. Frauen in der deutschen Literatur.* Ed. Marianne Burkhard. Amsterdam: Rodopi, 1980. 83–108.

Frederiksen, Elke and Monika Shafi. "'Sich im Unbekannten suchen gehen' Bettina Brentano-von Arnims *Die Günderode* als weibliche Utopie." *Frauensprache-Frauenliteratur?: Für und wider einer Psychoanalyse literarischer Werke.* Ed. Inge Stephan and Carl Pietzcker. Tübingen: Niemeyer, 1986. 54–67.

Friedrichsmeyer, Sara. *The Androgyne in Early German Romanticism.* Bern: Lang, 1983.

———. "The Subversive Androgyne." *Women in German Yearbook.* Ed. Marianne Burkhard and Edith Waldstein. Lanham, MD: University Press of America, 1986. 3: 63–75.

Hammacher, Klaus. *Unmittelbarkeit und Kritik bei Hemsterhuis.* München: Wilhelm Fink, 1971.

Hampshire, Stuart. *Spinoza.* Middlesex, England: Penguin, 1951.

Hausen, Karin. "Die Polarisierung der 'Geschlechtscharaktere'—Eine Spiegelung der Dissoziation von Erwerbs- und Familienleben." *Seminar: Familie und Gesellschaftsstruktur.* Ed. Heidi Rosenbaum. Framkfurt a.M.: Suhrkamp 1978. 161–194.

Hoffmann, Volker. "Elisa und Robert oder das Weib und der Mann, wie sie sein sollten. Anmerkungen zur Geschlechtercharakteristik der Goethezeit." *Klassik und Moderne. Die Weimarer Klassik als historisches Ereignis und Herausforderung im kulturgeschichtlichen Prozeß.* Ed. Karl Richter und Jörg Schönert. Stuttgart: Metzler, 1983. 80–97.

Laqueur, Thomas. "Orgasm, Generation and the Politics of Reproductive Biology." *Representations* (Spring, 1986) 14: 1–41.

Lewald, Fanny. *Eine Lebensfrage.* Leipzig: Brockhaus, 1845.

Moenkemeyer, Heinz. *Francois Hemsterhuis.* Boston: Twayne, 1975.

Möhrmann, Renate Ed. *Frauenemanzipation im deutschen Vormärz. Texte und Dokumentation.* Stuttgart: Reclam, 1979.

Riley, Helene M. Kastinger. "Tugend im Umbruch. Sophie Laroches *Geschichte des Fräuleins von Sternheim* einmal anders." Helene M. Kastinger Riley *Die weibliche Muse. Sechs Essays über künstlerisch schaffende Frauen der Goethezeit.* Columbia, S.C.: Camden, 1986. 27–52.

Spickernagel, Ellen. " 'Helden wie zarte Knaben oder verkelidete Mädchen.' Zum Begriff der Androgynität bei Johann Joachim Winckelmann und Angelika Kauffmann." *Frauen Weiblichkeit Schrift.* 99–118.

Waldstein, Edith. *Bettine Brentano-von Arnim and the Politics of Romantic Converstation.* Columbia, S.C.: Camden House, 1988.

Weigel, Sigrid. "Frau und 'Weiblichkeit'. Theoretische Überlegungen zur feministischen Liternaturkritik." *Feministische Literaturwissenschaft. Dokumentation der Tagug in Hamburg vom Mai 1983.* Ed. Inge Stephan and Sigrid Weigel. Berlin: Argument, 1984. 103–113.

Wienpahl, Paul. *The Radical Spinoza*. New York: New York University Press, 1979.

Zur Rolle der Frau in der Geschichte des deutschen Volkes (1830–1945). Eine Chronik. Ed. Hans-Jürgen Arendt, Kurt Baller, Werner Freigang, Jürgen Kirchner, Joachim Müller, Siegfried Scholze, Fritz Staude. Leipzig: Verlag für die Frau, 1984.

III

Politics and Gender

Bettina Brentano-von Arnim's Relations to the Young Hegelians

Heinz Härtl

The works of Bettina Brentano-von Arnim that earned her the greatest recognition were published in the years between 1835 and 1844. During that decade the Young Hegelians also published texts "more emancipatory and revolutionary than anything that had ever been kindled in the minds of the German bourgeoisie" (das Freisinnigste und Revolutionärste was jemals vom deutschen Bürgertum hervorgebracht wurde).[1] The year 1835 witnessed not only the publication of Brentano-von Arnim's first book (*Goethe's Correspondence with a Child* [Goethe's Briefwechsel mit einem Kinde) but also that of the first work of David Friedrich Strauß, *The Life of Jesus* (Das Leben Jesu), a critique of the Gospels which sparked the Young Hegelian movement. After 1844 when *The Spring Wreath* (Clemens Brentanos Frühlingskranz) was released and the Young Hegelian movement slackened, Brentano-von Arnim's later publications received much less attention. The fact that the simultaneous notoriety of Bettina Brentano-von Arnim and the Young Hegelians was far more than a superficial coincidence shall be demonstrated in the following through the reconstruction of their relationship in the context of the times.

For this purpose the position of the Prussian Protestant orthodoxy yields the greatest insight. Its critique of Brentano-von Arnim's work stressed her intellectual relationship with Strauß and the Hegelian

Left. In the *Newspaper of the Protestant Church* (Evangelische Kirchen-Zeitung), which was edited by the Berlin professor of theology Ernst Wilhelm Hengstenberg, Brentano-von Arnim was sharply attacked, first in 1837/1838 because of the *Goethe-Book* and then in 1844 because of her text *The King's Book* (Dies Buch gehört dem König). In 1837 she was accused of "idolatry" and of confusing "in a sad delusion Goethe with God".[2] A year later, the Duisburg clergyman Johann Peter Lange, another opponent of Strauß,[3] testified to her "dependence" on "the modern intellectual movement" (Weltgeist).[4] He again accused her of "idolatry" and "worship of human beings," called the *Goethe-Book* "a bad omen" for "the spread of idolatry and worship of man, particularly the worhip of genius" and declared the glorification of Napoleon a further example of the "cult of genius in our time".[5] In 1844 the Halle historian Heinrich Leo also denounced Brentano-von Arnim in the *Newspaper of the Protestant Church* on account of *The King's Book*. As a defender of "Prussia's life breath, *Law* and *Order*,"[6] he insinuated that she was taking a leading role against state and religion. "That horrible old hag"[7] who, in *The King's Book*, "grinned at Frau Rat (Goethe's mother) from under a saddle"[8] during the looting of the Frankfurt Arsenal, is interpreted as a warning figure masking Brentano-von Arnim herself. "Woe! And three times woe . . . if you let a gang of depraved minds gain wider influence, lying and infecting others more than they already have, fighting along with this old woman who grins from under a saddle."[9] He had already proposed the expressions "gang" and "sect" for the philosophical avant garde in 1838 in his polemic treatise "The little Hegelians" (The Hegelingen).[10]

The persistence with which the Prussian orthodoxy raised its militant voice to connect Brentano-von Arnim with the Young Hegelians corresponds to the real nature of their relationship. As early as the fall of 1838 Strauß had written an essay "The Transitory and The Enduring in Christianity" (Vergängliches und Bleibendes im Christentum) in which he responded to the attack against his *Life of Jesus* in the *Newspaper of the Protestant Church*. In this essay he turned the anti-Brentano-von Arnim polemic into a positive statement.

> The Protestant Church Paper was quite right when it condemned the worship of the man on the Vendome column [Napoleon] and the Olympian of Weimar as a new idolatry. In fact these are gods which threaten . . . the God of the Protestant Church Paper. While Heine

[*Die Nordsee* (1826) Third part. On the chroniclers of Napoleon] compared the accounts of O'Meara, Antommarchi, and Las Casas to Mat-
thew, Mark, and Luke, how long will it be until people see a new gospel
according to John in Bettina's letters? . . . It is the tendency of the time
to worship the manifestation of God in those creative minds who have
influenced and vitalized humankind. For educated human beings in
these times there is only one cult which has survived the religious decay
of the preceding era—lament it or praise it, but you will not be able to
deny it—and that is the worship of genius.[11]

In his essay Strauß also tried to establish a connection between
reason and religion. As "the desire and ability of humans as finite
beings," reason "puts us and all that is given to us into a relationship
with what is higher and highest and makes this relationship as close
and real as possible so that all human thinking, feeling, and willing is
in greatest harmony." In this respect it is "nothing other than religion,
and the founder of that religion is then the one who enables humanity
to develop this sensibility, without which a human being cannot exist
and would not conceive of culture, state, art and philosophy."[12]
Strauß's statements about the "cult of genius," about the identity
of reason and religion, and about the dignity of the "founder of
religion" can be shown to be part of the spiritual substance of
Brentano-von Arnim's book *Günderode* (Die Günderode) also, in
the discussions between Bettine and Günderrode, about the possibility of each to become a genius (for God "recreates himself as genius
in the minds of human beings"),[13] about the connection between
prayer and thought ("Thinking is Praying" ["*Denken ist Beten*"])[14]
about a "floating religion" ["*Schwebe-Religion*"], and about the intent "to found a religion in which humanity feels whole again" (eine
Religion [zu] stiften für die Menschheit, bei der's ihr wieder wohl
wird).[15] The homage to persons of genius in *Günderode* corresponded
to the requirements of the Young Hegelians to focus attention on the
most progressive representatives in the history of humankind. The
emphasis on Mirabeau and Napoleon converged with the Young Hegelians' interest in the French Revolution. The respect with which
Brentano-von Arnim describes her grandparents La Roche corresponded to the relation of the Hegelian Left to the Enlightenment.
Brentano-von Arnim's critique of religion resembled that of the
Young Hegelians. They agreed also that the evil of the present would
have to be changed by the next generation to a better future.

However in one essential point, Brentano-von Arnim differed from the Young Hegelians. To be sure she intended, while working on *Günderode* to continue to proclaim the "idolatry of human beings" of which she had been accused, indeed to perfect it;[16] and she also acknowledged a "great respect"[17] for Strauß. But in contrast to the notion of philosophy as a science she proposed an all-inclusive and creative way of gaining knowledge. In a letter written between May 27 and May 30, 1839 she says:

> What is philosophy?—The free choice of all intellectual searching and desires. Even more: everything that emanates from the basic principles of particularity, be it thought or action or simply the instinctive use of individual strengths. . . . Free thought generates ultimate truth.

> Was ist Philosophie?—Der freie Wahlplatz aller geistigen Strebungen; ja mehr noch: alles was aus dem Urprinzip der Eigenthümlichkeit hervorgeht sei es Dencken, sei es Handeln, sei es blos instincktmässiges Üben einzelner Kräfte. . . . Freies Dencken ist Erzeugen der Wahrheit.[18]

Contradicting the author of the essay "The Transitory and The Enduring in Christianity" she argued in the same letter: "if Dr. Strauß takes miracles apart, he does something superfluous, and poets should defend themselves against this destruction of the crystals of divine power" (wenn der Docktor Strauß die Wunder wegdemonstrirt so thut er etwas überflüssiges, und die Poeten sollten sich gegen ihn wehren, daß er die Kristalle göttlicher Fähigkeiten zerstört.)[19] In all probability this critique was the result of her reading the re-issue of Strauß's essay in *Two Peaceful Papers* (Zwei friedliche Blätter) which was published in the spring of 1839.[20] Brentano-von Arnim juxtaposed poetry against the discipline of philosophy, the affirmation of the miraculous against the logical dissection of miracles, feeling against detached judgment. And against thinking in systems she proposed an unsystematic worldview, a conglomerate of all realizations which the philosophical traditions had attained, and her principle that "the balance of the senses is the gate to all wisdom"(Sinnliche Gerechtigkeit ist die Pforte zu aller Weisheit).[21] It is difficult therefore to reconstruct a philosophical discourse in the strict sense of the word between Brentano-von Arnim and the movement of the Young Hegelians. More rewarding and more illuminating as to Brentano-von Arnim's intentions is to reverse the approach and examine the opinions of the Young Hegelians about her.

An essay written by Strauß about Brentano-von Arnim in 1838 was not published, neither then nor later. Strauß had sent it to Joseph Savoye, editor of the *Panorama de l'Allemagne* in Paris who was to have published four volumes of this work. However, only the first one, without Strauß's essay, did in fact appear.[22] The well-known positions of the Bible critic towards "Germany's undisputably foremost woman author"[23] make it patent that he did not intend to analyze her work according to philosophical or theological criteria, but he appreciated them as poetical achievements. He was convinced of the "independent poetical worth"[24] of the *Goethe-Book* and he similarly extolled the "artistic value"[25] of the letters in *Günderode*. "From a historical viewpoint"[26] as well as in the attempt to portray "the idea, the total picture"[27] of the title characters, both these books he considered better in conveying the mood of the time than the labored philological critiques of Friedrich Wilhelm Riemer and Johann Friedrich Heinrich Schlosser. These critics had tried to reduce Brentano-von Arnim's reputation as author by accusing her of fictionalizing, to which Strauß remarked "On the contrary, whenever you discredit the chronicler you must credit the poet" (Im Gegentheil! was ihr der Erzählerin nehmt, legt ihr der Dichterin zu).[28] Strauß had had to pay for his controversial views by retreating into private life, and when *Günderode* appeared he was inclined to identify with the friend of Brentano-von Arnim's youth: "I cannot imagine a lovelier girl than this Günderode, I carry her image in my innermost heart" (Ein lieblicheres weibliches Wesen als diese Günderode ist nicht zu denken; ich habe ihr Bildnis in meinem Innersten aufgestellt).[29] He confessed that his interest was somewhat pathological: "The flight from reality plays a part in it."[30] On October 12, 1840 he wrote a letter to the author[31] in which he gratefully acknowledged the book as a literary monument to Günderrode:

Your Highness
    Have given me great surprise and joy by presenting me with your book *Günderode*. I had already read the book when it first appeared, and I read it so quickly and uninterruptedly that I was totally enraptured and captivated by it. Your purpose to preserve the memory of your deceased friend and to endear her to a receptive audience has been entirely successful, if I may judge by my own experience. The beautiful picture irresistibly bewitches one's mind with its gentle magnificence. The pure white light in the letters of one writer and the glow

and change of rich colors in those of the other complement each other and heighten the effect. But an infinite anguish remains in the reader's mind, that such a beautiful and harmonious life had to end so early and in such harsh dissonance. And this emotional and personal interest, which transcends the purely aesthetic, makes one wish that one day circumstances might allow you to inform your readers in greater detail about your friend's tragic decision and about its motivation and gradual formation. Your charming description has made me long, too, for her likeness, and I would be very grateful if you could inform me if her portrait still exists somewhere.

I am delighted that your highness has confidence in my appreciation of your writing. Works such as your two correspondences are for me true food for the mind. The view of the world and emotional attitude represented in them and the images which they conjure up form parts of something positive which compensates for the negative which I must condemn in so much of what is sacred to others; or put differently, those new gods expel the old ones from the temple.

Searching among my things for something appropriate to present to you I find only the enclosed little book which I commend to your friendly reception. It was written during a bad time and in a depressed mood which, thank God, has now passed for me. It was beneficial to the first essay but an obstacle to the second—the last half is of no value.

Finally, kindly accept the feelings of heartfelt gratitude and sincere reverence with which I remain
Your devoted
D. F. Strauß
Stuttgart, Oct. 12, 1840

The "little book" was *Two Peaceful Papers* with the revised edition of the two essays on "Justinus Kerner" and on "The Transitory and The Enduring in Christianity." The same year that saw the publication of *Günderode* also saw that of the first volume of Strauß's second main work *Christian Doctrine* (Die christliche Glaubenslehre), in which he sharply criticized church dogma and postulated a new religion based on more recent religious experiences. Brentano-von Arnim's *Günderode* had proclaimed such experiences and announced a non-dogmatic emancipated religion.

The example of Strauß contradicts the widely held view that the Young Hegelians maintained a principled hostility to anything Romantic.[32] More correctly, their relation to Romanticism in general, and to Brentano-von Arnim in particular, was divided; the manifesto by Ruge

and Echtermeyer "Protestantism and the Romantic" (Der Protestant-
ismus und die Romantik) which was published by the main journalistic
organ of the Young Hegelians—the *Halle Yearbooks for German Art
and Science* (Hallesche Jahrbücher für deutsche Wissenschaft und
Kunst)—between October 1939 and March 1940 was not an expression
of a uniformly held anti-Romantic attitude. Although polemics against
the convergence of Romantic subjectivism and reactionary politics
dominated the *Yearbooks*, the authors of several articles differentiated
between Romanticism as an aesthetically legitimate expression of that
which is subjective and psychological and Romanticism as a political
ideology.[33] In articles not contained in the *Yearbooks* the generaliza-
tions of the manifesto were even attacked directly. It is significant that
Eduard Meyen reproached Arnold Ruge:

> Honestly speaking, you go too far in your polemic against Romanti-
> cism, for you are becoming a fanatic. Oppose Romanticism and the
> erroneous direction of Romanticism as much as you like, but do not
> entirely destroy for us Romanticism as the world of emotions and
> feelings. I can demonstrate as well as you do what is unclear in the
> works of the Romantic poets, but I love them all the same. I will not let
> Eichendorff, Brentano, Arnim and Tieck be taken away from me.
>
> Aufrichtig gesagt: Sie treiben Ihre Polemik gegen die Romantik zu weit,
> denn Sie werden fanatisch. Bekämpfen Sie den Romantismus, die
> verkehrte Richtung der Romantik, soviel Sie wollen, aber töten Sie uns
> nicht die Romantik, die Welt der Gefühle. Ich weiß sehr gut so wie Sie
> nachzuweisen, was unklar ist an den Produktionen der romantischen
> Dichter, aber ich liebe sie darum doch, ich lasse mir Eichendorff,
> Brentano, Arnim, Tieck nicht rauben.[34]

He [Meyen] claimed it was "general opinion" that the manifesto presented Romanticism in a "tendentiously significant and important
way but not exhaustively and absolutely."[35]

Meyen himself contributed to a more balanced assessment of Romanticism. For the *Halle Yearbooks* he wrote a detailed and favorable
review of the first volumes of Achim von Arnim's *Collected Works*
(Sämmtliche Werke). They were published beginning in 1839 by Wilhelm Grimm at Brentano-von Arnim's request.[36] He also defended
Bettina Brentano-von Arnim and progressive Romanticism in other
journals. From a letter by Karl Friedrich Köppens to Karl Marx we
know that [Meyen] had allowed an open letter of hers to be published

in the *General Newspaper of Augsburg* (Augsburger Allgemeine
Zeitung).[37] In the letter she had supported Berlin's chief music director, Spontini, who had been charged with lèse majesty: in the Berlin
journal *Athenäum* Meyen acknowledged Bettina Brentano-von Arnim
with respect to *Günderode* as "a phenomenon unparalleled in its kind,
and without equal in any other literature at any time" (eine Erschein-
ung, die einzig in ihrer Art ist, wie sie keine andere Literatur keiner
Zeit aufzuweisen hat).[38] She seemed "in many ways to be a better
representative of German Romanticism than the poets of the Romantic School themselves, because she has made *herself* the subject of her
poetry, herself with all her fancies, her feelings, thoughts and her entire
natural being" (in vieler Beziehung eine reichere Verkünderin der
deutschen Romantik, wie die Dichter der romantischen Schule selbst,
denn *sie selbst* hat sich zum Stoff des Dichtens gemacht, sie selbst mit
all' ihren Neigungen, Empfindungen, Gedanken, ihrem ganzen natür-
lichen Sinn).[39] As late as 1843 he remarked that she belonged "in her
basic direction to the era of Romanticism" and represented the "least
clouded, clearest and most characteristic product of German Romanticism" (das ungetrübteste, reinste und eigenthümlichste Product der
deutschen Romantik) while avoiding its "errors." [40]

Among the Young Hegelians an illuminating discussion arose in the
Halle Yearbook (after July 1841: German Yearbook [*Deutsche Jahrbücher*]) about the book *Günderode*. It began with the publication of
an article by Moriz Carrière, Brentano-von Arnim's most ardent supporter. Turning against ideologues who did not attribute any real validity to Romanticism, Carrière made the following differentiation:

> *Bettina's Romanticism is the Romanticism of the future*, the all-pervading
> breath of spring's rapture. She does not live in the *past*: For her only the
> eternal prevails. It has its roots there and flowers in the present. . . . The
> Romanticism of the past looks for firm ground to anchor its own idées
> fixes. It turns to Catholicism in whose affirmative attitude its sensual
> restlessness achieves a finite external satisfaction; the Romanticism of
> the future constructs a *floating religion* from the premonitions of the
> heart, the experiences and thoughts of the present as a joyful temple to
> living beauty.
>
> *Bettina's Romantik ist die der Zukunft*, der alldurchathmende Hauch
> der Frühlingsbegeisterung. Sie lebt nicht in der *Vergangenheit*: ihr gilt
> nur das Ewige, welches dort Wurzel gefaßt hat, daß es in der Gegen-
> wart blühe . . . Die Romantik der Vergangenheit sucht das Feste, um

die eigenen fixen Ideen daran anzuknüpfen, sie wendet sich zum Katholicismus, in dessen Positivität ihre sinnliche Ruhelosigkeit zu einer endlichen äußerlichen Befriedigung kommt; die Romantik der Zukunft erbaut aus den Ahnungen des eigenen Herzens, aus den Erlebnissen und Gedanken der Gegenwart *eine schwebende Religion* als den heitern Tempeldienst des lebendigen Schönen.[41]

The "main idea of this wonderful book," Carrière declares, is *"that everything in nature strives toward the infinite and finds itself in the spirit"* (wie alles in der Natur zum Unendlichen strebt und im Geiste sich findet).[42]

Arnold Ruge, along with Echtermeyer, was not only the author of the manifesto "Protestantism and Romanticism" but also the editor of the *Halle Yearbook*. He had some reservations about Brentano-von Arnim, "the old hag,"[43] but he accepted the enthusiastic review of her apologist. He wrote to Carrière that she turned out to be "somewhat lyrical" and "not to be used as basis for objective opinion; nothing gets spoiled more easily than such a vain lady" (man könne darauf nicht fußen, wenn man ein objectives Urtheil haben will, und nichts ist leichter verdorben, als so ein eitles Frauenzimmer).[44] The differences among the Left about Brentano-von Arnim stemmed not only from their relation to Romanticism, but above all from personal religious convictions and the announcement of a new religion in *Günderode*. This was revealed in a letter which Heinrich Bernhard Oppenheim wrote to Ruge.

the whole difference between you and Carrière seems to me to be the fact that you reject Christianity as an antiquated superstition, as medieval heretics did long ago, before Montesquieu's *Lettres Personnes*, while he still believes in the possibility of incorporating modern culture and thereby salvaging certain concepts and feelings which he continues to describe as Christian, because an abrupt break in the development of religious consciousness among the general population is unthinkable.— Judging by your convictions you must be a pantheist, as he is, in the Hegelian manner transcending Spinoza. . . . with all respect for her in other matters, I do not see *Bettine* as the canonical work of a new religion. But that it contains much of this religious pantheism, a version of which is appropriate for a strong people, like that of Schelaleddin-Ranis [Dschelaled-Din Rumi, 1207–1273, a mystic pantheistic poet] was for Persia, I cannot deny. Nor can I disagree on this with Carrière, a man of such poetic sensitivity.

scheint mir der ganze Widerspruch zwischen Ihnen und Carrière der zu
sein, daß Sie das Christenthum als einen antiquirten Aberglauben
verwerfen, wie das im Grunde vor Montesquieus Lettres Personnes
schon manche mittelalterliche Ketzer gethan, während er die moderne
Bildung noch glaubt in ein Gebiet der Vorstellung und Empfindung
retten zu können, deren Gebilde er dann noch christlich nennt, weil in
der Entwicklung des religiösen Bewußtseyns im Volke kein Bruch
denkbar ist.—Sie sind, dem Inhalte Ihrer Überzeugungen nach, gewiß
Pantheist, wie er, auf Hegel'sche Weise über Spinoza hinaus. . . . ich
halte ebenso wenig, bei aller sonstigen Verehrung, die *Bettine* für das
canonische Buch der neuen Religion. Aber daß in ihr viel von dem
Gehalt dieses religiösen Pantheismus ist, von einem Pantheismus, der
für ein thatkräftiges Volk paßt, wie der Schelaleddin-Ranis [Dschelāled-
Din Rumi, 1207–1273, mystisch-pantheistischer Dichter] etwa für
Persien, ist, glaube ich, nicht zu läugnen oder doch einem poetischen
Gemüthe, wie dem Carrière's, nicht abzusprechen.[45]

Shortly after this letter the religious-philosophical reservations of
the Left Hegelians against Carrière and his interpretation of *Günderode* became the subject of public controversy. To be sure, he was
not attacked by name and the critique included Brentano-von
Arnim's other interpreters. On May 23rd and 24th, 1842, Edgar
Bauer's essay "Bettina as Founder of a Religion" (Die Bettina als
Religionsstifterin), was published in the *German Yearbook*. It is
possibly the most important contemporary statement with regard to
Brentano-von Arnim and *Günderode*. Chronicling the events that
led to the publication of this essay gives some idea of the ideological
tensions of the years 1841 and 1842 in which not only the second
part of Strauß's *Christian Dogma* was published but also Ludwig
Feuerbach's *The Character of Christianity* (Wesen des Christentums)
and Bruno Bauer's *Critique of the Protestant Interpretations of the
Evangelists* (Kritik der Evangelischen Geschichte der Synoptiker).
The significance of these works for Young Hegelians has been sum-
marized in this way:

On the basis of Feuerbach's critique of religion and the reorientation of
Hegel's doctrine to a philosophy of self-consciousness by B. Bauer, a
new philosophy of emancipation was developed which was directed
against the whole intellectual and political situation of the time. The
radical exponents of this school became atheists and revolutionary
democrats.

Insbesondere auf Grund der Feuerbachschen Religionskritik und der Umbildung der Hegelschen Lehre zur Philosophie des Selbstbewußtseins durch B. Bauer wurde eine Emanzipationsideologie geschaffen, die man gegen den gesamten geistigen und politischen Zustand der Zeit kehrte. Die radikalen Vertreter der Schule wurden Atheisten und politisch revolutionäre Demokraten.[46]

In a letter written by Edgar Bauer to his brother Bruno on January 18, 1842, he relates that he first wanted to publish his essay in the Berlin *Yearbook for Scientific Critique* (Jahrbücher für wissenschaftliche Kritik), but that the editorial board rejected it.[47] In Ruge's opinion this was typical of "straight-laced, doctrinaire Berlin attitudes, an over-intellectualized exclusive arrogance."[48] One reason for the rejection was probably the fact that the publishers did not want to accept a review that was indirectly antithetical to the somewhat more conservative article on *Günderode* which had already been published in their journal by the Leipzig aesthetician Christian Hermann Weiße. Although Weiße had been sensitive in his analysis of the aesthetic qualities of *Günderode*, he had spoken out against its political tendencies, manifest in its dedication "To the Students" and in general against authors who "claim that their poetry and genius exempt them from the yoke of the law" (welche sich rühmen, durch Poesie und Genialität vom dem Joche des Gesetzes emancipirt zu sein).[49] Another reason, possibly the main one, for the rejection of the essay was its position on religious philosophy. Edgar Bauer told his brother Bruno of what the secretary of the editorial board, Leopold Dorotheus von Henning, had reported.

> Unfortunately, he said, the decision is negative, because this article contains the same theological views as the "other" works of your brother. The board must therefore explain that it cannot associate itself with these. . . . Now they have returned it to me after having taken quite some trouble with it. Several of the most controversial places are marked. But they were so intent on their efforts that they included in this some of Bettina's own words which I had copied without quotation marks. I have now rewritten the essay and sent it to Ruge.[50]

Edgar Bauer turned against Brentano-von Arnim's "burdensome champions"[51] in his essay. He accused them of "transforming simple nature poetry into dogma, . . . simple naive poetry into religion, an author who as such belongs to all humankind, into the founder of a

religion and thereby making her a welcome object for theologians."
They had "put Arnim into a sphere . . . in which she did not belong.
They had intended to honor her, but had dishonored her instead. They
had intended to elevate her, but had denigrated her instead."[52] While
Carrière and others—particularly Theodor Mundt[53]—had praised
Brentano-von Arnim as the prophet of a new religion, Bauer claimed
her book "renounced all religion."[54] At the same time his essay was a
basic affirmation of the idea that religious fantasies had to be overcome
through the emancipation of human beings themselves: "These fools
have not realized that humanity is striving to rid itself of all dogmatic
fetters and remove all religious restrictions" (Die Thoren bedachten
nicht, daß die Menschheit dahin strebe, sich überhaupt dogmatischen
Fesseln, aller religiösen Beschränkung zu entkleiden).[55] According to
Bauer, religion sanctioned "original sin" itself, the "dichotomy between nature and mind, finiteness and infinity, word and flesh" something he saw as a "transition only," to a new union of these.[56] Human
beings must achieve this goal through intellectual autonomy and activity. Bauer described the approach which Brentano-von Arnim had
taken in connection with an interpretation of her views.

Only the genius in us, if we allow it free reign, gives us divine freedom;
only when it lives in us, do we live in a divine element. This genius has
no need of a mediating revelation, it speaks to us in everything, in the
bloom and scent of the rose, in moonshine and the gurgling brook, in
the rustling treetops. And the gospel with which the western wind fans
the violets is the true gospel of the spirit to our spirit. Therefore the life
of nature which explores wild abysses, ignorant of divine genius but not
denying it either, is not what is objectionable. It is the cultivated life of
virtue which is objectionable when it shuts out genius and practices
virtue in its own wisdom. Self discipline means to subject oneself trust-
ingly to genius. Yield to the care of nature's genius, expel all fear of
nature from your mind, and it will nourish you lovingly. The bee has
lost its sting and the snake its poison. That is what Bettine teaches. . . .
You, and the genius in you, have to free yourself from the selfish "I" by
following your inner voice. Find your own self and you will shed all
fetters. . . . "At night, all alone in the open, it seems as if Nature were
a spirit which seeks redemption from humanity." And there you have
it, what shall be redeemed in this new religion. Not human beings
because they can redeem themselves, but Nature, which cannot. A
religion for the world of plants and stones and animals. As the Christian religion sends a human-god down to earth to redeem humanity, so

Bettine asks the natural human or human nature, to once again reconcile nature and humanity. It is not a new religion for human beings or
an exclusive prophesy. Everyone redeems himself and nature. The "I"
shall not transpose its God into another world again, to Heaven, so
that the word may descend from there and become flesh. No, genius
shall evolve from nature, flesh will become spirit.

Nur der Genius in uns, wenn wir ihn ungehemmt herrschen lassen, bietet
uns göttliche Freiheit; nur wenn er in uns lebt, leben wir im göttlichen
Element. Dieser Genius aber bedarf keiner vermittelnden Offenbarung; aus Allem spricht er uns an: aus dem Blühen und Duften der
Rose, aus dem Schein des Mondes, aus dem Murmeln des Baches und
aus den rauschenden Wipfeln des Baumes. Und das Evangelium,
welches der Westwind den Veilchen zufächelt, ist das wahre Evangelium
des Geistes an den Geist. Darum ist nicht das Verwerflichste jenes
Naturleben, welches durch wilde Abgründe schweift, den göttlichen
Genius nicht kennend, aber ihn auch nicht verläugnend; jenes cultivirte
Tugendleben ist verwerflich, welches den Genius von sich ausschließt
und Tugend übt aus eigner Weisheit. Und das ist Selbstbeherrschung,
wenn Du Dich vertrauensvoll dem Genius unterwirfst. Ueberliefere
Dich der Pflege, welche der Genius der Natur an Dir übt, verbanne alle
Furcht vor der Natur aus Deinem Geiste, und sie wird liebend Dich
nähren, und die Biene hat ihren Stachel, die Schlange ihr Gift verloren.
Solches lehrt Bettine. . . . Du selbst, der Genius in Dir, sollst Dich
freimachen von Deinem eignen selbstischen Ich, und zwar indem Du
nur der Stimme in Dir folgst. Finde Dich selbst und Du bist aller Fesseln
ledig. . . . 'Wenn man so einsam Nachts in der freien Natur steht, da
ist's, als ob sie ein Geist wär', der den Menschen um Erlösung bäte.' Da
haben wir ja, was in der neuen Religion erlöst werden soll. Nicht der
Mensch, denn er erlöst sich selber. Die Natur ist es, denn sie kann sich
nicht selbst erlösen. Eine Religion für Pflanzen, für Steine, für Thiere!
Und wie die christliche Religion einen Gottmenschen auf Erden sendet,
die Menschheit zu erlösen, so fordert Bettine den reinen Naturmen-
schen oder die reine Menschennatur, um die Natur zum versöhnenden
Bunde mit der Menschheit zurückzuführen. Also keine neue Religion
für Menschen, keine exclusive Prophetie. Jeder Mensch ist Erlöser,
seiner selbst und der Natur. Nicht von Neuem soll das Ich seinen Gott ins
Jenseits, in den Himmel versetzen, damit von dort erst das Wort
herabsteige und Fleisch werde. Nein, aus der Natur heraus soll sich der
Genius entwickeln, das Fleisch soll Geist werden.[57]

Edgar Bauer's interpretation of Brentano-von Arnim's natural philosophy was unique among his contemporaries. And even later his

insight has never been equaled. Only Turgeniev came close in his view that Brentano-von Arnim, through her "compassion" with nature which humanity had abandoned, removed the differences between them.[58] In agreement with Strauß Bauer acknowledged *Günderode* as an extraordinary poetic achievement. He however surpassed Strauß in one respect; he emphasized Brentano-von Arnim's poetic competence as well as distanced himself from her "immediacy."[59] This immediacy he thought difficult for other people, who had to reach "by means of philosophy" what was "immediate" for her.[60]

> Bettine does not need these concepts and she is therefore free to ask of us that we trust our instincts, the genial natural desires. . . . Bettine may claim that . . . all this history is not useful to her. But the rest of us who can only live in history because we are rooted in it, we cannot simply dispose of the external world, this 'facticity,' in so ingenious a manner, we do not even know anything which we have not assimilated through learning.

> Die Bettine ist des Begriffes nicht bedürftig, und es steht ihr daher frei, uns aufzufordern, daß wir uns dem Instincte, dem genialen Naturtriebe anvertrauen. . . . Die Bettine mag behaupten, daß die . . . ganze Geschichte ihr nichts nütz sei. Wir aber, die wir allerdings nur daduch, daß wir auf der Geschichte fußen, in der Geschichte leben können, wir dürfen uns freilich nicht mit dieser Genialität über die Außenwelt, über die "Facticität" hinwegsetzen. Wir wissen einmal nichts, als was wir uns durch Lernen gegeben.[61]

Another Young Hegelian response to Brentano-von Arnim's work varied the themes of Edgar Bauer's essay. Franz Szeliga Zychlin von Zychlinski, who later became a Prussian general, versified Brentano-von Arnim's gospel—that humans find realization in continual exchange with nature—in a poetic contribution to *The Spring Wreath* (1844). Zychlinski's poem, constructed as a dialogue between the main characters of *The Spring Wreath*, "Bettine" and "Clemens," is a "poetic recapitulation of the work" (dichterische Rekapitulation der Dichtung).[62] However he distances himself from Brentano-von Arnim's enthusiam for nature. "Clemens" not only regrets that he does not feel qualified to share in this, he also objects to the claim of exclusivity that it is "nature that heals all wounds" (Natur, die alle Wunden heilen soll)[63] and to the carefree way in which his sister affirms her immediate appreciation of reality and rejects the philosophical. "What you disdain as useless, the thinker regards as the permanent and eternal" (Was Du den Rest verächtlich nennst, begreift / Als Bleibendes und Ewiges der Denker).[64] As representative of modern awareness, Clemens was conscious only of doubts: "Can I be happy in this knowledge? No, I am rather sad, because it remains a mystery to me, where it's going to take me" (Kann ich heiter sein / Mit dem Bewußtsein? Nein mir ist recht traurig, / Daß mir ein Räthsel bleibt, wohin mich/s treibt).[65] Zychlinski's ambivalent relation to Brentano-von Arnim becomes clearer in a prose introduction to his poem. It is actually the second part of a discourse with her of which the first has to do with *The King's Book*. That part also recapitulates and quotes essential themes of Brentano-von Arnim's work. He programmatically defines poetic imagination as "reason itself in one of its sensual forms" (Vernunft selbst in einer ihrer sinnlichen Formen).[66] It is recognized as a legitimate, but not an autonomous means of knowing. At the end of the first part he openly admits that Brentano-von Arnim's imagination was suspect to her interpreter: "The previous century had the quick and excited pulse of a child and adolescent. Now it is time for calm and reflection" (Das vorige Jahrhundert hatte den schnellen, aufgeregten Puls des Kindes und Jünglings. Es ist Zeit, daß wir zur Ruhe und Besonnenheit kommen).[67] Since this disclaimer occurs at a significant point of the prose text and directly ahead of the poem, the dominance of Brentano-von Arnim's views are therefore decidedly qualified. Zychlinsky's line of action must have been motivated by literary politics. The consensus with Brentano-von Arnim was essentially meant for outsiders; at the same time the initiated were to be made aware of his distance from her. Zychlinsky's views were published in the *North German Journal for Criticism, Literature and Entertainment* (Norddeutsche Blätter für Kritik, Literatur und Unterhaltung) edited by the brothers Bruno and Edgar Bauer. They therefore also represented the basic position of the editors who dominated the radical Young Hegelians among the so-called *Liberated* in Berlin. The dependence of Zychlinsky's contribution on the position Edgar Bauer had developed in his essay is as evident as his epigonic approach to intellectual and poetic matters in general.

Eduard Meyen, another member of the *Liberated*, published a critique of *The King's Book* in 1843 in which he was much more argumentative than Zychlinsky concerning Brentano-von Arnim's relative proximity and distance to the Young Hegelian positions. While she defended "the natural right to free emotions" (das

Naturrecht der freien Empfindung) the radical theoreticians regarded
"self-awareness . . . the complete emancipation of the mind" (das
Selbstbewußtsein . . . die vollendete Freiheit des Geistes).[68] She
touched, he said, "the principles of the new philosophy without
getting a real grip on it."[69] Meyen limited Edgar Bauer's position on
the "renunciation of all religion" decisively. Brentano-von Arnim,
he said, professed a "beautiful and lovable Pantheism but nowhere
near the highest truth and freedom" (einen schöne[n], liebens-
werthe[n] Pantheismus, wenn auch noch lange nicht die höchste
Wahrheit und Freiheit).[70] In contrast to Bauer's retrenchment from
Brentano-von Arnim's immediate relation to nature, Meyen found a
need to mediate between this and the philosophy of self-esteem.
Through their idealism, Brentano-von Arnim and the women of her
time had to be credited with having "served philosophy and prepared a way for it . . . [their idealism led philosophy] to its reunion
with nature."[71] On the other hand he noted that Brentano-von
Arnim had been influenced by the "spirit of radicalism born of the
most recent trends in German philosophy."[72] Brentano-von Arnim
had been "touched" by it and through a combination of her "enthusiasm for nature" and the "recognition of ultimate spiritual freedom"
she had reached a new rung in her development: "She had transformed herself into a democrat" (Sie hat sich zur Demokratin
umgestaltet).[73] In Meyen's review therefore the exploration of the
differences between the views of the Young Hegelians and those of
Brentano-von Arnim was connected to an understanding of their
mutual rapport and influence which, they confessed, had been relevant and educational in their development. Meyen also occupied a
middle position with regard to the political motivations of *The
King's Book*. To be sure, he declared Brentano-von Arnim's hope
for a "political Christ" to be "an error" compared to the Young
Hegelian alternative that "people need to emancipate themselves by
becoming intellectually free and then letting the awareness of this
freedom be the highest authority" (dass das Volk sich selbst befreien
müsse, indem es sich geistig frei macht, und das Bewusstseyn seiner
Freiheit zur Herrschaft erhebt).[74] Still, Meyen supported Brentano-
von Arnim with a *Captatio benevolentiae* in her plea to the king, that
"he above all has need of true knowledge of his time and the un-
veiled description of the condition of his people," for knowing that
the monarch knows all is also "progress for the people."[75]

In the chapter of his book *A complete History of Party Fights in the Years 1842–1846* (Vollständige Geschichte der Partheikämpfe in Deutschland während der Jahre 1842–1846) which is called "The Autocrat" (Der Selbstherrscher), Bruno Bauer returned in 1847 to the main expectations of liberals and democrats at the time of *The King's Book*. They had thought reforms by the king and more direct relations between him and others could lead to solutions of acute political problems. Brentano-von Arnim had given this "naive hope" a more "concrete form" by stating that the king had "no will of his own" but followed "outside influences," be they those of his entourage or those of his *good fairy*."[76] The politically radical Young Hegelians rejected the notion of a constitutional monarchy, which becomes evident from contemporary journalistic responses to *The King's Book* and Brentano-von Arnim's reactions to these as constituting essential issues of her book.[77] However not all Young Hegelians shared the positions of Eduard Meyen and Bruno Bauer. Adolf Stahr, for instance, who early on confessed to liberal views, even propagated the idea of a constitutional monarchy in his pamphlet "Bettina and her 'King's Book'." And even among the positions of the radicals a clash between praxis and theory was imminent as seen in Meyen's postulate on the intellectual self-emancipation of the people.

The political differences between Brentano-von Arnim and the radical Young Hegelians become evident also in the connection between her enthusiam for revolution in *The Spring Wreath* and corresponding statements of Edgar Bauer. While she praised the Girondists and stylized Mirabeau into a popular hero, he despised the "Girondist types,"[78] whom he confronted, as his brother Bruno did, by taking a positive stand for the Jacobins. He cautioned against regarding Mirabeau, who held the people in contempt, "as a saint."[79] This warning can be found in the second of the series of pamphlets published by the brothers Bauer in 1843–1844 and entitled *Memoirs of the History of modern Times since the French Revolution* (Denkwürdigkeiten zur Geschichte der neueren Zeit seit der Französischen Revolution). In the copies preserved in the Brentano-von Arnim library in Weimar a few underlined parts and marginal notes coincide with views expressed in *The Spring Wreath*. To be sure the handwriting is that of Brentano-von Arnim's son Friedmund, who was friendly with the brothers Bauer, but the similarities between the parts of *Memoirs* and *The*

Spring Wreath are so pronounced that it can be assumed that Brentano-von Arnim was aware of them. They make it clear that she and Edgar Bauer, while disagreeing on Mirabeau and the Girondists, shared views on other aspects of the French Revolution.[80]

For the study of Brentano-von Arnim's reception a similar case of proximity as well as distance is significant in Max Stirner's *The Individual and his Property* (Der Einzige und sein Eigentum). In it quotations from *The King's Book* were re-interpreted as anarchistic, because she laid the cause for criminality on the state itself. He described Brentano-von Arnim as "benevolent enough to think of the state as sick only and hoping for its recovery" (guthmütig genug, den Staat nur für krank zu halten und auf seine Genesung zu hoffen).[81], but Stirner's individual remains "an inveterate criminal in the state."[82] It was precisely these passages about criminals in *The King's Book* that influenced German anarchism. The reception of this idea follows a direct line of descent from Stirner to Gustav Landauer, who counted Brentano-von Arnim "and many other women" among the "colleagues" on his journal *The Socialist* (Der Sozialist)[83] in which he published excerpts from *The King's Book* under the title "The Criminals" (Die Verbrecher).

While previous scholars had attributed a review of Stirner's book to Brentano-von Arnim, later research has proved that it was her son Friedmund's.[84] It is not documented whether she was familiar with *The Individual and his Property* and, with one exception, it is not known if she read any of the systematically theoretical treatises of the Young Hegelians. The exception, Bruno Bauer's three volumes *Critique of the Protestant Interpretation of the Gospels* (Kritik der Evangelischen Geschichte der Synoptiker) 1841–1842, she was said "to have read . . . in part."[85] Her remarks, though, leave room for doubt that she seriously appropriated its contents. These remarks were addressed provocatively to Heinrich Bernhard Oppenheim, who had doubts about Bauer's teachings and who found his book "too learned for quick perusal" (zum Durchlesen zu gelehrt). To this Brentano-von Arnim replied that she had read it with her daughters "from beginning to end" and they

> found it very interesting particularly since they had commented previously on all the parts from the bible and had admitted freely that they had disposed of all that already in connection with their confirmation but had not wanted to rile anyone with their views.

durchaus lebhaft intressant war um so mehr da sie jede Bibelstelle schon im voraus comentirten und frei eingestanden daß sie bei ihren [!] Confirmation dies alles schon beseitigt hatten, aber niemand mit ihrer Ansicht Aergerniß geben wollte.[86]

So far it has only been possible to make assumptions about Brentano-von Arnim's borrowing from Bauer's ideas in his theoretical works, and some congruences have been pointed out,[87] but direct dependence cannot be shown. More detailed comparisons have to be made to obtain any certainty. As long as no positive proof is available, one will have to take Brentano-von Arnim's assurance on face value, when she states that the "sensual complexion" of her "mind" does not allow her "a study of philosophy" ("sinnliche Complexion" ihres "Geistes" verbiete ihr "das Studium der Philosophie").[88] She preferred theological and philosophical discussions with authors to scientific scrutiny of their works. Her account of mutual inspiration from her conversations with Schleiermacher at the start of the 1830s represents the best known testimony of intellectual exchange through discourse. Several visitors to "Mrs. von Arnim's Sibylline cave" (Frau von Arnims sibyllinischer Höhle)[89] gave witness to it around 1840.

The theoretical head of the Young Hegelians, Bruno Bauer, was Brentano-von Arnim's favorite discussion partner. He belonged to the radical Berlin group of the *Liberated*, as did his brother Edgar and Meyen and Stirner. Brentano-von Arnim became personally acquainted with him at the beginning of October 1841 through Karl Varnhagen von Ense from whom she had asked an introduction[90] and to whom she then reported "with great joy"[91] about the new acquaintance. Shortly after that she spent a "whole hour [exchanging ideas] about present and future" with Bruno Bauer.[92] "His whole personality" had become "especially dear to her" and she stated that "such respectability was seldom if ever accompanied by such modesty" (Er war ihr "seinem Wesen nach ungemein lieb geworden," und sie fand, "daß sich selten, vielleicht nie eine so freie Sittlichkeit mit Bescheidenheit vermählte).[93] In November and December of 1841 she defended Bruno Bauer against Oppenheim's accusation that Bauer refuted without enthusiasm existing educational patterns and the *The Moral Stature of Jesus Christ* (Sittliche Grösse von Christus).[94] On the contrary, she stated, Bruno Bauer "contributes to the effort of our times, bringing the Truth to light with childlike devotion" (an dem Werk unserer Tage, die Wahrheit ins Licht zu stellen mit dem Eifer

einer naiven unbedingten Hingebung).[95] He represents, she argued,
the "libertine principle" (das befreiende Prinzip)[96] and shakes "the
massive pillars of superstition in the sweat of his brow" (und rüttele
"im Schweiß seines Angesichts an den gewaltigen Pfeilern des Af-
terglaubens).[97] To Oppenheim's complaint that Bruno Bauer did not
want "to recognize . . . the freedom of the individual,"[98] Brentano-
von Arnim, whose values were founded on the belief in individual
freedom, responded with a historical challenge to Christianity.

> Humanity and its ethical moral relationships have existed longer than
> Christendom which has put them into words. But it has not re-
> spected . . . *individual freedom*, rather it made itself into a snare for
> this individuality and hitched it in pairs to a cart full of the state's refuse
> which was to be spread as fertilizer for the growth and glory of the royal
> throne.

> Das Menschengeschlecht und die Reinheit seiner moralischen Bezie-
> hungen bestehen länger als das Christenthum in dem sie ausgesprochen
> sind, aber es hat die *freie Individualität* . . . nicht respecktirt sich im-
> mer noch zum Netzgarn brauchen lassen diese Individualität zu paaren
> zu treiben, und in Karren gespannt den Staatsdünger auszubreiten für
> des Thrones ausgepolsterte Herrlichkeit.[99]

The critique of Christianity as state religion which hindered the development of free individualism is evident in Brentano-von Arnim's
statement as is its proximity to the most avant-garde positions of her
contemporaries regarding the critique of religion and society, and in
particular those of Bruno Bauer in whose defense it was written and
with whom she had intensive communication while she so decisively
and completely denounced Christian religion.[100]
   Particularly in 1843 when *The King's Book* was published there
was much mention of her friendly relation to Bruno Bauer. She was
said to hold him "in great regard"[101] and he did not seek anyone's
company "except *Bettina's* . . . , and with her he is good friends."[102]
"Bettina and Bauer are given to philosophizing," the young Swiss
Heinrich Grunholzer wrote in his diary.[103] A confidante reported that
"because she defended Bruno Bauer's views on religion [she had
gotten] into conflict" with her relatives in Frankfurt.[104] Another confidential report even mentioned that two acquaintances had found
"whole pages" in *The King's Book* "which her intimate friend Bruno
Bauer had dictated to her."[105] Brentano-von Arnim herself declared

though that "the philosophy in it . . . did not come from Bruno Bauer . . . but from *Günderode*. She does not want to have anything to do with B. Bauer's" (die Philosophie darin . . . gehöre nicht Bruno Bauer . . . , sondern der Günderode zu. Von der des B. Bauer will sie nichts wissen).[106] Only occasionally is a particular topic recorded.

> It is not long ago that he [Bruno Bauer] had a conversation with her about the immortality of the soul. To his claim, that he did not believe in immortality, *Bettina* replied mischievously: she did not know what would happen to his, but about her own she was quite convinced.

> Nicht lange ist's, was [!] er [Bruno Bauer] mit ihr ein Gespräch über die Seelenunsterblichkeit hatte; auf seinen Ausspruch, er glaube nicht an die Unsterblichkeit, meinte *Bettina* boshaft: Wie es mit seiner Unsterblichkeit stehe, wisse sie nicht, von ihrer Unsterblichkeit jedoch sei sie vollkommen überzeugt.[107]

The assumption that Brentano-von Arnim preferred controversial discussions with Bruno Bauer about immortality is indirectly supported by central passages from a text by Friedmund von Arnim published in 1843 under the title *Good Things about the Soul* (*Die gute Sache der Seele*). It was dedicated to Bruno Bauer who deserved "greatest respect."[108] Bauer's "stubborn refutation of God and personal immortality"[109] had given rise to this text, which aimed to question this negation. According to Friedmund von Arnim, in the course of history, individual bliss continued beyond death and did not end for the good of the species. Doubtlessly Brentano-von Arnim agreed with her son on this point. Disregard of death and belief in immortality were tenets in which she had long believed. Although Achim von Arnim (1831) Goethe (1832) and Schleiermacher (1834) were dead, none had died for her in a higher sense. In her view they had simply reached a different form of existence which made genuine intercourse with them "a truer and deeper communion than was possible while they lived" (eine wahre, tiefere Gemeinschaft, als die das Leben erlaube).[110] In *The King's Book* immortality is a Leitmotif[111] about which she talked not only with Bruno Bauer at the time of its publication. She said to Grunholzer:

> I am of the opinion that after death our bodies evolve differently. We experience a new world of the senses. I do not therefore believe in crude physical resurrection, but there exist spirits.

Ich bin nämlich der Ansicht, daß wir uns nach dem Tode körperlich anders entfalten; eine neue Sinnenwelt geht uns auf. Ich glaube deswegen nicht an eine plumpe Auferstehung des Leibes. Aber Geister gibt es.[112]

With David Friedrich Strauß, too, Brentano-von Arnim discussed her favorite topic on the occasion of a visit in Sontheim on January 10, 1843. This visit is documented vividly in a picturesque letter of Strauß's.

Last Tuesday between light and dark, in the worst storm and rain—did you have horrible storms too? We could hardly sleep for several nights and I wondered whether your high chimney had held up—just then, at dusk, Bettina arrived here en route to Stuttgart. Imagine our surprise! She could stay only a little while because her carriage was waiting downstairs, but it was interesting enough for us to make her acquaintance—a little person like quicksilver not really pretty but again not ugly, with the most intelligent eyes. She talks incessantly and vivaciously, often full of wit, often confused. She challenged me on the issue of immortality of which she is fervently convinced, fell in love with my wife, and drove off again in the midst of the most ghastly weather.

Vorigen Dienstag zwischen Licht und Dunkel im gräulichsten Sturm und Regen—ei habt Ihr auch so gräßliche Stürme gehabt? wir konnten mehrere Nächte kaum schlafen, ich dachte, ob's Euer hohes Kamin nicht mitgenommen?—fuhr Bettina bei uns an auf einer Reise nach Stuttgart,—denkt Euch unsere Überraschung! Sie konnte sich nur kurz verweilen, weil der Wagen unten hielt, doch war es uns interessant genug, sie kennen zu lernen—ein kleines Figürchen wie Quecksilber, keineswegs hübsch, aber auch nicht widrig, höchst geistvolle Augen. Spricht unendlich viel und lebhaft, oft geistreich, oft confus. Nahm mich wegen der Unsterblichkeit auf's Korn, die sie eifrig glaubt, verliebte sich in meine Frau, und fuhr im gräßlichsten Wetter wieder davon.[113]

Brentano-von Arnim shared with Strauß a conviction in human perfectability beyond death. It can be assumed that she was impressed with his opposition to the chief dogma of Christianity, that the deeds on earth are rewarded in the next world, and therefore sought discourse with him.

So you do not believe in immortality? Forget the malevolent consequences. I do not deny them, but I base them on something totally different from the need for reward or retribution . . . the more I renew and purify my strength at this moment, the more I prepare for a similarly liberating development in the future and thereby joy and bliss. . . . For the apostles afterlife represented retribution, for us it is a continuation.

Also läugnest du die Unsterblichkeit? / O stille mit den böswilligen Consequenzen! Ich läugne sie nicht; aber ich begründe sie auf etwas ganz Anderes, als auf die Nothwendigkeit einer Vergeltung . . . je frischer und reiner ich meine Kraft in jedem Augenblicke entwickle, desto mehr bereite ich mir auch für die Zukunft eine ähnliche freie Entfaltung derselben, und damit Lust und Glückseligkeit, vor. . . . Den Aposteln war das andere Leben Vergeltungszustand: uns ist es Fortentwickelung.[114]

Apart from the issue of immortality there is no exact record of Brentano-von Arnim's conversations with Young Hegelians. Outsiders only report that they had similar opinions. Overriding was certainly their common basic opposition to the intellectual and sociopolitical situation in Germany. Differences on concrete questions pale in comparison to this fundamental agreement. In the content and form of *The King's Book* this intellectual proximity is probably more generally reflected rather than exhibiting concrete cases of influence. Compared to Brentano-von Arnim's earlier works, the abstract philosophical passages became longer and dialogue determined their structure. It is remarkable that even contemporary reviews of *The King's Book* dispensed with proofs of direct dependence in favor of emphasizing more general correspondences. The best example is Eduard Meyen's review. However the influence of the Young Hegelians on Brentano-von Arnim also had negative consequences for *The King's Book*. The liberal commerce with the philosophy of self-awareness diminished its poetic sensuality. Particularly significant was Strauß's disappointment: it was

an unfortunate text . . . , a tendentious work with a laudable intent . . . ; but the preaching and philosophizing never befitted the author, even in her earlier works; here it becomes the main thing and the colorful, magically illuminated images from the inner and outer world which were the charm of those earlier letters are totally lost.

ein verunglücktes Produkt . . . , ein Tendenzbuch, die Tendenz zwar ganz löblich . . . ; aber das Doziren und Philosophiren stand der

Verfasserin schon in ihren früheren Werken schlecht—hier ist es zur
Hauptsache geworden und die farbigen, magisch beleuchteten Bilder
aus der inneren und äußeren Welt, worin der Zauber jener früheren
Briefe bestand, fallen ganz weg.[115]

Brentano-von Arnim was not only interested in the oppositional
ideas of the Young Hegelians, she also sympathized with them as
oppositional and social outsiders. A person's thoughts and his or her
personality formed a unit for her. The unconventionality and originality of an intellectual/physical individual constituted for her essential
criteria for the image of a whole person. Whosoever did not conform
to the prevalent norm fitted into hers. And when rulers attacked
outsiders, she came to their defense. The greater the injustice and
need they suffered, the greater her support. Among the Young Hegelians she particularly wanted to help the brothers Bauer. In 1843,
immediately after their publication, the Prussian police interdicted
Edgar Bauer's *The Critics' Conflict with Church and State* (Streit der
Kritik mit Kirche und Staat) as well the first volume of Bruno Bauer's
*History of Politics, Culture and Enlightenment of the Eighteenth Cen-
tury* (Geschichte der Politik, Kultur und Aufklärung des achtzehnten
Jahrhunderts). The publisher of these books, another brother Egbert
Bauer, was also discredited. Although they could not revoke his license they intended "to get his new publishing house in another way
soon."[116] At the turn of the year 1843–1844 Brentano-von Arnim
parted with her fourth publisher Eduard Heinrich Schröder who had
printed *The King's Book*. On April 29th Adolf Stahr related:

Bettina socializes a lot with the *Bauers* nowadays. She praised their
courage in their conflict with the censor, spoke highly of Bruno B.'s
new book on the history of the 18th century and told me that she
would let the brothers publish her new books. The police chief, who
watches "subversive" writers very carefully here, had made a vain
attempt at warning her of the morals of her new protégés. She did not
believe him, she had answered . . . The boys really are somewhat
wild morally—they are the genuine enfants perdus of the German
social and intellectual revolution—the true Sansculottes.

Bettina verkehrt jetzt sehr viel mit den *Bauer'n*; sie rühmte deren
Tapferkeit im Kampfe mit der Censur, pries Bruno B.'s neustes Buch
über die Geschichte des XVIIIten Jahrhunderts und sagte mir, daß sie
den Brüdern ihre neuen Bücher in Verlag geben wolle. Vergebens hat ihr

der Polizeipräsident, der die 'subversiven' Literaten hier sehr genau bevigilirt, Mittheilungen über die Sittlichkeit ihrer neuen Schätzlinge gemacht. Sie glaube das nicht, hat sie ihm geantwortet . . . Sittlich verwildert aber sind die Burschen sicher—es sind die ächten enfants perdus der Deutschen sozialen und geistigen Revolution—ächte Sanscülloten.][117]

Not only did Brentano-von Arnim let the Charlottenburg house of Egbert Bauer publish her new book *The Spring Wreath* in May 1844, but in October of the same year she also published there a text by the Swede Georg Svederus "On Industrialism and Poverty" (Über Industrialismus und Armuth) which belonged to her *Poor Book* (Armenbuch) project. Furthermore she entrusted the brothers Bruno, Edgar and Egbert Bauer with the remainders of her previous works as well as the *Collected Works* of Achim von Arnim; and they obligated themselves loyally to take over her affairs and sales on commission. *The Spring Wreath*, she said, she gave to Egbert Bauer "for no other reason than to support communism where it is not advocated senselessly but founded on a moral sentiment" (aus keinem andern Grund, als um den Communismus zu unterstützen da wo er nicht albern angebracht ist sondern auf sittliches Gefühl gegründet ist).[118] Less noteworthy than the use of a current political slogan—of whose theoretical basis of which Brentano-von Arnim could have had only a vague conception three years before the *Communist Manifesto*—is the remark about the ethical basis for politics and theory. In a more detailed explanation for her aid she argued from a moral viewpoint without minimizing the political discrimination. Her support for a publisher "who was trying to get through waste and morass on two crude, awkward stilts and getting stuck every minute" (der auf zwei groben ungeschickten Stelzen durch sein Koth und Morastland sich durcharbeitet, und jeden Augenblick stecken bleibt)[119] was linked to an accusation against the lack of solidarity exhibited by his colleagues.

> The other publishers just look on and reassure each other *he won't get through* . . . and it does not occur to any of these gentlemen that they could do something to prevent it. I do not dispute their claim to a sense of honor in spite of their preoccupation with their earthly prosperity. But here, where they could manifest this sense of honor in a way beneficial to general sentiment and opinion, they remain obstinate.

Die anderen Herrn Buchhändler sehen zu! und versichern einander: *Er wird nicht durchkommen!* . . . und keinem von diesen Herrn fällt es ein, irgend etwas zu thun um es zu verhindern. Obschon sie noch ausser für den irdischen Wohlstand noch Gefühl für Ehre zu haben behaupten, und ich will ihnen diese auch garnicht abschneiden. Aber hier wo sie ihr Ehrgefühl manifestiren könnten auf eine der allgemeinen Tendenz und Gesinnung so heilsame Weise, sind sie widerwillig![120]

The absurd measures to censor *The Spring Wreath* in May and June 1844 were in reality directed at the publisher and at Brentano-von Arnim's defense of the brothers Bauer—"as a revenge for extending a helping hand so they could build an existence as honest citizens of the state" (Aus Rachegeist daß man ihnen emporhelfe damit sie doch als honnete Bürger im Staate ihre Existenz begründen können).[121] Brentano-von Arnim could only guess at all this, but the Prussian minister of the interior made it very clear to his king

that the confict 'en question' was not between Bettina and the censor but between the police and the notorious publisher Edgar [should actually have been Egbert] Bauer. Bettina must have a particular predilection for the regulars of her salon, the well known Bruno Bauer, Egbert [actually Edgar] and the third of these little clover leaves, Edgar [actually Egbert] whom she chose as publisher of her masterworks. (Egbert [actually Edgar] Bauer came out of a pub in a drunken state the other day and fell into the gutter. He was picked up by kind passersby and taken to the police station whence his honorable brother took him home.) [If she associates with people like this] she will have to suffer the consequences . . . . nothing like that has ever happened to an *honest* book seller.

der Kampf en question nicht zwischen der Censur und Bettina sondern zwischen der Polizei und dem berüchtigten Buchhändler Edgar [richtig: Egbert] Bauer stattfindet. . . . Wenn Bettina aus besonderer Vorliebe für die habitués ihres Salons (Bruno Bauer, wohlbekannt, Egbert [richtig: Edgar] Bauer, der neulich aus einer Branntwein-schenke betrunken in den vorüberfließenden Rinnstein fiel, von mild-herzigen Vorübergehenden auf der Polizey abgeliefert und dort durch seinen schätzbaren Bruder abgeholt wurde) das dritte Blättlein dieser Kleepflanze, Edgar [richtig: Egbert] Bauer, zum Verleger ihrer Geistes-werke auswählt, so muß sie sich schon die folgen gefallen lassen . . . einem *honnetten* Buchhändler ist dergleichen noch nie begegnet.[122]

Among these consequences was the fact that after the book was finally released Friedrich Wilhelm IV warned Brentano-von Arnim on June 23, 1844: "Today is the summer solstice, a good time to draw water from a well. . . . Maybe you have already done that. But I am asking you kindly, do not pour this noble liquid into the trough of peasants [word play on the name Bauer, which means peasant]" (Eben ist Johannis-Nacht. Da ist gut Wasser schöpfen. . . . Nun, Sie werden es wohl schon gethan haben; aber dann bitt' ich gar schön: gießen Sie halt die edle Flut nicht in unedler "Bauern" Gefäße!).[123] In an entry in Karl August Varnhagen von Ense's diary the negative effect of the royal letter on Brentano-von Arnim is noted. It appears that she took the allusion to be a "misunderstanding of poor folk" (Mißkennen des armen Volkes) and a warning not to publish her *Poor Book* (Armenbuch) after the riot of the Silesian weavers.[124] However it must have been clear to her what he meant with the "peasants." This assumption becomes more credible since in the following year Brentano-von Arnim apparently interceded with Friedrich Wilhelm IV in favor of the brothers. On May 9, 1845, Edgar Bauer was apprehended after three consecutive lawsuits. At first he was accused of subversive tendencies in his book, *The Critics' Conflict with Church and State*, then of its publication in Bern by the publisher Jenni and Son, and lastly of the publication of papers pertaining to the first suit by the same Swiss publishing house.[125] He was taken into custody not "for security reasons," as Brentano-von Arnim knew, but "as a punishment for not taking the hint to leave the state!" (sondern gleichsam zur Strafe, daß er die Winke zum Davongehen nicht benutzt habe!).[126] The reason was "that they naturally wanted to get rid of him and in the process claim that he had been afraid of the government and fled. But that did not come off" (man wünschte natürlich ihn loszuwerden, und dabei ihm die Blamage anzuhängen daß er sich vor der Regierung fürchte und ausreisse. Aber daraus ward nichts).[127] On August 14, Rudolf Baier, Brentano-von Arnim's young assistant, quoted a letter in his diary which she had written to Klara Mundt on August 4 and in which she had expressed her sympathy with Friedrich Wilhelm IV and alluded to the dangers from his entourage "but with infinite delicacy and cleverness; she had done this to show the king 'look here this is what I think and this is how I defend your interests' but she did it only to help Edgar Bauer" (aber unendlich fein und klug; sie hatte das gethan, um dem König damit zu zeigen: Sieh' so denke ich und so vertrete ich dich! und das namentlich war geschehen um von ihm etwas für Edgar Bauer zu erlangen).[128] The content of the letter became "known" and those "on top were strongly inclined to favor her."[129] Neither the letter[130] nor the extant draft[131] show any evidence of an intercession on behalf of the prisoner. However two undated documents have also been preserved which had previously not been recognized as drafts for a letter to Friedrich Wilhelm IV. One of them has a handwritten note[132] which had been omitted in the printed version, "To the king about Bauer;"[133] the other is more explicit.

How many malicious insults and accusations!—did they not denigrate me to the king because I chose as publisher the brother of a man who has been hunted by the police? Why I did that I will herewith explain, first because the pursuit of an honorable civil occupation is not contrary to the interest of the state and because the government nevertheless tried to suppress this business in a way which would be difficult to justify. . . . for a start they confiscated, quite illegally, all the books that appeared with this publisher for months, indeed for half a year, thereby damaging him greatly. Secondly, again quite illegally, they even prevented the tobacconist from plying his trade on Sundays in Charlottenburg when that is his best time for making a profit and while all his neighbors were allowed to keep their shops open. It was done under the pretext that he also had a publishing firm and therefore could not open his tobacco shop on Sundays, and this was the only source of income for a family of five small children and also the subsidy for his publishing enterprise, which was not yet making a profit but which was intended to support his brothers and his father.

Wie vielen muthwilligen Beleidigungen wie viele Anschwärzungen!— hat man nicht mich bei dem König verkleinert weil ich den Bruder eines von der Polizei verfolgten Schriftstellers zum Buchhändler nahm?— Warum ich aber dies gethan habe will ich hier darlegen weil erstens ein ehrenvolles Bürgerliches Gewerk zu unternehmen gar nichts dem Staate zu wider laufendes ist, weil aber dennoch die Regierung diesen Buch- handel unterdrückte auf eine Weise die zu rechtfertigen eine sehr schwürige Sache sein würde. . . . fürs erste hat man dieser Buchhand- lung alle Bücher die in ihrem Verlag herausgekommen ganz widerrecht- lich, Monatelang ja halbe Jahre lang confiscirt wodurch man die Buch- handlung sehr bedrängte fürs zweite hat man widerrechtlich in diesem Augenblick sogar den Tabackshändler verboten am Sonntag in Char- lottenburg wo er doch allein die größte Einnahme hat, während alle Nachbarn ihren Handel treiben können, unter dem Vorwande daß weil er auch einen Buchverlag habe, so dürfe er am Sonntag das Tabacksgeschäft nicht treiben! Hiervon aber ernährt er eine Familie von 5 kleinen Kindern, und hiermit unterstützt er seinen bis jezt nur Kosten machenden Buchhandel, von dem seine Brüder und Vater leben sollten.[134]

The draft ends at this point. Thus Brentano-von Arnim stood up for the whole Bauer family. Whether and how she argued for Edgar Bauer in particular remains unclear. It does not appear that she accomplished much for him, possibly some relief while he was in custody. He was sentenced to four years imprisonment. On August 26 Brentano-von Arnim informed her son Friedmund that Edgar Bauer had been brought to Magdeburg under "abhorrent" circumstances, on foot, at first, accompanied by two police officers, then on a wagon "together with a thief and another criminal! That is deeply insulting to any decent citizen." (mit einem Dieb, und noch einem andern Verbrecher!—So etwas muß einen bürgerlichen Charakter sehr tief kränken).[135] In Magdeburg he was relatively well treated, his brother Bruno related, "he was able to spend most of his day in the open and . . . work there diligently" (er könne den ganzen Tag im Freien sein und . . . soll dort fleißig arbeiten).[136] Edgar Bauer remained in jail until the revolution in March 1848.

At the end of 1845 the publishing business became the cause for a falling-out between the brothers Bauer and Brentano-von Arnim, who had had conflicts with all her other publishers also. Her "generosity to the persecuted Bauer" (Hochherzigkeit für den verfolgten Bauer)[137] had resulted in financial losses for her. Egbert Bauer seemed to have owed her "about 1506 Thaler;"[138] according to another letter it was "at least 1500 Thaler."[139] Working on commission did not seem profitable either for him or his brothers. "Could he not simply have acted straightforwardly and confessed that he regretted taking on my work on commission, rather than making snide remarks about how hard he had to work for nothing?" (Konnte er nicht besser einfach gehandelt haben, und mir aufrichig bekennen daß die Übernahme meiner Commission ihn nachträglich reut, als immer mit Bemerkungen kommen wie sehr er sich umsonst anstrengen müsse?), Brentano-von Arnim asked.[140] She claimed that Egbert Bauer accused her "of having tried to fleece them" (schindermäßig ihnen die Haut über die Ohren ziehen zu wollen) and make them work for nothing.[141] She wrote to Bruno Bauer:

When I began to take an interest in your publishing enterprise it was *your* views in particular which you had made known to me and the principles with which *you* intended to conduct your business that made it desirable for me to enter into the relationship. I counted on a stable situation which would save me anxiety and effort and also give me the necessary moral backing for my . . . position. I also held the firm belief that such a valuable and rich branch of literature . . . would substantially contribute to the success of your enterprise, in spite of all the aggravating circumstances, and would therefore be doubly important for a business which was not yet solidly connected. It was therefore all the more unpleasant and disappointing that your brother raised these belated objections, after the fact and beyond the course of all *honorable practice*.

Als ich darauf einging mich für Ihr Buchhändlerisches Unternehmen zu intressiren, waren es grade *Ihre* mit mitgetheilten Ansichten und Grundsätze nach welchen *Sie* das Geschäft zu leiten gedachten, welche mir dies Verhältniß wünschenswerth machten, weil ich dabei auf eine gesicherte Stellung rechnete die mir Verdruß und Bemühung erspare und die nothwendige moralische Garantie gewähre für welche ich . . . selbst einzustehen habe. Auch hatte ich den Glauben, daß ein so werthvoller und reichhaltiger Zweig der Literatur . . . trotz allen erschwerenden Umständen, sehr wesentlich zum Gelingen Ihres Unternehmens beitragen könne und die daher Ihnen noch nicht consolidirten Geschäftsverbindungen doppelt wichig sein mußten. Um so mehr haben diese nachträglichen, über alle Gebühr eines *aufrichtigen Verfahrens*, verspäteten Einwendungen Ihres Bruders mich unangenehm überrascht.[142]

Brentano-von Arnim was especially annoyed that the "activities of the Bauers' publishing business" prevented Achim von Arnim's *Collected Works* from appearing on schedule, something "which caused incalculable damage and confusion, and gave cause to insufferable troubles every day" (woraus ein nicht zu berechnender Schade und Verwirrung entstanden und unerträgliche Mißhelligkeiten noch täglich daraus hervorgehen).[143] Edgar Bauer's "plan to discount the net worth of *22,000* volumes for 12,000 Thaler," which could not expect for another five years did not seem realistic to her.[144] Further details of her conflict with the brothers Bauer is illuminated in the draft of a letter written around 1847 or 1848 by P.L. Jenatz who was then in charge of Brentano-von Arnim's affairs. It was addressed to the president of the superior court, Heinrich Leopold von Strampff:

Several unpleasant circumstances have obliged Mrs. von Arnim to terminate the contract which had been made with the hon. Edg. Bauer.

This happened in February 1846; in April 1846 Bauer delivered everything he held for her and at the same time gave her a final account. . . .
This account was audited and . . . approved. In the second year, 1847,
Mr. Bauer was obligated by contract to account for the copies that were
sent to him in between January and April 1846 and for those at his
disposal in 1846. When none of this took place, and after several re-
minders, proceedings were instituted against him. He was taken to
court, and he declared then that the contract which he himself had
drawn up and signed was quite wrong and, according to a new one
which he had just written, he owed nothing more, indeed, he actually
had money coming back to him.

Mehrere mißliche Umstände mußten Frau v Arnim veranlassen, den mit
H. Egb. Bauer geschlossenen Commissions-Vertrag zu kündigen. Dies
geschah im Februar 1846; im April 1846 lieferte Bauer alles bei ihm
Vorräthige ab und übergab gleichzeitig einen 'Haupt Abschluß' . . .
Dieser Hauptabschluß wurde . . . geprüft und für richtig befunden. Im
zweiten Jahre—1847—sollte H. Bauer nach dem geschlossenen Con-
trakte für die vom Jan[uar] April 1846 versandten und ihm im Jahre 1846
zur Disposition gestellten Ex[em]pl[a]re aufkommen. Nachdem Herr
Bauer nach mehrmaligen vorhergegangenen Mahnungen dies nicht
that, wurde man klagbar gegen ihn. Vors Gericht gefordert, erklärte er
nun, der ganz von ihm abgefaßte und durch seine Unterschrift vollzo-
gene Abschluß sei unrichtig, er habe nach einem neuen Abschlusse, den
er jetzt angefertigt, nichts mehr zu zahlen, im Gegentheile bekäme er
noch Geld heraus.[145]

Brentano-von Arnim then asked for the immediate return of all
books which had been consigned to Bauer on commission as well as,
perhaps, two-thirds of their list price. Her claim was rejected by the
city court of Charlottenburg on November 18.[146]

At the time of these difficulties in the book trade the brothers
Bauer had not been able to develop their radical views from the early
1840s any further. Bruno Bauer distanced himself from the common
people, disappointed that his critical theories received no resonance
among them, and Edgar Bauer concentrated on non-philosophical
journalism, inasmuch as he was able to publish at all. It was not
surprising therefore that from the mid 1840s on Brentano-von Arnim
no longer exhibited an interest for the intellectual achievements of the
brothers Bauer. In spite of the fact that they became intellectually
independent from one another and in spite of the business disagreements they had had, she remained loyal to them in a manner that

became evident in a later lawsuit. Brentano-von Arnim had started her own publishing business in the summer of 1846, the "Expedition des v. Arnimschen Verlags." But while she was suing Egbert Bauer, she became implicated in a suit by the Berlin magistrate because she was carrying on a business there without having acquired Berlin citizenship.[147] She took it upon herself to make this dispute public and in the course thereof she proclaimed her story and made the magistrate look ridiculous. She was a master of indiscretion when it was a matter of broadcasting her convictions, but she was equally a master of discretion when it came to protecting the less well-respected from public opinion. To her contemporaries and even to researchers of later years the controversy with the book business of the Bauers remained a secret by Brentano-von Arnim's own directive: "So much prejudice exists against the Bauers and it would become a very painful experience for me if this affair were to increase it" (Es ist so viel Vorurtheil gegen die Bauers und es würde mir eine der schmerzlichsten Erfahrungen sein wenn dem durch diese Sache Vorschub geleistet würde).[148]

Notes

This chapter was translated from the German by Dorothee E. Krahn.

A shorter German version of this article was presented at the German Studies Association Conference in Milwaukee on 6 October, 1989. Since the article contains a large number of quotes, the German original is given only if the quote is by Bettina Brentano-von Arnim or if it is important for the context. Since the list of notes is extensive a works cited list was not added.

1. Heinz and Ingrid Pepperle, eds., Introduction, *Die Hegelsche Linke: Dokumente zur Philosophie und Politik im deutschen Vormärz* (Leipzig: Reclam, 1985) 25.
2. "Menschenvergötterung," *Evangelische Kirchen-Zeitung* 30 [Berlin] 15 Apr. 1837: col. 237.
3. A[dolph] Hausrath, *David Friedrich Strauß und die Theologie seiner Zeit* vol. 1 (Heidelberg: Bassermann, 1876) 298-304.

4. [Johann Peter Lange], "Bettine," *Evangelische Kirchen-Zeitung* 27–29 [Berlin] 4,7, 11 Apr. 1838; col. 210. Cp. concerning the question of authorship: Bettine von Arnim. *Clemens Brentano's Frühlingskranz. Die Günderode*, ed. Walter Schmitz (Frankfurt a. M.: Deutscher Klassiker Verlag, 1986) 941–943; 945–964, 995–997, 1005–1007, 1024–1033, 1119–1121 contain sources and information about the relationship between Bettina and the Young Hegelians.
5. [Lange] 214, 217, 229, 231.
6. H[einrich] L[eo], rev. of *Dies Buch gehört dem König*, by Bettina von Arnim, *Evangelische Kirchen-Zeitung* 35, 36 [Berlin] 1 May and 4 May 1844: col. 286. Concerning the question of authorship see: Anneliese Krige, "Geschichte der Evangelischen Kirchen-Zeitung unter der Redaktion Ernst-Wilhelm Hengstenbergs (vom 1. Juli 1827 bis zum 1. Juni 1869): Ein Beitrag zur Kirchengeschichte des 19. Jahrhunderts," part 2, diss., Rheinische Friedrich-Wilhelms-Universität Bonn, 1958, 60.
7. Bettina von Arnim, *Dies Buch gehört dem König* (Berlin: E.H. Schroeder, 1843) 326; L[eo], Review, col. 284.
8. Arnim 325.
9. L[eo], review, col. 285.
10. Heinrich Leo, *Die Hegelingen: Actenstücke und Belege zu der s.g. Denunciation der ewigen Wahrheit zusammengestelt* (Halle: Anton, 1838).
11. David Friedrich Strauß, *Zwei friedliche Blätter: Vermehrter und verbesserter Abdruck der beiden Aufsätze Ueber Justinus Kerner und Ueber Vergängliches und Bleibendes im Christenthum* (Altona: Hammerich, 1839) 99–101.
12. Strauß 108.
13. Bettina von Arnim, *Die Günderode. Clemens Brentanos Frühlingskranz*, ed. Heinz Härtl (Berlin and Weimar: Aufbau Verlag, 1989) 174.
14. Arnim 167.
15. Arnim 166, 162.
16. Reinhold Steig, "Ein Besuch bei Frau Bettina von Arnim [1839]," *Vossische Zeitung* [Berlin] No. 385. 19 Aug. 1909.
17. *"An einen unbekannten Empfänger"*, 10 September 1839. Manuscript in Varnhagen von Ense Archive. Biblioteka Jagiellońska, Kraków. It will be referred to as BJ.
18. Werner Vordtriede, ed. "An Julius Döring." In "Bettina von Arnims Briefe an Julius Döring," *Jahrbuch des Freien Deutschen Hochstifts* (1963): 393.
19. Werner Vordtriede 393.
20. Strauß 84: "how often is wine created most naturally from a vessel in which water was once found . . .

I see wine created later from a vessel that was once filled with water: must therefore the water have been changed into wine, and only it perhaps remained unnoticed by me, how the water was poured out and the wine poured in?" And Bettina to Döring, 27–30 May 1839; Vordtriede, "Bettina von Arnim's letters to Julius Döring," p. 393 ff.: Strauß "could certainly have said, that it is no miracle, that Christ could walk on water, that it was no miracle, that he could change water to wine; because the Philistines also change wine to water . . . You also have changed water to wine, my lips have tasted it and my senses tested its spirit."

wie oft wird aus einem Gefäße, in dem früher Wasser sich befunden hatte, später auf die natürlichste Weise Wein geschöpft . . . Ich sehe aus einem früher mit Wasser gefüllten Krug nachmals Wein schöpfen: muß darum das Wasser in Wein verwandelt worden sein, und blieb mir nicht vielleicht nur unbemerkt, wie das Wasser aus-, und der Wein eingegossen wurde? Und Bettina an Döring, 27.–30. Mai 1839; Vordtriede, "Bettina von Arnim's Briefe an Julius Döring," p. 393 f/: Strauß "hätte freilich sagen können es giebt kein Wunder, denn Christus konnte auf den Wassern gehn, das war kein Wunder, er konnte Wasser in Wein verwandlen; denn die Philister verwandlen ja auch Wein in Wasser . . . Du auch hast Wasser in Wein verwandelt, und meine Lippe hat ihn gekostet, und meine Sinne haben seinen Geist geprobt."

21. Werner Vordtriede, ed., 364.
22. Cp. Heinrich Heine, *Heinrich Heine: Säkularausgabe*, vol. 25 (Berlin and Paris: Akademie-Verlag, Editions du CNRS, 1974) 169, 201.
23. [David Friedrich] Strauß, review. *Mittheilungen über Goethe: Aus mündlichen und schriftlichen, gedruckten und ungedruckten Quellen*, by Dr. Friedrich Wilhelm Riemer, *Deutsche Jahrbücher für Wisssenschaft und Kunst* 25, 30 July 1841, 98.
24. Strauß, *Deutsche Jahrbücher für Wissenschaft und Kunst* 98.
25. "To Wilhelm Strauß," 6 Dec. 1840, *Ausgewählte Briefe von David Friedrich Strauß*, ed. Eduard Zeller (Bonn: Strauß, 1895) 95.
26. Strauß, *Deutsche Jahrbücher für Wissenschaft und Kunst* 98.
27. Strauß, *Deutsche Jahrbücher für Wissenschaft und Kunst* 98.
28. Strauß, *Deutsche Jahrbücher für Wissenschaft und Kunst* 98.
29. Adolph Rapp, ed., "To Ernst Rapp," 9 Sept. 1840, *Briefwechsel zwischen Strauß und Vischer*, vol. 1 (Stuttgart: Klett, 1952) 298.
30. Rapp, ed., "To Ernst Rapp," 12 June 1841, 298; ibidem.
31. *An einen unbekannten Empfänger*. Ms. in BJ.
32. Cp. Karl Heinz Bohrer, *Die Kritik der Romantik: Der Verdacht der Philosophie gegen die literarische Moderne* (Frankfurt a.M.: Suhrkamp, 1989) 182–202.
33. Cp. Else von Eck, *Die Literaturkritik in den Hallischen und Deutschen Jahrbüchern (1838–1842): Ein Beitrag zur Geschichte der deutschen Literaturwissenschaft* (Berlin: Ebering, 1925) 48.
34. 20 May 1840; Heinz and Ingrid Pepperle, eds. 799–800.

35. Heinz and Ingrid Pepperle, eds. 801.
36. Cp. E[duard] Meyen, "Achim von Arnims sämmtliche Werke," ed. Wilhelm Grimm, vol. 1 and 2, *Hallische Jahrbücher für deutsche Wissenschaft und Kunst* [Leipzig] (1839): 31 Oct., No. 261; 1 Nov., No. 262, cols. 2081–2086, 2094–2096.
37. 3 June 1841; MEGA², vol. 1, Berlin 1975, 361. Cp. *Allgemeine Zeitung* [Augsburg] 19 May 1841, No. 139, p. 1108.
38. Ed[uard] Meyen, "Die neueste belletristische Literatur," *Athenäum: Zeitschrift für das gebildete Deutschland* No. 2 [Berlin] 9 Jan. 1841: 29.
39. Meyen, *Athenäum: Zeitschrift für das gebildete Deutschland*.
40. Eduard Meyen, "Bettina's Politik: Dies Buch gehört dem Könige," *Allgemeine Literatur-Zeitung (Ergänzungsblätter)* [Halle] November 1843; No. 98 and 99, cols. 778–779. Concerning authorship: Articles which appeared in the "Rhein Newspaper" in 1842 were likewise signed "E.M." by Meyen. (Zur Verfasserschaft: Ebenfalls mit "E.M." zeichnete Meyen seine 1842 in der "rheinischen Zeitung" erschienenen Beiträge.) Cp. Wilhelm Klutentreter, *Die Rheinische Zeitung von 1842/43 in der politischen und geistigen Bewegung des Vormärz.* [Teil 2.] *Dokumente.* Dortmund 1967, S. 215 (Dortmunder Beiträge zur Zeitungsforschung, vol. 10, part 2).
41. Moritz [!] Carrière, review, *Die Günderode*, *Hallische Jahrbücher für deutsche Wissenschaft und Kunst* (1841): 283–284. [Leipzig] 24 and 25 March 1841, No. 71 and 72. Quoted page 283 ff. Reprint in Moriz Carriere, "Achim von Arnim und die Romantik. Die Günderode." *Studien für eine Geschichte des Deutschen Geistes* 1 (Grünberg: W. Levysohn, 1841) 28–44.
42. Carrière, review. 287.
43. Paul Nerrlich, ed., "To Adolf Stahr," 5 May 1840, *Arnold Ruges Briefwechsel und Tagebuchblätter aus den Jahren 1825–1880* vol. 1 (Berlin, 1886) 205.
44. Paul Nerrlich, ed., "To Adolf Stahr," 10 Mar. 1841, 225.
45. 1 May 1842. Ursula Püschel, ed., " . . . *und mehr als einmal nachts im Thiergarten." Bettina von Arnim und Heinrich Bernhard Oppenheim. Briefe 1891–1848.*, *Bettina von Arnim Studien*, vol. 1, ed. Ursula Püschel (Berlin: FSP-Fotosatz und Spezielle EDV-Programme GMBH, 1990).
46. Heinz and Ingrid Pepperle 899.
47. Cp. *Briefwechsel zwischen Bruno Bauer und Edgar Bauer während der Jahre 1839–1842 aus Bonn und Berlin* (Charlottenburg: E. Bauer, 1844) 166–168.
48. Arnold Ruge, Introduction for 1841 edition of the *Deutsche Jahrbücher*. Heinz and Ingrid Pepperle, eds., 225.
49. [Christian Hermann] Weiße, rev., *Die Günderode*, *Jahrbücher für wissenschaftliche Kritik*, vol. 2 [Berlin] (1840), No. 96–98, cols. 800–824.

50. *Briefwechsel zwischen Bruno Bauer und Edgar Bauer während der Jahre 1839–1842 aus Bonn und Berlin* 167–168.

51. Edgar Bauer, "Die Bettine als Religionsstifterin," *Deutsche Jahrbücher für Wissenschaft und Kunst* [Leipzig] 23 and 24 May 1842, No. 122 and 123, (1842): 484.

52. Bauer 484.

53. Cp. Theodor Mundt, "Bettina und der Cultus des Genius," *Der Freihafen: Galerie von Unterhaltungsbildern aus den Kreisen der Literatur, Gesellschaft und Wissenschaft* [Altona: Hammerich] No. 2 (1841): 319–329.

54. Bauer 484.

55. Bauer 484.

56. Bauer 484.

57. Bauer 486–487.

58. I.S. Turgénev, "To Bettina," The end of 1840 or beginning of 1841 *Polnoe sobranje sočinenje i pisem*, Pisma, vol. 1 (Moscow and Leningrad: Chudožest v. Literatury, 1961) 213–214.

59. Bauer 487.

60. Bauer 487.

61. Bauer 488.

62. Bettine von Arnim, *Clemens Brentanos Frühlingskranz. Die Günderode.* 1024.

63. Szeliga [Franz Szeliga Zychlin von Zychlinski], "I. Dies Buch gehört dem König. II. Clemens Brentano's Frühlingskranz," *Norddeutsche Blätter für Kritik, Literatur und Unterhaltung* No. 2 (1844): 14.

64. Szeliga 14.

65. Szeliga 18.

66. Szeliga 1.

67. Szeliga 10.

68. Meyen, "Bettina's Politik: Dies Buch gehört dem Könige," *Allgemeine Literatur-Zeitung (Ergänzungsblätter)* col. 784.

69. Meyen, "Bettina's Politik: Dies Buch gehört dem Könige," *Allgemeine Literatur-Zeitung (Ergänzungsblätter)* col. 784.

70. Meyen, "Bettina's Politik: Dies Buch gehört dem Könige," *Allgemeine Literatur-Zeitung (Ergänzungsblätter)* col. 783.

71. Meyen, "Bettina's Politik: Dies Buch gehört dem Könige," *Allgemeine Literatur-Zeitung (Ergänzungsblätter)* col. 778.

72. Meyen, "Bettina's Politik: Dies Buch gehört dem Könige," *Allgemeine Literatur-Zeitung (Ergänzungsblätter)* col. 781.

73. Meyen, "Bettina's Politik: Dies Buch gehört dem Könige," *Allgemeine Literatur-Zeitung (Ergänzungsblätter)* col. 781.

74. Meyen, "Bettina's Politik: Dies Buch gehört dem Könige," *Allgemeine Literatur-Zeitung (Ergänzungsblätter)* col. 786.

75. Meyen, "Bettina's Politik: Dies Buch gehört dem Könige," *Allgemeine Literatur-Zeitung (Ergänzungsblätter)* col. 791.

76. Bruno Bauer, *Vollständige Geschichte der Partheikämpfe in Deutschland während der Jahre 1842–1846*, vol. 2 (Charlottenburg, 1847) 11–12.

77. Cp. Heinz Härtl, "Die zeitgenossische publizistische Rezeption des Königs-Buches," *Bettina von Arnim-Studien*, vol. 2, 1992.

78. Edgar Bauer, "To Bruno Bauer," 18 Jan. 1842, *Briefwechsel zwischen Bruno Bauer und Edgar Bauer während der Jahre 1839–1842 aus Bonn und Berlin* (Charlottenburg: E. Bauer, 1844) 170.

79. Edgar Bauer, *Frankreich vom Juli bis zum October 1789, oder die ersten Kämpfe des constitutionellen Princips mit dem Königsthum und der Volksparthei. Denkwürdigkeiten zur Geschichte der neuern Zeit seit der Französischen Revolution* (Charlottenburg: E. Bauer, 1843) 42. Based on sources and original memoirs edited by Bruno and Edgar Bauer. 2.

80. Cp. Heinz Härtl, "Mirabeau im *Frühlingskranz*," *Germanica Wratislavensia* 80 (1990), 137–147.

81. Max Stirner, *Der Einzige und sein Eigenthum* (Leipzig: Wigand, 1845) 263.

82. Stirner 263.

83. Gustav Landauer, "To Ernst Joel," 24 Dec. 1915, *Sein Lebensgang in Briefen*, ed. Martin Buber, vol. 2 (Frankfurt a.M.: Insel, 1929) 114.

84. Gertrud Meyer-Hepner, "Ein fälschlich Bettina zugeschriebener Aufsatz," *Weimarer Beiträge* 6.1 (1960): 132-134.

85. Undated and unaddressed letter draft to Heinrich Bernhard Oppenheim, 28 Dec. 1841. Ursula Püschel,"Bettina von Arnim. Werke und Briefe," diss., Freie Universität Berlin, 1965, 298. Cp. the dated continuation of this letter in *Bettina von Arnim. Werke und Briefe*, ed. Joachim Müller. (Frechen: Bartmann, 1961) 496–498.

86. Püschel 299.

87. G. A. van den Bergh van Eysinga, "Bettina von Arnim en Bruno Bauer," *Godsdienstwetenschappelijke Studien* 9 (1951): 36, 40.

88. "To Hermann Karl von Leonhardi," 24 Nov. 1838. Heinz Härtl, "Zwei Briefe Bettina von Arnims an Hermann Karl von Leonhardi," *Wissenschaftliche Zeitschrift Martin-Luther-Universität Halle-Wittenberg. Geisteswissenschaftliche Reihe*, 41, No. 1 (1992) 10.

89. *Bilder aus Karl Sievekings Leben: 1787–1847*. Part 2 of Vol. 2 of *Bilder aus vergangener Zeit nach Mittheilungen aus großentheils ungedruckten Familienpapieren*, ms., (Hamburg: Agentur des Rauhen Hauses, 1887) 183.

90. Cp. *Tagebücher: Aus dem Nachlaß Varnhagens von Ense*, ed. Ludmilla Assing, vol. 1 (Berlin: Brockhaus, 1861) 340–341.

91. *Tagebücher: Aus dem Nachlaß Varnhagens von Ense* 346.

92. "To Julius von Hardegg," 12 Oct. 1841, ms. located in Deutsches Literaturarchiv im Schiller-Nationalmuseum, Marbach.

93. "To Friedmund von Arnim," 27 Oct. 1841." Karl-Heinz Hahn, *Bettina von Arnim in ihrem Verhältnis zu Staat und Politik*, (Weimar: Böhlau, 1959) 33.

94. Püschel 298.

95. Püschel 296.

96. Püschel 296.

97. Püschel 297.

98. Püschel 299.

99. Püschel 299.

100. Ursula Püschel, "Bettina von Arnim und Friedrich Wilhelm IV," *Internationales Jahrbuch der Bettina-von-Arnim-Gesellschaft* 3 (1989) 102.

101. Cp. Heinrich Grunholzer, *Tagebuch* (26 Feb. 1843) ms., Paul Kläui-Bibliothek, Uster, Switzerland.

102. Franz Thomas Bratranek to Ignác Jan Hanuš, 2 Dec 1843. Jaromir Loužil, "Franz Thomas Bratranek—ein Vermittler der deutschen Philosophie im böhmischen Vormärz," *Ost und West in der Geschichte des Denkens und der kulturellen Beziehungen: Festschrift für Eduard Winter zum 70. Geburtstag* (Berlin: Akademie-Verlag, 1960) 604.

103. Grunholzer (10 Aug. 1843).

104. Karl Glossy, ed., "26 September 1842," *Literarische Geheimberichte aus dem Vormärz* part 1 (Vienna, 1912) 319.

105. approx. 1843; see Püschel, 43. Endnote 45.

106. Martha Becker, ed. *Anton Schindler der Freund Beethovens: Sein Tagebuch aus den Jahren 1841–43* (Frankfurt a.M.: Kramer, 1939) 100 (3 August 1843).

107. Loužil 604.

108. [Friedmund von Arnim], *Die gute Sache der Seele, ihre eigenen Angelegenheiten und die aus dem Menschen und der Vergangenheit entwickelte Geschichtszukunft* (Braunschweig: Otto, 1843) 3.

109. Friedmund von Arnim 3.

110. Alfred Dove, ed., "Leopold von Ranke an Heinrich und Selma Ranke, 24 März 1831," *Leopold von Rankes Sämmtliche Werke* vol. 53/54 (Leipzig: Duncker & Humblot, 1890) 250.

111. Cp. [von Arnim], *Dies Buch gehört dem König* 27, 32, 33, 38, 64, 83, 84, 92, 101, 112–114, 145, 194, 230, 233–235, 241–242, 257, 258, 285, 369, 394, 401, 405–407, 427, 431, 451, 520–522.

112. Grunholzer (18 May 1843).

113. To Wilhelm Strauss, 16 Jan. 1843. Strauß, *Ausgewählte Briefe von David Friedrich Strauß* 145. Cp. Emma von Niendorf, [Emma von Suckow], *Aus der Gegenwart* (Berlin: Alexander Duncker, 1844) 147.

114. Strauß, *Zwei friedliche Blätter* 65–69.

115. "To Ernst Rapp," 29 Sept. 1943. Strauß, *Ausgewählte Briefe von David Friedrich Strauß* 153–154.

116. *Tagebücher: Aus dem Nachlaß Varnhagens von Ense* vol.2 (Berlin: Brockhaus, 1861). 208. (20 August 1843)

117. Ludwig Geiger, ed., "An Carl Stahr, 29. April 1844," *Aus Adolf Stahrs Nachlaß. Briefe von Stahr nebst Briefen an ihn von Bettine von Arnim [u.a.]* (Oldenburg: Schulze, 1903) 88.

118. Kurt Gassen, ed., "An Rudolf Baier, 9. Oktober 1845," *Bettina von Arnim und Rudolf Baier: Unveröffentlichte Briefe und Tagebuchaufzeichnungen. Aus den Schätzen der Universitätsbibliothek zu Greifswald* 11 (Greifswald: Bamberg, 1937) 61–62. Cp. Otto Mallon, "Bettinas Buchhändlerepistel: Ein bisher unbekannter Brief," *Zeitschrift für Bücherfreunde* 38.3 (1934): 2–4.

119. "To Baier," 9 Oct. 1845. Gassen, ed. 62.

120. Gassen, ed. 62.

121. Ludwig Geiger, ed., "An Adolf Stahr, Ende Mai 1844," *Bettine von Arnim und Friedrich Wilhelm IV: Ungedruckte Briefe und Aktenstücke* (Frankfurt a.M.: Rütten & Loening, 1902) 61.

122. Adolf Heinrich Graf von Arnim-Boitzenburg to Friedrich Wilhelm IV, 6 June 1844. Geiger, ed. *Bettine von Arnim und Friedrich Wilhelm IV: Ungedruckte Briefe und Aktenstücke* 58–59.

123. Manuscript. Goethe- und Schiller-Archiv der Stiftung Weimarer Klassik, Arnim-Nachlaß Sign. 350a. (will be referred to as GSA)

124. *Tagebücher: Aus dem Nachlaß Varnhagens von Ense* vol. 2 315. (24 June 1844)

125. Cp. Erik Gamby and Edgar Bauer, *Junghegelianer, Publizist und Polizeiagent: Mit Bibliographie der E. Bauer-Texte und Dokumentenanhang. Schriften aus dem Karl-Marx-Haus Trier 23* (Trier: Karl-Marx-Haus, 1985) 21–23.

126. *Tagebücher: Aus dem Nachlaß Varnhagens von Ense* 73.

127. "Bettina an Friedmund von Arnim," date unknown, ms., GSA 386.

128. Gassen, ed. 36–37.

129. "Bettina an Siegmund von Arnim," 5 Oct. 1845, ms., GSA 388.

130. ms., Freies Deutsches Hochstift—Frankfurter Goethe-Museum, sign. 13265.

131. Manuscript. GSA 472a.

132. GSA 422.

133. Bettina von Arnim, *Werke und Briefe* vol. 5 (Frankfurt a.M.: Frechen and Köln, 1986) 498–499.

134. GSA 422.

135. Manuscript. GSA 386.

136. Manuscript. GSA 386.

137. Baier to Bettina, 9 Oct. 1845, ms., GSA 413.

138. "Bettine an Friedrich Klein, ms., GSA 423.

139. Bettine an Friedmund von Arnim," ms., GSA 386.

140. To Baier, Dec. 1845. Gassen, ed. 79.
141. Gassen, ed. 80.
142. Undated letter to an unknown recipient, Dec. 1845, ms., Biblioteka Jagiellońska, Kraków.
143. Undated letter to an unknown recipient, approx 1846. GSA 455,5.
144. Undated letter to an unknown recipient," Dec. 1845, ms., Biblioteka Jagiellońska, Kraków.
145. Manuscript, GSA 455, 5.
146. Cp. GSA 455, 5.
147. Cp. Gertrud Meyer-Hepner, *Der Magistratsprozeß der Bettina von Arnim* (Weimar: Arion Verlag, 1960).
148. "Bettine an Rudloff," 15 Feb. 1846, ms., Biblioteka Jagiellońska, Kraków.

Bettina Brentano-von Arnim's "Tale of the Lucky Purse" and Clemens Brentano's "Story of Good Kasperl and Beautiful Annerl"[1]

Birgit Ebert

1.

Bettina Brentano-von Arnim's *Poor Book* (Armenbuch), her great project documenting the plight of the poor, was supposed to appear in the summer of 1844.[2] However, on June 9 news of the Silesian weavers' revolt reached Berlin, and Alexander von Humboldt urgently advised Brentano-von Arnim against publishing the book.[3] For the time being she delayed publication. Brentano-von Arnim would have been subject to prosecution from the board of censors; but probably more important to her in making this decision was the fact that her desire to prevent the weavers' revolt had already been frustrated (Frühwald, "Weber" 275). She did not drop the project completely; she continued to collect documents and to write until at least 1852. The book was never published during her lifetime.

Not until nearly 120 years later were the materials for the *Poor Book* published, and then only in fragments. In 1962, in his critical edition of selections from Brentano-von Arnim's handwritten manuscripts of the *Poor Book* papers, Werner Vordtriede included a prose text from 1845, the "Tale of the Lucky Purse" (Erzählung vom Heckebeutel).[4] This piece has since enjoyed only minimal attention. Yet this "treasure of Bettina's narrative art" (Kostbarkeit Bettinischer Erzählkunst) (Vordtriede 497) is a story that deserves close reading.

185

Woodcut: The Misery in Silesia, in: "Fliegende Blätter," no. 135, 1848.
(Staatsbibliothek Preußischer Kulturbesitz, Berlin. Photo: Bildarchiv
Preußischer Kulturbesitz).

Bettina Brentano-von Arnim's "Tale of the Lucky Purse" has been
discussed in relation to a novella by her brother, Clemens Brentano,
the "Story of Good Kasperl and Beautiful Annerl" (Geschichte vom
braven Kasperl und dem schönen Annerl) (1817). "How very much
like Brentano this story is" (Wie brentanosch diese Erzählung doch
ist) Vordtriede himself has observed (518). There may well be a number of shared elements in the two works, since the two authors were

very close for many years; Bettina was, nevertheless, quite capable of maintaining her intellectual independence from her brother. Three years after his death, in the summer of 1845, the ending of the "Tale of the Lucky Purse" was written, the year after Brentano-von Arnim had published the reworked correspondence between her brother and herself in *The Spring Wreath* (Clemens Brentanos Frühlingskranz) (1844). At this time she had been involved intensely with her brother's work. Thus, we are concerned here with the "Tale of the Lucky Purse" from a double perspective: on the one hand as it contrasts with Clemens Brentano's novella, and on the other hand within the context of Brentano-von Arnim's own work. Before turning to these perspectives and for the purpose of orientation, a short overview of the content of both texts will be given.

In the story of the "Lucky Purse" we have something quite different from the other papers in the *Poor Book*, that is, we have a narrative. It is a report to the Prince of Prussia concerning the uses to which a sum of money given by him had been put. At its center is the description of an old woman. The author-narrator Frau von Arnim tells the story of an eighty-nine-year-old herb-gatherer, mother of big grenadiers, and guardian of her grandchildren, who comes to her door. This aged grandmother tells of her poverty and asks Frau von Arnim for financial support with the greatest of rhetorical skill. We learn how the family of the old woman, brothers and sisters, husband and children, have been destroyed in Prussian wars and by illnesses, and how the survivors have had to battle with economic misery. After many visits to the Brentano-von Arnim household and many loans from the "Lucky Purse," Frau von Arnim's poor-fund, the old woman develops a plan by which she can help herself. She wants to start a grocery business with a dogcart in order to insure that her grandchildren will have means of support after her death. Misfortunes continually preclude any progress for her undertaking. Undaunted, the old woman never loses sight of her aim. Although openended, the introduction, commentary, and afterword by the narrator give the story a deeper significance. In the life of this woman the history and the courage of the people are mirrored.

In Brentano's novella the figure of an old peasant woman also has a central position. The "Story of Good Kasperl and Beautiful Annerl" tells the tragic story of Kasperl and his fiancée Annerl from the point of view of Kasperl's grandmother. The stories of both characters come into contact with each other only through the person of the old peasant woman, who relates them bit by bit to a second narrator figure, a poet-author. Kasperl takes part as a cavalryman in the Napoleonic wars, returns and shoots himself out of "lost honor" when he discovers that his father and brother have stolen his regimental horse. Annerl, god-child of the old woman, is engaged to Kasperl, moves to the city, is seduced by a nobleman, becomes pregnant and, at the end of the story, is executed as the murderer of her child. Personal guilt, the confusion of moral standards, and secret demonic powers determine the destinies of Kasperl and Annerl. These two stories-within-a-story are imbedded in a dramatic frame, in which the grandmother comes to the city during the night before Annerl's execution, in order to fight for an honorable grave for her grandson and godchild.

2.

Bettina Brentano-von Arnim probably met the old woman from her "Lucky Purse" story personally. In her report she assures us:

> This little story of the poor has been written completely according to the truth and not a single word has been added to what the woman actually said; I wrote it down because my children told me that Your Majesty had ordered them to tell him how the two gold pieces had been used.

> Diese kleine Armengeschichte ist ganz nach der Wahrheit geschildert und ist selbst dabei kein Wort hinzugesezt [sic] von dem was die Frau gesagt hat; ich habe sie niedergeschrieben weil meine Kinder mir sagten seine Königliche Hoheit habe ihnen anbefohlen die Verwendung der beiden Goldstücke ihm mitzutheilen. (Heckebeutel 515)

The Prince of Prussia is, as Vordtriede suspects, Prince Waldemar, who was often a guest in Brentano-von Arnim's home and to whom she dedicated *The Spring Wreath*.

A comparison of the two main versions of the story also indicates an actual meeting. Details, the natural sincerity of the old woman, and some authentic, colloquial expressions from the speech of the grandmother have been left out of the second version in favor of a stronger stylization. The impression arises that the first version was a close narration written after a real meeting. In the second version, Brentano-von Arnim changes the appearance of the grandmother;

she leaves out, among other things, her hiking cane, which seems to give her an even more erect and imposing figure (Heckebeutel 498, 504), the spontaneous, heartfelt embraces of the old woman (Heckebeutel 498, 503), and her figures of speech recalling old sayings (Heckebeutel[1] 505, 507). In the second version, (and in the final variant in someone else's handwriting), Brentano-von Arnim is obviously more concerned to present the spiritualized, mythic grandeur of the old woman, the "old Sybille" ("alte Sybille" [sic]) (Heckebeutel 515). This is certainly evident with respect to the effect which Brentano-von Arnim might have wanted to achieve in the eyes of the specific audience to whom this story was addressed, the Prussian Prince. The story was probably to be given a higher, more exemplary significance, since Brentano-von Arnim begins it purposely: "For example: [. . .]" (Zum Beispiel: [. . .]) (Heckebeutel 498).

Since the documents from the poor lists (which actually constitute the bulk of Brentano-von Arnim's *Poor Book*) have not been accessible in print, it has yet to be determined to what extent these writings provided source material for the story.[5] But a series of essential details are contained in the report from the Vogtland "Experiences of a Swiss in the Vogtland" (Erfahrungen eines Schweizers im Vogtland) by the twenty-four-year-old student, Heinrich Grunholzer, which makes up the ending of Brentano-von Arnim's *The King's Book* (Dies Buch gehört dem König) (1843). Here she obtained information about the varied attempts of the poor to help themselves. This "piece of social reporting" (sozialwissenschaftliche Reportage) about the poor colony outside the Hamburg Gate in Berlin was probably edited and reworked by her (Hirsch 91). Here unemployed laborers speak out, expressing the courage and desire to make themselves independent, if they were given starting capital (Köln 3: 248). But the requirement by the monarchical state, that the poor first buy a merchant's license at the considerable price of twelve Talers, prevents many from acquiring money on a legal basis, so that the hungry often have no other choice than to beg (Köln 3: 247). Brentano-von Arnim charges: "Thus, when poverty becomes impoverished through its business, it must still bleed to death from the attempt to work its way up!" (Also wenn die Armuth verarmt bei ihrem Gewerb, so muß sie sich am Versuch verbluten, sich empor zu arbeiten!) (Heckebeutel 510). This license, an absurd requirement considering the circumstances of the poor, acquires symbolic significance in Brentano-von Arnim's literature. Even when her business cannot be continued, the grand-mother must still pay the fee for a whole year.

The strategies for survival in the story, which the old woman uses in order to deal with her desperate situation, originated with the poor in the Vogtland. Grunholzer reports how even a complete lack of money fails to prevent one man from losing his good disposition. The commentary notes that a broken spirit seems to be the prerequisite for receiving charity from the state:

> Any cheerfulness on the part of the poor is often the cause of reproach and can even prevent their receiving financial support. 'He doesn't need anything; he's doing well enough' people think; as if one had to allow one's misery to depress one's soul completely.

> Der Frohsinn wird dem Armen sehr häufig zum Vorwurfe gemacht und kann sogar die Unterstützung verhindern. 'Der braucht nichts; es ist ihm wohl genug,' heißt es; gleichsam als müßte man sich durchs Elend an der ganzen Seele niederdrücken lassen. (Köln 3: 236)

Brentano-von Arnim develops a different point of view. In the report from the Vogtland, the central element is her socially critical transformation of begging into the art of persuasion. When a shy mother of five children invites him into her dwelling, her reporter relates:

> I was not offended that she wanted to show me into her room and expected a few groshen in advance. When I saw the poor condition of the children, however, I was glad at the woman's behavior. I could read in her eyes that her love for her children triumphed over feminine shyness. The boldness of beggars is often annoying. But one should not allow oneself to be overly influenced by the first unpleasant impres-sion. What makes the beggar bold is what is best about him.

> Ich nahm es derselben nicht übel, daß sie mich durchaus in ihre Stube führen wollte und zum voraus einige Groschen erwartete. Wie ich aber die Not der Kinder sah, freute ich mich über das Benehmen der Mut-ter. Ich konnte dieser in den Augen lesen, daß in ihr die Liebe zu den Kleinen über die weibliche Schüchternheit triumphierte. Die Dreistig-keit der Bettler belästigt oft. Man darf sich aber ja nicht von dem ersten unangenehmen Eindruck bestimmen lassen. Was den Bettler dreist macht, ist gerade das Beste an ihm. (Köln 3: 248/9)

This "best" is the courage of the poor woman to articulate; to use one's own voice means to step into public life. When the socially disadvantaged beg, they become for Brentano-von Arnim advocates of their own cases. But the woman does not ask for herself, she asks for her children. Love motivates her actions. She acts out of the same emotion that motivated the grandmother's actions in relation to her grandchildren. This love is the source of life and the central power in all of Brentano-von Arnim's works. As Böttger explains:

As a new higher principle, which was not made by governments and courts, but is something absolute, love is the order of the day with its ability to be empathetic toward everything living. It works, as Bettine believes, as a revolutionary power, which will change the social structure of Prussia, Germany, even Europe.

Als neues höheres Prinzip, das nicht von Regierungen und Gerichten gemacht wurde, sondern etwas Absolutes ist, steht die Liebe auf der Tagesordnung mit ihrem Einfühlungsvermögen in alles Lebendige. Sie wirkt, wie Bettine meint, als revolutionäre Kraft, die die Gesellschaftsstruktur Preußens, Deutschlands, ja Europas verändern wird. (Böttger 292)

Bettina Brentano-von Arnim's socio-political views in this story—the concept of self-help, for example, and the right of the poor to participate in the common wealth of society—were already formulated in *The King's Book* as well as in other manuscripts in the *Poor Book* project. Research has pointed out repeatedly that many of her socially critical views were based on her perpetuation of ideas from the Enlightenment and Early Romanticism into the Vormärz. Brentano-von Arnim renews in her own way "the poetic conception of the Heidelberg Romantic school within the Vormärz movement" (die Poesiekonzeption der Heidelberger Romantik im Vormärz) (Härtl, "Romantikerin" 33). *The Boy's Magic Horn* (Des Knaben Wunderhorn) (1805/1808), the lieder-collection of her brother Clemens Brentano and his friend Achim von Arnim, was the characteristic work of the late Romantic period of Heidelberg. There individual and folk poetry combine, just as life and poetry finally seem one and the same to these poets (Härtl, "Romantikerin" 29). Brentano-von Arnim's story shows these relations. The invention of the fairy tale-like "lucky purse," a pouch "in which money (like the famous hedge-penny) is constantly renewed, as often as it is given out on great occasions" (worin das Geld gleich jenem berühmten Heckpfennig sich immer wieder erneut, so oft es auch bei erheblichen Anlässen verausgabt wird) (Heckebeutel 498), gives the "true" report a Romantic aura.[6]

In this context the references of the author to Brentano's "Kasperl and Annerl" can be discussed. In addition to the Romantic character of this most well-known of Brentano's novellas, with its influences and source materials from folk songs, chronicles, and sagas, which the poet reworked towards the "construction of a seemingly naive folk-like tone of voice" (Konstruktion eines scheinbar naiven Volkstons) (Frühwald, "Volkston" 270), a basic social content to this magical, fairy tale-like story has now become apparent.[7] For the figure of the old woman herself, who belongs to the stock of figures in Romantic poetry, no evidence in the sources can be found. Even so her function as storyteller is reminiscent of the mother of Luise Hensel, who is supposed to have related to Brentano the stories of the soldier and the child murderer (Kluge, *Materialien* 63, 143).

3.

In Brentano's and in Brentano-von Arnim's stories the figure of the single-minded, strong-willed woman is the focus. She is presented in Brentano's novella in the following manner: "An old peasant woman sat on the stairs. . . . There was something very strange, even grand about the way the good old woman knew so well what she wanted" (Eine alte Bäuerin saß auf der Treppe. . . . Es hatte etwas sehr befremdendes, ja schier großes, wie die gute alte Frau so sehr wußte, was sie wollte) (Brentano 19: 401). Her quiet, ceremonious appearance is described, the "mysteriously deep . . . and earnest . . . voice" (wunderlich tiefe . . . und ernste . . . Stimme) (19: 402), "that certain, earnest tone, her security in life" (ihr bestimmter ernster Ton, ihre Sicherheit im Leben) (19: 403). She is eighty-eight years old, she relates. In her view the duke should not disrespect her since three of her sons died in his service and even her only grandson (Kasperl, as we find out) just bid his farewell (in a double sense, from the duke's services and from life altogether). It soon becomes clear that life no longer means anything to the old peasant woman, she has already prepared herself for death. Consequently she is fighting, as the plot develops not for a reprieve for her godchild, Annerl, but for Annerl's honorable grave in preparation of judgment day. The life preceding death appears meaningless to her. She sees it as a chain of repetitions, which can no longer surprise her (Kluge, *Materialien* 102). The old woman's compass is her belief. She guides herself throughout life with the sentence: "Honor God alone" (Gieb [sic] Gott allein die Ehre) (19: 409).

The many interpretations of this text agree on one point: the old peasant woman is in the center of the narration.[8] "She is the only one who does not owe her existence to the story, but comes from farther away" (Sie ist die einzige, die nicht von Gnaden der Geschichte lebt, sondern von weiter herkommt), writes Alewyn (107). The grandmother comes from a different world. She is a genuinely Romantic figure: old people and old things are recurring motifs in Romanticism, signifying a mysterious depth of time. Her magic world might represent the motherly safety Brentano was looking for all his life, in the faith of the common people and in folk songs, and later in life in the return to his childhood church (Alewyn 112). This peasant grandmother has a mythic character and she is the source of narration and speech. For a long time, the narrator is merely repeating to us what the old woman has told him in trust; he tries to alter the narrative only by stepping into the action of the story near its end. Still he cannot change Annerl's destiny and death but the grandmother achieves her goal seemingly without effort. For the first-person narrator the grandmother is an expression of the strength of the people, which he obviously admires. At the same time, however, he vacillates as to whether or not the traditional values are the correct ones, for he also sees their social relativity expressing itself in the social differences within the story. Thus the question of proper proportion in life in general remains (Kluge, "Perspektivismus" 162). It is important, however, that the old peasant woman dies in the arms of the poet at the end. With her death, the story line ends. What remains is an afterword, a report on the static circumstances, and perhaps still a call for help from a "life yearning for release" (nach Erlösung sich sehnenden Lebens) (Alewyn 137).

Brentano-von Arnim begins her story with what would seem to be the same grandmother that appeared in Brentano's "Kasperl." Particular phrases have the effect of transformed quotations: an old woman comes to her door,

great as those chosen women of Germany who have done their part for
the Prussian Grenadier-regiments. That I did, the old woman said; I
am the mother of three big strong Grenadiers, and I had another son,
but he did not grow to be very big.

groß wie jene auserlesnen Frauen Deutschlands welche zu den Preus-
sischen Grenadier-Regimentern das ihre gethan haben. Das hab ich
auch, sagt die alte Frau; von drei mächtig großen Grenadieren bin ich
die Mutter, und noch einen Sohn hatte ich, der war aber nicht groß
gewachsen. (Heckebeutel 498)

However as the old woman tells the story of her life we discover
that her three sons have died not for an unnamed duke, but for
Prussia. This reference clarifies from the start that we are not about
to hear a Romantic fairy tale but a narrative that points to grim
historical reality. This woman is "great" (groß) not only in the physical sense, but in the spiritual sense, like Brentano's female figure. She
too wants to carry out a final battle. Moreover, alluding to Novalis
and the Early Romantic tradition, "desiring greatness" (groß sein
wollen) is the task of every human being, for every human being is
born towards the ideal (Härtl, "Romantikerin" 31). Consistent with
this idea, Bettina Brentano-von Arnim sees this potential not only in
poetic genius but also in the character of her old woman.

However, Brentano-von Arnim's character takes a different path
from Kasperl's grandmother from the very beginning: she focuses on
life, not death. Her story about her children and grandchildren are
reports that portray the suffering of this family and every poor family
during the coalition wars against France and under the politics of the
Prussian aristocracy. A crass light falls on the effects of military mod-
ernization: the conscription of troops and the maintenance of the
soldiers occur through an exploitation of the people. Neither personal
misbehavior nor demonic powers are responsible, as in Brentano's
narrative, but solely the political and social circumstances. They
alone lead to the death of husbands, brothers, children, and grandchildren. Here again Brentano-von Arnim's story combines the motifs of
Romanticism with the social reality of Vormärz. The alms which the
narrator and Count Grossinger throw into the lap of Kasperl's grandmother become the gold pieces of the lucky purse, which Brentano-
von Arnim's old woman knows how to get for herself.

Wolf Kittler assigns a special significance to these gold pieces. For one taler the poet-narrator, in one sense, buys the rights of the story from the grandmother:

> Like the songs from the Boy's Magic Horn he is going to sell it as poetry. Thus the Romantic poet appears not as the producer of what he publishes. Rather, it is the truth when he calls himself a stenographer. This is what he is in a literal sense: stenographer of poetic discourse, which the people, in the shape of women, produce.

> Wie die Lieder aus des Knaben Wunderhorn wird er sie als Poesie verkaufen. So erscheint der romantische Dichter nicht als Produzent dessen, was er publiziert. Es ist vielmehr die Wahrheit, wenn er sich einen Schreiber nennt. Er ist es im buchstäblichen Sinn: Aufschreiber des poetischen Diskurses, den das Volk in Gestalt von Frauen produziert. (Kittler 236)

The narrator reveals that the women in this story are seduced victims of men, but he himself changes nothing about this situation; even he exploits the grandmother's speech (Kittler 236–237). Brentano-von Arnim's old tradeswoman does *not* allow the rights to her discourse to be bought; on the contrary, she produces it in order to keep her grandchildren alive with the earnings herself. Ironically the narrator of this story turns into eloquence what the rich call begging.

Narrating itself becomes a topic when the joy of the old woman about her strength of intellect is repeated as a leitmotif throughout the story. This gift of "eloquence" (Beredsamkeit) is the poetic discourse of the old woman. On another level, it is the same gift which Frau Rat Goethe develops in *The King's Book*. Indeed, eloquence represents the basic strategy of Brentano-von Arnim's poetics in her socio-political letters and writings. Her narrator-persona Frau von Arnim relates episodes, allows the old woman to narrate until "the I (Bettine's) breaks through in the text" (das Ich [Bettines] im Text durchbricht) (Drewitz 225) and Brentano-von Arnim herself interprets the old woman as the mother of the people in her commentary, mythologizing what has been experienced.

The old woman, who attempts, by using her own powers, with "superhuman, unbroken optimism" (übermenschlichen ungebrochenen Zuversicht) (Heckebeutel 509) to work her way out of her misfortune and to secure a future for her grandchildren, becomes a heroine.

This woman, *old as a stone* , had attempted the impossible, in order to secure an independent existence, in her ninetieth year, by means of her own abilities. That these were not enough, was to be expected. If, however, an old warrior, winner of many victories, finally steps into a last duel and cannot help using the weapons himself, even if he should lose; he is still the greater hero!

Die *Steinalte*, hatte das Unmögliche versucht um im 90sten Jahr noch mit eignen Kräften eine unabhängige Existenz zu erwerben, diese langten nicht aus, das war voraus zu sehen. Wenn aber ein alter Krieger der vielen Siegen voran stritt, endlich noch in eine lezte [*sic*] Fehde verwickelt, selbst die Waffen zu führen sich nicht enthalten kann; sollte er auch unterliegen; so ist er dennoch der größere Held! (Heckebeutel 508)

That it can only be a woman who saves the future generations, that Brentano-von Arnim places her higher than the heroes of the battle-fields, gives this myth a matriarchal component. Courage, optimism, and future orientation, her own positions, are also the attributes of this woman, old as stone. The old woman is aware of the sacrifice she makes for the king. Her honor is her self-respect and dignity, the pride of the people in their own strength. Her piety is the belief in the good in all human beings. The help of God is self-help, for God helps those who are clever enough to understand his subtle direction (Heckebeutel 507). Brentano-von Arnim transforms these concepts from her brother's novella and gives them a strong social significance.

The great old woman, the most obvious parallel to the "Story of Good Kasperl and Beautiful Annerl," however, is a figure shaped by the author's own creativity. Together with the historical personages of Goethe, her brother Clemens, and the poetess Karoline von Günderrode, this simple, clever, and practical old woman represents one of the most influential figures in Brentano-von Arnim's writing. She appears in the epistolary novel *Günderode* (1840) as the "Grandmama" of Bettine, the writer Sophie von La Roche; there and in *The King's Book* as the mother of Goethe, Frau Rat Goethe, and as mythical Sibylle; and in many other figures, such as a milk woman, a widow, an aged woman. Old people, particularly old women, play a central role in the work of Bettina Brentano-von Arnim; they give, receive, and educate life, they retain in narration and in memory both human values and the past; they connect past and future (Hoock-Demarle, "Frau und Stadt" 56).

The author closes her book *Günderode* with an impressive report about the Jew Ephraim. Here, too, we see a worthy old figure, who takes care of the grandchildren. As a symbol of eternal, spiritual youth, his beauty is similar to the beauty of the herbalist from the "Tale of the Lucky Purse." Brentano-von Arnim writes: "I know nothing anymore about getting old, fading, since I looked at this man" and "I thirst for the blessing of old people, ever since I learned about death; so it seems to me the last period of a person's life is something holy" (ich weiß nichts mehr von Veralten, Verwelken, seit ich diesen Mann angeschaut hab) (Weimar 2: 294) and (mich durstet nach dem Segen alter Leute, seitdem ich vom Tod weiß, so deucht mir die letzte Lebenszeit eines Menschen etwas Heiliges) (Weimar 2: 323–324).

This transfigured view of age stands in contrast with Brentano-von Arnim's social observations on the powers of resistance, especially in the women of the people. In *The King's Book* the mayor of Frankfurt reports on the plundering of the arsenal during the invasion of the "redcoats." A dreadful old woman, "the depth of decay, the scum of humanity" (der Abgrund des Verderbens, der Schlamm der Menschheit) (Köln 3: 144) had grinned at him from underneath a stolen saddle that protected her from the rain. Frau Rat Goethe takes upon herself the defense of the demoralized woman:

> What is the German's fatherland? Not Pommerania, not Swabia; it is the country of old women! . . . . There are old cats that strangle their young and the horrible old woman, who jeered at the worthy civil servant from under the saddle is truly a prophetic image. . . . The old women are an abomination to you; you'd like to drown their insolent grinning from their faces, and if an opportunity arose, you wouldn't hesitate.—Who are these old women?—They are the ones whose sons, whose husbands became cannon-fodder in war, or came home as cripples! They are the ones who have become a pack of thieves in order to feed their families. That was welcome satisfaction for their provoked revenge, malice and deception!

> Was ist des Deutschen Vaterland? Nicht Pommerland, nicht Schwabenland; es ist das Alteweiberland! . . . . Es gibt so alte Kater, die ihre Jungen würgen, und die schauderhafte Alte, die unterm Sattel hervor die würdigen Beamten so verhöhnte, ist wahrhaft ein prophetischer Anblick. . . . Die alten Weiber sind Euch ein Greuel; ihr freches Angrinsen möchtet ihr ihnen eintränken, sowie sich Gelegenheit dazu findet, werdet ihr nicht säumen.—Wer sind diese alten Weiber?—Es

sind die, deren Söhne, deren Männer im Krieg Kanonenfutter wurden,
oder als Krüppel heimkamen! sie sind Raubgesindel geworden, die
ihrigen zu ernähren, das war ihrer erregten Rache, Bosheit und Tücke
willkommne Genugtuung! (Köln 3: 144–145)

It is an old woman like this from the "dregs of the people" (Hefe des
Volks) (Köln 3: 144) who comes to the author's door. But in a marve-
lous transformation of perspective, a frightening and threatening market woman becomes the figure of a great old woman with inalienable
human dignity: "how contented she now went with the basket on her
back under her own roof, completely without effort, the umbrella was
fastened to the basket" (wie vergnügt ging sie nun mit der Kiepe auf
dem Rücken unter ihrem eignen Dach, ganz ohne Mühe, der Schirm
war an der Kiepe befestigt) (Heckebeutel 506). The symbol of the
roof has been taken from *The King's Book*; in place of the saddle, the
tradeswoman uses an umbrella to protect herself from the rain.
Brentano-von Arnim demonstrates here in a very concrete way that
these women are responsible even for the roofs over their own heads.

4.

A comparison of the narrative structure of the "Tale of the Lucky
Purse" and the "Kasperl" story shows some parallels on a formal
level. Both texts have been given a story-within-a-story structure,
each however with a different function. Brentano-von Arnim introduces the institution of the money-purse for the poor and creates as
narrative motivation the connection to her aristocratic public. In both
texts we find two narrators: in Brentano-von Arnim's tale the old
herbalist and Bettina-as-herself, and in Brentano's story the grandmother and the poet-narrator, who shows some distant resemblance
to the author, Clemens.

In the "Story of Good Kasperl and Beautiful Annerl" two stories-
within-a-story are contrasted to the whole. A symbology is created by
constant repetition of certain words and motifs: destiny, honor, the
grace of God, a folk song, the coin, the rose, the veil. All these
elements refer to a knowledge which is God's. The symbolic, magic-
divine order created in this way appears to regulate the life of the
characters. To be sure, the author adds several levels of meaning to
this apparently closed system by constantly changing the meaning of

the central theme of "honor," and this frustrates its closure. He ends his story with the scene at the grave, which eternalizes the symbolic order of things in stone, and still, in its artificiality, also questions this very order. The different perspectives of both narrators, grandmother and poet, contribute to the fragmentary and indirect narration.[9] The structure of this novella is artistically construed. The constant repetition of things "as self-citation" allows them, as Kluge explains, to become ever more meaningful and increases thereby the artistic character to the level of the aesthetic perfection of an "artistic construction closed in itself, sealed on all sides almost hermetically" (in sich geschlosse[n], nach allen Seiten hin abgedichtete[n], fast hermetische[n] Kunstgebilde[s]) (102–103).

In the "Tale of the Lucky Purse" the story-within-a-story and the overall narrative are mutually interdependent. The author as "Frau Brentano-von Arnim" relates to both, interweaves both, and remains within the dialogue, with the old woman, who also speaks; with the prince as the donor; and with the readers as the actual public. In a swift change of perspective, the "I" of the old woman and the "I" of the narrator alternate with each other. In the earlier version, the old woman herself intervenes in the communication with the royal house: "Oh, write the Prince of Prussia that he can depend on my honor" (Ach schreiben sie doch dem Prinzen von Preußen, daß er sich auf meine Ehre verlassen kann) (Heckebeutel 516), but the author-narrator takes over this task herself in the later version by means of her great, penetrating commentary, which addresses itself not only to Waldemar, but also in the final passage to the rich and powerful in general, to those "lords of the world" (Herren der Welt) who surround themselves with hypocrites, philistines, and opportunistic civil servants. Brentano-von Arnim claims that the old woman is right in pursuing her goal and, turning to the reader, she asks to honor the woman's sincere efforts:

No one should think the wrong thing here, as if she hadn't had the earnest will to do what she proposed. . . . A princely state of mind will not give room to a slanderous opinion, or believe the bad, where it can presume the good.

Keiner denke hier das Falsche, als habe sie nicht den ernsten Willen gehabt zu dem Vorhaben. . . . Eine fürstliche Gesinnung wird keiner verläumderischen [sic] Ansicht Raum geben, noch das Böse glauben, wo sie das Gute vorraussetzen darf. (Heckebeutel 509)

Here it becomes clear in the structure, how Brentano-von Arnim connects her personal experiences—her meeting with the old herb-seller—with her socio-political concerns. Six episodes, meetings with the old woman, are reported, which each time reach their climax in a loan from the lucky purse. An intensification is provided by the project with the dogcart, the result of which remains open. How the story will end for the old woman is not important, really; the author is pursuing another aim. The process counts, not the result. This episodic narration makes clear that the important concern is a stylistically good text, but not a closed artistic artifact.

Brentano-von Arnim's way of writing exists within the context of the style of journalism, influenced by Heine, and emerging in the Vormärz, a journalism which develops "society-forming power" ("gesellschaftsbildende Kraft") (Drewitz 188). Meier notes that in this context her distance to Romanticism becomes clear. While the Romantic fairy tales want to allow "a more actual being" (ein eigentlicheres Sein) behind reality to shine through, the fairy-tale-like in Brentano-von Arnim, as in Heine, serves to throw a socially critical light on reality itself (Meier 446). The author's intent is social communication.

There are obvious differences between the two texts, not only in structure, but also in the way time is used in the narration. While the story of Kasperl is traditionally categorized as a novella on the basis of its temporal closure, Brentano-von Arnim's tale presents itself to us as a text held open in its narrative time, a report without an end. Kasperl's and Annerl's stories come together out of the past into the narrative time of the present in one night. The plot begins slowly, increases in its pace, continues at an even faster rate, becomes concentrated in order to end after its climax (Annerl's execution in the early morning) almost contemplatively. In contrast, Brentano-von Arnim begins her narrative at an apparently arbitrary time: "For example: an old woman comes to my door" (Zum Beispiel: Eine alte Frau kommt an meine Thüre) (Heckebeutel 498) and continues the report loosely over the time period of about six months, from winter through Easter and Whitsuntide until summer. What the old tradeswoman relates grows into an image of her changing life, instead of a real story. Just as the narrative times of the past and the present are not clearly delineated—the dates of Prussian battles are the fixed points in the memory of the old woman—the future is also open in the narrative. Where Brentano places a demonstratively excessive ending with the bizarre and artificial tableau of the monument, Brentano-von Arnim's text ends where it actually should have begun, that is, with the information about the use of the goldpieces from the Prussian royal house. Life is a process, a "continual becoming of the future" (fortwährendes Werden der Zukunft) (Köln 3: 184).[10] In spite of the obvious futility of the old woman's undertaking, Bettina Brentano-von Arnim is hopeful that this is the way by which the people could achieve independence, if the state were to make some compromises.

The "Tale of the Lucky Purse" is seen as an attempt to rework the intentions of the *Poor Book* in a literary manner. Vordtriede formulates the thesis that this project of Brentano-von Arnim's, in which she wanted to educate the Prince outside the context of self-portrayal, is atypical of her. Whether this contradiction could have been the reason that the *Poor Book* project was never finished, remains to be discussed. Waldstein argues convincingly that Brentano-von Arnim's dialogic way of writing stood in contrast to the overwhelming concern of the *Poor Book*, which is to defend an objectified standpoint:

> In the process of writing and revising, she was ultimately unable to write herself out of the text. Moreover, she was not able to eliminate the voice of the poor in an analysis of them. With the material she had, Bettine [*sic*] von Arnim could not create a conversational genre that combined the political and the personal in such a way as to reflect authentically the situation of the underclass. (90)

While this may be an accurate description of the project on the whole, she was nevertheless successful, in my opinion, in her conception of the poor tale. She integrated herself in the narrative as an "I," not as the Bettine figure of her epistolary novels, but in the person of the Berliner Frau von Arnim, and entered into a dialogue with the voice of the poor. However, the main emphasis of the text remains her concern to portray the mythic-realistic old woman as emblematic of the primal power of the people upon whom the king is dependent. Brentano-von Arnim proposes a maternal figure in contrast to that of Brentano's. Both are narrators, voices of the people. But the peasant grandmother, oriented to the fact of death, is turned into a "Sybille" [*sic*], a prophetess of life. A yearning for life replaces a yearning for death.

As we have seen, Brentano-von Arnim's story is closely linked with the theme and the material of *The King's Book*. Her references to the novella of her brother appear as transformed quotations on a level of language and motif, which she integrates into her text in Late-Romantic fashion, in order to change their significance.

5.

Clemens Brentano and his sister Bettina were not only very close in their youth, but they later inspired each other with ideas about art and literature. Ever since Joseph von Eichendorff's essay "Brentano and his fairy tales" (Brentano und seine Märchen) (1847) the similarities and differences between brother and sister have been discussed in the secondary literature.[11] What differentiates the later Bettina Brentano-von Arnim in her method of writing from her "twin-like talented brother" (zwillingsgleich begabten Bruder)?

Bettina Brentano first met her seven-year-older brother Clemens, who had been raised by an aunt, in 1797. From 1800 on they turned to each other. This relationship lasted, with varying intensity, until Brentano's return to the Catholic church in 1816/1817. It proved to be of deep emotional significance for both of them, as can be seen in the surviving parts of their correspondence as well as in comments on the missing letters. About the lost original correspondence between brother and sister, which formed the basis of Brentano-von Arnim's *The Spring Wreath*, the catalog of the Wiepersdorf Auction states in 1929:

> the . . . letters of the brother and sister . . . give evidence that Bettine was to a certain extent the religion of the religion-thirsty Clemens, until he himself returned . . . to the lap of the Catholic Church. . . . The . . . correspondence leaves the impression that Clemens was the receptive, Bettine the giving one.

> die . . . Briefe der Geschwister . . . geben Zeugnis davon, daß Bettine gewissermaßen die Religion des immer religionsdurstigen Clemens war, bis er selbst in den Schoß der katholischen Kirche . . . zurück-kehrte. . . . Der . . . Briefwechsel hinterläßt den Eindruck, daß Clemens der Empfangende, Bettine die Gebende war. (qtd. in Gajek 172)

These sentences strengthen the impression that there was a strong emotional and intellectual influence of Bettina upon Clemens for many years, besides the well-known poetic influence which the Romantic poet Brentano had on the young Bettina (Böttger 42–51). Brother and sister worked together on some of Brentano's early texts (Riley 24). Later Bettina contributed to *The Boy's Magic Horn*, the edition of old and new lyric folk songs, which her brother and his friend Achim von Arnim, her future husband, published together (Böttger 58).

In the images of Brentano and of herself which she created in the *The Spring Wreath* from these letters of the years 1801–1803, she reinvented how she communicated to Clemens in an exchange of ideas, idealism, imagination, and emotional security; how she defended herself against his teaching attempts with irony and banter; and how she finally convinced him to respect her intellectual autonomy. Here it becomes quite clear what differences Brentano-von Arnim saw between herself and her brother in their conception of art. Out of the Romantic yearning for harmony in nature and in spirit, life, and art, there remains for the character Clemens sadness over his inner confusion of mind and disharmony. Where Clemens does not succeed in embedding art into life, where art becomes something deadly, the character Bettine oversteps the boundary between art and life, and brings herself into the field of this magic power. Bettina Brentano-von Arnim's aestheticism is sensual. Love and the vitality of life impart to this aestheticism a positive energy which conquers everything. For this reason it is understandable that Clemens Brentano's novella appears as a closed, but inwardly dissonant work of art, torn from the life of the poet, while Bettina Brentano-von Arnim's story presents itself as open, dialogic, and related to action. Its author refused to become a poetess in Brentano's sense, because she did not want to recognize this separation.

The method of integrating suggestions of others into one's own texts and reworking them into something new, is not only an element of the Romantic method of writing in general, but one particularly practiced by Clemens Brentano. Helene Kastinger Riley gives this method its own name—Brentano's "contamination style" (Kontaminationsstil) (20). Beside the conscious mutual inclusion of others' ideas in "fraternal working method" (fraternaler Arbeitsweise) Riley sees the existence of a subtler, psychological variant: Brentano attempted to achieve in the creative combination of ideas an indissoluble mental-spiritual union with his (female) partner. It appears, however, that he knew how to maintain his own dominance, when he tried to transform his beloved into her "true essence" (wahres Wesen) and to integrate into his work what was spiritually her own (Riley 24).

Brentano-von Arnim took up this Romantic principle of combination from early in her youth as the point of departure for her own work. She rejected the confessional religiosity of her aging brother. For this reason she created an image of the young poetic Clemens in the *The Spring Wreath* in opposition to her conservative family, which was more concerned after Brentano's death to repress his early work.[12] She included a number of at-that-time unknown poems of Brentano's and continued work on some of his drafts.[13] The motif quotations in the "Tale of the Lucky Purse" are thus highly considered choices. Consciously and openly she includes elements of the "Kasperl" novella and reworks them anew. On the linguistic level, she concerns herself intensely with Brentano's imagistic language, as Frühwald has shown, and turns it into a social one (Frühwald, "Weber" 278). This confrontation is only one aspect of this text, but an important one. In its content and form she pursues her own political vision and her own aesthetics, which, despite many commonalities, differentiate themselves strikingly from the views of her brother.

The author pleads rigorously for the independence of women. She combines in this "central piece" (Kernstück) (Härtl, "Armenbuch" 132) of her prose for the *Poor Book* socio-political engagement and female perspective.[14] In her poor story she takes on a special, personal relationship to this old mother of the people. This relationship arises not through identification, but through the production of an affinity, which includes both proximity and difference.[15] In dialogue and commentary their two voices are intermixed, yet heard as distinct from each other at the same time. The old woman is not an object of Brentano-von Arnim's socio-political interest or the producer of a story; she is the subject: *She* initiates the relationship with the narrator and motivates the report by means of her actions and plans. Although Frau von Arnim raises herself above the old woman's incapacity with Romantic irony, seeing that her objective in "the continual circulation of hope and failure" (ständigen Kreislauf[. . .] von Hoffnung und Scheitern) (Meier 446) will never be reached, there remains in this contradiction the affinity between the two women. For Brentano-von Arnim the old woman is still right despite her mistake to recognize the futility of her endeavor.

The "Tale of the Lucky Purse" was interpreted in close relationship to Brentano's novella. Ingeborg Drewitz had already pointed to the general validity of the Romantic fairy tale motif in the story in 1969, but without generating any further discussion (224). "How Brentano-like this story is" Vordtriede had argued

> This old, single-minded woman, who comes to the city from the country, we know in a different form as the grandmother in Clemens Brentano's "Good Kasperl and Beautiful Annerl." Thus here in Brentano's circle, reality has imitated Brentano's art.

> Diese alte unbeirrte Frau, die aus dem Lande in die Stadt kommt, kennen wir ja in anderer Gestalt als die Großmutter in Clemens Brentanos 'Bravem Kasperl und schönen Annerl.' So hat hier in Brentanoschem Umkreis die Wirklichkeit die Brentanosche Kunst nachgeahmt. (518)

Following Vordtriede, who had suggested this connection, Gerhard Kluge added the text in 1979 to his comprehensive edition of commentary and background material for the "Story of Good Kasperl and Beautiful Annerl." He considered the "ninety-year-old woman drawn 'exactly according to reality' . . . to be unthinkable without the model of the grandmother from Brentano's 'Story . . . .' " ('genau nach der Wahrheit' gezeichnete alte neunzigjährige Frau . . . ohne das Vorbild der Großmutter aus Brentanos 'Geschichte . . . ' [für] undenkbar) (Kluge, *Materialien* 153). In his socio-historical analysis of the *Poor Book* in 1985, Wolfgang Frühwald even saw the text as a linguistic "contrafact" (Kontrafaktur):

> In the *little poor story* about the gold pieces in the lucky purse, she wrote a contrafact to Clemens Brentano's "Story of Good Kasperl and Beautiful Annerl" and made the figure of the old woman, *who was as great as those select women of Germany who had done their part for the Prussian Grenadier regiments*, a symbol of the poor in Prussia.

> In der *kleinen Armengeschichte* von den Goldstücken im Heckebeutel schrieb sie eine Kontrafaktur zu Clemens Brentanos *Geschichte vom braven Kasperl und dem schönen Annerl* und machte die Gestalt der alten Frau, *groß wie jene auserlesenen Frauen Deutschlands welche zu den preußischen Grenadierregimentern das ihre gethan*, zur Symbolfigur der Armen in Preußen. (278–279)

Brentano-von Arnim's "Tale of the Lucky Purse" was completely overshadowed by her brother's; the text seemed to its first critics to be little more than an imitation. Bettina Brentano-von Arnim's narrative of the great mother of the people does not, however, in my opinion, fulfill the requirements of a "contrafact." In contrafact, the adaption of a written source for one's own argumentative intentions, the source remains the dominant constructive factor (Verweyen/Witting 28, 49). Brentano-von Arnim, however, creates, as we have seen, a completely different prose in form and content, in which motifs from Brentano's novella are woven together in the sense of a contamination with material from other works. The fairy tale of the poor is "Brentano-like" only at first sight; under the scrutiny of a closer reading, it is evident how very much this story arises from Brentano-von Arnim's own work.

Recently Böttger has suggested a common significance for the figure of the grandmother in Brentano's novella and Frau Rat Goethe in *The King's Book* as two symbolic figures which point to Classic-Romantic notions of matriarchy (285). Similarly, Marie-Claire Hoock-Demarle points to the dominance of the figure of the old woman in Brentano-von Arnim's prose even before Brentano-von Arnim began to confront the work of Brentano.

As yet the only commentary I have found on the "Tale of the Lucky Purse" that is not completely overshadowed by Brentano's novella was written by Albert Meier. Here the structure as well as the socio-historical context is examined. But Meier's final judgment, that this text expresses a tendency to resignation, does not find my complete agreement. Brentano-von Arnim combines her socially critical accusation against the inhuman circumstances of the time with the portrayal of a matriarch who transcends this historical situation in her contradictions and in her strength.

In my opinion, the "Tale of the Lucky Purse" has been undervalued. Points of intersection between Brentano and Brentano-von Arnim ought not to be seen automatically as the sister's appropriation of the 'poetic genius' of her brother. That Bettina Brentano-von Arnim created her own work, which is not to be measured by that of Clemens Brentano, can no longer be overlooked. Christa Wolf's famous question from her Bettina letter of 1980 has, to be sure, not lost its validity:

> Couldn't it be, I ask myself and you, that the often, sometimes even hypocritically deplored lack of feminine artistic "genius" has to do not only with the living circumstances of women but also with their inability to fit themselves to an image of the genius tailored to men?

Könnte nicht, frage ich mich und Sie, der öfter, manchmal auch
heuchlerisch beklagte Mangel an weiblichen Kunst-'Genies' außer mit
den Lebensumständen der Frauen auch mit ihrer Untauglichkeit zusam-
menhängen, sich dem auf den Mann zugeschnittenen Geniebild einzu-
passen? (Wolf 608)

Notes

This chapter was translated from the German by Patrick McGrath.

1. The original version of this article was written for the seminar "Novella
   and Short Prose" at the University of Maryland 1985 (conducted by Elke
   Frederiksen).
2. Among the materials she collected were reports, statements, and lists of
   poor people. These papers document the mass pauperization in Berlin's
   working-class suburb, Vogtland, and among the Silesian cottonweavers.
   Since the beginnning of the century tremendous population growth,
   agricultural crises, epidemics, and growing industrial competition had
   triggered the rapidly worsening deterioration of a proletariat of ever-
   increasing numbers.
3. An overproduction crisis in the textile industries in 1844 left cotton
   spinners' and weavers' families on the verge of starvation. On June 4,
   1844, the weavers revolted, only to be suppressed by Prussian troops on
   June 6.
4. I refer to the story as "Heckebeutel." Werner Vordtriede's comments are
   quoted as "Vordtriede." A synopsis of two basic versions and two variations of the closing passages are to be found on pp. 497–517. Unless noted
   differently as "Heckebeutel[1]," my analysis refers to the second version
   and to the "fair copy of the ending." Vortriede's article was reprinted in a
   revised form in 1969 and again in an expanded form in 1981 by the Insel
   Publishing Company. Only in these editions was the title of Brentano-von
   Arnim's story added. Under the title "The Lucky Purse" (Der Heckebeutel), and with the addition of a commentary, the story was reprinted
   yet again in 1985 in *Meistererzählungen der deutschen Romantik* , ed. by
   Albert Meier et al., (München: Deutscher Taschenbuch Verlag) 329–338.
   Brentano-von Arnim's story, according to the date beneath the last variation, was not finished before June 1845. It is open to question whether the
   story fits into her original plan for the *Armenbuch*. In fact, any of the

collected papers may or may not have been included in a finished edition of the book never published. A reconstruction and critical edition of the *Armenbuch* has yet to be accomplished. The status of Brentano-von Arnim's "Tale of the Lucky Purse" will have to be discussed in this context. (See Schultz 224–233, and Härtl, "Armenbuch.")

5. The manuscripts of the *Armenbuch* published by Vordtriede and an additional eleven lists and reports concerning the status of the poor are among the literary estate papers of Bettina Brentano-von Arnim in the Freies Deutsches Hochstift in Frankfurt am Main. Further documents are to be found in Karl August Varnhagen von Ense's papers in der Biblioteka Jagiellońska in Kraków, in the Stiftung Weimarer Klassik in Weimar, in the Central State Archives in Potsdam, and in various other archives. Approximately seventeen sheets which were printed in 1844 are supposed to have been lost. (See Härtl, "Armenbuch" 128.)

6. Grimm's dictionary points out that these Romantic-ironic fairy tale motifs were widely used by authors from Musäus to Jean Paul. Grimm/Grimm, columns 744–749.

7. Frühwald and Kluge comment on Brentano's stand for reform in the army, on his discussion of the different roles of authors in Germany and France, and on the death penalty for child murder, which was controversial amongst contemporaries (Frühwald, "Ehre" 74–80; Brentano 19: 828–833, 840). Riley stresses Clemens Brentano's political interests and engagements, which have often been denied (Riley 102,105). Heinz Rölleke und Gerhard Kluge have collected a multitude of sources concerning Brentano's novella. (See Rölleke, Kluge, Materialien, and Kluge's commentary in Brentano 19: 801–842.)

8. Bibliography see Riley 106–107. Here I would like to follow the conclusions of Alewyn, Frühwald, Kluge, and Kittler.

9. See Alewyn 113–114; Kluge 105.

10. This thought can already be found in the last chapter of Brentano-von Arnim's epistolary novel *Die Günderode*. In a great symbolic closing act the narrator Bettine tells about Ephraim, her old Jewish mathematics teacher, about the blooming rosebush he presented her, and, turning to the Vormärz, about the young and politically hopeful students. "As I left Ephraim he placed his hand on my head and said: 'All becoming is for the future (Als ich wegging von Ephraim, legte er mir die Hand auf den Kopf und sagte: 'Alles Werden ist für die Zukunft') (Weimar 2: 470).

11. See Härtl, Weimar 2: 951; Schmitz, Frankfurt 1: 1033–1035. See also Härtl, Weimar 2: 906–920.

12. For the use of his letters and poems compare the commentaries of the editors in the two most recent Brentano-von Arnim editions: Härtl, Weimar 2: 952–972, and Schmitz, Frankfurt 1: 1014–1022.

13. Härtl explains:

Bettina enclosed in *The Spring Wreath* twenty poems by her brother. No less than seventeen were published here for the first time; many of these are or were at least for a long time known only in the version in which they are printed in Bettina's book. Considering that some of the poems appearing in *The Spring Wreath* were among the most famous poems by Brentano, a fact hardly appreciated up to now becomes evident: the significance of the book as a medium of tradition and popularization of Brentano's poetry. Since some of the poems circulated by *The Spring Wreath* are (probably or obviously) reworked by Bettina, Brentano cannot be seen as their sole author.

Bettina fügte in den "Frühlingskranz" zwanzig Gedichte ihres Bruders ein. Nicht weniger als siebzehn davon wurden zum ersten Mal veröffentlicht, und viele von ihnen sind oder waren doch lange Zeit nur in der Fassung bekannt, in welcher sie in Bettinas Buch stehen. Bedenkt man, daß einige der im "Frühlingskranz" erschienen Gedichte zu den berühmtesten Brentanos gehören, so wird die noch kaum angemessen gewürdigte Bedeutung des Buches als Medium der berlieferung und Popularisierung Brentanoscher Lyrik evident. Einige der durch den "Frühlingskranz" verbreiteten Gedichte sind auf Grund der (mutmaßlichen oder nachweisbaren) berarbeitungen Bettinas kaum eindeutig Brentano als alleinigem Verfasser zuzuweisen. (Weimar 2: 962)

14. Three trends coexist in contemporary research. Each seems to examine a different Bettina Brentano-von Arnim: the eccentric Romantic, the political author of the Vormärz, and the author of a feminist poetics. Nevertheless we can demonstrate in our story, which used to be attributed to the political Brentano-von Arnim, that Romantic, political, and feminist aspects are interconnected as inseparable parts of Brentano-von Arnim's oeuvre.

15. On the term "affinity" in a feminist theory of reading see Patrocinio P. Schweickart 54.

Works Cited

Alewyn, Richard. "Brentanos 'Geschichte vom braven Kasperl und dem schönen Annerl'." *Deutsche Erzählungen von Wieland bis Kafka*. Ed. Jost Schillemeit. Frankfurt am Main, Hamburg: Fischer, 1966. 101–150.

Arnim, Bettina von. "Erzählung vom Heckebeutel." Ed. Werner Vordtriede. *Jahrbuch des Freien Deutschen Hochstifts*. (1962): 497–517. Tübingen: Max Niemeyer Verlag, 1962.

————, *Werke und Briefe*. Vol. 3: *Dies Buch gehört dem König*. Ed. Gustav Konrad. Frechen/Köln: Bartmann-Verlag, 1963. (Referred to as Köln.)

————, *Werke und Briefe in drei Bänden*. Vol. 1: *Clemens Brentanos Frühlingkranz, Die Günderode*. Ed. Walter Schmitz. Frankfurt am Main: Deutscher Klassiker Verlag, 1986.

————, *Werke 2: Clemens Brentanos Frühlingkranz, Die Günderode*. Ed. Heinz Härtl. Berlin and Weimar: Aufbau-Verlag, 1989. (Quotations from *The Spring Wreath* and *Günderode* according to this edition, which is referred to as "Weimar.")

Böttger, Fritz. *Bettina von Arnim. Ein Leben zwischen Tag und Traum*. Berlin: Verlag der Nation, 1986.

Brentano, Clemens. "Geschichte vom braven Kasperl und dem schönen Annerl." *Clemens Brentano. Sämtliche Werke und Briefe*. Vol. 19: *Prosa IV: Erzählungen*. Ed. Gerhard Kluge. Historical-critical edition arranged by Deutsches Hochstift. Stuttgart, Berlin, Köln, Mainz: W. Kohlhammer, 1987. 401–439. Lesarten und Erläuterungen. 801–842. (Referred to as Brentano 19.)

Drewitz, Ingeborg. *Bettine von Arnim. Romantik–Revolution–Utopie*. Düsseldorf: Diederichs, 1969. München: Heyne, 1969. Fourth edition 1982.

Frühwald, Wolfgang. "Die Ehre der Geringen. Ein Versuch zur Sozialgeschichte literarischer Texte im 19. Jahrhundert." *Geschichte und Gesellschaft. Zeitschrift für Historische Sozialwissenschaft*. 9(1983): 69–86.

————. "Die artistische Konstruktion des Volkstons. Zu Clemens Brentanos 'Der Spinnerin Nachtlied'." *Gedichte und Interpretationen*. Vol. 3: *Klassik und Romantik*. Ed. Wulf Segebrecht. Stuttgart: Reclam, 1984. 269–279.

————. "Die Not der schlesischen Weber. Zu Bettine von Arnims Armenbuch 1844." *Herzhaft in die Dornen der Zeit greifen. Bettine von Arnim 1785–1859. Katalog der Bettine-von-Arnim Ausstellung des Freien Deutschen Hochstifts*. Ed. Christoph Perels. Frankfurt am Main: Freies Deutsches Hochstift, Frankfurter Goethemuseum, 1985. 269–280.

Gajek, Bernhard. *Homo poeta. Zur Kontinuität der Problematik bei Clemens Brentano*. Frankfurt am Main: Athenäum, 1971.

Grimm, Jacob and Wilhelm Grimm. *Deutsches Wörterbuch. Vierten Bandes Zweite Abtheilung*. Prepared Moriz Heyne. Leipzig: Verlag von S. Hirzel, 1877.

Härtl, Heinz. "Bettina von Arnim. Romantikerin und Demokratin. Eine Annäherung." *Bettine von Arnim. Romantik und Sozialismus. (1831–1859)*. Trier: Karl-Marx-Haus, 1987. 27–40.

————. "Bettina's 'Armenbuch': Das überlieferte Material und seine Editionen." *Internationales Jahrbuch der Bettina-von-Arnim-Gesellschaft*. 3 (1989): 127–136.

Hirsch, Helmut. *Bettine von Arnim. Mit Selbstzeugnissen und Bilddokumenten*. Reinbek bei Hamburg: Rowohlt, 1987.

Hoock-Demarle, Marie-Claire. "Frau und Stadt: Erlebnis und Erfahrungen der Bettina Brentano-von Arnim." *Bettina von Arnim. Romantik und Sozialismus. (1831–1859).* Trier: Karl-Marx-Haus, 1987. 41–57.

———. "The Nineteenth Century: Insights of Contemporary Women Writers." *Women as Mediatrix. Essays on Nineteenth-Century European Women Writers.* Ed. Avriel H. Goldberger. New York/Westport/London: Greenwood Press, 1987. 1–12.

Janz, Marlis. *Marmorbilder. Weiblichkeit und Tod bei Clemens Brentano und Hugo von Hofmannsthal.* Königstein im Taunus: Athenäum, 1986.

Kittler, Wolf. "Familie, Geschlecht und Poesie. Brentanos 'Geschichte vom braven Kasperl und dem schönen Annerl'." *Germanistik in Erlangen. Hundert Jahre nach Gründung des Deutschen Seminars.* Ed. Dietmar Peschel. Erlangen: Universitätsbund Erlangen-Nürnberg e.V., 1983. 231–237.

Kluge, Gerhard. "Vom Perspektivismus des Erzählens. Eine Studie über Clemens Brentanos 'Geschichte vom braven Kasperl und dem schönen Annnerl'." *Jahrbuch des Freien Deutschen Hochstifts* (1971): 143–197. Tübingen: Max Niemeyer, 1971.

———. *Clemens Brentano. "Geschichte vom Kasperl . . . ." Text, Materialien, Kommentar.* München/Wien: Hanser, 1979.

———. "Brentanos Erzählungen 1810–1818. Beobachtungen zu ihrer Struktur und Thematik." *Clemens Brentano. Beiträge des Kolloquiums im Freien Deutschen Hochstift 1978.* Ed. Detlev Lüders. Tübingen: Max Niemeyer, 1980. 102–134.

Meier, Albert. Commentary on "Der Heckebeutel." *Meistererzählungen der deutschen Romantik.* Ed. and annotated Albert Meier, Walter Schmitz, Sibylle von Steinsdorff, and Ernst Weber. München: Deutscher Taschenbuch Verlag, 1985. 442–448.

Riley, Helene M. Kastinger. *Clemens Brentano,* Stuttgart: Metzler, 1985.

Rölleke, Heinz. "Quellen zu Brentanos ' Geschichte vom braven Kasperl und dem schönen Annerl'." *Jahrbuch des Freien Deutschen Hochstifts* (1970): 244–257. Tübingen: Max Niemeyer Verlag, 1970.

Schultz, Hartwig. "Bettine von Arnim's *Armenbuch'.* Probleme einer kritischen Edition." *editio. Internationales Jahrbuch für Editionswissenschaft.* 1(1987): 224–233. Ed. Winfried Woesler. Tübingen: Max Niemeyer Verlag, 1987.

Schweickart, Patrocinio P. "Reading Ourselves: Toward a Feminist Theory of Reading." *Gender and Reading. Essays on Readers, Texts, and Contexts.* Ed. Elizabeth A. Flinn and Patrocinio P. Schweickart. Baltimore and London: Johns Hopkins University Press, 1986. 31–62.

Verweyen,Theodor and Gunther Witting. *Die Kontrafaktur. Vorlage und Verarbeitung in Literatur, bildender Kunst, Werbung und politischen Plakat.* Konstanz: Universitätsverlag Konstanz, 1987.

Vordtriede, Werner. "Bettina von Arnims Armenbuch." *Jahrbuch des Freien Deutschen Hochstifts* (1962): 379–518. Tübingen: Max Niemeyer Verlag, 1962.

Waldstein, Edith. *Bettine von Arnim and the Politics of Romantic Conversation*. Columbia: Camden House, 1988.

Wolf, Christa. " 'Nun ja! Das nächste Leben geht aber heute an.' Ein Brief über die Bettine." (first in: *Sinn und Form*. 2(1980): 392–418). *Die Dimension des Autors. Essays und Aufsätze, Reden und Gespräche*. Darmstadt und Neuwied: Luchterhand, 1987. 511–610. Included in this volume.

Questioning the "Jewish Question": Poetic Philosophy and Politics in *Conversations with Demons*

Claire Baldwin

In Bettina Brentano-von Arnim's famous letter of 1839 to Friedrich Karl Savigny, she includes among her political concerns the discrimination against Jews in Germany; she wishes to dedicate a "romantic heroes' fire" (ein romantisches Heldenfeuer) to them (Köln 5: 318). Her informed interest in the status of Jews in Germany can be traced throughout her literary opus as well as in her letters. In *Goethe's Correspondence with a Child* (Goethes Briefwechsel mit einem Kinde) (1835), *Günderode* (Die Günderode) (1840), and *Clemens Brentano's Spring Wreath* (Clemens Brentanos Frühlingskranz) (1844) passages that are primarily anecdotal indicate her awareness of the fate of the Jews in Germany and offer her positive depiction of Jewish characters. Yet it is in her last published novel *Conversations with Demons* (Gespräche mit Dämonen) (1852) that she dedicates her most focused literary effort on behalf of the Jews and develops a sustained argument for their legal emancipation and acceptance in society.

Brentano-von Arnim weaves multiple concerns inextricably in the ambitious political and aesthetic project of *Conversations*. She offers her work as a literary contribution to the political and social debates of the 1840s and 1850s. The contemporary relevance of her treatment of Jewish status in Germany in the first extended section of the novel has rarely been considered; the section, entitled "The Cloister Berry. In reminiscence of the Frankfurt Jewish Ghetto" (Die Klosterbeere. Zum Andenken an die Frankfurter Judengasse) has been read primarily as a memoir of Brentano-von Arnim's youth.[1] Although Brentano-von Arnim does date "The Cloister Berry" to 1808, this designation is part of an elaborate dating artifice designed to position it in an historical trajectory that will emphasize her work's contemporary and future significance. *Conversations* aspires to stimulate informed debate and to instigate political change.

The political and the poetic dimensions of *Conversations* are motivated and united by Brentano-von Arnim's conception of nature as a transcendent spiritual guide. The truths of nature are precepts that ought to shape political and social reforms. Brentano-von Arnim aims to communicate these messages in an innovative aesthetic form akin to the structure of nature's spiritual language. Her strategies to devise such a form for her novel and to overcome the limitations of literary convention feature the principles of dialogue and music. Before turning to how her poetic and political programs are delineated in the novel, a short historical sketch of the status of Jews in Prussia may be useful.

Historical-Political Context

The edict issued by Chancellor Karl August von Hardenberg in March 1812 was the first major legislative step toward political emancipation of the Jews in Prussia.[2] Although Friedrich II had proclaimed religious tolerance when he came to power in 1740, his policies toward the Jews followed the restrictive measures introduced in 1730. The Revised General Regulation of the Jews (1750) tightened the conditions of residency privileges and raised their cost. Sharper distinctions were drawn between Protected Jews (Schutzjuden) having letters of protection applicable only for their lifetimes and those having letters which could be bequeathed to the oldest sons, and the rights of the family after the death of the patriarch were curtailed. The king granted social privileges only to a tiny group of so-called Court Jews who were entrusted with the monarchy's mint and other financial tasks. In short, his policies toward the Jews were aimed at securing the financial basis of the state and increasing revenue through higher taxes on privileges, while otherwise restricting Jews' social freedom as much as possible.

The edict of 1812 decreed that Jews who already possessed letters of protection were now full Prussian citizens. In practice, the edict's stipulations were often not implemented, and the regulations left much latitude for administrative interpretation. Nevertheless, it appeared to many to be the promise of full legal emancipation and social esteem. This hope was still pervasive in the Jewish community when, in 1813, Friedrich Wilhelm III issued his appeal "To my People" for support of the Wars of Liberation against Napoleonic rule (1813–1814). For the first time Jewish citizens were eligible for military service; here many saw the chance to demonstrate unequivocally their Prussian patriotism and integrity. In 1813, 170 Jewish men were drafted as soldiers; 561 reported voluntarily to fight for the Prussian cause (*Juden in Preussen* 178). Such personal engagement as well as the financial and ideological support of the Jewish communities for the war contributed to the national victory over Napoleon in 1814, but still this debt and Jewish rights to freedom went unacknowledged. Traditional Christian doubts as to the moral fiber of the Jews resurfaced, prohibiting all but a few of those who had earned the Iron Cross for bravery from receiving military positions, despite their legal claims.

In 1815, all Jews were compelled to resign from state-appointed positions (with a very few exceptions, cf. Fischer 54f). The author Ludwig Börne, for example, whose brother was a soldier in the war, was removed from his job in civic administration because he was Jewish. Börne describes the hypocritical actions of the state:

> A large number of Jews took up arms against Napoleon and fought for the freedom of their German fatherland. Yet when they returned among the victors, they were immediately placed among the helots again, despite the acclaimed German faithfulness and sense of justice.

> Es hatten eine große Menge Juden gegen Napoleon die Waffen ergriffen und für die Freiheit ihres deutschen Vaterlandes gekämpft. Doch als sie unter den Siegern zurück gekehrt, wurden sie gleich wieder unter die Heloten gesteckt, trotz der gerühmten deutschen Treue und Rechtlichkeit.[3]

Instead of social and legal recognition, new waves of anti-Jewish sentiment and legal restrictions were felt after the Congress of Vienna in 1815. The stipulations of the 1812 edict were not expanded to cover the new territorial gains of Prussia.[4] Instead, the monarchy maintained a multitude of laws governing Jewish status: nearly every province had its own ordinances, and conflicting regulations often existed within the same area. Wilhelm Freund depicts this legal chaos still felt in 1843, commenting that King Friedrich Wilhelm II could never have imagined when passing the 1812 edict

> that after more than thirty years there would be, besides this one constitution, seventeen other ordinances concerning the Jews in the Prussian state which belong to the most varied epochs and epochal views, and that nearly one thousand special ordinances for the elaboration and explanation of these different constitutions would be in existence.
>
> daß nach mehr als dreißig Jahren im preußischen Staate neben dieser Einen Verfassung noch siebenzehn andere, den verschiedensten Zeiten und Zeitansichten angehörende Juden-Verfassungen einhergehen werden, und daß zur Ergänzung und Erläuterung dieser verschiedenartigen Verfassungen nahe an tausend Specialverordnungen vorhanden sein werden. (7)

In 1816 only 52.8 percent of the Jews in the Prussian monarchy had rights of citizenship (Fischer 69). This number decreased: prior to the new constitution in 1848, less than one fourth of the 125,000 Jews in Prussia held such rights (Grab 26).

The reactionary trend in political and legal spheres was current in social interactions as well. In the profoundly conservative, nationalistic, and anti-Semitic pamphlet *On the Claims of the Jews to German Citizenship* (Über die Ansprüche der Juden auf das deutsche Bürgerrecht) of 1815, Friedrich Rühs attributed negative characteristics to the "Jewish nation" and proposed that Jews wear identifying marks of differentiation from Christians "so that a German . . . will recognize his Hebrew enemy" (damit ein Deutscher . . . seinen hebräischen Feind erkenne).[5] The pamphlet sparked a flood of responses, both supporting and opposing its positions. Saul Ascher's criticism of Rühs ("Germanomie" 1815) was among the works burned symbolically at the nationalist Wartburg Festival (October 1817), eliciting Heinrich Heine's prophetic lines "where one burns books, one will end up burning people" (dort wo man Bücher verbrennt, verbrennt man auch am Ende Menschen) (Grab 27). In 1819, nationalist and anti-Jewish emotions erupted in violence against Jews in Hamburg, Würzburg, Frankfurt, and elsewhere in the Hep-Hep riots. A hate pamphlet of the time incites to brutality, proclaiming "Let our battle cry be Hepp! Hepp!! Hepp!!! Death and destruction to all Jews. You must flee or die" (unser Kampfgeschrey sey Hepp! Hepp!! Hepp!!! Aller Juden Tod und Verderben. Ihr müßt fliehen oder sterben).[6]

One Jewish response to such hatred was articulated by The Club for the Culture and Science of the Jews (Verein für Kultur und Wissenschaft der Juden), founded in 1819 by the Young Hegelians Eduard Gans and Leopold Zunz, whose circle included acquaintances of Bettina Brentano-von Arnim's. The club aspired to raise recognition of Jewish cultural achievements; it reacted in part to those opponents of Jewish emancipation who insisted that political rights could be granted only after Jews culturally assimilated to the larger community. Yet other anti-Semitic positions, such as that expressed by Rühs, were founded conversely on Christian fears of a lack of visible differentiation. Averse to any free development within the Jewish community whatsoever, the state resisted the assimilation and acculturation it often prescribed as a prerequisite for legal rights. The laws of 1823, for example, prohibited reforms in Jewish rites and branded them "sectarianism" (Geiger 1871, 152).

Many Jewish leaders and political liberals, discontented with the hypocritical regime of Friedrich Wilhelm III, placed their hopes for social and legal reform in the Crown Prince. However, these aspirations were soon disappointed after his coronation in 1840. The policies of Friedrich Wilhelm IV toward his Jewish subjects, proclaimed in 1841, were based on the principle of the Christian state. This concept was articulated and more fully developed in 1847 by Friedrich Julius Stahl, a prominent convert from Judaism. It prevented Jews from occupying any position with executive power; most civil and military appointments fell under this rubric. Furthermore, Friedrich Wilhelm IV wished to replace the conditions of 1812 with laws based on his notion of a Jewish corporation, a body functioning parallel but external to the political governance of Prussia. His policies would have granted rights to the Jewish communities, but not to individuals within these communities. The king's position was severely criticized not only by Jewish leaders and many other Prussians, but even by members of his own cabinet.[7]

The king's legislative plans and a new wave of anti-Semitic writings, the most prominent of which was Bruno Bauer's "The Jewish Question" (Die Judenfrage), unleashed a flood of responses from

Jewish community leaders as well as from non-Jewish intellectuals. The essays furthering this vehement debate, which appeared in major periodicals or as separate publications, included the article "On the Jewish Question" (Zur Judenfrage) by Karl Marx, in which he argued against Bauer's "theological" approach.[8] Marx claimed that Bauer confounded political and human emancipation. Marx considered the Jewish desire for political emancipation valid, but only a step toward human emancipation. He located the empirical basis of Judaism in the spirit of commercialism which structures bourgeois society and contended that the pending task was the emancipation of humanity from the inhumane "Judaism" of this deleterious social structure.

The debates on the so-called "Jewish Question" were increasingly publicized in the 1840s. There was much controversy within the Jewish communities on education, acculturation, and religious reform, converging in the rabbinical conferences in the mid-1840s (Toury, 1966). Conflicts on the matter of Jewish legal rights also raged during the 1840s. The legislation which was eventually passed in July 1847 by the general Prussian assembly (*Vereinigter Preußischer Landtag*) did largely unify the regulations governing the status of the Jews in Prussia, yet by no means represented the full legal emancipation many hoped for: it exempted the Posen Jews and imposed limitations on professional positions Jews could occupy (Toury 1977, 286f).

The revolution of 1848 finally brought about full legal emancipation of the Jews in the constitutions of both Prussia and the German Confederation in 1849. Almost immediately, however, in many of the German states the rights granted to the Jews were either explicitly rescinded, practically annulled by other articles in the constitution (as in the Prussian clause in Article 14 of the revised constitution of 1850 dictating a Christian state), or simply not implemented in practice. Once again, the promises of legal equality proved to be illusory.[9] Jacob Toury concludes that, while the laws following the revolution achieved an improvement in legal status for 20 percent of the German Jews in fifteen states, the reaction in eleven other states led to a status either equivalent to or worse than that prior to the revolution (1977, 307). Furthermore, the revolutionary events of 1848 were accompanied by an extensive wave of some eighty anti-Jewish riots across the German states, reminiscent of those of 1830 and often seen as early manifestations of modern anti-Semitism (1977, 290).

Brentano-von Arnim's Offering:
Dedication and Prayer

This assessment, then, describes the bleak situation facing the German Jews one year after the publication of Bettina Brentano-von Arnim's *Conversations with Demons*. Brentano-von Arnim followed and participated in the discussions about the status of Jews in Germany, a topic of major concern in her social circle, which included many prominent representatives of conflicting positions. "The Cloister Berry," in which Brentano-von Arnim develops her appeal for Jewish emancipation, addresses many of the familiar issues from the political arena, presenting them with a fundamental critique of the Christian church and state. This section of *Conversations* is preceded by two short passages opening the novel. The first is a dedication, the second a "prayer" or dialogue with nature. Both intriguingly introduce Brentano-von Arnim's joint political and poetic project and establish complex historical, personal, and poetic patterns that frame the main body of the text.

In the dedication, Brentano-von Arnim considers her novel's potential political influence by recalling the history of her relationship to King Friedrich Wilhelm IV.[10] The first sentence evokes a point in the past when he was positively inclined toward her: "It has been quite a few years since I stood before a king full of reverent will toward me" (Es ist schon manches Jahr her, da stand ich vor einem König voll huldreichem Willen zu mir) (Köln 3: 259). This could refer to 1839 when their personal interaction began or more probably to 1843 when she published *The King's Book*, the companion volume to *Conversations with Demons*. Brentano-von Arnim had optimistically conceived of her *King's Book* as a vehicle through which to "save the king" from his advisors by "telling him the truth" about the social and political ills in his realm.[11] Although the king accepted the dedication of the work, he spurned Brentano-von Arnim's efforts to persuade him to institute political reforms addressing the unjust social conditions she depicted and condemned.

In 1849, the date Brentano-von Arnim specifies here as the year in which she composed "The Cloister Berry," the monarch "no longer sounded so friendly" (Köln 3: 259). She too is more wary of their interaction. Whereas the king's sanction in 1843 initially protected her work from censorship, in this second volume she acknowledges and points to her subversive thoughts through glaring "gaps of self-censorship" (Köln 3: 259). Finally, Brentano-von Arnim suggests a third new stage in her relationship to the king: "And now, after so long a time, I've heard the king's voice speaking to me again" (Und jetzt—nach geraumer Zeit hörte ich wieder des Königs Stimme, die redete zu mir) (Köln 3: 259). Yet the king again disappoints her hopes for dialogue.

Conversations with Demons, as the second part of *The King's Book*, has thus lost its original addressee, and the author must renounce her hope of influencing the Prussian monarch politically. She turns, therefore, to the reigning Turkish sultan, seen (due to reforms he instituted in 1839) as a liberal political ruler who fulfills her ideal of a people's king (Volkskönig). Brentano-von Arnim dedicates her work "To the Spirit of Islam represented by the magnanimous Abdul-Medschid-Kahn, emperor of the Ottomans" (Dem Geist des Islam vertreten durch den großmütigen Abdul-Medschid-Kahn Kaiser der Osmanen).[12]

Her dedication encompasses both an abstract, religious dimension and an historically concrete, political one, a duality that is sustained throughout *Conversations*. The spirit of Islam serves her as a guiding ideal, transcending the limitations of the historical moment. Yet the philosophical and religious tenets of the spirit of Islam are not divorced from history. They find historical expression through the emperor and they inspire fuller transformation of abstract ideals into specific political and social structures. The spirit of Islam speaks, comforting Brentano-von Arnim for her lack of current political influence with the promise of a future in which her writing will find resonance, her loyalty will be recognized, and her ideals vindicated. In this manner the historical trajectory sketched in the dedication is extended into the future, inspiring and justifying her literary and political engagement.

The second prefatory section of *Conversations* further develops the political and philosophical sanction for the work presented in the dedication, while also invoking Goethe and nature to authorize Brentano-von Arnim's unconventional literary style. Brentano-von Arnim deftly inscribes her relation to Goethe through the dates given to the various opening sections of her text.[13] "The Cloister Berry" is presented in the dedication as Brentano-von Arnim's poetic offering in honor of Goethe's hundredth birthday in 1849. The text itself is dated on Goethe's birthday in 1808 and is preceded by the short passage dated 1808 on her own birthday. This passage immediately follows her expression of hope "that perhaps some day my fame will yet resound in songs" (dass vielleicht einst in Liedern mein Ruhm noch erschallen werde) (Köln 3: 260). Brentano-von Arnim thus offers an appreciation of Goethe similar to the one she herself wishes to receive in the future and parallels her own poetic genius with his.

The juxtaposition of Brentano-von Arnim's and Goethe's birth dates (reminiscent of Goethe's astrological musings in the opening passages of *Poetry and Truth* (Dichtung und Wahrheit) underscores the notion of a "natural" affinity between the two authors, and their poetic parity is further elaborated in the prayer. The character Bettine expresses her longing for an intellectual and spiritual union with the universe: "I want to become the great spirit that encompasses everything!" (Ich will der grosse Geist werden, der alles umfasst!) (Köln 3: 261).[14] Indeed, the union envisioned embraces nature, God, genius, and Goethe: they are conflated in the prayer through recurring pronouns with shifting referents and through the interplay of images within a common metaphoric field spanning the section.[15] The senses, inspired by nature, nurture the life of the spirit and strive toward genius, for which Goethe is a symbol.

Nature, Bettine tells Goethe, counsels her to "silently absorb your poet's rays into my senses" in order to "learn to understand them" (stumm Deine Dichterstrahlen einsaugen in meine Sinne. Dann werd ich sie verstehen lernen) (Köln 3: 262). Bettine wishes to understand and to speak the related languages of Nature and Goethe. She longs to respond to Goethe with the fires of inspiration, a topos of artistic expression: "O why do I only speak words to you, why not flames?" (Ach, warum rede ich nur Worte zu dir, warum nicht Flammen) (Köln 3: 262). The Weimar classicist is figured here as poetic mentor, yet also as erotic and poetic partner: their union is one which inspires them both. The muse collects sweet discourse from their lips and evokes Goethe's voice (Köln 3: 262). His voice— simultaneously the poet's voice and that of the lover who speaks endearingly to Bettine ("Sole treasure of my heart" [Herz einzig Kleinod])—begets Bettine's art: "and more sweet sounds sigh from your breast in a holy form that transforms me, sprouting laurels and rooted in your breast.—Yes, the senses become spirit and ascend to genius" (und mehr süsser Schall stöhnt aus deiner Brust in heiligem Gepräg, das mich umwandelt, lorbeerersprossend und wurzelnd dir

im Busen.—Ja, die Sinne werden Geist, die aufsteigen zum Genius)
(Köln 3: 262).[16]

Bettine has "absorbed" Goethe's poetic prowess and appropriated
it as her own. The transference of genius simultaneously transfers
Goethe's poetic authority, in its turn authorized by natural wisdom
and truth, to Brentano-von Arnim's work and reiterates the equality
and partnership between the two suggested in the parallel dating. In
"The Cloister Berry," Bettine similarly ascribes her political insights
and poetic inspirations to the master. This topos of modesty is explained as constitutive of her text's aim to eulogize Goethe and only
thinly veils his functionalization as both muse and authority.

Nature's Language

Brentano-von Arnim's introductions to the "Cloister Berry" section
of *Conversations with Demons* establish the interdependence of her
political and aesthetic visions. Both are motivated by her philosophical interpretation of nature. "The Cloister Berry" further specifies
this symbiosis. Here Brentano-von Arnim praises nature as a benevolent source of transcendent truths and as guide to ethical conduct.
Nature prompts human beings to develop their innate capabilities and
ideally directs all of humanity toward perfect spiritual knowledge,
harmony, and freedom. Brentano-von Arnim's understandings of Nature's teachings not only have direct relevance for her religious convictions and political engagement, but also deeply influence the poetics
of the text.[17]

One foundation of Brentano-von Arnim's poetics in "The Cloister
Berry" is her distinction between nature's language and the codes of
human culture. This crucial semiotic difference reflects the divergence between the creative, spiritual intellect (Geist) and the inani-
mate letter which encodes and alienates original truths and becomes a
substitute for personal conscience and accountability:

> The spirit is a voice that reaches us so that we renounce the letter, so
> that we won't kill anybody and can ourselves live on in the spirit; and
> only that doubt is sin which sways between spirit and letter, for all
> knowledge encompasses love and it is all the same whether we acknowl-
> edge it in the one or in many, in the father or in the son.

> Der Geist ist eine Stimme, die an uns gelangt, dass wir dem Buch-
> staben absagen, damit wir niemand töten und selber fortleben im
> Geist; und nur der Zweifel ist Sünde, der zwischen Geist und Buch-
> staben schwankt, denn alles Wissen umschliesst die Liebe, und ob wir
> in dem einen sie anerkennen oder in vielen, im Vater oder im Sohn, das
> ist alles eins. (Köln 3: 265–66)

She valorizes the comprehensive, generative language of the spirit as
the language of love and knowledge, and rejects culture's slavish
clinging to the "letter which kills" (Köln 3: 265). This criticism, although reminiscent of polemics against Jewish adherence to Old Testament law, applies equally, if indeed not more specifically, to Christian
orthodoxy and to political laws counter to human dignity and reason.
Love and knowledge comprise for Brentano-von Arnim the essence
of religious truth in both the Old and New Testaments and are the
basis for religious tolerance.

The language of human culture, codified in such laws, documents,
and oaths of loyalty as those of the Prussian kings, is restrictive,
burdening, and static. Nature's language, in contrast, is freeing and
imaginative, harmonious and musical, encompassing and promising:

> anyone whom enthusiasm entrusts to phantasy misses nothing; he sees
> everything at the right time and in the right light—and speaks with
> Nature, chiming in with her whispering, her coolness and smiling si-
> lence. She rings out promises to him which the heart willingly believes.

> der versäumt nichts, den Begeisterung der Phantasie antraut; er sieht
> zur rechten Zeit alles und im rechten Licht—und spricht mit der Natur,
> mitlautend in ihr Säuseln, ihre Kühle und lächelnde Stille, sie tönt ihm
> Verheissungen, denen glaubt das Herz willig. (Köln 3: 265)

The musical language of nature is, furthermore, a language which
transcends words. It speaks in smiling silence, through life and individual manifestations of that life such as the snowdrop (Köln 3: 261).

Bettine assigns herself the task of interpreting this silent embracing
language: "If only I could fully understand what you give, Nature.
What you lay on the snowdrop's lips, why don't I understand it?" and
"[M]y vows are to raise my eyes toward heaven and to interpret its
language which imposes no fetters on the spirit" (Könnt ich doch ganz
verstehen, was du gibst, Natur?–Was du dem Schneeglöckchen auf
die Lippe legst, warum versteh ich's nicht? [Köln 3: 261]; [M]eine

Gelübde sind, die Augen erheben zum Himmel und seine Sprache
mir deuten, die keine Fesseln anlegt dem Geist (Köln 3: 265). Yet
Bettine is not content merely to interpret nature. By speaking to her
imagination and senses as well as freeing her intellect, nature inspires
her to campaign actively for its truths. Bettine clearly articulates this
motivation for poetic creativity; she wishes to ally herself with nature
by opposing social ills and misguided constructs of culture through
nature's principles:

> And couldn't we then respond to your language? How can I manage
> never to deny you, in all that life gives and takes? To shed human law
> with your spirit and to combat its absurdity with your tenet in my
> breast. O, raise me beyond its forms and customs.

> Und könnten wir deine Sprache alsdann nicht erwidern?—Wie mach
> ich's doch, daß ich nie dich verleugne bei allem, was das Leben gibt
> und nimmt?—Dass ich die Menschensatzung abstreife mit deinem
> Geist, und ihren Widersinn bestreite mit deiner Lehre in meiner Brust!
> Ach du, heb mich hinaus über ihre Formen und Bräuche. (Köln 3:
> 261–262)

Brentano-von Arnim avows the truth of nature in her literary
strategies as well as in her philosophical tenets. She seeks to respond
in the newly learned language, and to articulate and communicate her
political and philosophical insights in a commensurate literary form.
She longs to speak and, paradoxically, to write nature's inspiring
language, to manifest the freedom and the wisdom of the spirit in her
linguistic expression.[18] Brentano-von Arnim's aspiration is to translate her understandings into a language comprehensible to her audience without succumbing to the form of the "dead letter" she is
combatting.

Nature's language reveals a realm of creative sensual imagination,
of knowledge greater than rational understanding, which Bettine
wishes to access. She shares the Romantic desire to reach the absolute in effusive, unbounded literary expression and to combine art
and life in sublime poetic representation. Yet in order to be as encompassing as nature, as free and as freeing, she would have to remain
silent, for only nature's silent expression would fully facilitate fluidity
and motion while resisting stasis and fixation.

Goethe's natural poetic genius and Bettine's communion with it
are figured in these terms: nature answers her "with the cloud-flakes

in the heavens, with the snowdrop which defies winter;" Bettine is to
absorb Goethe's poetic rays *silently*. Goethe teaches her the immortality of the spirits and stars with a silent gaze while her senses swirl
around him in intoxication like air or water (lustrauschen) (Köln 3:
262). Ludwig Börne found such sensibility for nature's language in
Brentano-von Arnim's first novel, yet in his enthusiastic review of
Goethes Correspondence with a Child he pointedly denied Goethe the
affinity with nature Brentano-von Arnim ascribed to him: "She is the
happy playmate of the flowers, the confidante of the nightingale; she
understood the language of silence which Goethe was deaf to, and
knew how to interpret the pantomime of silent nature" (Sie ist
glückliche Gespielin der Blumen, vertraute der Nachtigall; sie verstand die Sprache der Stille, der Goethe taub war, und wußte das
Mienenspiel der stummen Natur zu deuten) (Köln 2: 867).

Dialogue

Brentano-von Arnim strives for a poetic form which can approach
nature's vivacity and overcome the limitations of written language.
One strategy she develops to achieve this goal of immediacy is to use
dialogue as a structuring poetic principle of her work. She builds the
illusion of the spoken word, of the openness and sociability of dialogue, into her writing. In *Conversations*, the dialogic principle is
already in play in the dedication, with her evocation of past discussions with the king. There she also speaks with another powerful
ruler, the sultan, as well as with fantastic demons and spirits, and in
her "prayer" Bettine directly addresses both nature (Köln 3: 261) and
Goethe (Köln 3: 262). Brentano-von Arnim structures her arguments
in "The Cloister Berry" through a fictional dialogue between her
narrator-persona "Bettine" and the prince-primate Karl Theodor von
Dalberg, elector of Mainz, a Christian ruler holding political and
ecclesiastic authority over Frankfurt under Napoleon. As Bettine
wishes to translate Nature's powerful messages for the primate, her
adversary in discussion, Brentano-von Arnim aims to do so for her
readers.

Edith Waldstein has coined the term "conversational novels" for
The King's Book and *Conversations with Demons*. She describes this
genre as Brentano-von Arnim's mode of incorporating the sociability
(Geselligkeit) of Romantic salon culture into her literary work (also

Dischner 25–33). The poetic strategy of the conversational novel involves readers in an attempt to achieve a completed act of communication, in which artistic and political visions can inspire efforts to help
shape the future. Brentano-von Arnim conceives of her conversational
aesthetic project as an agent of historical change. She demands historical consciousness from her audience from the outset of *Conversations*.
The complex system of dating in the opening sections of the novel
insists on historical specificity and detailed historical knowledge. "The
Cloister Berry" is introduced from the perspective of 1849 as a portrait
of the Frankfurt Jewish ghetto from 1808. It looks back from the position of apparent legal rights gained through the revolution to the conditions imposed on the Jews forty years earlier. The initial image is thus
one of political success, implying that the critique of the Christian ruler
is outdated.[19] Yet Brentano-von Arnim actually wrote from the early
1850s: the achievements of the revolution had been annulled, and the
Jews were still living under severe political and social restrictions. To
read the past of 1849 and 1808 from the standpoint of 1852 is to read
with the knowledge of the failure to achieve important liberal political
goals, including Jewish emancipation.

Brentano-von Arnim wishes to channel this historical consciousness
raised in her audience toward conscious and constructive engagement
in shaping a better future. This indeed is the ultimate significance of
historical awareness, she argues: "Why would the past concern us if it
were not the vehicle of our future? Reflex of Becoming in us, for whom
the spirit mirrors the enticements of our own ideal in dreams" (Was
kümmerte uns Vergangenheit, wäre sie nicht Organ unserer Zukunft!
Reflex des Werdens in uns, dem der Geist in Träumen die Lockungen
des eigenen Ideals vorspiegelt!) (Köln 3: 285). Brentano-von Arnim
designs to inspire her audience to propel the future by revealing relationships between the past and the future, and to communicate the
ideals shown by the spirit through her work in a literary form commensurate with her understanding of the spirit's language.

Brentano-von Arnim's aesthetic and political projects are thus in-
tricately linked. The battle for Jewish emancipation is the first cause
she adopts in her venture of combatting the "absurdity of human
laws" with nature's precepts in *Conversations*, a literary project of
direct political and social commitment akin to that of the young German writers.[20] The innovations of the novel's joint poetic and political
enterprise are sanctioned by placing Brentano-von Arnim's work explicitly in an authoritative literary tradition. In keeping with the

novel's principle of dialogue, a conversational context is evoked thereby. The event which elicited her concern for the Jews, she claims, was a discussion with Goethe about Gotthold Ephraim Lessing's *Nathan the Wise* (1779). In his wisdom and humaneness, the title character of this drama had come to serve as the literary prototype for the Jew of enlightenment rationality.

Brentano-von Arnim emphasizes the influence of both Lessing and Goethe as literary role models on the young Bettine's perception and understanding, but also clearly distances her own position from Lessing's:

> Now I no longer pass wise Nathan's brothers indifferently and shyly, I see with amazement the narrow, dark houses; everything teems, not a single place to be alone, to reflect. . . . A stream of people surges in the street, so many children run around in rags, learn to earn money; and the old ones, day and night, are eager to bring them into prosperity. People begrudge them that and curse them as bothersome.

> Nun gehe ich nicht mehr gleichgültig schüchtern an des weisen Nathan Brüdern vorüber, ich betrachte mit Verwunderung die engen dunklen Häuser; alles wimmelt, kein Plätzchen zum Alleinsein, zum Besinnen. . . . Ein Volksstrom wogt in der Straße, da laufen so viele Kinder herum in Lumpen, die lernen Geld erwerben, und die Alten, Tag und Nacht sind eifrig, sie in Wohlstand zu bringen, das wehrt man ihnen und schimpft sie lästig. (Köln 3: 267)

Engaging in intertextual dialogue with Lessing, Brentano-von Arnim situates herself in literary succession to the enlightenment author while simultaneously offering a contemporary revision of his work, recasting Lessing's philosophical drama of religious tolerance in historically and politically specific terms. The direction of Brentano-von Arnim's refashioning was already suggested in the dedication by her address to a specific Islamic ruler of the nineteenth century. By expanding the discussion of religious tolerance and specifically "the Jewish question" to include graphic depiction of everyday life and conditions of the Jewish community, Brentano-von Arnim brings her work into the realm of social documentation and asserts contemporary authority.

Political and philosophical arguments supporting equal recognition of the Jewish culture Brentano-von Arnim portrays are presented with recourse to metaphors and analogies from the natural realm:

Whatever lives under the sun has equal claims; just as the multitudes of stalks in the field imbibe sunlight to produce seeds of grain, so too should everything fructify itself through the spirit of the sun with grand thoughts. They should thrive in the Jew as well as in other people, as the grain thrives in the stalk.

Was unter der Sonne lebt, hat gleiche Ansprüche; tränken sich die Scharen der Halme auf dem Feld mit ihrem Licht, um Körner zu gewinnen, so soll auch durch der Sonne Geist alles sich befruchten mit großen Gedanken! Sie sollen im Juden so gut gedeihen wie in andern Menschen, und wie in den Halmen das Korn gedeiht! (Köln 3: 269)

Brentano-von Arnim attempts both to render nature's forms and to interpret them, offering the reader this interpretation as translation. Her words, that is, do not simply draw the forms through which nature speaks to her but also give them voice: she offers herself as mouthpiece of nature from within its realm.[21] Here spiritual and intellectual development are presented as natural rights and needs of all human beings through the image of the seed which flourishes under proper conditions, the concept of entelechy applied to the human soul.

Such interpretation of natural phenomena provides the basis for her political philosophy. Brentano-von Arnim transposes Kant's notion of ethical responsibility for one's own development from the individual to the political sphere: the relationship between the people and political rulers—the king, the primate—must be such that the people can develop their potential to the fullest, and anything that hinders one group or nation from achieving this aim will necessarily harm the community of humanity. She similarly believes that if a ruler is not pursuing politics that strive for the sublime, based on the natural religious principles as she sees them (love, faith, personal conscience, and movement toward greater knowledge and spirituality), he or she is not performing responsibly.

Comparing a good ruler's care of subjects to a conscientious gardener's care of plants, Bettine describes how a political leader—particularly one who also claims spiritual leadership—must treat Jewish citizens:

And to advance the Jews after such a long life of neglect, they must also be treated carefully and gently like exotic plants and be nourished with what makes the soul great, and no path must be closed to them except the one which can degrade them.

Und die Juden emporbringen nach so langem Darben, da müssen sie auch vorsichtig und zärtlich behandelt werden wie die ausländischen Pflanzen, und genährt mit dem, was die Seele groß macht, und muß ihnen keine Laufbahn verschlossen bleiben als nur, die sie erniedrigen kann. (Köln 3: 269)

Brentano-von Arnim alludes to the image of Jews as foreigners in Germany, but argues that they should therefore be given privileged attention. She clearly embeds reference to the long Jewish struggle for admission to various public careers. One of the crucial measures of the general emancipatory laws of 1849 was to proclaim, theoretically, Jewish eligibility to state-appointed positions. Yet in practice most states continued to discriminate against the Jews, indicating the true level of intolerance still pervading at the time Brentano-von Arnim's book was published.

Both Bettine and the primate regard the Jews as a separate "nation" or people from the Christian Germans, a notion which many Jews vehemently resisted. While it was so often used to justify anti-Semitic laws and attitudes, this concept also carried positive weight in definitions of Jewish identity (e.g., in shaping proto-Zionist thought). In *Conversations,* the primate's anti-Semitic conclusions drawn from his understanding of a Jewish nation are promptly refuted by Bettine. Although she also finds Old Testament law harsh and irrational, she values it as the basis for self-respect and identity of the Jews. "They feel their national existence in exile secured" through their faith, she argues, "their temple is their resting place on their journey through the world as refugees" ["sie fühlen sich . . . ihres nationalen Daseins in der Verbannung gesichert; ihr Tempel ist ihre Ruhestätte auf ihrer Flüchtlingsreise durch die Welt) (Köln 3: 274).

As noted above, it was commonly argued in the debates on emancipation that the Jews needed to prove themselves worthy of the rights they sought before these could be granted to them. Even Jewish representatives often accepted this view publicly. For example, they encouraged the "German heroism" of Jewish soldiers in the Wars of Liberation and pointed to their valor afterwards as a reason for granting emancipation. The position that rights must be earned was put forward by Christian Dohm, influenced by Moses Mendelssohn, in his treatise *On the Civil Improvement of the Jews* (Über die bürgerliche Verbesserung der Juden) (1781), often considered the beginning of the public debate over the social and political emancipation of the

Jews in Germany. Dohm's ideas, echoed in *Conversations* by the primate, are flatly rejected by Bettine:

> The right to free development of healthy abilities cannot be predicated upon prerequisites, still less can it be denied those whose natural tendencies are not allowed to run freely in cheerful streams of life. First give air, how soon then the light will shine!—This flame—this simple flame reaching into the heavens—and penetrating Nature and the world, it smolders, too, in the heart and soul of the Jew.

> Das Anrecht freier Entwicklung seiner gesunden Anlagen kann um keiner Voraussetzung willen einem vorenthalten werden, noch weniger ist's denen abzusprechen, deren Naturanlagen nicht in heiteren Lebensbächen dahinzurauschen vergönnt ist. Gebt erst Luft, wie bald wird dann Licht leuchten!—Diese Flamme!—diese einfache himmelermessende—Natur und Welt durchgreifende Flamme, sie lodert auch im Innern des Juden. (Köln 3: 273)

Again this position is strengthened by referring to qualities of the human spirit that have been suppressed in the Jews through restrictions on the fulfillment of their natural needs. Freedom and air, the "breath of Nature" (Köln 3: 261), will reignite the spiritual flame and lead the Jews to the human dignity currently denied them.

Music

Bettina Brentano-von Arnim shares the enlightenment belief that education, in addition to basic freedom and respect, is the foundation on which the Jews can assert this dignity. Johann Gottfried Herder, for example, criticized the "continuing barbarism of the state which suffers such laws from barbarous times" (die fortwährende Barbarei des Staates, der aus barbarischen Zeiten solche Gesetze duldet) (1802) and stressed the state's duty to provide its Jewish subjects with access to education.[22] Bettine emphasizes music as the primary factor in her educational program, which would include "riding, fencing, dancing . . . natural sciences, philosophy, history . . . and the first among all elements of education would have to be music! ("reiten, fechten, tanzen . . . Naturwissenschaft, Philosophie, Geschichte . . . und das erste aller Erziehungselemente müsste sein die Musik!") (Köln 3: 269).

Interestingly, her belief in the importance of music parallels that of many Jewish reform leaders. The incorporation of organ music into Jewish synagogue services, for example, was advocated as a means of bringing order and propriety into the Jewish rites. This was a fervently debated issue in the Jewish community, for many saw it as an unacceptable, radical deviation from Jewish tradition, in essence a "Christianization." In *Conversations*, the primate reflects the interpretation of the role of music as a Christianizing force, suggesting that even given such education and reform, Jews could or would not deny their Jewishness, thus—in his view—rendering Bettine's project unsuccessful. Bettine, however, does not conceive of music's influence as one that Christianizes Judaism, a process Brentano-von Arnim does not approve of in the least.[23] The status she ascribes to music is rather reminiscent of Plato's evaluation of music's primary role in education—clearly alluding to a pre-Christian tradition.[24]

Brentano-von Arnim frequently employs musical metaphors to compare Judaism and Christianity. Judaism is positively valued for its musical sensitivity. She finds it more attuned to nature, more genuine, and therefore closer to the goal of achieving spiritual growth and fulfillment than the Christian religion. Jewish prayers "harmonize with the universe of creation" (ins All der Schöpfung einklingen) (Köln 3: 270), while Christianity, conversely, is blamed for the discord it creates in the cosmic order. Its aggression and "dissonance of persecution" (Mißtöne[n] der Verfolgung) (Köln 3: 270) are contrasted negatively to "the pure tone of Judaism" (den reinen Ton des Judaismus) (Köln 3: 271). Musical metaphors take on a metaphysical dimension, evoking a utopian vision of an encompassing nonsectarian religious sensibility, of tolerance and harmony in the "moral firmament" (moralisches Firmament) (Köln 3: 271).

In this respect, Brentano-von Arnim's conception of music clearly differs from one current in Romanticism that relies on a Christian interpretation of the absolute to be reached through music. Novalis, for example, uses musical metaphors quite close to Brentano-von Arnim's in "Christianity or Europe" (Die Christenheit oder Europa) (1799), yet he identifies the salvation of "holy music" with Christianity (Köln 3: 523).[25] Brentano-von Arnim, in contrast, argues that music can transcend limitations imposed on the spirit through circumstances such as the Christians' repression of the Jews or the deadening weight of philistine learnedness in the Christian church to spur the senses on to yet a higher understanding:

Music brings the scale of the soul, which has become fully toneless
through Christian loosening and is out of tune, into the purest temperament. Music does not issue solely out of spirit and sentiment, the senses
fructify it even far more and make it capable of that which the intellect
does not yet grasp. Music is the renaissance for spiritual Nature.

Die Musik bringt die Skala der Seele auf die reinste Temperatur, die
durch christliches Herabspannen ganz tonlos geworden und verstimmt
ist. Musik geht nicht allein aus Geist und Gemüt hervor, weit mehr
noch befruchtet sie die Sinne und befähigt sie zu dem, was der Geist
noch nicht faßt.—Sie ist die Wiedergeburt für die geistige Natur. (Köln
3: 269)

Thus she differs from Novalis in her belief that music's realm sur-
passes that of any positive religion, yet she shares with Romanticism
the assessment of music as the privileged art form providing access to
a realm of knowledge not apprehensible through mere intellect. She
underscores its power and import by incorporating musical accents
into her literary composition.

Bettine's confrontation with the primate is enclosed by a dramatic
musical framework. She criticizes his repressive laws against the Jews,
but:

[The primate] claims this reproach doesn't apply to him, Nathan's wisdom makes sense and he is not indifferent to the Jews' misery, but
wouldn't they abuse their freedom and, as soon as they had breathing
space, wouldn't they parry Christian injustice with Jewish audacity? We
were next to the concert hall when the primate said that, the entering
drums roused my courage.

Er meint, ihn treffe dieser Tadel nicht, des Nathan Weisheit leuchte
ihm ein, und das Elend der Juden sei ihm nicht gleichgültig, aber ob sie
ihre Freiheit nicht mißbrauchen und die christliche Ungerechtigkeit, so
wie sie Luft haben, mit jüdischer Keckheit ausparieren. Es war neben
dem Konzertsaal, wo der Primas das sagte, die einfallenden Pauken
steigerten meinen Mut. (Köln 3: 267–268)

This passage, which once again stresses the contrast between Lessing's Nathan taken as the representative Jew and Brentano-von
Arnim's concern with the reality of the community, is the structural
reference for a later point of division ending the long discussion:
"Here a strong drumbeat of the Haydn symphony ended the concert
and simultaneously my intercession for the Jews" (Hier endigte ein

derber Paukenschlag der Haydenschen Symphonie das Konzert und zugleich meine Judenverwendung) (Köln 3: 279).

More importantly, however, Brentano-von Arnim presents music as the liberating force that enables Bettine to challenge the primate and as the fictional framework in which the author herself may articulate her ideals. All the qualities that music carries for Brentano-von Arnim are empowering: music transmits knowledge of the divine or spiritual sphere, which is impossible to reach through fettered intellectual reasoning. Bettine's arguments are thus motivated by knowledge gleaned through music; this lends her voice conviction and courage.

By endowing her persona Bettine with musical inspiration, Brentano-von Arnim justifies the exalted language and free artistic experimentation in her presentation of arguments for Jewish emancipation both narratively and philosophically. Her literary style strives for movement, spontaneity, immediacy—all expressions of the intellectual and spiritual freedom and honesty to which she wishes to inspire her readers. Brentano-von Arnim anticipates the criticism of a lack of logical clarity in her argumentation by quietly ridiculing the primate, who is unable to keep pace with her imaginative presentation. Her invectives against those who allow themselves to be limited in their understanding by the confines of written codes make evident that the language she consciously chooses is meant to be that of nature and the spirit rather than that of the pedantic letter.

Just as she describes the interaction between Jews and Christians in musical terms, she presents the figures in her dialogue as musical voices in concert, working to transform her conversational novel into a symphonic one. She boldly seeks a communicative form for her literature that transcends even the immediate word spoken in dialogue. These literary strategies illuminate her position between the enlightenment ideal of rational, direct communication and the romantic conception of music as the non-linguistic art form able to mediate between the listener and the realm of highest truth.

Bettina Brentano-von Arnim foresees an age of bliss and harmony, to be attained through mutual development and positive influence, in which "Jew and Christian feel in common that God is with them" (Jude und Christ gemeinsam fühlen, Gott sei unter ihnen) (Köln 3: 270). The political implication of this vision, namely that the principle of the Christian state cannot be morally upheld, is explicitly delineated by Bettine for the benefit of the Christian ruler. Christianity, she says, will have to realize "that it does not have, along with the heaven of the Christians, sole claims to the world, leaving only hell over for heretics, pagans, and Jews" (daß sie mit dem Christenhimmel nicht auch die irdische Welt gepachtet habe und die Hölle für Ketzer, Heiden und Juden allein übrigbleibe!) (Köln 3: 270).

Brentano-von Arnim's conviction that her ideals could be achieved through just political leadership is the impetus for the debate between Bettine and the cynical primate: "If we were both to rule humankind, the primate over the Christians and I over the Jews, we would see who would have more success" (Sollten wir beide die Menschheit regieren, der Primas die Christen und ich die Juden, wir wollten sehen, wer besser fertig würde) (Köln 3: 268). Both this discussion and the later one between the sleeping king, the good demon, and the national spirits deeply affect the primate, who is present as a listener through-out the entire novel. Now he must admit that he is "possessed by the demon, which I must condemn as pagan, and enraptured by its wis-dom, which I abandon to the eternal fire as heretical" (besessen vom Dämon, den ich als heidnisch verdammen muß, und hingerissen von seiner Weisheit, die ich als ketzerisch dem ewigen Feuer preisgebe! (Köln 3: 407). Bettine's response, the final words of the book: "Yes, eternal fire glows in the breast of one who indulges in this wisdom" (Ja, ewiges Feuer lodert im Busen dem, der dieser Weisheit frönt), trans-forms the fires of hell to the inspirational fire of the spirit's wisdom, which she has successfully imparted to the prince-primate and has clearly wished to impart to her readers as well.

Reception

Most contemporary reviewers of the novel criticized its style and chose not to engage with the political vision offered. Yet one review of *Con-versations with Demons* ignored by subsequent criticism did take Brentano-von Arnim's political statements on this issue seriously. Writ-ten by Ludwig Philippson for his influential *General Newspaper of Judaism* (Allgemeine Zeitung des Judenthums) in 1853, it deserves closer scrutiny, since it is outstanding in its sensitivity to Brentano-von Arnim's literary and political concerns. Philippson first evaluates the date 1808 which Brentano-von Arnim gives "The Cloister Berry." He does not read it unquestioningly as a literal indication of the time the section was written, but concludes that it must be taken as a depiction of the Jewish situation in Frankfurt from that year:

and thus the entire fragment about the Jews would be a legacy from the year 1808, that is, 45 years old. The content also attests that this is so, for just as it externally presupposes the Frankfurt Alley as the ghetto of the Frankfurt Jews, it also presupposes internal conditions of the Jews from centuries ago.

und so wäre das ganze Fragment über die Juden wirklich ein Ueberkommnis aus dem Jahre 1808, also 45 Jahre alt. Und daß es dies ist, bezeugt auch der Inhalt; denn wie er äusserlich die Frankfurter Gasse noch als Ghetto der Frankfurter Judenschaft voraussetzt, so noch innerlich die Juden in einem Zustande vor Jahrhunderten. (388)

Philippson is concerned with the contemporary image the Jewish community presents to the Christian world. He reminds his readers that most of the Jewish acculturation to the larger community in education, the professions, and the arts was unperceived by outsiders. Thus, he finds Bettina von Brentano-von Arnim's rendering anachronistic. However, he does accord her literary work contemporary social and political relevance:

Therefore the fragment under consideration is even more interesting for us from two points of view: it shows on the one hand, how, such a short time ago, Jews appeared even to well disposed eyes—and this comparison is a tribute to us—on the other hand it offers us a means with which to gauge which prophecies of the author, who so vehemently demands our freedom, we have realized, and which we have not.

Darum ist das vorliegende Fragment aus zwei Gesichtspunkten um so interessanter für uns, indem es einerseits zeigt, wie noch vor so kurzer Zeit die Juden selbst günstigen Augen erscheinen mußten—und dieser Vergleich ist ein Ehrenzeugniß für uns—andrerseits uns einen Maßstab darbietet, an dem wir abmessen können, was wir von den Prophezeiungen der, unsre Freiheit ungestüm fordernden Verfasserin verwirklicht haben, was nicht. (388)

The reviewer accepts the necessity of proving oneself worthy of rights as a Jew—according to him, some reproaches the primate levels against the Jews were justified in 1808. He insists on the accomplishments of the Jews realized since that time and observes that, while Brentano-von Arnim envisioned emancipation as a necessary prerequisite for acculturation, Jewish acculturation to the larger society (which he views as a positive, autonomous achievement) preceded political rights. Philippson primarily discusses Brentano-von

Arnim's program of educational, professional, and moral betterment. On the crucial point of full legal, political, and social emancipation he suggests a careful analysis of the present situation to his readers, yet beyond that remains expressively silent. Clearly in his view the primary positive changes for the Jewish community between 1808 and 1853 have occurred culturally rather than legally.

In Philippson, not an unconditional admirer of the novel, Brentano-von Arnim certainly found a reader who fulfilled his role in the partnership she hoped to form through her literary work. He responded seriously to the political and social content of her novel, noting its relevance for the 1850s, and added impetus to the discussion through his review. Subsequent essays on "Bettina and the Jews" in Jewish papers failed to recognize the strong political motivation for Brentano-von Arnim's literary engagement.[26] Her Jewish audience gave her credit for her unique outspokenness, her positive attitudes towards the Jews, and her support of emancipation. However, her concern became strictly personalized, while the literary expression of her social and political beliefs was largely ignored. Her works were read as autobiographical documents to support the myth of Brentano-von Arnim as the loving child genius, whose innate goodness, sincerity, and compassion made her the friend and "little protector" of the Jews.

Current criticism generally justifies the negative reception of *Conversations* as appropriate neglect, and considers the work merely as the less successful second volume of *The King's Book*. While most scholars mention in passing Brentano-von Arnim's interest in the Jewish situation, even those who state this concern most emphatically (Drewitz, Dischner, and Staff) do not pursue the topic through textual analysis of her last novel. This is also true of some more recent, laudable efforts to differentiate between myths about Brentano-von Arnim and her actual life, which tend to blur distinctions between her literary texts and biographical material and seem to question the sincerity of her literary engagement on behalf of the Jews.[27] While anti-Semitic remarks Brentano-von Arnim may have expressed in her younger years ought not to be ignored or exonerated, her later explicit and vehement propagation of Jewish emancipation in an often hostile environment—a position which can be found throughout her literary opus culminating in *Conversations with Demons*—should be accorded proper recognition.

Bettina Brentano-von Arnim's work remained ineffective in achieving its aims: to stimulate "conversation" and to elicit serious response. One reason for the greater success of the first volume of the *King's Book* was its publication date. There was certainly more revolutionary fervor and readiness for political debate in 1843 than during the renewed reaction of the 1850s.[28] The novel's failure in this regard can also be read as a measure of the literary experimentation it manifests. Brentano-von Arnim fused fact with fiction, autobiography with fictional dialogues, social documentation with political argumentation, and real historical figures as characters and imaginatively invoked demons. This overwhelming synthesis proved itself too demanding of her readers, despite her educational efforts within the novel itself. Moreover, her attempts to overcome the boundaries inherent in language in order to transmit musical "knowledge" in her novel often contribute to the difficulties of reading her text and work against her aims of direct communication.

Rather than attributing this style prematurely to artistic ineptitude, one should attempt to understand Brentano-von Arnim's artistic expression on her own terms. In Christa Wolf's reading of *Günderode*, her experimentation and individual style are interpreted as the means of attaining the creative space enabling her to write, and as an explicit statement against the established aesthetic norms (310). In the same vein, Elke Frederiksen has stated that Brentano-von Arnim defies the traditional patriarchal codes of her time most strongly in her social and political writings (106). Edith Waldstein's concept of the conversational novel is a productive one with which to define Bettina Brentano-von Arnim's deviation from the literary expectations of her time—an initiative I have attempted to follow here. By appreciating the complexity of Brentano-von Arnim's literary endeavors, one can perhaps avoid reductive readings and do greater justice to her work as a carefully composed text.

Notes

1. Read by early reviewers as a formless and chaotic document of Brentano-von Arnim's personal quirks, it has also been largely ignored by contempo-

rary criticism. See the reviews reprinted in the Konrad edition (Köln 3: 491–500). Geiger (1902) and Frels praise the spirit of Brentano-von Arnim's later work while denying it literary quality. Recent studies that aim to cover Brentano-von Arnim's opus generally concentrate on *The King's Book* and only treat *Conversations* cursorily (e.g., Liebertz-Grün and Waldstein). Drewitz, Schmitz, and particularly Staff do consider *Conversations* in its contemporary context; only Staff focuses on the status of the Jews. Dischner and Hirsch thematize this issue by citing lengthy passages from "The Cloister Berry" without engaging in textual analysis.

2. This summary relies primarily on the histories of the Jews in Germany by Elbogen/Sterling, Fischer, Geiger, and Toury, and the exhibit catalogue *Jews in Prussia* (Juden in Preussen). See also Rürup and Silbergleit.

3. In *Menzel der Franzosenfresser* (1835), here Köln 3: 955. Börne repeatedly responded to prejudice against the Jews in a series of essays, each entitled "For the Jews" (Für die Juden), for example after the Congress of Vienna (1: 170–179) and after the anti-Jewish riots of 1819 (1: 871–880).

4. They remained limited to the four provinces of Brandenburg, Silesia, Pomerania, and East Prussia and continued to apply only to Jews with letters of protection.

5. Cited from Elbogen/Sterling, 188. Rühs revived a strand of nationalist anti-Jewish sentiment and the notion of a German-Christian people found in works by other influential intellectuals such as in J. G. Fichte's "Addresses to the German Nation" (Reden an die deutsche Nation) of 1807–1808, in which hatred against the foreign rule of the French fuelled prejudice against the Jews, considered a foreign nation within Germany. Jakob Friedrich Fries soon followed his teacher Rühs with a pamphlet *On the Threat to German Prosperity and Character from the Jews* (Über die Gefährdung des Wohlstandes und Charakters der Deutschen durch die Juden), Heidelberg, 1816. Börne called these and other such writings "a bouquet of dried poisonous herbs" (Blumenlese von getrockneten Giftkräutern) (cf. Elbogen/Sterling 188/189).

6. Cited from Elbogen/Sterling 192. The cry "Hep Hep" was a shortened version of the cries of the crusaders on entering Jerusalem. See also *Jews in Berlin* (Juden in Berlin) 66.

7. Cf. Fischer 170f. Frels describes the king's plans, generally disapproved of, as a central topic of concern in Berlin from January to June 1842 (29). Frels also documents the negative response to the policies of Eichhorn, the minister of culture, who drafted new ordinances on Sunday observances and called for a "Club for the Reacquisition of Jerusalem" (27–29).

8. In *Early Writings* (Frühe Schriften), 451–488. Marx continues his polemics with Bauer in chapter six of *The Holy Family* (Die heilige Familie) (*Frühe Schriften*, 769–773; 779–785; 794–811). See also Bauer's responses to criticism in his *General Literature Paper* (Allgemeine Literaturzeitung) (1: No.

1, 1–17; No. 4 10–19; 2: No. 9, 7–16); Ludwig Philippson's responses to Bauer in the *AZJ* (cf. Johanna Philippson, 270–273); and those positions in the "Literarisches Feuilleton" of Freund's publication, No. 2, 211ff.

9. Toury 1977, 299ff: twenty-four states had full legal equality in 1848/1849; nine of these fully abrogated those rights directly or in new interpretative legislation; five others withdrew legal rights in discriminatory practice.
10. See Geiger (1902), Frels, and Püschel on this relationship.
11. Frels relates this information, as noted by Karl August Varnhagen von Ense and Moritz Carrière (14–15). He also points out that Arnim's view of the king's relationship to his advisors was not idiosyncratic, but was shared by many in her time (17). Frels reads Brentano-von Arnim's later texts in general as a seismograph of the intellectual climate in Berlin in the 1840s.
12. Cf. Tekinay (48). Drewitz (258) and Konrad (Köln 3: 489–490) refer to Karl August Varnhagen's notes which state that Brentano-von Arnim hoped to gain help from the sultan for a poor Turkish family in Berlin and that she expected him to help finance her monument to Goethe.
13. Cf. Bunzel (7–10) who considers how dating constructs in *Goethes Briefwechsel mit einem Kinde* are part of that text's poetic strategy.
14. I will use the spelling "Bettine" to refer to the character in Brentano-von Arnim's text.
15. Thus Bettine prays by speaking to nature about "Him who shines in everything you give and to whom you bear witness in form and life;" at the end of the passage she claims "Today is my birthday, Goethe, I have spoken with nature about you." Initially Bettine sends her prayer up to heaven to "drink its gentle light" which nature exudes; likewise nature advises her to soak up Goethe's poetic rays and to make eternal vows to him. (So steige auf mein Gebet zum wolkendurchflockten Himmel, mit den Sinnen sein zärtlich Licht zu trinken und mit Dir Natur, zu reden über Ihn der in Allem erglänzt was Du gibst und Zeugnis gibst in Form und Leben von Ihm" and "Heute ist mein Geburtstag, Goethe, da hab' ich mit der Natur geredet von Dir . . . . Sie antwortet mit den Wolken-flocken am Himmel . . . . Ich soll nicht von Dir lassen, sagt sie, stumm Deine Dichterstrahlen einsaugen in meine Sinne. Dann werd ich sie verstehen lernen, wenn ich Dir Gelübde tue, ewige) (Köln 3: 261–262).
16. Brentano-von Arnim's syntax here, as elsewhere, remains flexible, allow-ing multiple alignments of references. "Lorbeerersprossend" can refer (at least) to both "Schall" and "mich." "Umwandeln" can mean enwrapping, encircling, and transforming, furthering multiple associations of "Gep-räg." In general, my translations cannot aspire to literary quality; they are offered as assistance in reading only.
17. Brentano-von Arnim's conceptions of nature and religion were deeply influenced by the Romantic philosopher Schleiermacher. Cf. Frels (esp. 66–74) and Bäumer (91–102).

18. For a differing view of Arnim's "natural writing" see Kittler, who presents her as a dancing "writing machine."
19. The Jews in Frankfurt, crowded in the Jewish ghetto established in 1462, were first granted legal rights (for which they, as usual, had to pay large sums) under Napoleonic rule. These were largely restricted after Napoleon was defeated.
20. In the letter to Savigny from 1839 cited above, Brentano-von Arnim identifies the situation of the Young German authors as one of her pressing political concerns. Her sympathies for their socially engaged writing and her personal acquaintance with the prominent authors of this movement, as well as the enthusiastic reception of her work in the publications of the Young Germans, attest to commonalities (without denying their many differences) in their endeavors. See also the comments of Hartwig Schultz in *Herzhaft* 105–113, esp. 105–109.
21. Liebertz-Grün's study takes Brentano-von Arnim's insistence "that her texts, like nature, appear as a chaotic jumble and, like nature, are built according to rigid rules" (daß ihre Texte wie die Natur als ein chaotisches Gewirre erscheinen und wie die Natur nach strengen Regeln gebaut sind) (3) as the key to her readings of Brentano-von Arnim's "Romantic novels." She also points to Brentano-von Arnim's sense of identity with nature, the "all-powerful, all-benevolent Great Mother" (die allmächtige allgütige Große Mutter) in *Günderode* (51).
22. Herder, *Adrastea*, (61ff, here 71–72). See also Dischner (161–163) on similarities between Arnim and Herder with respect to the "Jewish question."
23. Cf. for example Brentano-von Arnim's letter to Goethe of July 28, 1810: "the Jewish women sit together after the meal and unravel the old gold borders, and that always occurs in High German, has cramps, the children are baptized, have to make the sign of the cross, the divine Unzelmann recites in the evening" (die Jüdinnen setzen sich nach Tisch zusammen, und fasern die alten Goldborden aus, und das geht immer ganz hochdeutsch, hat Krämpfe, die Kinder sind getauft, müssens Kreuz machen, die göttliche Unzelmann deklamiert am Abend) (Köln 5: 84).
24. Brentano-von Arnim studied Plato with Schleiermacher. On the importance of Platonic dialogue as a model for Brentano-von Arnim, cf. Liebertz-Grün (76) and Bäumer (99f).
25. For example in describing the effects of the hatred of religion which "turned the infinite creative music of the cosmos into the monotone banging of an enormous mill" (machte die unendliche schöpferische Musik des Weltalls zum einförmigen Klappern einer ungeheuren Mühle) (Köln 3: 515). Nahrebecky discusses Brentano-von Arnim's views on music in the context of Romanticism, yet he is more interested in her thematic statements on music and with her image of Beethoven (208–214) than in how her understanding of music informs her poetic work.

26. For example the essays by Hirschberg (1904), Lachmanski (1934), and Kayser (1958).
27. See Bäumer (266–239) and Hirsch's articles and monograph (122f).
28. The new edition of *Conversations* which appeared during the Munich *Räterepublik* is indicative of the general interdependence between political interests and aesthetic predilections. It was bound in red and bore the subtitle *Bettina von Arnim's Call to Revolution and to the League of Nations* (Bettina von Arnim's Aufruf zur Revolution und zum Völkerbunde). (Ed. Curt Moreck. Munich: Schmidt, 1919)

Works Cited

Allgemeine Literaturzeitung: Monatsschrift. Ed. Bruno Bauer. Charlottenburg, 1844. 2 vols.

Arnim, Bettina von. *Werke und Briefe.* Ed. Gustav Konrad. Vols. 1–4. Frechen and Köln: Bartmann Verlag, 1959–1963. Briefe. Ed. Johannes Müller. Vol 5. Frechen and Köln: Bartmann Verlag, 1961. (Quoted as Köln.)

Bäumer, Konstanze. *"Bettine, Psyche, Mignon" Bettina von Arnim und Goethe.* Stuttgart: Akademischer Verlag H.D. Heinz, 1986.

Börne, Ludwig. *Sämtliche Schriften.* Ed. Inge and Peter Rippman. 5 vols. Düsseldorf: Joseph Metzler, 1964.

Bunzel, Wolfgang. "Phantasie ist die freie Kunst der Wahrheit." *Internationales Jahrbuch der Bettina-von-Arnim-Gesellschaft* 1 (1987): 7–28.

Dischner, Gisela. *Bettina von Arnim. Eine weibliche Sozialbiographie aus dem 19. Jahrhundert.* Berlin: Wagenbach, 1977.

Drewitz, Ingeborg. *Bettine von Arnim. Romantik—Revolution—Utopie. Eine Biographie.* Düsseldorf: Claasen, 1984.

Elbogen, Ismar, and Eleonore Sterling. *Die Geschichte der Juden in Deutschland.* Frankfurt/Main: Europäische Verlagsanstalt, 1966.

Fischer, Horst. *Judentum, Staat und Heer in Preußen im frühen 19. Jahrhundert. Zur Geschichte der staatlichen Judenpolitik.* Tübingen: Mohr, 1968.

Frederiksen, Elke. "Die Frau als Autorin zur Zeit der Romantik: Anfänge einer weiblichen literarischen Tradition." *Gestaltet und Gestaltend.* Ed. Marianne Burkhard. Amsterdam: Rodopi, 1980. 83–109.

Frels, Wilhelm. *Bettina von Arnims Königsbuch.* Schwerin: A. Schmidt, 1912.

Freund, Wilhelm. *Zur Judenfrage in Deutschland, vom Standpunkte des Rechts und der Gewissensfreiheit. Im Verein mit mehreren Gelehrten herausgegeben.* Berlin: Veit, 1843.

Geiger, Ludwig. *Bettine von Arnim und Friedrich Wilhelm IV. Ungedruckte Briefe und Aktenstücke.* Frankfurt/Main: Rütten & Loening, 1902.

———. *Geschichte der Juden in Berlin.* Berlin, 1871.

Grab, Walter. "Der preussische Weg der Judenemanzipation." *Juden in Preussen.* 24–29.

Herder, Johann Gottfried. *Sämtliche Werke.* Ed. Bernhard Suphan. Vol. 24. (1886) 33 vols. Berlin: 1877–1913.

"Herzhaft in die Dornen der Zeit greifen . . . ." Bettine von Arnim 1785–1859. Ed. Christoph Perels. Frankfurt/Main: Freies deutsches Hochstift, 1985.

Hirsch, Helmut. *Bettine von Arnim.* Reinbek bei Hamburg: Rowohlt, 1987.

———. "Jüdische Aspekte im Leben und Werk Bettine von Arnims." *Internationales Jahrbuch der Bettina-von-Arnim-Gesellschaft* 1 (1987): 61–76.

———. "Zur Dichotomie von Theorie und Praxis in Bettines Äußerungen über Judentum und Juden." *Internationales Jahrbuch der Bettina-von-Arnim-Gesellschaft* 3 (1989): 153–172.

Hirschberg, Leopold. "Bettina und die Juden." *Ost und West* 10 (1904): cols. 697–796.

Juden in Berlin 1671–1945. Ein Lesebuch. Berlin: Nicolai, 1988.

Juden in Preussen. Ein Kapitel deutscher Geschichte. Ed. Bildarchiv Preussischer Kulturbesitz. Dortmund: Harenberg, 1981. Official catalogue of the exhibit "Juden in Preussen."

Kayser, Rudolf. "Bettina von Arnim and the Jews." *Historica Judaica* 20 (1958): 47–60.

Kittler, Friedrich. "Writing into the Wind, Bettina." *Glyph* 7 (1980): 32–69.

Lachmanski, Hugo. "Bettina von Arnims jüdische Sendung." *Central-Verein Zeitung* 5 Oct. 1934 (13 No. 40).

Liebertz-Grün, Ursula. *Ordnung im Chaos. Studien zur Poetik der Bettine Brentano-von Arnim.* Heidelberg: Winter, 1989.

Marx, Karl. *Frühe Schriften.* Ed. Hans-Joachim Lieber and Peter Furth. 4th ed. Darmstadt: Wissenschaftliche Buchgesellschaft, 1981. Vol. 1 of *Werke. Schriften in 6 Bänden.* 6 vols. 1962.

Nahrebecky, Roman. *Wackenroder, Tieck, E.T.A. Hoffmann, Bettina von Arnim. Ihre Beziehung zur Musik und zum musikalischen Erlebnis.* Bonn: Bouvier, 1979.

Novalis. [Hardenberg, Friedrich.] *Schriften, Die Werke Friedrich von Hardenbergs.* 4 vols. and an accompanying vol. Ed. Paul Kluckhohn and Richard Samuel. Stuttgart: Kohlhammer, 1960–75. Accompanying volume 1988.

Philippson, Johanna. "Ludwig Philippson und die Allgemeine Zeitung des Judentums" *Das Judentum in der deutschen Umwelt 1800–1850.* Ed. Hans Liebeschütz and Arnold Paucker. Tübingen: Mohr, 1977. 243–293.

Philippson, Ludwig. "Literarische Nachrichten." *Allgemeine Zeitung des Judenthums* 17 No. 30 (25 July 1853): 387–389.

Püschel, Ursula. "Bettina von Arnim und Friedrich Wilhelm IV." *Internationales Jahrbuch der Bettina-von-Arnim-Gesellschaft* 3 (1989): 93–126.

Rürup, Reinhard. *Emanzipation und Antisemitismus. Studien zur "Judenfrage" der bürgerlichen Gesellschaft.* Göttingen: Vandenhoeck & Ruprecht, 1975.

Schmitz, Walter. " ' . . . die freie Kultur eines idealischen Sinnens' Bettine von Arnims Alterswerk 'Gespräche mit Dämonen.' " *Internationales Jahrbuch der Bettina-von-Arnim-Gesellschaft* 3 (1989): 137–152.

Silbergleit, Heinrich. *Die Bevölkerungs- und Berufsverhältnisse der Juden im Deutschen Reich.* Berlin: Akademie-Verlag, 1930.

Staff, Ilse. Introduction. *Dies Buch gehört dem König* by Bettina von Arnim. Frankfurt: Insel, 1982.

Tekinay, Alev. "Zum Orient-Bild Bettina von Arnims und der jüngeren Romantik." *Arcadia* 16 (1981): 47–49.

Toury, Jacob. "The Jewish Question. A Semantic Approach." *Leo Baeck Institute Yearbook* 11 (1966): 85–106.

———. *Soziale und Politische Geschichte der Juden in Deutschland, 1847–1871.* Düsseldorf: Droste, 1977.

Waldstein, Edith. *Bettine von Arnim and the Politics of Romantic Conversation.* Columbia: Camden House, 1988.

Wolf, Christa. " 'Nun ja! Das nächste Leben geht aber heute an.' Ein Brief über die Bettine." *Lesen und Schreiben Neue Sammlung.* Darmstadt: Luchterhand, 1980. 284–318. Included in this volume.

IV

Translating Experience

Letters in Sufferance and Deliverance: The Correspondence of Bettina Brentano-von Arnim and Karoline von Günderrode[1]

Patricia Anne Simpson

"Thus it is that what the 'purloined letter,' nay, the 'letter in sufferance' means is that a letter always arrives at its destination."
—Jacques Lacan, "The Seminar on the Purloined Letter"

Bettina Brentano-von Arnim inscribed the life and letters of her friend and teacher, Karoline von Günderrode, into the problematic, provocative literary genre of the epistolary novel.[2] In their actual and fictional exchanges, these two women of the German Romantic era realign the potentially unequal power relationship between author and text, subject and object, self and other. In so doing, they approximate a feminist aesthetic that is constituted in and by their correspondence. The texts produced during this period in German literary history have occupied the center of speculative thought about literary theory. Recent post-structuralist insights into the nature of language, cognition, and gender invite a re-examination or a re-reading of this particular epistolary novel. In this essay, I will claim that the Günderrode/Brentano-von Arnim exchange marks a significant contribution to contemporary theories of figurative language, even to the discussion of the relationship between gender and aesthetics. For Bettina Brentano-von Arnim and Karoline von Günderrode, the truth, expressed as the relationship between language and desire, is written into their fiction.

The genre of the epistolary novel automatically questions the sources and circumstances of the "original" or "authentic" correspondence.[3] The truth value of the letters, their signatures, and their designated readers raise the the questions of biography and autobiography.[4] In the case of *Günderode* (Die Günderode) (1840), Brentano-von Arnim inscribes the person (Günderrode) and the persona (Günderode, here Karoline) of her friend, positing both a factual and a fictional existence for them both. In so doing, she writes over their biographical disagreements and instead preserves the mutually illuminating friendship, even or only after Günderrode's suicide in 1806. The inscription of historical into the fictional truth transforms life into a pretext for the epistolary novels Brentano-von Arnim produces. Absence, death, and memory are the constitutive modes for this genre. In *Günderode*, Brentano-von Arnim provides both a monument to and a document of Günderrode's life and letters and "forwards" the letters to the present. Together, their contribution to a Romantic theory of language is constituted precisely by the mutual dependence of their thought and writing processes and by the apparent suspension of power in the subject-object dialectic. Language is for them an equal, if not a symmetrical, exchange between two subjects.

Brentano-von Arnim's work consists primarily of epistolary novels based on historically corroborated exchanges between her and her subjects. She is most noted for *Goethe's Correspondence with a Child* (Goethes Briefwechsel mit einem Kinde) (1835), *The King's Book* (Dies Buch gehört dem König) (1843), and *The Spring Wreath* (Clemens Brentanos Frühlingskranz) (1844), the product of her correspondence with her brother Clemens Brentano. The inscription of her life into her work accounts in part for the attention to Bettina Brentano-von Arnim's biography and her place at the center of the Romantic circle. She achieved notoriety as well for her unconventional deportment, her political activism, her salons, and her marriage to Achim von Arnim.[5] Her work, however, remains to be read on its own terms. Her female/feminist aesthetic seeks truth in speculation, reality in fantasy, and life in literature. In language, she posits a fictional identity, inscribing a textual space for the crossover between life and letters. Her representation of Günderrode may not be "historical," but it is no less legitimate.

It becomes the burden of scholarship to "read" the relationship between biography and literature, particularly with regard to *Günderode*, in order to acknowledge Brentano-von Arnim's contribution to literature and literary theory (as well as to literary history). For this epistolary novel, in part the product of her exchange with Karoline von Günderrode, is an impressive and innovative literary monument, full of speculation about the project of poetry and the nature of language. Their mutual meditations, modified by the authorial persona Bettine, are the product of actual and fictional exchanges between the two women. Günderrode as teacher and friend is the object of Brentano-von Arnim's work, but she is also the contributing authorial subject whose poetry is incoporated into the final product. The historical figures (Bettina Brentano-von Arnim and Karoline von Günderrode) can be distinguished from their fictional figures (Bettine and Günderode, here Karoline) only in reading the almost imperceptible difference in the signature of their names.[6] Bettine in effect suspends Karoline's death sentence textually. This tendency to write over the historical truth and to put poetic language in the center of existence are evident in the nature of their thoughts about the kiss. For Bettine, the kiss of nature is the source of poetic inspiration; for Karoline, it becomes the kiss of death. For both women, however, the kiss plays a crucial part in representing the originary power of figurative language.

With the letters that remain of the life, Bettina Brentano-von Arnim shapes her version of Günderrode as *Günderode*. Her operating principle is one of inclusion, rather than selection, for she deposits in the novel form the letters written and unwritten, letters addressed to other recipients, Günderrode's verse, fictive discourses, and playlets in prose and poetry. In a sense, the novel is more a monument than a document. It memorializes both the person and the pen of Günderrode. This act of positing, of prosopopoeia, governs the novel; this giving voice to the dead becomes an uncanny kind of mouth-to-mouth resuscitation. Only in the written trace can Bettine write over absence and represent Karoline and her work.

Günderrode quite literally lived and died through letters: she sustained her life in epistles, used letters as vehicles for her poems and playlets, and wrote missives to connect herself, and, finally, to sever connections to the world. She initially established and maintained contact with Bettina Brentano (later Brentano-von Arnim) in an appropriately epistolary mode.[7] Günderrode's letters from the secular convent for the daughters of the impoverished nobility (and from other locations) were the first vehicles of her poetry, prose, and private mythology, and they were also her epistles of desire. These letters, in the "original," kept the author in touch with her private readers.

The publication history of Günderrode's work, literally the making public of her private life and letters, constitutes a story of its own.[8] Before the complete works appeared in print under Günderrode's own name, Brentano-von Arnim's publication of the exchange made Günderrode and her work accessible to the reading public. The combination of truth and fiction present in the epistolary novel informs the reception of this work, for the scholarship on *Günderode* tends to fall into two categories: the first emphatically distinguishes between the "fact" and the "fiction;" the second celebrates the suspension of such rigid definitions. These separate trends tend to break down along the lines of sexual difference, though there are exceptions.

The scene of writing, then, becomes for some the scene of the crime. The publication history reflects this split in the novel's community of readers, receivers, and revisionists: the truth is engendered in the speculation about nature, writing, and desire, symbolized in the theory of the kiss. Following the itinerary of one letter containing a sonnet and postscript Günderrode sent to Karl von Savigny, then in revised form to Brentano-von Arnim, and chosen here for its thematization of origins—of desire, of poetic language—requires the kind of detective work the character Dupin undertakes in the Edgar Allan Poe story analyzed by Lacan in the "Seminar on 'The Purloined Letter'." In the essay, Lacan returns to and revises the Freudian concept of repetition compulsion to repetition automism, displacing the drive (Zwang) from the self to the text in what he calls the "insistence of the signifying chain."[9] This revision of the concept points to the general trajectory of writing and desire.[10] The relationship is significant for Günderrode's work, for the sonnet "The Kiss in the Dream" (Der Kuß im Traum)[11] centers on a forbidden desire (for a man on the verge of marriage to someone else) as a source of poetic inspiration. The issue in the context of Günderrode's letters "in sufferance," or en route to their destination, is one of delivery. Her letters can be counted as representations of a desire for writing. Brentano-von Arnim's textual production and reproduction account for their delivery, even though her theory of writing differs from that of Günderrode. On behalf of her friend, Brentano-von Arnim gathers that which would otherwise be written to the wind.[12]

Works of literature and literary scholarship resurrected the literary corpus and saved Günderrode's epistles from consignment by edgy or indifferent readers—or peculiar packaging—to the dead letter file. A lineage of critics and committed readers has kept the letters and their enclosures in circulation. The letters remained private immediately after Günderrode's suicide. Friedrich Creuzer, the philologist and classical scholar, was the recipient of Günderrode's apparently requited but withdrawn love. Entrusted with the manuscript for her third volume of verse (penned under the pseudonym Jon), Creuzer first sold the volume, but withdrew it from consideration after her death at the urging of his friend Daub.[13] He thus succeeded temporarily in erasing traces of himself from her work.[14] Certain of her letters, in an ironic twist, emerged in the 1830s from his wife's legacy, the Leske estate.[15] The details of the publication history are revisited here as part of the story itself: of textual sabotage reversed not only by diligent scholarship and discovery, but by creative revisions that give voice to the dead.

The publication history of Günderrode's work reflects the split in scholarly reception between the historically inauthentic and the fictional truth posited in Brentano-von Arnim's *Günderode*. Responding to the revealed incompleteness of previous editions, Dr. Leopold Hirschberg edited a version of Günderrode's work in 1920. Even though he attempted to take Günderrode's work seriously and present it authentically, he trivializes her life in his introduction: "The Fairy-Tale of the Beautiful Karoline" (Das Märchen von der schönen Karoline) (1:iv). Describing her biography as a fairy tale, Hirschberg collapses her work into her life and aestheticizes her death. His impulse is to do justice to his subject by writing a fairy-tale, "instead of a dry biography in the usual sense, as has been told a hundred times" (Statt einer trocknen Biographie im gewöhnlicen Sinne, wie sie hundertmal erzählt ist) (1:iv). Time and again, editors reach the limits of conventional scholarship when dealing with Bettina von Brentano-von Arnim and Karoline von Günderrode. In Hirschberg's case, however, good intentions do not guarantee illuminating conclusions.

Not the ugly, most bombastic Karsch—rather the beautiful, dreamy Günderode [*sic*] deserves the epithet "German Sappho." Like the Greek, Günderode [*sic*] played her strings only in praise of the gods of love; like Sappho, she commited suicide, as Eros and Aphrodite disdained their victims.

Nicht der häßlichen, schwülstigen Karschin—der schönen, schwärmerischen Günderode [*sic*] gebührt der Beiname der "deutschen Sappho."

Wie die Griechin rührte sie ihre Saiten nur zum Preis der Gottheiten
der Liebe, ging wie sie freiwillig in den Tod, als Eros und Aphrodite
ihre Opfer verschmähten. (1:xxii)

Hischberg sets up a beauty contest between the two German female
poets, Anna Louisa Karsch (1722–1791) and Günderrode, which the
latter wins. Though he judges their poetry in slightly different terms,
Hirschberg's comparison to Sappho reveals a telling essentialism: female poets seem to constitute a separate category for evaluation.[16]
Moreover, the selective reference to the Greek poet thoroughly en-
chants Günderrode's suicide. He fails to compare the form and content of their respective lyric productions, and connects the two figures
only as female poets.

Walther Rehm's article in the "Goethe Calendar for the Year
1942" (Goethe-Kalender auf das Jahr 1942) concentrates on the literary rather than biological attributes of her corpus. In his essay on
Günderrode's poetry, he shifts the focus from her biography to the
philosophical disposition of other Romantics. He compares her to
Friedrich Hölderlin, stressing their kinship with the "family of decline" (Familie des Untergangs) (95). He reads and classifies her life
in terms of her male contemporaries, failing to acknowledge Günderrode's literary singularity.

Günderrode belongs in the world of Kleist, Hölderlin, and Novalis; not
so much due to poetic accomplishment—seldom does she achieve the
heights of the others—rather because of the decided power of her
heart that forged ahead even to its own end. . . . In such a community,
Günderrode also shares with the others the unmistakable road to destruction, to the realm of the dead, to the dark night of the graves, to
the ground of the abyss.

In die Welt Kleists, Hölderlins, Novalis' gehört die Günderrode, nicht
durch das Maß bewiesenen Dichtertums—nur sehr selten naht sie sich
der Höhe der andern—,sondern durch die entschlossene, bis zum
eigenen Ende hinschreitende Kraft ihres Herzens. . . . In solcher
Gemeinschaft teilt die Günderrode mit den andern auch den
unbeirrbaren Weg nach unten, zu den Toten, in die dunkle Nacht der
Gräber, zum Grund und Abgrund. (96)

Rehm, though somewhat dismissive of her work, nonetheless locates
Günderrode's sensibility within a larger context populated by Höl-

derlin, Kleist, and others. The common denominator, as Rehm perceptively notices, is the relationship in their work between writing and death. Brentano-von Arnim, too, will make this point in her correspondence.

Dissertations by twentieth-century critics like the French Germanist Genviève Bianquis and later Annelore Naumann demonstrate that Günderrode's work is as interesting as her life and that the two are mutually illuminating. The crossing of fact and fiction is a common point in the Günderrode/Brentano-von Arnim correspondence, for both women are attentive to the literary nature of their relationship and are aware of the necessity of writing as their only medium. Writing, an act of representation contingent upon absence, grounds their relationship to each other and to language.

Before proceeding with a closer analysis of the work, I will return briefly to the problem of "authentic" and "apocryphal" in the publication history to make a point about textual truth and reliability. In his introduction to his version of the "complete" works, editor Friedrich Götz cautions the reader to distinguish between the authentic and the apocryphal in Brentano-von Arnim's epistolary novel: "Cp. Bettina 'Günderode.' . . . The poems contained therein by Günderode [sic] are all authentic and identical; however, the letters signed 'Caroline' are, according to authentic report, apocryphal, freely shaped by Bettine's poetic reminiscences and philosophemes" (Vergl. Bettina 'Die Günderode.' . . . Die darin mitgetheilten Gedichte der Günderode [sic] sind alle ächt und gleichlautend; die mit 'Caroline' unterzeichneten Briefe jedoch authentischem Vernehmen nach apokryph, nach poetischen Reminiscenzen und Philosophemen von Bettine freigestaltet) (x).[17] Götz expectedly briefs the reader on authenticity, on the reliability of the texts. Yet his own claims for the completeness of his edition prove untrue: the third volume of Günderrode's verse and prose, *Melete* (Melete), was included in the "complete" works only in 1920.[18] The epistemological ground seems unstable when anyone asserts the absolute truth or untruth of a text, for the guarantees themselves, the material manuscripts, are contained within the narrative strategy, as in the case of the epistolary novel (Bettina Brentano-von Arnim's *Die Günderode*), or in archives or estates (Karoline von Günderrode's original letters). The attempt to reconstruct an authentic, organic whole of a literary and biographical "body" is thwarted by the assumption that there is some kind of totality to be recovered in the first place. Whether a work is authentic or apocryphal is central to the critical enterprise. "Apocryphal" means primarily "of doubtful authenticiy, counterfeit, fabulous." It also means non-canonical. Brentano-von Arnim's Günderrode book is not the forgery some scholars claim; rather it is non-canonical.[19] Her fragments and embellishments come close to telling a "truth" about her friend's life and work. The presence of the novel destabilizes the concept of canon, elicits a different kind of reading: of texts in contexts, of life in letters, of criticism that informs without deforming.

Both scholarly and non-scholarly attempts to trace a literary matrilineage have taken the form of revisions or "translations" constituted by visionary criticism that revives suppressed figures while it participates itself in the literary form of that tradition. One of the first documents, or monuments, of this kind is Brentano-von Arnim's somewhat rhapsodic epistolary novel *Günderode* (1840), full of her response to her friend's work as well as the work itself. In it the letters are not exchanged, but rather forwarded with commentary from private to public readers. Later in the nineteenth century Margaret Fuller translated excerpts from the novel, which she referred to in the translator's preface as a work not "subject to the canons of literary criticism, but a simple product of private relations" (v).[20] In this century, Sarah Kirsch traces the same genealogy, engaging Bettina von Brentano-von Arnim in a fictive discourse about women in writing, in politics, in the context of her [Kirsch's] exquisitely lyrical "Wiepersdorf" cycle.[21] This desire to engage in fictive dialogue locates Christa Wolf in this matrilineage. Her efforts to recuperate the past, to let the dead speak, are evident in her edition of Günderrode's work *The Shadow of a Dream* (Der Schatten eines Traumes). A similar form of resuscitation occurs in her fictive discourse between Kleist and Günderrode: it takes place "no place on earth," only in Wolf's text. Though scholars have noted similarity in their work and in their biographies, there is no evidence that Kleist and Günderrode actually ever met. Wolf realizes their affinity in the fictive dialogue of *No Place on Earth* (Kein Ort. Nirgends). This practice of resurrection continues in her re-edition of Karoline, the afterword of which takes the form of a postscript, a letter written by Christa Wolf to a friend about Bettina Brentano-von Arnim and Karoline von Günderrode. Wolf's speculation and scholarship attempt to weave over the silence of women writing—the suppression of texts from publications and from literary canons—evident in her more recent yet more distant work with the Cassandra myth.

In another medium, Margarethe von Trotta's film *Sheer Madness* (Heller Wahn) (1982) can be read in the context of reception-revision, though neither of the central figures aligns perfectly with the two Romantic predecessors. The Karoline figure, Ruth (played by Angela Winkler), is shy, depressive, and withdrawn, a private painter. She is befriended by the Bettine figure, a literary scholar, Olga (played by Hanna Schygulla), who encourages her work and creates tension between Ruth and her husband. Ruth's diffidence is offset by the confident Olga, who is teaching the work of Brentano-von Arnim and Günderrode.[22] Von Trotta visually and thematically cites the tradition of female friendship within her film. Her revision is subversive, for Ruth does not die in the film; the suicide is displaced by an ambiguous scene of homicide in which Ruth kills her husband.

Although some scholars have demonstrated a need to categorize and catalogue the "truth" of Brentano-von Arnim's literary production, their attempts are thwarted by the recalcitrant and self-sufficient object of study. Brentano-von Arnim writes as part of the natural process of creation with little attention to scholarly accuracy. Waldemar Oehlke's study of the epistolary novels painstakingly chronicles the documented letters and their reappearance. He concludes the chapter on *Günderode*:

> For, the attempt to classify the material, compiled from letters, as an epistolary publication on the grounds that it fulfills the conditions of the genre, leads to the opposite result. We have before us an individually crafted work of art, which, on the one hand exhibits historical accuracy, but on the other, a completely disorderly use of the limited authentic material; not letters, not even parts of letters: epistolary thoughts are the components of this book.

> Denn aus dem Versuch, das zu ordnen, was als Briefpublikation zu der Voraussetzung berechtigte, es sei aus Briefen zusammengestellt, ergibt sich das gegenteilige Resultat: wir sehen ein individuell gearbeitetes Kunstwerk vor uns, das zwar historische Treue, nicht minder aber völlig ordnungslose Verwendung des geringen echten Materials aufweist; nicht Briefe, auch nicht Briefteile: Briefgedanken sind des Buches Komponenten. (246)

Noteworthy is Oehlke's willingness to set aside his cautious method and comment on the achievement of the work itself, even if, or perhaps because, it resists control and disobeys orders.

Brentano-von Arnim's braiding of fact and fiction in the novel
constitutes an attempt to keep Günderrode and her work in circulation in an instance of writing and re-creation. Given the death of
Günderrode and the suppression of her work, this project could only
be accomplished in an act of writing and rewriting. Brentano-von
Arnim makes no scholarly claims. Instead she relies on her fictionalizing of life and letters to document those of her friend. This
type of revisionary activity may not be gender-specific, but Brentano-
von Arnim's interpolating and embroidering of the historical truth
and the actual texts continue to inspire women artists to occupy ab-
sences with their own imaginations, as evidenced in the creative reception outlined above. In the "originary" epistolary novel, the temporal
shifts throughout the work characterize a sedimentation of form and
content in the interdependent writing of the two women. Their shared
thoughts grow together, but their representation maintains the integrity of both figures. Brentano-von Arnim, as well as Günderrode, is
both subject and object of her own book. *Günderode* presents readers with a challenge similar to *The Autobiography of Alice B. Toklas.*
Whose is it, the reader asks, and why does the question matter?
Again, the impulse to determine the truth value, or the reality, in or
behind literature is compelling, but equally confounding. In the
novel, Bettine and Karoline are participants in the subject-object
relationship, but both are also writing subjects, even in the context of
the former's novel that bears the latter's name. Their historical, interpersonal relationship informs, but does not limit the correspondence.
The language Brentano-von Arnim employs to describe the correspondence between the two women relates directly to her theory of
language which is central to an understanding of the larger context of
German Romanticism. For Brentano-von Arnim articulates specifically the relationship between natural and divine language. Poetic,
figurative language is for Brentano-von Arnim the kiss of nature: a
de-eroticized expression of divine inspiration. For Günderrode, however, the language of desire, contingent upon the absence of the
desired object, can only be the desire for writing. Only in writing can
absence be represented, if not recuperated.

More constant than any other identifiable theme is the self-
consciousness focused on the acts of reading and writing. The question of Bettine's natural and Karoline's formalized language recurs
throughout the novel, providing a red thread for an unsystematic
work. Bettine continually comments on her friend's poetry and prose,

which inspire her own rhapsodizing about the nature of language. She concludes that the nature of language is the language of nature. The persistent difference between the two women is a matter of style. Bettine provides an example of this difference.

> I think it's so lovely to contemplate everything with you, we walk around Grandma's garden, in the magnificent summer days, or in the thicket where there are such dark paths through the foliage, whenever we pretend, we walk there and let everything unfold in conversation, then, in the evening, I write it all down and send it to you in the city with the Jew who takes the mail, and then you put it into a poetic form, so that some day, when other people find it, they'll respect and believe it all the more, it is a lovely joke, but don't take it just as a joke, I am serious, for why shouldn't we think together about the well-being and needs of humanity.

> Ich denke mir's so schön, alles mit Dir zu überlegen, wir gehen dann zusammen hier in der Großmama ihren Garten auf und ab, in den herrlichen Sommertagen, oder im Boskett, wo's so dunkle Laubgänge gibt, wenn wir simulieren, so gehen wir dorthin und entfalten alles im Gespräch, dann schreib ich's abends alles auf und schick Dir's mit dem Jud in die Stadt, und Du bringst es nachher in eine dichterische Form, damit, wenn's die Menschen einst finden, sie um so mehr Ehrfurcht und Glauben dran haben, es ist ein schöner Scherz, aber nehm's nur nicht für Scherz, es ist mein Ernst, denn warum sollten wir nicht zusammen denken über das Wohl und Bedürfnis der Menschheit. (Weimar 2:165–66)

Bettine imagines the two women in a conversation, set in her grandmother's garden, and assigns her friend the task of putting the thoughts they think together in poetic form to enhance reverence and belief. Bettine, speculating about the "Floating-Religion" (Schwebe-Religion), posits the relationship between divine creation, thought, and prayer: "Whoever does not think shall not learn to pray" (Wer nit denkt, lernt nit beten) (Weimar 2:166), which Karoline revises: "Thought is prayer" (Denken ist Beten) (Weimar 2:167). Karoline's is the task of concision in formal, poetic language. Bettine's style amplifies, associates, and expands.

Bettine always entertains; Karoline edifies. Bettine supplies family anecdotes, encounters with her history tutor and assorted guests, the mysterious figure of the postman. Karoline offers advice and encouragement, occasionally reproachment. Bettine is truly a woman of correspondence: she is connected to her context. In some cases that context is nature, in some culture. Even in *Günderode*, Brentano-von Arnim's political activism, her concern with the power structures of her time, is apparent in the rousing dedication to Germany's students, as well as in the above-mentioned concern with the well-being of humanity in general. Karoline, conversely, lives a disconnected life. Her texts provide her only context, and her only tenuous connections to the world. Letters provide the lifeline during her lifetime, in all the pathos this situtation implies. The distinction between the narrator and the narrated collapses in the epistolary novel, but the differences between Bettine and Karoline prevail in their respective divergent relationships to language. Both women use the image of the kiss to express this relationship.

Brentano-von Arnim's and Bettine's relationship to nature informs her/their relationship to language, and consequently, to Günderrode and Karoline. In writing, she recuperates or reshapes experiences from memory and/or imagination. As the novel unfolds, the kiss becomes the figure for inspiration. Bettine acknowledges but ignores certain conventions; she is subject, however, to received notions about the tedium of certain disciplines (especially dry, abstract philosophy) which she contrasts with the natural beauty of art and poetry. Bettine further splits writing into the practice of form or style and her own writing. She does, however, praise her friend's concision and precision in language, and contrasts it to her own expansive style. Nature, she asserts, is the source:

> —I cannot write poetry like you, Günderode, but I can speak with Nature when I am alone with her, but no one else should be behind me, for precisely the soliditude allows me to be with her.

> —Ich kann nicht dichten wie Du, Günderode, aber ich kann sprechen mit der Natur, wenn ich allein mit ihr bin, aber es darf niemand hinter mir sein, denn grad das Alleinsein macht, daß ich mit ihr bin. (Weimar 2:43)

Bettine's self-described dialogue with nature resembles the end effect of the epistolary novel. The dialogue can only be a monologue, for the conversation partners, invoked by writing, cannot ever be present, but only represented. The exchange of letters takes the place of presence for Bettine and Karoline, but not for Brentano-von Arnim and Günderrode, for writing can only figuratively revive the dead.

Bettine criticizes but justifies her own writing and contrasts it to that of Karoline, her echo, her mirror. In her letters to Karoline, Bettine offers insight into the complexities of language and her occasional frustration with its manipulation. Bettine asserts that she has no control over her writing, but that language as an expression of nature controls her work. The reversion to nature as the ultimate source leads one step further, to pantheism, and Bettine's private religion. Even this conviction has a linguistic motivation: Bettine believes in the performative power of language. Language is the originary act of creation. Speaking constitutes a moment of creation. In a later letter, Bettine refers to the creation by focusing on divine utterance. Here she approximates the theory of symbolic totality familiar from the dialectic of the general or universal contained within the specific, the concept of one-in-all.

—The Holy Spirit is the soul of the world.—It touches everything, it awakens the dead, and if I did not have it, then everything would be dead.—And life means to awaken life, I was amazed, when the spirit told this to me.—I wondered whether I awaken life, or whether I am dead.—And it occurred to me that God said: Let there be, and that the language of God is creation;—and I wanted to imitate that.

—Der heilige Geist ist die Weltseele.—Er berührt alles, er weckt von den Toten auf, und hätt ich ihn nicht, so wär alles tot.—Und Leben ist Leben wecken, ich war verwundert, als der Geist mir's sagte.—Ich besann mich, ob ich Leben wecke oder ob ich tot sei.—Und da fiel mir ein, daß Gott sprach: Es werde, und daß die Sprach Gottes ein Erschaffen sei;—und das wollt ich nachahmen. (Weimar 2:185)

Here Bettine connects the dialectic of the specific and the general to the performative utterance. She continues as the novel weaves on to make connections between nature and the divine dimension of language. She hopes to imitate God's language in the act of creation, frequently referring to God as the primal poet—"God is a poet" (Gott ist Poet) (Weimar 2:163). Bettine goes one step further, concluding that God is also poetry, and that writing poetry becomes an act of divine inspiration.

—But the one thing I have retained, that God is poetry, that the human being is created in his image and likeness, that we are therefore born poets, that all are called and few chosen, that I know unfortunately

from my self, but still I am a poet, even though I can make no rhyme, I
feel it when I walk in the open air, in the forest or in the hills, there a
rhythm lies in my soul, and I have to think to its measure, and my tone
changes to the beat.

—Aber das eine hab ich behalten, daß Gott die Poesie ist, daß der
Mensch nach seinem Ebenbild geschaffen ist, daß er also geborner
Dichter ist, daß aber alle berufen sind und wenige auserwählt, das muß
ich leider an mir selber erfahren, aber doch bin ich Dichter, obschon
ich keinen Reim machen kann, ich fühl's, wenn ich gehe in der freien
Luft, im Wald oder an Bergen hinauf, da liegt ein Rhythmus in meiner
Seele, nach dem muß ich denken, und meine Stimmung ändert sich im
Takt. (Weimar 2:164)

Bettine associates the rhythm of nature with that of poetry and both
with divine creation. While she acknowledges the achievement of
Karoline's poetry, Bettine redeems her own creative nature, though
her natural "poetry" cannot be read or written.

In another passage about the relationship between nature and language, Bettine writes about her amazement at the packaging of the
chestnut and its form. Here she affirms and extends her previous
comments about the nature of divine speech. While she comprehends
the larger order of things, she admits difficulty in understanding the
specifics of creation. The example she uses is that of the chestnut
tree.

It is impossible that there be a form unless it came forth from God's
word "Let there be." Now, that which comes forth from the eternal will
of creation, that must have its own language, that must speak out for
itself and answer itself. Your life must lead its own language, for otherwise it is nothing.

Es ist unmöglich, daß eine Form sei, sie ist denn durch Gottes Wort
"Es werde" hervorgegangen. Nun, was durch den ewigen Erzeugungs-
willen hervorgeht, das muß doch eine Selbstsprache haben, das muß
sich nämlich aussprechen und sich auch beantworten. Dein Leben muß
doch eine Sprache führen, denn sonst ist es ja nichts. (Weimar 2: 231)

In subsequent paragraphs, Bettine sermonizes about the dialogue
between God and the faithful, mediated by nature. In the above
passage, however, she uses language as an overarching concept, not
as an instrument of communication or a sign system with specific

and general modes of signification, but as an ultimate category to explain phenomena not readily accessible to human understanding. The form of the chestnut is the obedient product of God's utterance, "Let there be," but it also speaks its own language in order for its kind to persist. Bettine reads genetic and generic coding into the language of nature, which extends to include human nature. Without "leading" a language, she concludes, life is nothing. Bettine alternates between desiring to write, to produce poetic language, and recognizing the self-sufficiency of nature, which confidently speaks its own originary language. Nature is indifferent to writing, but Bettine can never be indifferent to nature.

The itinerary proceeds through a growing self-consciousness about the power of language, especially of figurative language, to express. Bettine often refers to her sense of bewilderment, even enchantment, at the unpredictability of language, especially in the act of writing. Bettine expresses her frustrated attempts to write everything she thinks. Writing as an expression of her thoughts proves an inadequate but necessary form of mediation.

> I can tell you many stories from here, I have many thoughts that I cannot write down, sometimes I jump up, as if I had to go to you and immediately tell you some newly thought thing—.

> Ich kann Dir auch viel von hier erzählen, ich hab eine Menge Gedanken, die ich nicht aufschreiben kann, manchmal spring ich auf, als müßt ich zu Dir und Dir gleich was ganz neu Gedachtes sagen—. (Weimar 2: 81)

Bettine provides self-commentary within her letter. She informs Karoline about her own process of selection: she could write about events, and will in the end rehearse the quotidian details of her existence, for her thoughts, she implies, outrun her hand. But the impulse remains the same: she writes to achieve an immediacy with Karoline. In response to Karoline von Günder(r)ode's "The Shades" (Die Manen), Bettine writes:

> . . . Voigt and I strolled to a green spot and I read aloud from your letters, I read him the "Shades" and attached all sorts of ideas to it, that I really cannot articulate; I cannot speak with anyone the way I can with you.

> . . . ich schlenderte mit dem Voigt nach einem grünen Platz und las ihm
> vor aus Deiner Brieftasche, ich las ihm die "Manen" vor und knüpfte
> allerlei Ideen dran, die ich nicht recht aussprechen konnt, ich kann vor
> niemand sprechen wie vor Dir. (Weimar 2: 91)

Bettine is convinced that her difficulty in articulating such thoughts
does not extend to her relationship with Karoline. Apart from the
minor inconveniences that prohibit a coherence between her thinking
and speaking (and writing), Bettine's expressed frustration stems
from the more general, always troubled relationship between thought
and language. In Bettine's hands, perhaps in itself, language seems
out of control.

Her response to language as a process and product of nature abdicates a certain responsibility: she as a subject is not the source, rather
she is a writing instrument for the greater dictates of nature and the
divine. Still, she has the capacity to recognize correspondences.
Bettine is highly aware of the performance of writing itself and incorporates this consciousness into her missives. Often she comments on the
actual circumstances under which she is writing: "I wrote this page by
moonlight, you will not be able to read it" (ich hab diese Seite im
Mondschein geschrieben, Du wirst nicht lesen können.) (Weimar 2:
57). Bettine inscribes the scene of writing into her letters. The process,
the act of writing itself, informs her content, just as Brentano-von
Arnim includes the letters in a novel. This alignment between the two
forms of inclusion provides the basis for Brentano-von Arnim's aesthetic, constituted by the capacity of writing to represent a past event.
Bettine writes by the dim light of nature. In another letter, Bettine
comments: "I write it down, that I feel so well today, because the sun
shines on my paper and lights up my thoughts; there I read so well in
my heart" (Ich schreib's dahin, daß mir's so wohl ist heut, weil die Sonn
mir auf's Papier scheint und meine Gedanken beleuchtet, da lese ich so
deutlich in meinem Herzen) (Weimar 2: 134).[23] The sun, the natural
source of light, illuminates her thoughts, and enables her to "read" in
her heart. Here Bettine posits a form of natural inscription that provides the basis of her relationship to herself. The consciousness of her
writing context embraces her relationship to nature, to language, to
her political and social circumstances. Whether by the light of the
moon or the light of day, Bettine asserts that she writes through natural
inspiration: she is "kissed" by it, and constantly aware of the "presence" of nature, lighting her thoughts as well as the material paper.

On the other hand, Karoline's seclusion, or lack of context, shapes her work. She inhabits a textual world of myth, history, philosophy. Her writing is disciplined by form in a way Bettine's is not. This premeditatedness Bettine calls poetry. Bettine, it seems, can only write about things she has experienced; Karoline can only write about things she has not experienced. Whereas Bettine fills her letters with details about her life, her thoughts, and her relatives, Karoline responds to Bettine, and writes mostly of her private myths and dreams, the most poignant example of which is the kiss in the dream.

This difference in style prompts Bettine to chastise herself for her "scribbling" (Schreiberei), echoing the criticism of her brother Clemens—who wants her to write a book—(Weimar 2:141) in the following excerpt:

> I noticed, when I was writing, the self-satisfied, idle chatter that is so easy to carry on, that seduced me, and now all at once I have had enough. How gracefully and pleasantly you said everything and with your magic wand you playfully drew a circle in which you joked with me, and I lashed out around me with thorns and nettles and thistles; ah, I feel a reluctance toward my scribbling from yesterday.—

> Ich merkt es, als beim Schreiben das selbstgefällige Geschwätz, was sich so schön fügte, mich verführte, und nun auf einmal bin ich's satt. Wie anmutig und scherzend hast Du alles ausgesprochen und mit Deinem Zauberstab Dir spielend einen Kreis gemacht, mit mir drin zu scherzen, und ich hab mit Dornen und Nessel und Disteln um mich gepeitscht; ach, ich fühl einen Widerwillen gegen meine Schreiberei von gestern.— (Weimar 2: 101)

It is difficult to interrupt Bettine. To cut into the text and present pieces of the prose is like changing the course of a rapidly moving stream. In this moment of self-criticism, Bettine downgrades a sonnet she wrote the previous night in sadness and "super-cleverness" (Hyperklugheit) (Weimar 2:101). At the same time, she praises Karoline's magic wand, a figural pen which demarcates the difference between the two styles of writing. Karoline comments, in the context of the novel, on her pen friend's letters:

> You speak a language one could call style, if it were not in violation of all customary rhythm. Poetry is always genuine style, for it only streams forth from the spirit in harmonic waves, and what is not worthy

of this spirit, should not be allowed to be thought at all, or rather all experience should only touch the spirit poetically, otherwise it suffers from disrupture, as I experienced this morning when an old family bill for 17 Flr. from the shoemaker reached me from Hanau, and which I unfortunately cannot pay, in order to dissolve my embarassment poetically, I am sending you the little Apollo as a hostage together with Türkheim's laurel wreath, give me the money.

Du führst eine Sprache, die man Stil nennen könnte, wenn sie nicht gegen allen herkömmlichen Takt wär. Poesie ist immer echter Stil, da sie nur in harmonischen Wellen dem Geist entströmt, was dessen unwürdig ist, dürfte gar nicht gedacht werden, oder vielmehr darf alles Ereignis den Geist nur poetisch berühren, sonst leidet er Abbruch, wie ich das heute morgen habe erfahren müssen, wo mir von Hanau eine veraltete Familien-Schuhmacherrechnung von 17 Flr. zugeschickt wurde, die ich nicht bezahlen kann, meine Verlegenheit poetisch aufzulösen, schicke ich Dir den kleinen Apoll als Geisel samt Türkheims Lorbeerkranz, gib mir das Geld. (Weimar 2: 109)

Karoline fills her letter with generalities that would sound like poetic platitudes if not mitigated by the subtle self-irony with regard to her "unpoetic" debt. Significant in this letter is the quiet counterattack on Bettine's hypertrophical intelligence or "philistinism" (Philistergeist) (Weimar 2:101). Karoline reverses the assumed priority of thought over language; if a thought cannot be expressed poetically, then it should not be thought in the first place. This radical position leads directly to the disruptions of the quotidian: the unpaid, unpayable bill. From these casual exchanges emerge two separate, willful, and discerning theories about the constitutive relationship between epistemology and rhetoric, thought and its expression. Bettine writes everything she thinks with little attention to style or form: Karoline asserts that only thoughts that can be expressed poetically should be thought in the first place. Bettine would insist on the primacy of thought over its expression; Karoline on the primacy of expression over thought. Precisely this ongoing argument constitutes their legacy to literary theory.

The question of the relationship between thought and its representation comes up in the letters about Friedrich Hölderlin. Bettina Brentano-von Arnim and Karoline von Günderrode, as well as their fictional counterparts, share a fascination with Hölderlin, whom they read with enthusiasm but never knew. Bettine's attention to his work in *Günderode* can be located in the larger development of a theory of figurative language attributed to the thought of German Romanticism. After hearing his poems, read by Hölderlin's friend St. Clair, Bettine reports to Karoline:

> When I think of it—what harmony in his language!—His poems that St. Clair read to me—scattered in various calenders—ah, what a holy being is language. He was bound to it, it bestowed its most secret, innermost charm upon him, not, as Goethe, through the untouched intimacy of feeling, rather through its personal contact with him. So true! he must have kissed language.—Yes, so it goes, whoever associates so closely with the gods, for him they turn it into misery.

> Wenn ich bedenk—welcher Anklang in seiner Sprache!—Die Gedichte, die mir St. Clair von ihm vorlas—zerstreut in einzelnen Kalendern—ach, was ist doch die Sprache für ein heilig Wesen. Er war mit ihr verbündet, sie hat ihm ihren heimlichsten, innigsten Reiz geschenkt, nicht wie dem Goethe, durch die unangetastete Innigkeit des Gefühls, sondern durch ihren persönlichen Umgang. So wahr! er muß die Sprache geküßt haben.—Ja so geht's, wer mit den Göttern zu nah verkehrt, dem wenden sie's zum Elend. (Weimar 2: 146–147)

The bond between Hölderlin and divine language, so Bettine implies, leads to his insanity. No two styles could be more divergent than Hölderlin's exactingly precise prosody and Bettine's/Brentano-von Arnim's easily and ecstatically flowing prose. Günderrode's work, as Rehm suggests, comes closer to Hölderlin's in its rhythmic precision and premeditation.

The figure, however, that I would like to profile, is the image of the kiss: "So true! he must have kissed language" (So wahr! er muß die Sprache geküßt haben). The erotic, linguistic, immediate, mediated, natural, cultural aspects of the act of inspiration converge in the figure of the kiss.

The author Karoline von Günderrode uses the gesture of the kiss to figure the language of desire. For Bettine, the kiss is an expression of fullness; for Karoline, it is one of lack. Günderrode's sonnet "The Kiss in the Dream" first reached her beloved Savigny on the verge of his marriage to Gunda Brentano.[24] Günderrode's love for him shapes the dream frame of the sonnet, the postscript, and the details from her biography.[25] Unrequited love resembles an unanswered letter, or an imagined dialogue with nature or with a dead or absent friend in that the discourse is completely one-sided. Writing becomes a means of recuperating the experience of unanswered love. Here Günderrode risks double indemnity: both unrequited and unpublished.

A kiss has breathed life into me,
Stilled the deep yearning in my breast.
Come, Darkness, embrace me in night
That my lips may drink in new delight.

Such a life was dipped in dreams.
Thus I live, watching dreams forever.
I disdain the shine of other joys,
Because the night breathes such sweet balsam to me.

The day is poor in love-sweet delight.
It hurts me, the empty glitter of its light.
And these burning embers consume me.

So hide yourself, oh Day, from the light of earthly suns,
Cover yourself in Night, it stills your longing
And heals your pain, like Lethe's cool tides.

Es hat ein Kuß mir Leben eingehaucht,
Gestillet meines Busens tiefes Schmachten,
Komm, Dunkelheit, mich traulich zu umnachten,
Daß neue Wonne meine Lippe saugt.

In Träume war solch Leben eingetaucht,
Drum leb ich ewig Träume zu betrachten,
Kann aller andern Freuden Glanz verachten,
Weil mir die Nacht so süßen Balsam haucht.

Der Tag ist karg an liebesüßen Wonnen,
Es schmerzt mich seines Lichtes eitles Prangen,
Und mich verzehren diese heißen Gluten.

Drum birg dich, Tag, dem Leuchten ird'scher Sonnen,
Hüll dich in Nacht, sie stillet dein Verlangen
Und heilt den Schmerz, wie Lethes kühle Fluten.
(Weimar 2: 262)

Before focusing on the poem itself, I turn first to two comments on nineteenth-century language theory, both of which highlight the physical and metaphysical capacity of the mouth: one from Bettine, and one from Hegel. Bettine's comments on the nature of language and the language of nature correspond to a general Romantic preoccupation. Her random remarks, however, go beyond conventional associations of the feminine with nature. The product of Bettine's and Karoline's exchange approaches the conclusions of a higher authority, Hegel, who describes the various functions performed by the mouth. I quote the passage from his *Philosophy of Nature*: "In many animals the organs of excretion and the genitals, the highest and lowest parts in the animal organization, are intimately connected: just as speech and kissing, on the one hand, and eating, drinking and spitting, on the other, are all done with the mouth" (404). This moment in Hegel connects sensory perception with more elevated activity. This attention to the metonymy of the mouth marks a shift from the physical to the metaphysical. Bettine, too, recognizes this multiplicity of meanings, from the literal, corporeal functions of the mouth through the figural, metaphysical organ of inspiration and production. For Bettine, the body is the basis of figure.

Bettine rhapsodizes the relationship of perception and reception throughout the work. In the following passage from the novel, she ponders the natural "language" of the chestnut, the linguistic code by which nature programs its growth:

> Kissing is the taking the form and the spirit of the form into us, that which we touch, that is the kiss, yes the form is born within us. And for this reason language is kissing, each word in a poem kisses us . . . I have learned this from Nature, she kisses me constantly . . . she kisses me, and I am already so completely accustomed to it, that I meet her immediately with my eyes, for the eyes are the mouth that Nature kisses.

> Küssen ist, die Form und den Geist der Form in uns aufnehmen, die wir berühren, das ist der Kuß, ja die Form wird in uns geboren. Und darum ist die Sprache auch Küssen, es küßt uns jedes Wort im Gedicht . . . ich hab's von der Natur gelernt, sie küßt mich beständig . . . sie küßt mich, und ich bin auch schon so ganz dran gewöhnt, daß ich ihr gleich mit den Augen entgegenkomme, denn die Augen sind der Mund, den die Natur küßt. (Weimar 2: 249)

Here Bettine equates the eyes with the mouth: perception with poetry. She draws a parallel between the chestnut she admires above and the capacity for form born into her. This capacity governs the act of reading as well as writing, for receptivity is also a matter of sensibility. Understanding, for Bettine, is the kiss of nature. The moment, though, when Bettine reads her own image literally, an image of seeing with the mouth, is the moment the image becomes grotesque. If the kiss of language is the kiss of nature, then it retains the power of mutation. The power, or rather the possibility of natural mutation, instills within the natural order an unpredictability, the threat of a loss of control that gives figurative language its uncanny power.

"The Kiss in the Dream" turns on tropes of inspiration, of the fictitious kiss: the veil of night, the veil of light, that which is seen and unseen; tropes of desire and of forgetting, revolving on the necessary sublimation of the erotic into the somatic. The dream kiss, at the moment of writing, comes into consciousness only through language, not actual experience. This concept of creation is a reversal of Bettine's natural theory of inspiration. Günderrode's sonnet, however, also turns on the metonymy of the mouth for speaking, breathing, kissing. The kiss, for Günderrode, is a source of inspiration. For unlike Bettine, who would assert that nature or divine inspiration generate her writing, Günderrode is in control of even her subconscious desire. She may or may not have actually dreamt the kiss, but the inscription of it is fully conscious and controlled, attested to by the careful execution of the formal sonnet. For Günderrode, the kiss of the dream is ultimately the kiss of death, because language is the only vehicle for her desire. The poem comes to represent the things absent from a life of seclusion. For this reason, the dream frame is crucial to the sonnet "The Kiss in the Dream," which first appeared in 1804 in *Poems and Fantasies* (Gedichte und Phantasien) under the male pseudonym Tian. The poem is the realization of the dream.

Brenatano-von Arnim provides a different context for the sonnet. She locates the sonnet in a supplement or enclosure to a letter verifiably written by Günderrode. The sonnet is framed yet again. Both Günderrode and Karoline introduce the poem with the following warning: "and do not immediately think that I am too unhappy — poetry is the salve for that in life which is unfulfilled" (und glaub nicht gleich, ich sei zu traurig.—Gedichte sind Balsam auf Unerfüllbares im Leben) (Weimar 2:257). Writing is always an articulation of that absence, the emptiness which is always figured by the trope of prosopopoeia,[26] the rhetorical figure by which an imaginary or absent person is represented as speaking or acting. Brentano-von Arnim gives face and voice to Günderrode, sending the letters to the present. Through her use of the trope prosopopoeia, Bettine defies temporality: she both presents and represents Karoline in a fictitious dialogue. The record of this "dialogue," just as her "correspondence" with nature, can be delivered in texts. Absence, or death, is the inevitable precondition.

In a suggestive and substantial article on Bettina Brentano-von Arnim in *Glyph* 7 (1980), Friedrich Kittler addresses the issue of her theory of writing. He describes it as a kind of dance: "And so on, back and forth, until out of writing and rocking a dance is formed, until poplar, garden, stairs, table, and quill become a crazy and unique writing-machine."[27] And in this writing-machine "the book is only wastepaper" (35). Kittler characterizes Karoline von Günderrode's literary attempts, her efforts to write for her life that lead to the love affair with death. He writes: "The hostile world that prohibits love, the lonely self, silenced by love's pain but reaching toward a written language" (39). Such things, Kittler indicates, prompt Günderrode to give form to a loveless, amorphous life in verse: "Günderode's [sic] verses are not music but colonnades: gravestones to a self that has no substance, only the form of its sorrow. Yet precisely for that reason it is not willing to disappear, get carried away, and not despair. Günderode's [sic] writing of poetry is an exercise in dying" (39). Kittler highlights Günderrode's recognition of a fundamental equivalence between writing and dying; between death and representation. To substantiate oneself in terms of verse is to disappear—to write one's life is to die, for representation in any formal system of notation such as writing requires the absence of the thing represented. The sonnet literally takes the place of the poet who penned it. The letters, the epistolary novel also take Günderrode's place. Her absence predicates the possibility of representation by inscription in the first place. The material traces, the letters, remain.

Brentano-von Arnim is also aware of the link between writing and dying. Not accidently she comments on the relationship in the context of her letter about Hölderlin, his Oedipus translation, and myth:

—Ah, poetry! holy grave that silently collects the dust of the spirit and keeps it from injury.—Oh you let it rise again, let me ascend to it and extend my hand to it in a dream, that it may with its holy finger sow single golden seeds on my open lips and inspire me with the breath that it drinks from the breast of the gods according to their will. For I desire longingly to bear together the sorrow of the day and together to receive comfort in the dreams of the night.

—Ach Poesie! heilig Grabmal, das still den Staub des Geistes sammelt und ihn birgt vor Verletzung.—O du läßt ihn auferstehen wieder, laß mich hinabsteigen zu ihm und die Hand ihm reichen im Traum, daß er mit heiligem Finger die goldnen Saatkörner mir auf die offne Lippe streue und mich anblase mit dem Odem, den er nach dem Willen der Götter aus ihrem Busen trinkt. Denn ich begehr sehnsüchtig, mitzu-tragen gemeinsam Weh des Tags und gemeinsam Tröstung zu emp-fangen in den Träumen der Nacht. (Weimar 2: 149–50)

In her recognition of the relationship between writing and dying, Brentano-von Arnim sees, by contrast, poems as both epitaphs and the only way to a textual resurrection and her own personal ascent. She acknowledges her lack of logic and historical sense to Karoline, but then justifies her flight of fancy. In the passage just quoted, Bettine clearly rhapsodizes within the context of poetic laments, but in her further commentary, she locates herself and him in a mytholo-gized topography: "where Hölderlin sleeps above the grave of Oedi-pus" (wo Hölderlin schläft über dem Grabe des Ödipus) (Weimar 2:150). Poetry remains for her a medium for the spirit. She equates the writing of poetry with death and inspiration, but also with resur-rection and dreams. These are the themes of the sonnet in question.

In the sonnet, Günderrode elaborates the conceit of respiration and inspiration. The sonnet itself turns on the metonymy of the mouth for speaking, breathing, kissing: "A kiss has breathed life into me" (Es hat ein Kuß mir Leben eingehaucht). The impersonal struc-ture of the first line conveys more a life force than a sexual energy. The question of desire, of the trajectory of sexual energy, is displaced by the question of ontology. This is not a love poem. In a strict sense, the poem is about coming into being through language—a question-able coming into being.

For Günderrode, who also takes her own figurative language literally, it is the kiss of death. The sonnet in question turns from the kiss to respiration to inspiration: writing the dream. The conceit she elaborates exploits the capacity of language to achieve figurative as well as literal meanings, here contained in and conveyed by the verbs, which rely on the development from the physical to the meta-physical. The subjects of these verbs are the essential elements of air and water and fire: inhale, still (quiet), suck, dip in, breath (ein-hauchen, stillen, saugen, eintauchen, hauchen). They exemplify the move from breath to life, empty to full, but only in the context of the dream. Günder(r)ode opposes the meaning of this verbal weave with tropes of seeing in the dark during a dream, a revelation in concealment: shroud in darkness, observe, scorn, hide, cover (umnachten, betrachten, verachten, birgen, hüllen). These sets of verbs, of inspiration and of concealment, are interwoven with the verb to heal (heilen), when a simple simile is employed: "And heal the pain, like Lethe's cool tides" (Und heilt den Schmerz, wie Lethes kühle Fluthen). The healing capacity of Lethe's cool waters which quench desire is the capacity to forget. The life inspired and baptized by the kiss in the dream in the dark must be forgotten. To live, the poet must forget she lives in the dream. Thus springs the desire to see only by night, a logical impossiblity.

"Seeing" in a dream is an act of poetic voyeurism: the poet abdicates consciousness in the act of dreaming, but the act of inscription is fully conscious, fully culpable. At this point of disjuncture, direction and destination must be considered. The kiss in the first line breathed life into the "I" of the poem. The night, which she commands to envelope her (think of the resonance of madness of the verb to shroud in darkness, *umnachten*), provides the possibility of life. This life of the night begins in the second stanza with the verb to dip in, *eintauchen*, as a pen in ink. The sonnet turns on the last line: "Because the night breathes sweet balsam to me" (Weil mir die Nacht so süßen Balsam haucht).

In the body of the letter, Günderrode equates poems with a salve, provided here by the night, the cloak of darkness which permits "seeing" only in dreams. Night constitutes her exhalations, her poetry. In the sestet, Günderrode turns from the mouth to the eyes: from the capacity to kiss, breathe, and speak to the sense of sight. The poet invokes darkness to forget what she remembers from the dream, the kiss that does not take place. The dream constitutes the capacity of language, the danger of language to say anything. The sonnet is an attempt to forget the self's having come into being, only through language, which is not being at all. This is the same as remembering something that never happened. This moment is daunting, for the sense of subject is erased and replaced by the memory of future death.

Bettine employs the kiss as a symbol for the point of connection between the subject and nature. It is a generalized act of inspiration, of perception and reception. Her synesthetic evocation, confusing human organs of speech and sight, however, reminds us that nature, as well as language, can create mutants, with eyes for mouths, without intention. Günderrode's use of the kiss, even when safely contained in a dream frame, and even though it symbolizes an act of inspiration, can only express, not fulfill, desire. In contrast to Bettine's de-eroticized kiss, "The Kiss in the Dream" remains charged in its hypothetical existence. The kiss, like language, is only a possibility. The sonnet itself ultimately defuses the tension and itself fulfills the desire for writing.

Günderrode sends the love letter to Savigny, then to Bettina Brentano-von Arnim, who, as Bettine, sends it to the present. Brentano-von Arnim broaches private and public language, delivering the epistles in the form of an epistolary novel. Just as the poem searches for origination, we do the detective work, the work of remembering. This search for origins and the attempts to establish a matrilineage has been the work of Christa Wolf, among others, whose revisions of the relationship between Brentano-von Arnim and Günderrode recuperate the past and let the dead and silent be read. This transpires only in textual space; only in writing does the silence resonate; only here do we find the tropes crossing the limits of life and death, life and literature, conflating present, past, and future. Letters from the dead: the challenge, met with aplomb by Bettina Brentano-von Arnim through Christa Wolf, is to deliver the letters from the grave. It is the burden of criticism to pay the postage due.

Notes

1. I would like to thank the editors, an anonymous reader, and Mark Schneider for their careful reading of this essay, their criticism, and their comments.
2. See Goodman, 73 ff., esp. 90, on relationship between the epistolary novel and "radical autobiography."
3. For conventional definitions of the private letter and the epistolary novel, see *Grundzüge der Literatur-und Sprachwissenschaft,* 324 ff.

4. For an illuminating theoretical discussion of the "natural" relationship between women writers and the development of the epistolary novel, see Bovenschen, 200 ff. Bovenschen concludes: "The literary production of women was and is just as dependent on the cultural-institutional constellations and generic-poetic situations as on contemporary values and conceptual contents connected to the word womanhood" (Die Literaturproduktion der Frauen war und ist ebenso von den kulturinstitutionellen Konstellationen und gattungspoetischen Konjunkturen abhängig wie von den jeweiligen Einschätzungs- und Vorstellungsgehalten, die sich mit dem Wort Weiblichkeit verbinden) (220). All translations, unless otherwise indicated, are my own.

5. See Drewitz, *Bettine von Arnim. Romantik, Revolution, Utopie*, for a presentation of Bettina von Arnim's life against the historical and political backdrop of the nineteenth century.

6. See Frederiksen and Shafi, 54–67 for a reading of the illuminating relationship between Bettina Brentano-von Arnim's novel and Hélène Cixous's écriture féminine. Frederiksen and Shafi point to the radical nature of Brentano-von Arnim's epistolary novel, both in form and in content, particularly with regard to the attempted identity with body and text (55), the inscribing of a utopian society (56), the specifically feminine "double perspective" (Doppelperspektive) (57) of the two voices, and the motif of flight related to the "Floating-Religion" (Schwebe-Religion) (60).

7. It is not known when the two actually met (Härtl, 788–789). Brentano-von Arnim and Günderrode broke off their friendship and their correspondence before the latter's death: Brentano-von Arnim even asks for her letters to be returned (see Geiger, 160 ff. and Oehlke, 181).

8. My purpose in researching the sketchy details of this history is not to provide an exhaustive reference work of various editions, but rather to focus on certain themes of "making public" Günderrode's work. The motivations and methods of scholarly and revisionist reception are significant for an understanding of Brentano-von Arnim's work with the fate of Günderrode's life and letters. For a comprehensive publication history, see Morgenthaler, 3:11 ff.

9. Lacan, "Seminar," 39.

10. These complex concepts are crucial to Lacan's work. I, however, am borrowing selectively for the purpose of reading the epistolary novel in question.

11. Also "A Kiss in the Dream" (Ein Kuß im Traume). See Salomon, 103 and 483. The editor notes this and other variants in Brentano-von Arnim's publication of the poem.

12. I am referring here to the title of Kittler's essay, a paraphrase from the letters.

13. See Wolf, *The Shadow of a Dream* (Der Schatten eines Traumes), 49.

14. See Preisendanz, *The Love of Günderode* (Die Liebe der Günderode) for Creuzer's letters to her. I do not intend to overstate the point of "ownership" with regard to letters, whether they belong in collected works, and if so, whose. In this context, I want to trace the meaning of the signifying chain, as well as the signification of one individual letter.

15. See Wolf, *The Shadow of a Dream* (Der Schatten eines Traumes), 37. She notes the irony of this discovery.

16. For further references to Günderrode as the German Sappho, see Naumann, 14.

17. I cite the reference in this way to highlight the assertiveness of the editor. For Salomon's comments on his editorial shortcomings, see xvi. The inconsistency in his spelling can be attributed to stable variation in the virtual interchangeabilty of "c" and "k" in proper names. Götz differentiates Bettina Brentano-von Arnim, the historical figure, from the fictional narrator with the final "e." I thank my colleague Rosina Lippi-Green for her help in this matter. Hirschberg modifies his predecessor's opinion, but retains the "apocryphal" aspect of the work: "The letters Bettina passed on are apocryphal, but they give an incomparably beautiful ideal image of the spiritual and cognitive life of Günderode [*sic*]" (Weimar 2:281).

18. See Hirschberg, 1:iv. He puts "complete edition" (Gesammtausgabe, 1:iii) in quotation marks for obvious reasons.

19. Other scholars have recognized the problematic but productive relationship between truth and untruth in this type of fiction. See Geiger, 129 ff.; Mattheis, 39–40; and Wilhelm, 27.

20. See Härtl, 812, for the history of this translation.

21. Kirsch posits the personal and political connections by addressing Brentano-von Arnim in the ninth section: "Tonight, Bettina, all is/As it was. Always/We are alone when we write to the Kings/Those of the heart and those/Of the state" (Dieser Abend, Bettina, es ist/Alles beim alten. Immer/ Sind wir allein, wenn wir den Königen schreiben/Denen des Herzens und jenen/ Des Staats) (27).

22. See Bock, E4. In his summary of this film, he points out the allusion to the relationship between Bettina Brentano-von Arnim and Karoline von Günderrode, and to other literary influences on von Trotta's work.

23. See also Karl August Varnhagen von Ense, *Briefe von Stägemann, Metternich, Heine und Bettina von Arnim*, for less auspicious references to the scene of writing. Bettine refers to a "lack of paper" (Mangel an Papier) (315), to explain the brevity of one letter: "writing is becoming so difficult for me, I make more ink stains than individual letters . . . and finally I just don't have any more stationery" (das Schreiben wird mir so schwer, ich mache mehr Tintenfleckse als Buchstaben . . . und endlich hab' ich auch kein Briefpapier mehr) (336). She refers to her own physical condition as well as her immediate surroundings: in a postscript to

Varnhagen von Ense she writes that the letter was "badly written by the light of a lamp that is even worse and darker than the times" (Schlecht geschrieben, bei einer Lampe noch schlechter und dunkler als die Zeit) (390). It was written during an epidemic.

24. See Härtl, 2:786: "In April 1804 Günderrode wrote the sonnet she directed to Savigny, 'The Kiss in the Dream' (compare 262), the strict form of which attests more openly to an unfulfilled love than her mostly veiled letters. When she wrote the sonnet, she was living with Savigny and Gunda, who had gotten married on 17 April 1804. They were living at his manor, Trages, from which she returned to Frankfurt on 30 May."

25. See Wolf, *The Shadow of a Dream* (Der Schatten eines Traumes), 25: "She had to add a postscript to this letter, unambiguous enough—the page is in the German State Library on Unter den Linden—: 'S.—g: it is true. Little Günderrode dreams of such things, and of whom? of someone who is quite beloved and who will always be loved'."

26. See de Man, "Autobiography As De-Facement" in *The Rhetoric of Romanticism*, 75–76, for a discussion of the relationship between the rhetorical figure of prosopopeia and autobiography. He defines the trope in the following manner: "the fiction of an apostrophe to an absent, deceased, or voiceless entity, which posits the possibility of the latter's reply and confers upon it the power of speech. Voice assumes mouth, eye, and finally face, a chain that is manifest in the etymology of the trope's name, prosopon poien, to confer a mask or a face (prosopon)."

27. Kittler's article informs my work, particularly with regard to the relationship between writing and desire. He does not account for the work Brentano-von Arnim undertakes in collecting and "delivering" the correspondence, which, if written to the wind, would be unreadable.

Works Cited

Arnim, Bettina von. *Werke*. Ed. Heinz Härtl. Berlin and Weimar: Aufbau-Verlag, 1989. 2 vols. Vol. 2 *Die Günderode*. (Quoted as Weimar.)

Bianquis, Genviève. *Caroline de Gunderode. Ouvrage accompangé de lettres inédites*. Paris: Librairies Félix Alcan et Guillaumin réunies, 1910.

Bovenschen, Silvia. *Die imaginierte Weiblichkeit. Exemplarische Untersuchungen zu kulturgeschichtlichen und literarischen Präsentationsformen des Weiblichen*. Frankfurt/M: Suhrkamp, 1980.

Burwick, Roswitha. "Bettina von Arnim's *Die Günderode*. Zum Selbstverständnis der Frau in der Romantik." in Vol. 6 of *Kontroversen, alte und neue. Akten des VII. Internationalen Germanisten-Kongresses, Göttingen 1985*. Ed. Albrecht Schöne. Tübingen: Max Niemeyer Verlag, 1986. 62–67.

CineGraph: Lexikon zum deutschsprachigen Film. Ed. Hans-Ludwig Bock. Munich: edition text und kritik, n.d.

de Man, Paul. "Autobiography As De-Facement." *The Rhetoric of Romanticism*. New York: Cornell University Press, 1984. 67–81.

———, "The Rhetoric of Temporality." *Blindness and Insight. Essays in the Rhetoric of Contemporary Criticism*. Minneapolis: University of Minnesota Press, 1983. 187–228.

Dischner, Gisela. *Bettina von Arnim: Eine weibliche Sozialbiographie aus dem neunzehnten Jahrhundert*. Berlin: Wagenbach, 1977.

Drewitz, Ingeborg. *Bettine von Arnim. Romantik.Revolution. Utopie*. Düsseldorf: Eugen Diederichs Verlag, 1969.

Frederiksen, Elke and Monika Shafi. " 'Sich im Unbekannten suchen gehen': Bettina von Arnims Die Günderode als weibliche Utopie." in Vol. 6 of *Kontroversen, alte und neue. Akten des VII.Internationalen Germanisten-Kongresses, Göttingen 1985*. Ed. Albrecht Schöne. Tübingen: Max Niemeyer Verlag, 1986. 54–67.

Geiger, Ludwig. *Karoline von Günderode und ihre Freunde*. Stuttgart, Leipzig, Berlin, Vienna: Deutsche Verlags -Anstalt, 1895.

Goodman, Katherine. *Dis/Closures. Women's Autobiography in Germany Between 1790 and 1914*. New York, Berne, Frankfurt /M: Peter Lang, 1986.

Grundzüge der Literatur- und Sprachwissenschaft. Vol 1: *Literaturwissenschaft*. Eds. Heinz Ludwig Arnold, and Volker Sinemus. Munich: Deutscher Taschenbuch Verlag, 1980.

Günderrode, Karoline von. (Pseudonym: Tian) *Gedichte und Phantasien*. Hamburg und Frankfurt: J.C. Hermannschen Buchhandlung, 1804.

———, *Gesammelte Dichtungen von Karoline von Günderode. Zum ersten Mal vollständig herausgegeben*. Ed. Friedrich Götz. Mannheim: Verlagshandlung von Friedrich Götz, 1857.

———. *Günderode*. Trans. Margaret Fuller. Boston: E.P. Peabody, 1842.

———. *Poetische Fragmente von Tian*. Frankfurt/M.: F. Wilmans, 1805.

———; *Sämtliche Werke und ausgewählte Studien. Historische-kritische Ausgabe*. Ed. Walter Morgenthaler. Basel, Frankfurt/M: Stroemfeld/Roter Stern, 1991. 3 vols.

Hegel, G.W.F. *The Philosophy of Nature*. Trans. A.V. Miller. Oxford: Clarendon Press, 1970.

Hirschberg, Leopold. Introduction. in Vol. 1 of *Gesammelte Werke der Karoline von Günderode*. Berlin-Wilmersdorf: O. Goldschmidt-Gabrielli, 1920–22. 3 vols. ix–xxii.

Kirsch, Sarah. "Wiepersdorf." *Rückenwind*. Ebenhausen: Langewiesche-Brandt, 1977. 18–29.

Kittler, Friedrich. "Writing into the Wind, Bettina." *Glyph* 7 (1980): 32–69.

Lacan, Jacques. "Seminar on 'The Purloined Letter'." Trans. Jeffrey Mehlman. French Freud: Structural Studies in Psychoanalysis. *Yale French Studies* 48 (1972). 38–72.

Lacoue-Labarthe, Philippe and Nancy, Jean-Luc. *The Literary Absolute. The Theory of Literature in German Romanticism*. Trans. Philop Barnard and Cheryl Lester. Albany: SUNY Press, 1988.

Mattheis, Margarete. *Die Günderrode. Gestalt, Leben und Wirkung*. Berlin: Junker und Dünnhaupt Verlag, 1934.

Naumann, Annelore. "Caroline von Günderrode." Diss. Berlin, 1957.

Oehlke, Waldemar. *Bettina von Arnims Briefromane*. Berlin: Mayer & Mueller, 1905.

Preisendanz, Karl, ed. *Die Liebe der Günderode. Friedrich Creuzers Briefe an Caroline von Günderode*. Munich: Verlag R. Piper, 1912. Bern: Herbert Lang Verlag, 1975.

Rehm, Walther. "Über die Gedichte der Karoline von Günderrode." *Goethe-Kalender auf das Jahr 1942*. 35 (1942): 93–121.

Salomon, Elisabeth. Preface. *Karoline von Günderode. Gesammelte Dichtungen*. Munich: Drei Masken Verlag, 1923.

Trotta, Margarethe von, dir. *Heller Wahn (Sheer Madness* also *Friends and Husbands)*. With Hanna Schygulla and Angela Winkler. Films du Losange-Westdeutscher Rundfunk, 1983.

Varnhagen von Ense, Karl August, comp. and ed. *Aus dem Nachlaß Varnhagen's von Ense. Briefe von Stägemann, Metternich, Heine und Bettina von Arnim, nebst Briefen, Anmerkungen und Notizen von Varnhagen von Ense*. Leipzig: F.A. Brockhaus, 1865.

Wilhelm, Richard. *Die Karoline. Dichtung und Schicksal*. 1938. Bern: Herbert Lang, 1975.

Wolf, Christa. *Cassandra. A Novel and Four Essays*. Trans. Jan van Heurck. New York: Farrar, Straus and Giroux, 1984.

———, Introduction. *Der Schatten eines Traumes. Gedichte, Prosastücke. Zeugnisse von Zeitgenossen*. By Karoline von Günderrode. Ed., comp. with an introduction by Christa Wolf. Darmstadt: Luchterhand Verlag, 1979. 5–40.

———, Afterword. *Die Karoline. Mit einem Essay von Christa Wolf*. By Bettine von Arnim. 1925. Leipzig: Insel Verlag, 1983. 545–584.

———, *Kein Ort. Nirgends. Erzählung*. Darmstadt: Luchterhand, 1979.

———, No Place on Earth. Trans. Jan van Heurck. New York: Farrar, Straus and Giroux, 1982.

A Language of Her Own: Bettina Brentano-von Arnim's Translation Theory and Her English Translation Project

Marjanne E. Goozé

> In a very specific way, the translator "re-experiences" the evolution of language itself, the ambivalence of the relations between language and world, between "languages" and "worlds." In every translation the creative, possibly fictive nature of these relations is tested.
>
> —George Steiner

George Steiner makes this observation in his study of translation, *After Babel: Aspects of Language and Translation* (235), pointing out how the translator encounters the essence of language through the act of literary translation: "Thus translation is no specialized, secondary activity at the 'interface' between languages" (235).[1] Here Steiner lays the groundwork for a discussion of translation theory by clarifying the relationships between translator and author, and an original text and a translation. Because translation is not a "secondary activity," the translator is not the author's servant, nor is the translation subservient to an "original" or "source" text. Once the translation exists, it and the original can be treated as co-equal literary productions. The only essential difference between them then is that the original may be reproduced again as a translation, whereas the translation may not. When analyzing a translation, the encounter between the translator and language and the fact that the translator is not the author's servant must always be kept in mind.

Bettina Brentano-von Arnim's translation into English of her first book, *Goethe's Correspondence with a Child* (Goethes Briefwechsel mit einem Kinde) (frequently known as *The Goethe Book* [Das Goethe Buch]), and her accounts of her work on this project document her "re-experience" of the "evolution of language." Brentano-von Arnim worked on the translation from 1834 to 1838—a significant portion of her publishing career. There have been only two studies of her English translation of *Das Goethe Buch*: Werner Vordtriede's "Bettinas englisches Wagnis" and H. P. Collins's and P. Shelley's "The Reception in England and America of Bettina Brentano-von Arnim's *Goethe's Correspondence with a Child*." Vordtriede presents the history of the translation project, while the second article investigates the reception of the German edition and the translation in England and America. Vordtriede insightfully describes *Goethe's Correspondence with a Child* as "a new Bettinaish work" (ein neues Bettinasches Werk) and "a separate part of Bettina's works" (ein selbständiger Teil von Bettinas Werken) (271–272).[2] He is particularly referring to the third volume (*The Diary of a Child*), which Brentano-von Arnim translated without assistance. It is the task of this essay to elaborate this thesis by examining how Brentano-von Arnim's theory of translation as outlined both in the "Preamble" to *The Goethe Book* and in related documents contributes to the theoretical discussion of her day. More specifically, this essay looks at how her theory enables the creation of a translation which is in itself a separate literary work. First will be outlined how Bettina Brentano-von Arnim decided to publish her Goethe book in English and why she chose to translate it herself. Second, a few examples from the translation will be examined. It is not possible to undertake a thorough, detailed analysis of the translation itself here. And third, her theories will be analyzed in the context of eighteenth- and nineteenth-century translation theories, focusing on how hers both reflect and subvert their gendered definitions of translation and the translator.

In the "Preamble" to the third volume of *The Goethe Book*, titled the *The Diary of a Child*, Brentano-von Arnim explains how she came to translate part of the work and her theory of translation. Much of what she says in the "Preamble" is also found in her letters.[3] She initiated her project by seeking a translator and English distributor. A physician, Dr. Nikolaus Heinrich Julius, acted as intermediary and in May 1834 contacted Sarah Austin to translate and the publisher Longman to distribute (Collins & Shelley 97–98). Mrs. Austin, who had translated other German authors, appeared to be the ideal choice, but she only planned to translate the narrative parts of the book (Vordtriede 276). Bettina Brentano-von Arnim mentions Sarah Austin in the "Preamble," but states in error that Austin first came to her: "the well renowned Mrs. Austin, by regard for the great German Poet, proposed to translate it" (Arnim, *Goethe's Correspondence* 3: i).[4] Austin later refused the job because she felt that the book was untranslatable and incomprehensible to English readers (3: vii–viii). Brentano-von Arnim had wanted to publish the German and English editions simultaneously, but only the German edition was issued in 1835 because Brentano-von Arnim refused to consent to an abridged and censored translation (Pückler 206).

In spite of the delays, Bettina Brentano-von Arnim became firmly convinced of the desirability of having the book translated into English because of the highly favorable reviews the German edition had received in England. She was determined

> that it should be read and liked by the English, and as their Reviews at least proved so finely their feeling-out of the primitive element of this love, and how unimpaired, undisturbed, and how much plainer than to my countrymen appeared to them that paternal relation of Goethe's delicious hearty affection to the *child*, from whose ecstacy he explored a sweet nurture for his immortality. (3: viii)

She was not mistaken in her reading of the praise the reviewers bestowed on the book, but she definitely misjudged the appeal all the parts of it would have. The passages that had been translated in the reviews were the most straightforwardly narrated of the book—those on Goethe's childhood, Madame de Staël, and Beethoven, among others. The review in the London *Athenaeum* of October 17, 1835, motivated Brentano-von Arnim to produce a translation. The book was called "a publication, the equal of which, in vivacity and original character, we have not met with for many a day" (774). The erotically-charged nature of Bettina Brentano-von Arnim's language and precisely that "primitive element" and "ecstacy" in which Goethe found "sweet nurture" made the full-length text an unlikely success in early Victorian England.

Except for the third volume and the Goethe sonnets which Brentano-von Arnim translated herself, it is difficult to determine who translated most of the first two volumes. Vordtriede contends

that Austin or a group of English students translated the first volume
and the first half of the second. Three British student assistants can
also be traced: Charles McCarthy, Mr. Wood, and Mr. Simpsone
(*Herzhaft* . . . 58). In the "Preamble" Brentano-von Arnim calls
them "my translators" (3: iii), but later she refers to them more
directly in a mixture of English and German as "die Kembrid-
schmember und Ochsfordmember" (Köln 2: 490) or "the seven wise
masters" (die sieben weisen Meister) who all speak a different English and cannot agree on anything (*Lebensspiel* 304).

Bettina Brentano-von Arnim asserts that she began to learn English in 1835 to oversee the English translation: "I was not acquainted
with the English tongue, therefore relied upon the consciousness of
my translators; the recapitulation of their version I tried to follow
with comparing it to the German text" (3: iii). She was often unhappy
with her translators' efforts and retained final authority over the text.
While the first two volumes were being printed, Brentano-von Arnim
decided in the fall of 1837 to revise passages and continue the translation on her own: "I never could have guessed those difficulties that
fell more heavily upon me, than upon any knight-errant who tries
with the help of propitious spirits to overcome impossibilities" (3: iv).
And the impossibilities were significant. Discouraged from the very
start, Bettina Brentano-von Arnim committed herself to the task of
translation. With little command of English she became for the next
seven months "trapped in this herculean task" (gefangen in dieser
herkulischen Arbeit) (*Lebensspiel* 305). She vastly underestimated
the richness of the English language, believing that "it consisting but
in thirty thousand words—I thought, if I only did know them, to be
sure I would find the right" (3: iv).

She dramatized her fight against the odds in letters to Caroline von
Egloffstein, Wilhelm Grimm, Karl August Varnhagen, and Philipp
Nathusius, but she told the whole story only in the "Preamble." In the
accounts she emphasizes that she began with no knowledge of English
and no assistance. She declared to Varnhagen: "I didn't know any
English" (Ich konnte kein Englisch) (Varnhagen 330)[5] and wrote
Grimm: "I have translated my diary into English, since no English-
man and no German could come assist me" (ich hab mein Tagebuch
ins Englische übersetzt weil kein Engländer und kein Deutscher mir
zu Stand kommen konnte) (Grimm 29). She worked for more than six
months on the *Diary* alone. The *Diary* appeared at the end of April
1838, one year after the first two volumes. Brentano-von Arnim

translated considerable portions of the book herself and supervised all of it. In her November 10, 1837, letter to Varnhagen, she outlines which sections are hers and the order in which she translated them:

> The sonnets from the first volume are the first that I, fumbling in the dark, brought to light. Then I translated the second half of the second volume and finally fifty pages of the first. . . . I translated my diary in a foreboding dusk which was often transversed by fog.

> Die Sonette des ersten Bandes sind das Erste, was ich, im Finstern tappend, an's Licht brachte. Dann hab' ich die zweite Hälfte des zweiten Bandes und endlich funfzig [sic] Kartons des ersten übersetzt. . . . Mein Tagebuch hab' ich in ahnender Dämmerung mit häufig durchziehendem Nebel übersetzt. (Varnhagen 328)

The English version of the *Diary* also contains new passages which are not in the German edition. Bettina Brentano-von Arnim asserted in a letter to Wilhelm Grimm that these passages are from sections she chose not to include in the German edition: "I have translated probably about half a folio more of my papers that are not in the German edition, because I believed they would not be understood, but which in English are very comprehensible" (Ich habe noch wohl einen halben Bogen mehr aus meinen Papieren übersetzt die nicht in der deutschen Ausgabe sind, weil ich glaubte man würde sie nicht verstehen die im Englischen sehr verständlich sind) (Grimm 30). The passages all present reflections on the abstract themes of love, art, and genius.[6] But the content of the third volume was highly criticized and Brentano-von Arnim was also taken to task for the translation. A reviewer in *The Athenaeum* found the translation baffling: "Throughout the whole book we hardly know whether is the more remarkable,—the rhapsodical and mystical poetry of certain passages, or the comicality of the Anglo-German Malaprop in which they are rendered" (170). The American response was more favorable and the book was printed twice, in 1841 and 1848, in the United States (Weimar 1: 688). Margaret Fuller described the translation as "German English of irresistible naiveté" (Collins & Shelley 158).

Brentano-von Arnim embarked on the task of translation with limited tools—a grammar and Johnson's dictionary. Her unfamiliarity with English usage led her to choose archaic formulations and word usages. She uses the verb "ween" for "wähnen," "denken," etc., but the word went out of general use in the seventeenth century. She did make, however, a concerted effort not only to check her English usage, but also to compare German and English. She wrote Caroline von Egloffstein: "*every* word I had to look up, every construction I had to learn to comprehend in the most laborious way; for every expression I had to find examples from English authors and then translate these again into German, in order to compare them" (jedes Wort hab ich suchen müssen, jede Konstruktion mußte ich auf der mühseligsten Bahn begreifen lernen; zu jeder Wendung mußte ich Belege in englischen Autoren suchen und diese erst wieder ins Deutsche übersetzen, um sie zu vergleichen) (*Lebensspiel* 304). But neither dictionary nor advisers could dissuade her from her ultimate criterion that the words be euphonious and rhythmic. She had objected to portions translated by others precisely because she found in their work "words lack of musical rhythm" (3: iii), while in her own work she searched for the most "euphonical" expressions (3: v). This is why she did not allow anyone to extensively edit or correct the text. She wrote Grimm that she "could not allow it to be done to me that one change anything, because I had translated from deeper motives or by instinct exactly this way and not another" (konnte . . . mirs nicht antun lassen daß man mir etwas verändere, denn ich hatte aus tieferen Beweggründen oder aus Instinkt grade so und nicht anders übersetzt) (29–30). Bettina Brentano-von Arnim further insisted on what she calls "my wrong way of translating" (3: vi).

There is, however, a method in her wrong way and idiosyncratic employment of the English language. She was aware of the errors in grammar and syntax Mr. Simpsone pointed out to her when he did a cursory final edit of the *Diary*, characterizing it as: "a maze of labyrinthian intricate expressions, wrong words, wrong spelt works, wrong pronouns, whole sentences turned upside down, in almost every line which created so many incongruities and inconsistencies till I found it out" (*Herzhaft* . . . 58). Brentano-von Arnim, however, was proud of her creation, since like Hölderlin's Greco-German Sophocles translations, her English reflects her attempt to refashion the language through the act of translation. She declared in a letter to Caroline von Egloffstein: "You must study my new English language, which I have built only instinctively and in a feeling of harmony" (Sie müssen meine neue englische Sprache studieren, die ich nur instinkmäßig und im Gefühl der Harmonie gebaut habe) (*Lebensspiel* 305).

In order to create "my new English language," Brentano-von Arnim based her theory of translation on her linguistic feelings and

instincts of what is melodic and harmonic. Her musical metaphors are
not coincidental; they are expounded in detail in her second epistolary novel, *Günderode* (Die Günderode). Brentano-von Arnim felt
that it was the musical in language that connected it to the divine and
that ideally language should become music because the divine spirit
and humankind can only communicate through music (Weimar 2:
232).[7] She calls the dialogue between the two "dialogue of the gods"
(Göttergespräch) and "dialogue of love" (Liebesgespräch), and what
is important is "not the content" (nicht der Inhalt), but the music
which makes the dialogue and its content possible (Weimar 2: 232). In
January 1838 Bettina Brentano-von Arnim tested the musicality of
her English. A British friend of Rosa Maria Assing read parts of the
book aloud to her:

> What a great comfort to me was therefore the appearance of your dear
> friend, who with the most melodic voice read an English from my
> proofs that in grace and sweetness was in no way inferior to the song of
> the nightingales. O! I thought, if it sounds so beautiful, so must then
> certainly also the meaning be beautiful and comprehensible, and from
> the judgment of your friend Elisa Sloman I have acquired a very favor-
> able confidence in my translation, because your friend thinks, there
> may indeed be a language in it like no English she has ever read, but all
> the more moving and very clear and intelligible.

> Welch ein großer Trost war mir daher die Erscheinung Ihrer liebens-
> würdigen Freundin, die mit der melodischsten Stimme ein Englisch aus
> meinen Korrekturbogen herauslas, was an Grazie und Anmuth dem
> Gesang der Nachtigallen nichts nachgab. O! dachte ich, wenn es so
> schön klingt, so muß der Sinn gewiß auch schön sein und verständlich,
> und ich habe auf das Urtheil Ihrer Freundin Elisa Sloman eine sehr
> glückliche Zuversicht gewonnen für meine Uebersetzung, denn Ihre
> Freundin meint, es sei zwar eine Sprache darin, wie sie selbst noch kein
> English gelesen, aber um so rührender und ganz klar und deutlich. (In
> Varnhagen 331)

Here Brentano-von Arnim turns Elisa Sloman's politely phrased opinion to her own advantage. It is certainly understandable that Sloman
felt it was an English like she had never heard before, as the following
citations from the "Preamble" demonstrate.

Brentano-von Arnim's hope to sing like a nightingale and still be
understood is echoed in the "Preamble." She defended her decision
not to allow only excerpts to be translated by comparing her initial

work to that of a musician. She writes: "but as no musician ever likes to have only those passages of his composition executed that blandish the ear, I likewise refused my assent to the maiming of a work, that not by my own merit, but by chance and nature became a work of art, that only in the untouched development of its genius might judiciously be enjoyed and appraised" (3: i–ii). Her differences with her translators also centered on musicality: "Often my ear was hurt by words lack of musical rhythm, that in the German text by their harmonious sound, and even by the union of their single parts awake poetic sensation, I must yield to have them supplied by such as want all lofty strain" (3: iii). The riches of the English language soon seduced Brentano-von Arnim who once had doubted the expressive possibilities of the language: "What a copiousness of words with their flexure overflowed me, how abundantly gracious seemed to me those varieties of flexions, I would have them all interweaved in my version, and desponded in choosing the finest, the noblest, the most eloquent, and euphonical among all" (3: v). While searching for examples and verifying her "instinctive" choices, "I fell upon so beauteous expressions I would compound with my text" (3: v).

For my examination of the translation, I have chosen to emphasize the parts of *Goethe's Correspondence* we can be certain Bettina Brentano-von Arnim translated—the Goethe sonnets, and *The Diary of a Child*. Her translation technique is based foremost on sound and secondly on the word. Her translation practice and theories resemble Hölderlin's and Schleiermacher's, whose views will later be contrasted with hers. Also, the "Wörtlichkeit," the literalness, of certain passages are illustrative of Goethe's (and Walter Benjamin's) theory and ideal of interlinear translation. The term "Wörtlichkeit" refers here both to a practice of translating as much as possible word-by-word and to a kind of etymological literalness of word meaning. While it may be generally observed that Brentano-von Arnim's approach is more word-based than not, sometimes she translates rather freely.

First, I would like to present some very brief examples of Bettina Brentano-von Arnim's translation of some abstract terms. The translation is the least coherent when it renders Brentano-von Arnim's abstract ideas and observations; the narrative passages are much clearer. The beginning of the section from the *Diary*, *Fragments from letters written in Goethe's summer-house*, is loaded with such abstract German terms such as "Offenbarung," "Geist," "Ahnung," "Bedürfnis," and "Wollust" (Weimar 1: 529–532; 3: 196–199). An examination of a few of these words shows her various approaches to specific translation problems. Some words, such as "Geist," are consistently translated with one English word, "spirit." For other words, multiple equivalents are found. "Offenbarung" appears four times near the beginning of the passage. The first time it is translated as "inspiration," the other times as "revelation." In context, "I long for inspiration" seems clearer than: "Revelation is the only want of the spirit; for the sublimest is ever the onliest want" (Offenbarung ist das einzige Bedürfnis des Geistes, denn das höchste ist allemal das einzigste Bedürfnis). Bettina Brentano-von Arnim's "Wörtlichkeit" is evident here. At other places in this passage she embellishes the meaning without adding new material, taking the phrase rather than the word as her unit of translation. The phrase, "Nach Deinem Innern strebt die Liebe," becomes "Love strives to be imbosomed within thee." The unusual "imbosomed" has a sexual connotation not present in the German. There are also neologisms in the passage: "Thus spirit must imparadise itself" (So muß sich der Geist sein Paradies begründen), and "the young day's inarmings of light" (der junge Tag umfängt ihn mit seinem Licht). In order to create these new words, Brentano-von Arnim had to make nouns verbs and vice versa. Because of the effusion of such abstract terms in the German— which is itself often unclear—it is difficult to say whether her free translation is any better or worse than her word-for-word approach. An example of the latter is: "In thee I behold a thousand germs" (3: 41) for "In Dir seh ich tausend Keime" (2: 320). She always translates "Keim" and its derivatives as "germ," etc.

The most prominent example of the tenaciousness of her word-based translation and the danger of relying on an antiquated dictionary is her equation of the word "Wollust" with "voluptuousness." By the eighteenth century "voluptuousness" was not used as a personal attribute without a sexual connotation, although it can be used to describe luxurious objects. This equation leads to phrases such as: "Virtue which is not the highest voluptuousness" (2: 342), "this dolesome voluptuousness" (3: 55), "it is the blessed to whom all is voluptuousness" (3: 75), and "this sadness is voluptuousness to me" (3: 197). Brentano-von Arnim was fond of the word and uses the phrase "Voluptuousness-holyghost" in describing the translation to Nathusius (Köln 2: 491). She probably liked the word because it sounds like "Wollust" and even further intensified her erotically-charged language.

The more than forty pages of new material in *The Diary of the*

Child contain reflections upon the relationship between art, the spirit, and the senses as they strive towards the divine. It is on these new sections that an unbiased test of comprehensibility may be made, since there is no German text to rely on. I would contend that despite lines such as: "Love is of supernal nature the lofty pregnancy" (3: 246) and "my love is the hatching-warmth for spirit's offspring" (3: 236), the new sections, like the rest of the translation, may be understood by a diligent reader.

The sonnets are the least "wörtlich" of all her translations, and yet perhaps the most musical. Her Goethe sonnets maintain the rhyme scheme of the original and also sometimes the meter.[8] In the sonnet translations the demands of the rhyme scheme cause her to translate more freely than in the *Diary*. Bettina Brentano-von Arnim first tried her translation skills on the sonnets, as she told Varnhagen. It would seem, therefore, that when she began translating her approach was much freer than when she finished the *Diary* and wrote the "Preamble." Perhaps her renderings of Goethe's texts depart more from their originals than her translations of her own works because she is trying to gain authority over them. She is reclaiming the sonnets which she contended (often erroneously) she inspired. The sonnets appear in two locations in Brentano-von Arnim's *Goethe Book*, within the body of the text and in footnotes. In the most instances, both the translation and the original are provided so that Brentano-von Arnim's versions exist alongside Goethe's.

Goethe's poem, "If I did send thee now these pages white" (Wenn ich nun gleich das weiße Blatt dir schickte), was inspired by one of her original letters to him. Her rather free rendition exemplifies Brentano-von Arnim's whole process of "translation" in both literal and figural terms; it is a rendering from one language to another as well as an interpretation of the poem. Through the act of translation she reappropriates her own letter: Goethe "translated" her letter into poetry and then Brentano-von Arnim included the poem in the German edition of her book, *Goethes Briefwechsel*, claiming credit as muse. But by translating the poem into English, Bettina Brentano-von Arnim reasserts her rights as *author* of the text:

> If I did send thee now these pages white,
> Not filled with letters,—then perhaps to rhyme
> They should engage thee, and to charm my time
> Wouldst thou send back them, spending me delight. (1: 386)

Wenn ich nun gleich das weiße Blatt dir schickte,
Anstatt daß ich's mit Lettern erst beschreibe,
Ausfülltest du's vielleicht zum Zeitvertreibe
Und sendetest's an mich, die Hochbeglückte. (Weimar 1: 126)

Brentano-von Arnim wrote letters to Goethe as an expression of her
desire to be with him and because she believed that a kind of presence
was achieved through the act of exchanging letters. She offers her body
as blank page waiting, indeed asking for inscription by the male pen.
For her, sending blank or filled pages is not an either-or option. She
overlooks the word "Anstatt" (instead) thereby eliminating the chronology of writing and sending established in Goethe's poem. Her loose
translation of the third verse adds several elements to the poem. Goethe is to do more than "fill out" the papers, as the German version
implies. In Brentano-von Arnim's rendition he is to write a poem upon
them—"then perhaps to rhyme/They should engage thee." The inscription of the papers becomes then a much more serious task—an engaging one rather than one performed "zum Zeitvertreibe" (to pass the
time). Bettina Brentano-von Arnim interprets this differently; in the
translation, "Zeitvertreibe," becomes "to charm my time," putting the
focus on her own pleasure as recipient and reader rather than on the
writer. The return of the pages would make her "die Hochbeglückte."
This adjectival noun meaning, the woman who has been made very
happy, is not directly translated, but happiness is instead described as
"spending me delight." Her textual body is not wholly given over to the
poet: once inscribed, she wants it put back in circulation, so that she
can delight in it. The poet is to serve her pleasure as well as his. The
blank page initiates the correspondence and the exchange of pleasures.
Finally, however, Brentano-von Arnim strives to maintain control over
their entire relationship. It is she who first expresses the idea of the
blank page by writing of it on it. His poetic inscription does not fill her
blank page; it adds a layer to her own text. Her inclusion of the poem in
the *Goethe Book* again surrounds his text with her own. And finally,
Bettina Brentano-von Arnim's translation retains the original letter
without erasing or covering the other layers.

Such issues of authority and control do not present themselves in
the body of the prose translation. As both author and translator
Bettina Brentano-von Arnim can alter her text as she pleases. Because there is no need to reclaim her authorship, her translation can
remain closer to the original. The musical properties still take prece-

dence, but not to the degree they do in the poetry. The prose allows for greater "Wörtlichkeit" without sacrificing the melodic qualities she wants to preserve. It is, of course, impossible to prove by quoting specific passages that Brentano-von Arnim at certain points consciously sacrificed semantic clarity to musicality; what can be shown is that in both her word-by-word approach to the prose and her freer one in the poems, other aspects seem to take precedence over meaning. The only way of proving that she employed this policy when translating is by examining her theories as she explained them in the "Preamble," her letters, and *Günderode* (Die Günderode).

Brentano-von Arnim's own theory behind her translation practice can only be understood in the context of the German translation theory expounded by her precursors and friends—men such as Johann Georg Hamann, Johann Gottfried Herder, Humboldt, Goethe, and Friedrich Schleiermacher. Their ideas influenced Bettina Brentano-von Arnim both directly and indirectly. Brentano-von Arnim was indirectly influenced by the translation theories of Hamann and Herder. She was an active member of the intellectual community at the time and given her interest in language, it can be assumed that she was conversant with their theories. Also, Hamann's and Herder's theories are reflected later in Goethe's and Schleiermacher's writings on the topic. Bettina Brentano-von Arnim was acquainted with Humboldt and was friends with Schleiermacher; her knowledge of Goethe and his works at the time she was writing her books, especially the *Divan* from which she took some of the poems included in *The Goethe Book* and in which Goethe explained some of his translation theories, cannot be questioned.

In eighteenth-century Germany there was a debate in translation theory between the advocates of "freie"—free or non-literal translation—and "treue Übersetzung"—a translation which is to some degree literal, one in which the translator is "faithful" to the author. Those on both sides believed that a complete or perfect translation must be possible (Kloepfer 46). The idea of perfect translation as a unification of languages which would express humankind's linguistic situation before Babel is particularly espoused in then current mystical philosophies in which all language is defined as translation. The theories of Herder, Schleiermacher, and later Walter Benjamin reflect this mystical and religious aspect of translation (Huyssen 39–40). As we shall see, Brentano-von Arnim imbues language with divine import and these mystically-based philosophies of language

affect her own view of language as that which connects the human
and the divine. What André Lefevere has noted regarding Herder's
theory of translation applies to Brentano-von Arnim's too: "Translation is no longer a literary and/or linguistic activity. It becomes a
metaphor, a category of thought, and will remain so . . . . The divine is translated into the human in language. The spirit of the
infinite reveals itself in all languages and in all poetry—an idea later
to be taken up by Benjamin" (Lefevere, *Translating* 30). Hamann,
who greatly influenced Herder, declared: "Speech is translating—
from angel's language into human language" (Reden ist übersetzen—aus einer Engelssprache in eine Menschensprache) (2: 199).
These mystical approaches to translation de-emphasize the content
of the text to be translated and highlight language itself. Such an
approach results in a translation which, as Herder explained, refash-
ions the target language into the mold of the source language (Lefevere, "German" 14). An example of this kind of translation would
be Hölderlin's Greco-German Sophocles translations. Influenced by
these theories, the central question for translation theorists in the
nineteenth century evolved so that it was no longer one of fidelity to
a source text, but one of the nature of language itself. Goethe also
pushed the definition of translation beyond issues of semantic
equivalences. He wrote in his *Maxims and Reflections* (Maximen
und Reflexionen): "When translating one must approach the untranslatable; only then does one become aware of the foreign nation
and the foreign language" (Beim Übersetzen muß man bis ans
Unübersetzliche herangehen; alsdann wird man aber erst die fremde
Nation und die fremde Sprache gewahr) (12: 499). In speaking
about the *Divan*, Goethe defined three types or epochs of translation. The first two roughly equate respectively with "free" and "faithful," but the third poses a kind of synthesis. It is both the highest
and the final kind of translation, "where one would like to make the
translation identical to the original, so that one does not have one
instead of the other, but so that one may be valid in place of the
other" (wo man die Übersetzung dem Original identisch machen
möchte, so daß eins nicht anstatt des andern, sondern an der Stelle
des andern gelten solle) (2: 256). This type "ultimately approaches
the interlinear version" (nähert sich zuletzt der Interlinearversion)
(2: 258). Goethe's use of the term "interlinear" here to refer to the
replacement of the source text by the translation is unusual, since in
a standard interlinear version both texts coexist on the same page.

Goethe's "interlinear" translation is therefore not an overly literal translation, but one in which the translation would completely replace the original work.[9]

Friedrich Schleiermacher, along with Martin Luther and Walter Benjamin, is considered today to have been the most significant German translation theorist. Schleiermacher's theories are significant here because he played an important role in Brentano-von Arnim's life in the late 1820s and early 1830s. He often discussed his Plato translations with her, and in one letter Brentano-von Arnim claims that he called her his Plato (Köln 5: 232). Also, Schleiermacher had once offered to proofread and edit the German edition of *The Goethe Book*, but he died in 1834 before the manuscript was completed (Köln 5: 224). Konstanze Bäumer also points out that Schleiermacher, along with Pückler-Muskau, was just as important to the creation of the German *Goethe Book* as Goethe was (39).[10] Schleiermacher outlined his translation theory in a Berlin lecture in 1813. He identified two sorts of translation: author- or text-oriented and reader-oriented: "Either the translator leaves the author to the greatest extent possible in peace and moves the reader towards him; or he leaves the reader to the greatest extent in peace and moves the author towards him" (Entweder der Übersetzer läßt den Schriftsteller möglichst in Ruhe und bewegt den Leser ihm entgegen; oder er läßt den Leser möglichst in Ruhe und bewegt den Schriftsteller ihm entgegen). His own translation of Plato, like Hölderlin's Pindar and Sophocles, is text-oriented, recapturing as much as possible the structural and tonal elements of the Greek. For Schleiermacher, translation in depth demanded the accommodation of one's own language to the lexical and syntactic world of the original (Steiner 266). Schleiermacher believed that the musical and rhythmic aspects of language transmit a higher meaning beyond the content of the translated text. He stated that "the musical element in language that reveals itself in rhythm and change of tone has a distinguished and higher meaning" (das musikalische Element der Sprache, das sich in Rhythmus und Tonwechsel offenbart, eine ausgezeichnete und höhere Bedeutung hat) (53). As demonstrated by her sonnets, Bettina Brentano-von Arnim adopted much of Schleiermacher's technique of musicality and rhythm for her own project. Her diary is clearly an example of a text-oriented translation which strives to bring English and German together by Germanizing the English language, particularly through the neologisms seen in the examples given.

It is evident from the above overview of German translation theories that there is no agreement on translation terminology. In the eighteenth century, the debate was on the merits of "free" versus "faithful" translation (Kloepfer 46). Schleiermacher's distinctions rely on his hypothesis that language determines and frames thoughts, and concludes that the farther the translator moves from the author's language and towards the reader's, the greater the possibility for the distortion of the author's intent (Schleiermacher 43). Schleiermacher moves his reader towards the author, requiring the reader's accommodation not only to a foreign language, but also, like Goethe, to foreign thought content. Hölderlin makes similar demands on his reader in his Sophocles translations.

Hölderlin's translation theories also influenced Bettina Brentano-von Arnim. In *Günderode* she paraphrases passages from Hölderlin's commentaries on his Sophocles translations. Like Hölderlin and mystical translation and language theorists, she seeks the key to the divine language of the creator who made the world through the word: "And aren't there not still in language hidden powers that we do not yet have? . . . if we could only reach into there, to speak the unsaid . . . because the whole spirit is merely a translation of God's spirit in us" (Und ob's doch nicht noch in der Sprache verborgne Gewalten gibt, die wir noch nicht haben? . . . ob wir da hindringen könnten, das Ungesagte auszusprechen . . . denn der ganze Geist ist wohl nur ein Übersetzen des Geist Gottes in uns) (Weimar 2: 299). In Bettina Brentano-von Arnim's hierarchy, music assumes the superior position to language in bringing us closer to the divine. Ideally, "all language must be music" (alle Sprache muß Musik sein); language must free itself of categorical forms of expression in order to adequately express the spirit (Weimar: 2: 232).

Like her theoretical precursors, Brentano-von Arnim elevated translation in a mystical analogy between language and divine creation, declaring in *Günderode*: "And then it occurred to me that God spoke: *let there be*, and that God's language is a creation and that I wanted to imitate" (Und da fiel mir ein, daß Gott sprach: *Es werde*, und daß die Sprach Gottes ein Erschaffen sei;—und das wollt ich nachahmen) (Weimar 2: 185). Underlying this analogy are the two major definitions of the verb "to translate"—"übersetzen" and its related nominalized form "Übersetzung."[11] The first and most common use, even during Brentano-von Arnim's time, was that of "translation" (übersetzen) as rendering something said or written in one language into another. Figuratively "translation" approaches in meaning "interpretation." The second definition functions etymologically and the meaning takes on a spatial aspect: "setzen" as to "place," "put," or "set," and "über" as "over," designating either lateral or upward movement; translation is also transportation. This aspect of movement from one place to another is evident in Schleiermacher's theory. Goethe's vertical placement of one text over another in his definition of ideal translation, alludes to this meaning of the term. The ideal text, for Goethe, is set over the original text in the interlinear version, both coexisting with it above the line of the original and being set above it as a replacement. For mystical language theorists, translation transports language towards the divine by raising it above both the specific source and target languages so that it functions dialectically as a third term, as an ideal concept of language which approaches the divine language of creation. Walter Benjamin has called this third and ideal type of translation—a translation which is neither "free" nor "faithful" but a step beyond these mundane concerns—"real translation" (79) (wahre Übersetzung 18).[12]

Benjamin's essay, "The Task of the Translator" (Die Aufgabe des Übersetzers) is relevant to this discussion because in it he elucidates and expands upon the mystical translation theories that influenced Brentano-von Arnim and because he demonstrates how these theories circumscribe both translation as an act and the translator in terms of male gender and male roles. According to Benjamin, only "real translation" can fulfill the translator's messianic mission to redeem language from its post-Babelian state (15). The translator is to be a romantic cabalistic redeemer of what Benjamin calls "pure language" (74) (die reine Sprache" [13]), the seed of which lies buried in all languages (13). Through translation the interrelationship between all languages is revealed and within this revelation lies a seed of pure language.[13] Pure language is the essence of all language. A translation gives us a presentiment of what pure language is; it makes us aware of language as language (Derrida, Ear 123–124). For Bettina Brentano-von Arnim, literature and poetry in particular have the power to reveal pure language—"to illuminate the divine secret of language" (das göttliche Geheimnis der Sprache zu erleuchten) (Weimar 2: 265). The translator-poet has the power to unlock the door to divine language through his work (Weimar 2: 299). He, like the messiah, mediates between the human and the divine message independent of the surface meaning of the words.

For Bettina Brentano-von Arnim, like Hölderlin and others, this requires that the translator concentrate on the sound of language, rather than on the meaning. In fact, Benjamin believes that a communicatively (i.e., reader-oriented) based translation fails to reflect the essence of the literary work. In it, "Its essential quality is not statement or the imparting of information. Yet any translation which intends to perform a transmitting function cannot transmit anything but information—hence, something inessential" (Wesentliches ist nicht Mitteilung, nicht Aussage. Dennoch könnte diejenige Übersetzung, welche vermitteln will, nichts vermitteln als die Mitteilung—also Unwesentliches) (69). For this reason, the essential message of translation is not any specific surface content, but the lost unity of language and the utopian vision of reunification, of redemption through translation. The real translation illuminates pure language; in Brentano-von Arnim's terms, literature should illuminate (erleuchten), in Benjamin's: "A real translation is transparent; it does not cover the original, does not block its light, but allows the pure language, as though reinforced by its own medium, to shine upon the original all the more fully" (79) (Die wahre Übersetzung ist durchscheinend, sie verdeckt nicht das Original, steht ihm nicht im Licht, sondern läßt die reine Sprache, wie verstärkt durch ihr eigenes Medium, nur um so voller aufs Original fallen" [18]). As Goethe does, Benjamin posits interlinear translation of the Bible as his model: "The interlinear version of the Scriptures is the prototype or ideal of all translation" (82) (Die Interlinearversion des heiligen Textes ist das Urbild oder Ideal aller Übersetzung [21]). Translation ideally then brings languages closer together literally and figuratively, and thereby reveals the essence of pure language contained in every specific language.

If the translator is to act as a kind of linguistic messiah, as God's messenger, then this metaphor seems to demand interpretation in male-gendered terms. In Christianity and Judaism the messiah is male, and presumably then for these theorists the translator is male. The employment of masculine metaphors as references to both translator and translation evokes a whole complex of literary terminology and assumptions about male authorship and female texts, and about appropriate productive and reproductive roles. If, for example, the Bloomian metaphor of the author as father is adopted, the author is defined as a producer of a unique product, but a translator would logically then merely reproduce the author's texts, not fathering a work, but perhaps metaphorically mothering it by nurturing its growth. These translation theorists who re-evaluate the role of the translator in the literary process, give the act of translation a masculine cast. They want to masculinize translation and free it from its status as a reproductive (and therefore presumably feminine), as opposed to a productive, original, and masculine task (Chamberlain 455). So-called masculine and feminine tasks here can be linked directly with assumptions regarding the gender of the author and the translator. Lori Chamberlain has observed that translation is so overcoded with sexual metaphors because "it threatens to erase the difference between production and reproduction which is essential to the establishment of power" (466). The author and translator dispute paternity rights "because this is the only way, in a patriarchal code, to claim legitimacy for the text" (Chamberlain 466). It is perhaps ironic that Bettina Brentano-von Arnim and her translation find themselves in the midst of this argument over the paternity and the legitimacy of the text, because all of her works have had at some time their authorship and their legitimacy challenged. Her own approach to her translation and her work as a translator contribute to and challenge the arguments of her day.

In his interpretation of Benjamin's essay, Jacques Derrida deconstructs the gendered metaphor of translation. He takes Benjamin's statement, "Yes this task: in the translation to bring to fruition the seed of pure language" (80) (Ja, diese Aufgabe: in der Übersetzung den Samen reiner Sprache zur Reife zu bringen" [17]), and etymologically associates the seed (as "semen" as well as seed) with engendering, family and semantics. In this way Derrida continues to locate the word within patriarchal imagery. Derrida defines his own " 'task of the translator' " in terms of a marriage contract where the translator contracts with a virginal original mother text to produce a child ("Babel" 191–192). In this marriage two languages are also conjoined ("Babel" 200). He does expose how gender and its accompanying terms such as virginity and fidelity code definitions of translation, but he does not reach beyond them.

It is clear that these theories leave little room for the woman translator, just as literary theory with its metaphors of paternity excludes women authors. It is important to note that despite these definitions of the translator, Bettina Brentano-von Arnim did not step outside of prescribed gender roles when she translated her *Goethe Book*. In the eighteenth and nineteenth century Germany women were the primary translators of popular literature. Many of the first women authors in Germany were also translators—women such as Luise Kulmus Gottsched, Dorothea Schlegel, Caroline Schlegel-Schelling, Brentano-von Arnim's sister-in-law Sophie Mereau, and Mereau's sister Henriette Schubart, who earned her living by translating from English to German. The efforts by theorists to masculinize the role of the translator should not be seen then in an historical vacuum. The reassessment of the reproductive task of translation by men and its redefinition as productive task did not occur in a value-free environment.

Bettina Brentano-von Arnim's place within the trend to define translation as a male activity is problematic. Her theories of translation reflect those of Schleiermacher and others. But her gender also subverts these theories by implicitly challenging the gender constructs of literary production. How can she as a woman translator play a messianic role? Bettina Brentano-von Arnim further complicates theoretical constructs by translating her own work, as well as some of Goethe's. She is both the author and translator. Is she then both father and mother to her text? Does she play the mother and father role twice, once as author and once as translator? Brentano-von Arnim's self-translation points out the absurdity of the sexual metaphor of translation, but at the same time she makes use of it. She refuses in the end, as a jealous parent, to hand over her child, *Goethes Briefwechsel mit einem Kinde*, to a foreign translator who will become its surrogate parent. Adding to the confusion in this mother-father-child triad, within the book itself she is the "child" of the title, and Goethe the paternal figure. As translator of her own work, she both can protect her text and give birth to it—reproduce it—all over again.

Bettina Brentano-von Arnim creates the text anew by adding new passages and through the neologisms and new uses of English words. According to Brentano-von Arnim, this new language which is neither wholly English or nor wholly German is germinated through the technique of cross-pollination: "the strange etymologies even as blossomdust transported by sedulous bees from foreign lands to their homely field, variegating the flowerage of their words" (3: v). This use of the etymological dictionary and her pastoral metaphor make it apparent that Brentano-von Arnim's basic unit of translation is the word and not the phrase or the sentence. Benjamin describes this technique, seeing the sentence as a barrier, a wall between the languages and "literalness is the arcade" (79) (Wörtlichkeit die Arkade [18]). While Benjamin's metaphors are architectural, Bettina Brentano-von Arnim's are biological. Her male assistants were amazed by her self-described plantlike technique: "They are amazed at my syntax and are in awe of my phytologic technique" (Da staunen sie über meine Wortstellungen und haben eine heilige Scheu vor meinem phytonissischen Verfahren) (Köln 2: 491). As the horticulturist of words, the translator creates new varieties by facilitating the sexual union of words.

Through this metaphor, Bettina Brentano-von Arnim exhibits her dependence on a gendered theory of translation. The translator might not be a party to a marriage contract, as Derrida contends, but is at the very least a coupleur, a compounder of words and meanings. To "compound" words, as she observes in her "Preamble" (3: v), is both to conjoin them and to add to an existent number in a process comparable to God's originating "Let there be" (Es werde). She believes that the translator does not consciously express the divinity in language; therefore, instinct and feeling guide her work.

> Unconsciously I pursued my task, confiding in my genius, that would preserve me from doing any harm by unfit or even unusual expressions, and persisted often in my wrong way, when my advisers would have subverted my construction as they were absurdities, often my version larded with uncommon or obsolete expressions gave way to misunderstanding, then I could not ally the correction with my meaning, and would not be disputed out of my wits impassionated as I was for my traced-out turn, for which I had rummaged dictionary and poetry and never would yield. (3: vi)

Reliance on the unconscious and "genius" for inspiration and guidance is a theme common to all German Romantic literature. Bettina Brentano-von Arnim, however, is not content to play the role of mere muse to male genius; she envisions for herself both a messianic role and one as "genius." As a messiah in relatively traditional terms (in spite of being a female messiah), the god she serves is Goethe. It is the message of her god's "paternal" love for the "child" that she wants to carry to the English (3: viii). Her task as "the real translator" (die wahre Übersetzerin)—to paraphrase Benjamin—is to implant Goethe in foreign soil. She wants "to find a new fatherland for this book of love" (3: viii). At the same time, of course, she also propagates her own art and fame.

It is on this point of self-promotion that Brentano-von Arnim subverts the translator's messianic role defined by Benjamin and her precursors. Although her theory of translation echoes some of the male-gendered metaphors already discussed, she also uses maternal imagery. She proclaims herself in her roles as author and translator as a defender of both texts—the German and the English Goethe books. In the "Preamble" is a mother defending her young:

> I struggled for my version as does an animal for its young and suffers them not to be touched by an indiscreet hand, but licks them clean again; so it was with me, instinctively and with great labour I tried to overcome all the corrections by a deeper inducement, while people laughed at my relucting and said that I never would come to good issue. (3: vii)

Her protectiveness and proprietary hold over her "children" *Goethes Briefwechsel mit einem Kinde* and *Goethe's Correspondence with a Child* are evident here. She is mother to both texts, and her "god" and their father is Goethe. Since Goethe exists now in another realm, as spirit he cannot compete with, and more importantly, cannot challenge her text or her authority to speak for him. In speaking for him, Brentano-von Arnim displaces the father and usurps for herself on several levels all three roles in the family triad. She plays the "child" within the text, and as messianic child of her godfather she speaks his message for him. Her usurpation of the authority of the absent god is analogous to the Oedipal struggle between father and son, only she does not have to murder the father to take his place, since he is already dead. As a mother protecting her literary issue, her "children," Brentano-von Arnim subverts the cultural metaphor of author as father. She also plays havoc with the metaphor of the translator as messiah. Bettina Brentano-von Arnim is bearer of two messianic messages: Goethe's and her own. She is, therefore, not only the mother, father, and child of both texts, she is also a divine speaker of the word, or at the very least its chosen messenger. In translating between the divine and the earthly, Bettina Brentano-von Arnim reinforces her own importance, making herself more than the editor of a correspondence or the author of a fictional work; through the act of translation—both by "translating" figuratively Goethe's words in his letters in the German edition and by translating from German to English—her task assumes cosmic proportions and this is perhaps also why she was so reluctant to allow another to "transplant" Goethe's message and her own to English soil.

English readers were in general not receptive to this message and in the end, Bettina Brentano-von Arnim's hope of transplanting Goethe to foreign soil was disappointed. The reviewers were not enthusiastic about the first two volumes of the translation. The *Literary Gazette* reported that the correspondence "is an exotic that would find no growth in our quiet and cold soil; and we must frankly confess, we see no reason that it should" (651). The book's acceptability was questioned in *The Athenaeum*, which had praised the German version: "we doubt whether the work, taken as a whole, is likely to be acceptable to an English public; it is too essentially German" (769). The essential Germanness of the book lay in its erotic component. One reviewer for *Foreign Quarterly Review* complained "that the warmth of the unrestrained effusions of a glowing imagination . . . so far exceeds the bounds authorized by the English laws of decorum, that the work, faithfully translated, would not be tolerated on the table of any English family" (120–121).

Even though the English were not enthusiastic, *Goethe's Correspondence with a Child* and especially *The Diary of a Child* are a significant part of Bettina Brentano-von Arnim's collected works. They reveal a philosophy of language and translation which leaves neither source nor target language unaffected. The English text becomes a kind of transparent palimpsest, allowing, as Brentano-von Arnim proposes, the original to shine through the translation and enhance it at the same time. In her practice, Brentano-von Arnim's translation approaches Goethe's and Benjamin's ideal that the translation does not cover the original, but instead illuminates it (Benjamin 18). While the translation is not now nor was it then a replacement for the German version, it exists alongside the German as an independent work, mirroring and being mirrored by the German version. Through her translation Bettina Brentano-von Arnim creates a language of her own and discovers the seed of pure language bringing all languages closer to God's and our own before Babel.

Notes

I would like to thank the University of Georgia Humanities Center for supporting the completion of this essay.

1. In this essay, I will confine my discussion to literary and artistic translation. The theories examined in most cases do not apply to other types of
translation.

2. All translations, unless otherwise noted, are provided by the author.

3. I will quote extensively from the "Preamble" in this essay, since it is not
available in any of her currently published works. Quotations from the
"Preamble" will also familiarize the reader with Brentano-von Arnim's
English style. All the quotations taken from the first edition of the translation published in Germany, *Goethe's Correspondence with a Child*, 3
vols. (Berlin: 1837-1838).

4. This statement also reinforces the impression Brentano-von Arnim
wanted to give that the work contains more letters from Goethe than it
actually does and that it is an unedited record of their relationship. In
having Austin come to her she also implies that the book was widely
known in England.

5. In assessing her knowledge of English, Bettina Brentano-von Arnim is
quite typically exaggerating her ignorance. There is reason to believe
that she learned some English in her youth. There can be no doubt,
however, that many years later she had much to learn.

6. Two editors of Bettina Brentano-von Arnim's works, Gustav Konrad and
Heinz Härtl, consider these English passages so crucial to the book that
they included them in the appendices of the German editions. Härtl even
had them translated into German.

7. The edition of Brentano-von Arnim's works edited by Heinz Härtl and
published in Weimar will be used for references to *Goethes Briefwechsel
mit einem Kinde* and *Die Günderode*, and the edition edited by Gustav
Konrad (volumes 1–4) and J. Müller (volume 5) for *Ilius Pamphilius und
die Ambrosia* and some of the letters.

8. Some of the Goethe poems included in the book are not sonnets and
therefore demand different treatment by the translator.

9. Interlinear translation is most practiced in the translation of ancient
Greek, Latin, and biblical texts where the translation is inserted between
the lines of the source text.

10. For more information on the relationship between Bettina Brentano-von
Arnim and Schleiermacher see the articles by Moltmann-Wendel and
Patsch. Brentano-von Arnim wrote about her relationship with Schleiermacher in her correspondences with Julius Döring, and Pückler-Muskau,
and in her book *Ilius Pamphilius und die Ambrosia*.

11. This summary of dictionary definitions is based upon the entries in
Grimms Deutsches Wörterbuch, volume 11, section 2, pages 544–553.

12. The translated quotations from Benjamin's essay are taken from Harry
Zohn's translation of "The Task of the Translator." (For the complete reference, see the entry for Benjamin in "Works Cited.") Some minor changes

have been made by the author. Page references following the English quotations are from this translation. Page references following the original German are from the Suhrkamp edition of Benjamin. See "Works Cited."

13. "If the kinship of languages manifests itself in translations, this is not accomplished through a vague alikeness between adaptation and original. . . . Rather all suprahistorical kinship of languages rests in the intention underlying each language as a whole—an intention, however, which no single language can attain by itself but which is realized only by the totality of their intentions supplementing each other: pure language" (72–74). (Wenn in der Uebersetzung die Verwandtschaft der Sprachen sich bekündet, so geschieht es anders als durch die vage Aehnlichkeit von Nachbildung und Original. . . . Vielmehr beruht alle überhistorische Verwandtschaft der Sprachen darin, daß in ihrer jeder als ganzer jeweils eines und zwar dasselbe gemeint ist, das dennoch keiner einzelnen von ihnen, sondern nur der Allheit ihrer einander ergänzenden Intentionen erreichbar ist: die reine Sprache [Benjamin 13]).

Works Cited

Arnim, Bettina von. *Goethe's Correspondence with a Child*. 3 vols. Berlin: 1837–1838.

———. *Lebensspiel*. Ed. Willi Reich. Zürich: Manese, 1953. Letter to Caroline von Egloffstein. 28. March 1838.

———. *Werke*. Ed. Heinz Härtl. Berlin and Weimar: Aufbau Verlag, 1986 (vol. 1), 1989 (vol. 2). (Quoted as Weimar.)

———. *Werke und Briefe*. 5 vols. Eds. Gustav Konrad (Vols. 1–4: Frechen and Köln) and Joachim Müller (Vol. 5: Frechen and Köln: Bartmann, 1958–1963. (Quoted as Köln.)

——— and Julius Döring. "Bettina Brentano-von Arnims Briefe an Julius Döring." Ed. Werner Vordtriede. *Jahrbuch des freien deutschen Hochstifts* (1963): 341–488.

——— and J. and W. Grimm. *Der Briefwechsel Bettine Brentano-von Arnims mit den Brüdern Grimm. 1838–1841*. Ed. Hartwig Schultz. Frankfurt/M.: Insel, 1985.

Bäumer, Konstanze. *"Bettine, Psyche, Mignon": Bettina Brentano-von Arnim und Goethe*. Stuttgarter Arbeiten zur Germanistik 139. Stuttgart: Akademischer Verlag, 1986.

Benjamin, Walter. "Die Aufgabe des Übersetzers." *Gesammelte Schriften.* Frankfurt/M.: Suhrkamp, 1980. Vol. 4.1. 9–21.

———. "The Task of the Translator." Trans. Harry Zohn. *Illuminations.* New York: Harcourt, Brace & World, 1968. 69–82.

Chamberlain, Lori. "Gender and the Metaphorics of Translation" *Signs: Journal of Women in Culture and Society* 13 (1988): 454–472.

Collins, Hildegard P. and Philip A. Shelley. "The Reception in England and America of Bettina Brentano-von Arnim's *Goethe's Correspondence with a Child*" in Vol. 2 of *Anglo-German and American-German Crosscurrents.* Ed. Philip Shelley and Arthur Lewis. Chapel Hill: University of North Carolina Press, 1962. 97–174.

Derrida, Jacques. "Des Tours de Babel." *Difference in Translation.* Ed. and Trans. Joseph F. Graham. Ithaca: Cornell UP. 165–207.

———. *The Ear of the Other: Otobiography, Transference, Translation.* Ed. Christie V. McDonald. Trans. Peggy Kamuf. New York: Schocken, 1985.

Goethe, Johann Wolfgang von. *Werke.* Hamburger Ausgabe. Ed. Erich Trunz. 14 vols. München: Beck, 1977.

Hamann, Johann Georg. *Sämtliche Werke.* 2 vols. Ed. Josef Nadler. Wien: Verlag Herder, 1949.

Herzhaft in die Dornen der Zeit greifen . . . Bettine von Arnim 1785–1859. Ed. Christoph Perels. Frankfurt/M.: Freies Deutsches Hochstift, 1985.

Huyssen, Andreas. *Die frühromantische Konzeption von Übersetzung und Aneignung.* Zürcher Beiträge zur deutschen Literatur- und Geistesgeschichte 33. Zürich: Atlantis, 1969.

Kloepfer, Rolf. *Die Theorie der literarischen Übersetzung.* Freiburger Schriften zur romanischen Philologie 12. München: Fink, 1967.

Lefevere, André. "German Translation Theory: Legacy and Relevance." *Journal of European Studies.* 11 (1981): 9–17.

———. *Translating Literature: The German Tradition from Luther to Rosenzweig.* Amsterdam: Van Gorcum, 1977.

Moltmann-Wendel, Elisabeth. "Bettina Brentano-von Arnim und Schleiermacher." *Evangelische Theologie* 31 (1971): 395–414.

Patsch, Herrmann. " 'Ob ich dich liebe, weiß ich nicht.' Goethe und ein Wechselgedicht zwischen Bettina Brentano-von Arnim und Friedrich Schleiermacher." *Zeitschrift für deutsche Philologie* 104 (1985): 542–554.

Pückler-Muskau, Hermann. *Frauenbriefe von und an Hermann Fürsten Pückler-Muskau.* Ed. Heinrich Conrad. München & Leipzig: Georg Müller, 1912.

Steiner, George. *After Babel: Aspects of Language and Translation.* New York and London: Oxford UP, 1975.

Störig, Hans Joachim. *Das Problem des Übersetzens.* Darmstadt: Wissenschaftliche Buchgesellschaft, 1963.

Varnhagen von Ense, Karl August. *Aus dem Nachlaß Varnhagen's von Ense.*

Briefe von Stägemann, Metternich, Heine und Bettina Brentano-von Arnim, nebst Briefen, Anmerkungen und Notizen von Varnhagen von Ense. Ed. Ludmilla Assing. Leipzig: F. A. Brockhaus, 1865.

Vordtriede, Werner. "Bettinas englisches Wagnis." *Euphorion* 51 (1957): 271–294.

ENGLISH REVIEWS

The Athenaeum. Oct. 17, 1835: 416: 772–74

———. Oct. 14, 1837: 520: 769.

Foreign Quarterly Review. Oct. 1837: 20: 120–21.

Literary Gazette. Oct. 14, 1837: No. 1082: 651–52.

Bettina Brentano-von Arnim:
The Unknown Musician

Ann Willison

While music is a prevalent theme in Bettina Brentano-von Arnim's letters and epistolary novels, her aspirations and efforts to become a musician in her own right are relatively obscure. The handful of published musical compositions and pages of remaining manuscripts has left no mark on the course of music history, so that today few people are aware of the significant position music occupied in Brentano-von Arnim's life. Nevertheless, the scanty and largely unknown record of her musical career bears testimony to a talented woman—however troubled by feelings of her own inadequacy—with profound musicoliterary as well as personal sensitivities.

In her lifetime, Brentano-von Arnim published less than a dozen compositions, all of them songs for voice and piano. The first two were individual songs published with the literary works of Achim von Arnim (1781–1831) for which they were written, one before and one shortly after their marriage in 1811. Both appear under Brentano-von Arnim's pseudonym, "Beans Beor."[1] Brentano-von Arnim published compositions in her own name only once, in 1842. After she was already known as the author of two epistolary novels, she collected seven songs into a book (Spontini songbook). Two other song publications appeared during her lifetime, but Brentano-von Arnim was not recognized as the composer. Table 1 summarizes Brentano-von Arnim's song publications.

Table 1. Brentano-von Arnim's Songs Published in Her Lifetime

Song Title	Author of Text	Source of Pub.	Date
1. Romanze	A.v.Arnim	*Gräfin Dolores*	1810
2. Lied des Schülers	A.v.Arnim	*Novellensammlung*	1812
3. Klage und Trost	A.v.Arnim	*Liederbuch für dt. Künstler*	1833
1. Mondenschein	A.v.Arnim	Spontini Songbook	1842
2. Aus Faust	Goethe	"	
3. Aus dem 'Wintergarten'	A.v.Arnim	"	
4. Ein Stern der Lieb	A.v.Arnim	"	
5. Herbstgefühl	Goethe	"	
6. Duett (Abendstille)	A.v.Arnim	"	
7. Duett (Vom Nachen getragen)	A.v.Arnim	"	
questionable:			
Lied beim Scharpiezupfen	C. Brentano	*Viktoria*	1824

This small number of published works seems to indicate that music was only of secondary importance to Bettina Brentano-von Arnim. Yet a close look at her letters and music manuscripts gives a very different picture. They show that Brentano-von Arnim had sketches and ideas for at least fifty other songs that were either never completed or remained unpublished. In her twenties, Brentano-von Arnim expressed the desire to have music as a central part of her life. She studied voice, piano, composition, and harmony intensely and spent many hours practicing and composing songs. The manuscripts that have survived contain a wealth of sketches, fragments, and some completed songs. These provide insight into Brentano-von Arnim's compositional style, method, and skill, and help to establish a chronology of her works.

The Dannie and Hettie Heineman Collection of The Pierpont Morgan Library in New York houses Brentano-von Arnim's only extant music manuscripts. A 140-page music notebook (MS 9B) and a folder of loose pages (MS 30) comprise all of Brentano-von Arnim's autographed compositions known today. The notebook may originally have been intended only for settings of Achim von Arnim's poems, since roughly the first nineteen pages contain his poems set to music in clean ink copies.[2] Fragments and sketches in pencil to poems of Goethe, Achim von Arnim, Friedrich Hölderlin (1770–1843), and the little-known poet Amalie von Helvig (1776–1831) make up the middle section of notebook MS 9B. At some point, Brentano-von Arnim turned the notebook upside down and began filling it from the back with larger scale sketches of Achim von Arnim's dramatic poems. The notebook bears no date, but she could well have used it over the span of a decade or so, roughly from 1815 to 1827. If indeed Bettina Brentano-von Arnim intended to dedicate it to settings of her husband's poetry, the first ink entries were probably composed as early as 1805, then copied later into this book. She may have tired of the painstaking neatness required to produce the finished product, set the notebook aside, and later may have used it as a sketchbook for songs inspired by a variety of poets.

Many factors suggest that the sketches were conceived spontaneously and jotted down quickly. Time signature, key signature, and measure lines are often missing, and the rhythm and harmonization are frequently very sketchy or completely absent. Sometimes, in her haste to put her ideas on paper, Brentano-von Arnim skipped words of the text or used a kind of shorthand. Still, she almost always conceived her music in connection with a text; only about eleven passages contain purely instrumental music. Table 2 ignores some inconsistencies within sections but gives a general overview of the contents of notebook MS 9B.[3]

Occasionally, other people also wrote in this music notebook of Brentano-von Arnim's. One song, with an Italian text, may have been written in by a friend as a kind of souvenir (MS 9B 124). Pencil markings on the first ink pages appear be from another person, suggesting that Brentano-von Arnim may have asked for help in completing these settings. The entire last half of one song is written in another hand (MS 9B 19).

Loose sheets on which Bettina Brentano-von Arnim wrote songs and sketches, and miscellaneous other music manuscripts that were in her possession, are listed together as MS 30 of the Heineman Collection. The pages in Brentano-von Arnim's handwriting include

Table 2. Overview of Notebook, Heineman MS 9B

Pages*	#Poems	Poet[†]	Characteristics
1–19	11	A.v.Arnim	clean, completed songs, working copies, some fragments, in ink
20–53	7	Goethe	pencil sketches, many very short
	3	A.v.Arnim	long sketches (3–4 pages each)
	2	Hölderlin	long sketches
	2	Helvig	1 short sketch, 1 longer sketch upside-down
54–132	11	Goethe	pencil sketches, most entries upside-down, some blank pages
	6	A.v.Arnim	
	2	Helvig	
2 loose	1	Goethe	sketchy, in ink and pencil
pages	2	unknown	

*Pages were numbered later in pencil in the upper outer corner. 41 pages contain no notations.
[†]There are approximately 14 passages for which text and author have not yet been identified. Most of these are very short (one line or less), except for the two found among the loose notebook pages (see Table 2). Some could even be Bettina Brentano-von Arnim's text variations, as they appear together with known poems.

one clean, ink copy of the song "Romanze," as well as sketches to additional poems by Achim von Arnim, Helvig, and Goethe, and some passages without texts. A setting of Clemens Brentano's poem "Lied eines Müllers am Rhein"—in the handwriting of Brentano-von Arnim's niece Maximiliane Brentano—is most likely also her composition.[4] In addition, the manuscripts include ten sacred songs, settings of Achim von Arnim's poems, and some folk pieces. Finally, a large fragment of the song Ludwig van Beethoven dedicated to Brentano-von Arnim, a setting of Goethe's poem "Neue Liebe, neues Leben," is preserved with the other manuscripts. Thus, as

Table 3. Brentano-von Arnim's Manuscripts in *Heineman* MS 30

#Poems	Poet	Characteristics
2	A.v.Arnim	1 clean ink copy, 1 working copy
1	C.Brentano	clean ink copy by Maximiliane Brentano
3	Goethe	ink and pencil sketches
1	Helvig	ink and pencil sketch

shown in table 3, MS 30 contains the following compositions recognized as Brentano-von Arnim's own.[5] The Pierpont Morgan Library also houses the copyist's manuscript for the Spontini songbook. Transcriptions of some five other songs have been located in Germany.[6]

Several features emerge as characteristic tendencies in the corpus of Bettina Brentano-von Arnim's music. She composed Lieder almost exclusively, many of them in the simple folk song (volkstümlich) style of the Second Berlin Song School. With few exceptions, Brentano-von Arnim chose poems of male writers she knew personally as the texts for her songs and published very few of the songs she wrote or conceived. The limited opportunities available to women in nineteenth-century Germany could have contributed to Brentano-von Arnim's composing songs with texts by men and rarely publishing. Women were generally discouraged from composing or performing in public, although the ability to play for private home gatherings and to teach music to children were desirable qualities.[7] A certain basic level of musical instruction was therefore a part of the education of most young women in cultivated circles, but a thorough music education such as that received by Louise Reichardt (1779–1857), Fanny Mendelssohn Hensel (1805–1847), and Clara Wieck Schumann (1819–1896) was extremely rare for women because it was considered too intellectually rigorous, not to mention superfluous. The Lied, however, which flourished in the Romantic period, became an acceptable form of musical expression for women. Women could perform and compose this small chamber form within domestic confines while ceding the larger genres of orchestral composition and opera in the public arena to men.[8] Thus the Lied was a logical choice for Bettina Brentano-von Arnim when she began composing. Her songs were further legitimized when she was encouraged by her brother Clemens Brentano and his best friend, Achim von Arnim, to set their poems to music. They even urged her to publish her songs, but strangely enough, Brentano-von Arnim was reluctant. Her hesitancy may in part be due to an assimilation of the viewpoint generally held by the Vormärz society that it was somewhat immodest for women to publish.[9] Her reluctance to publish her songs, however, seems to have been more closely tied to her feelings of inadequacy as a composer and to her compositional method.

Bettina Brentano-von Arnim's musical gift was song—creating quasi-improvisational melodies for poetry that spoke to her on a deep, emotional level. Not only are Brentano-von Arnim's written melodies uniquely attractive, but her extemporaneous singing was enchanting. Her weaknesses lay in the more technical aspects of composition, such as applying a meter and constructing a harmony sophisticated enough to accompany her melody. Her sketch (Example 1a) for Goethe's "Wandrers Nachtlied" (Über allen Gipfeln ist Ruh) is typical in many ways, and shows how she approached the poem.

As demonstrated later in more detail, she frequently jotted down words to a poem, sometimes choosing verses seemingly at random from a long work. Then above the words, she quickly sketched in the pitches, matching the melodic contour to the contours of the words. In this example, it appears that the notes were written first, judging from the more erratic placement of the words. Since this poem is short, Brentano-von Arnim may have simply had the words in mind as she composed the melody. This could also account for the slight variations in the text. In her haste to get her ideas out on paper, she only wrote the clef and key signature on the first line, and omitted the time signature and barlines. Although the meter is often uncertain, she usually displayed concern for proper declamation, and took care that the rhythms and accents enhanced those of speech. This suggests that Brentano-von Arnim conceived of rhythm in its relationship to the words and melody, not necessarily in its relationship to the underlying meter of the piece. In this sketch, the stressed syllables receive longer note values (quarter notes), while shorter note values (eighth notes) are written for many unstressed syllables. In her attempt to convey the poem's meaning and emotion, special parts of the text

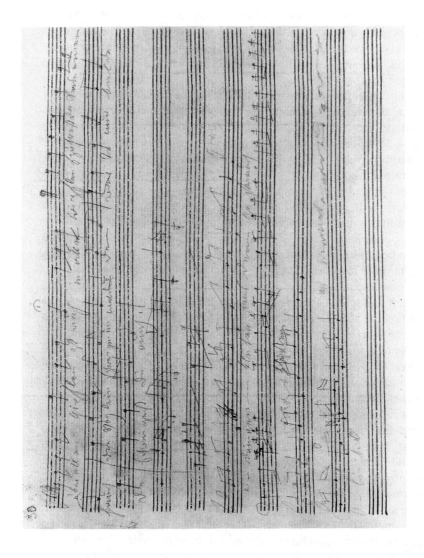

Example 1a. "Wandrers Nachtlied" sketch. The Dannie and Hettie HEINEMAN Collection in the Pierpont Morgan Library, New York. *Heineman* MS 9B 30.

Example 1b. "Wandrers Nachtlied" sketch, transcription.

might be highlighted musically with longer note values, high pitches, wide interval leaps, or tone painting. In the "Wandrers Nachtlied" sketch, Brentano-von Arnim suggests the tops of mountains and trees with the high notes on "Gipflen" [*sic*] and "Wipflen" [*sic*], while on the word "Ruh," the music reposes on a low note held by a fermata. All of this was conceived spontaneously upon reading the poem and allowing it to inspire the music.

The task of completing the song by writing in measure lines and providing a harmonic accompaniment was pure drudgery for Brentano-von Arnim. Often someone else, a teacher or musician friend, would assume this task for her or assist in the song's completion. Brentano-von Arnim's approach—allowing the poem to spontaneously inspire the music—provides a clue to understanding why she wrote Lieder almost exclusively, chose particular texts, and refrained from publishing.

Decades later, in the process of rewriting the letters dating from her years of music study, Brentano-von Arnim's view of her own musical worth underwent a transformation. In the first three epistolary novels—*Goethes Briefwechsel mit einem Kinde* (1835), *Die Günderode* (1840), and *Clemens Brentanos Frühlingskranz* (1844)—Brentano-von Arnim portrayed her young self as a natural talent empowered by a force higher than the theoretical rules her teachers imposed. This revised assessment placed a greater value on the genius of inspiration while devaluing the importance of more technical aspects of music. Thus, publishing her compositions, even if she did

receive help completing them, was no longer daunting or hypocritical. The inspiration of combining melody with words was her own,
and the harmonization was a mere technicality. With new courage
and a political cause, Brentano-von Arnim dedicated a book of seven
songs to Gaspare Spontini in 1842.[10]

Genius versus *Generalbaß*

The story of Bettina Brentano-von Arnim's musical pursuits is the
story of a rich imagination overflowing with melodies and of little
theoretical knowledge to refine them; it is a study of admiration of
genius and discouragement with the set of harmonic rules known as
Generalbaß.[11] Brentano-von Arnim believed her own compositions
were inspired by poetic genius, and she tried to conform her music to
the words' emotion. As a young woman Brentano-von Arnim studied
with a variety of teachers in pursuit of musical training. She struggled
to acquire a firm working knowledge of *Generalbaß*, if only so that
her compositions would be worthy of the words they accompanied.
She sang and composed spontaneous melodies, yet throughout her
years of formal musical training, felt that the mysteries of *Generalbaß*
eluded her. After seeing a different kind of genius in Beethoven—
isolated, reclusive, misunderstood—Brentano-von Arnim's attitude
towards knowledge of *Generalbaß* and conformity to the norms of
musical society began to change. Later, in the epistolary novels,
Brentano-von Arnim portrayed her teachers as Philistines and the
musical rules they enforced as destructive to her natural creativity.
    Bettina Brentano-von Arnim received her first musical training
while attending the Ursuline cloister school in Fritzlar from 1794 to
1797.[12] Upon her return to Frankfurt, Philipp Carl Hoffmann (1789–
1842) became her instructor in piano and music theory. Hoffmann, a
violist and music dilettante, infused a love and spiritual understanding
of music in his young pupil. In September 1804, as a young woman of
nineteen, she already saw music as her sole resource and nourish-
ment, as she wrote to her brother-in-law, Friedrich Carl von Savigny:
"I am taking piano lessons from Mr. Hoffmann again, despite the
temptations that I am exposed to; I am also diligently learning to sing,
and I am in the theater whenever operas are performed; music is now
my only resource and my refreshment" (Ich nehme wieder Klavier-
stunde bei H[errn] Hoffm[ann aus Offenbach], *malgré les tentations,*

denen ich ausgesetzt bin; singen lerne ich auch recht fleißig, und wenn Opern gegeben werden, so bin ich immer im Theater, überhaupt ist Musik jetzt meine einzige *ressource* und mein Labsal) (*Andacht* 21).

Showing a remarkable degree of independence for a woman at that time, Brentano-von Arnim traveled to Munich alone in 1809, after auditioning to study voice and composition with the opera composer and Bavarian *Hofkapellmeister* Peter von Winter (1754–1825). Winter was undoubtedly Brentano-von Arnim's most important teacher, and during her months under his instruction, her singing and musical skills improved noticeably (see *Andacht* 101, 104). She reported to Achim von Arnim and the Savignys that to make the most of her time, she filled her days with lessons and practice. In February 1809, she wrote that she had two 90-minute voice lessons daily with Winter, in addition to piano and Italian lessons with other teachers (*Andacht* 104). Winter, however, was a stricter taskmaster than Hoffmann had been, and after six months, Brentano-von Arnim could no longer endure or financially afford her lessons. Returning to Landshut, she took lessons in *Generalbaß* from a genial elderly man named Eixdorfer, who held the position of *Kanonikus* (Betz 274–275).

For a short time in 1810, Alois Bihler (1788–1857), a law student just three years her senior, assisted Brentano-von Arnim in transcribing her compositions. She referred to Bihler as her "Music transcriber" (Notenschreiber) and nicknamed him "Riemer" after Goethe's secretary (Steig 2:385). Their weekly sessions were mutually beneficial and full of lighthearted humor. While Bihler helped her with rhythm and harmony, she helped him with melody and counterpoint: "He gives rhythm to my music, I expand upon his melodies, he writes a purer bass setting for me, I invent the instrumental countermovements for him" (Er bringt mich in Takt, ich erweitere seine Melodien, er setzt mir einen reineren Baß, ich erfinde ihm die Gegenbewegung zu den Instrumenten) (Steig 2:385). Voice lessons with Vincenzo Righini (1756–1812) brought her formal music training to a close shortly after her marriage to Achim von Arnim in 1811.

Combining poetry with music in extemporaneous song was perhaps Brentano-von Arnim's strongest musical talent, one for which she consistently received approbation. "Irresistibly . . . Bettina ruled in the realm of song. Here she fully unfolded her wonderful individuality," reports Bihler. (Unwiderstehlich . . . herrschte Bettina auf dem Gebiete des Gesanges. Hier entfaltete sie völlig ihre wunderbare

Eigentümlichkeit.) (315) His account, colored with the popular ro-
manticized picture of Brentano-von Arnim as a type of Goethe's
Mignon, establishes that she often sang improvisationally and filled
the tones with feeling.

> She seldom chose written songs—singing she created poetry and creat-
> ing poetry she sang with a glorious voice in a kind of improvisation. For
> example, she knew how to pour a wealth of soulful emotion into the
> simple, slow scale as well as into the spontaneous improvisations
> welling up from within her, so that I listened enraptured by her creative
> genius.

> Selten wählte sie geschriebene Lieder—singend dichtete sie und
> dichtend sang sie mit prachtvoller Stimme eine Art Improvisation. So
> zum Beispiel wußte sie in die einfach getragene Scala ebensowohl als in
> die ihr momentan entquellenden Solfeggien eine Fülle der Empfindung
> und des Geistes zu legen, daß ich hingerissen ihrem schöpferischen
> Genius lauschte. (315)

The famous writer Ludwig Tieck heard Bettina sing at a private
Hauskonzert gathering and was emotionally stirred to the point of
tears. As Clemens Brentano recounted to Achim von Arnim in 1806,

> she sang before him so wonderfully and beautifully, the wild cry of her
> soul, no *Aria brillante* like she used to sing. . . . As for her singing, her
> extemporaneous singing—I saw him shedding tears, and he assured me
> that he, the church musician, had never heard anything like it and that
> he now knew how music originated.

> sie hat so wunderbar schön vor ihm gesungen, ihren wilden Seelen-
> schlag, keine *Aria brillante* so wie sie früher sang. . . . Was ihren
> Gesang betrifft, d.h. den extemporirten, so habe ich ihn Thränen dabei
> weinen sehen, und er versicherte, er der Kirchenmusikus, daß er nie
> etwas ähnliches gehört habe und daß er jetzt wisse, wie die Musik
> entstanden sei. (Steig 1:193)

Clearly, the songs Brentano-von Arnim created extemporaneously
roused the emotions of others.

Brentano-von Arnim's talent for improvisational singing is reflected in her compositions, both in her method of allowing the poem
to inspire the song and in the dominance of melody. She chose poems
of Goethe and Achim von Arnim that moved her deeply as texts for

her first compositions. Her habit of referring to the poems as Lieder
and to her compositions as Melodien indicates that she thought of the
song's *melody* as her essential contribution to a text already possess-
ing musical qualities. Furthermore, she describes her compositional
process in intuitive terms; as she read a poem, a melody came to her
as if given from an outside power. When Achim sent her eight poems
from *Gräfin Dolores*, she composed two immediately, "just the first
melodies that occurred to me at the first reading," she told him (grade
die ersten Melodieen, die mir bei dem ersten Durchlesen einfielen)
(Steig 2:385). She set several passages from Goethe's *Faust*, including
an overture, but told Achim von Arnim she would not compose the
whole work since some things did not correspond to her "musical
nature" (musikalischen Natur) (Steig 2:385–386). Her setting of "Ach
neige du schmerzenreiche" [sic] from *Faust* was probably good, she
wrote Goethe, for it "deeply moved" her (es hat mich innig gerührt)
(Köln 5:22). In February 1808 she claimed not to have composed, but
only to have "found" two additional "happy melodies to *Faust*"
(glückliche Melodien zum Faust) (Steig 2:106). Days before Goethe's
death in March 1832, von Arnim wrote that his poems were still a
source of energy as she attempted to capture their feeling in music:

> Truly today as then I still draw from you all my energy for living; as
> then, the song of your poetry tempers and strengthens my spiritual
> impulses, especially with my immature attempts at art, when I strive to
> model them after nature, and the eternal play, the continuous stream of
> life, flowing wave upon wave, confuses my senses. Then I concentrate
> my thoughts at the piano and compose any one of your poems whose
> rhythm corresponds to that of my feelings.

> Wahrlich heute wie damals sauge ich noch aus Dir alle Energie des
> Lebens, wie damals, mäßigt, kräftigt der Gesang Deiner Lieder meine
> geistigen Regungen, besonders bei meinen unmündigen Versuchen in
> der Kunst, wenn ich sie nach der Natur zu kopieren strebe, und mir das
> ewige Spiel, das ununterbrochene Well auf Welle Hinwallen des
> Lebensstromes die Sinne verwirrt. Dann geh ich zum Konzentrieren
> meiner Gedanken ans Klavier, und komponiere irgend eines Deiner
> Lieder, dessen Rhythmus dem meiner Empfindungen entspricht.)
> (Köln 5:128)

In short, the musicality of the poem, or Lied, had to correspond to
her feelings in order to inspire a song within her.

Because the poetry inspired the music, Brentano-von Arnim objected strenuously to substituting different poems for completed melodies. Achim von Arnim and Clemens Brentano solicited her help for
their folk song collection, *Des Knaben Wunderhorn* (1806–1808),
sending poems and requesting her to write tunes for them (Steig
2:14–18). When Achim proposed substituting different texts for the
melodies she had written, Bettina, believing that the text and melody
were bound together in the song's creation, personified the melodies
as slaves to the texts for which they were conceived: "it depends on
them [the texts], if they wish to allow them [the melodies] to go free,
or on your cunning and skill to entice them away or make them
disloyal and turn towards a new master, if you are not otherwise
ashamed of this deceit" (es kömmt auf diese an, ob sie dieselben
wieder freilassen wollen, oder auf Ihre List und Geschicklichkeit, sie
zu entwenden oder abtrünnig zu machen und einem andern Herrn
zuzuwenden, wenn Sie Sich anders des Betrugs nicht schämen) (Steig
2:19).

Although the melodies came to Brentano-von Arnim spontaneously, the task of forming them into complete songs took her much
longer, and she often needed assistance. She admitted that sometimes
she required one half hour to write a single verse (Steig 2:106). Furthermore, her lack of skill at completing her songs herself led to her
reluctance to publish. When Achim von Arnim offered to publish one
of her songs in 1808, she declined, saying she had not yet mastered
bezifferten Baß and still needed her teacher's help to complete the
composition.

> I have no desire to publish; in time, if I really learn something properly,
> then as far as I'm concerned you may publish these as well, but since
> now I am unable merely to set a song's rhythm or write it readably or
> set chords with it, and my teacher must do all this, it would be very
> unjust to publish a song as my own that I merely envisioned but did not
> create; it would be just as if someone had a painting done entirely
> according to his conception and wished to say he did it. I do have the
> sensibility, but not the practice, but in time I think I will obtain this as
> well and please you; then we can speak more about it.

> zum Herausgeben hab ich keine Lust; wenn ich wirklich mit der Zeit
> noch was ordentliches lerne, so magst Du meinetwegen auch diese
> herausgeben, aber da ich jetzt nicht vermögend, ein Lied nur in Takt zu
> bringen oder leserlich zu schreiben oder richtig in die Accorde zu

setzen, und dies alles mein Meister thun muß, so wäre es sehr unrecht,
ein Lied, das ich zwar gedacht, aber nicht gemacht habe, für mein
Werk auszugeben; es wäre grad, als wollt der, der ein Bild ganz nach
seiner Idee malen läßt, sagen, er hab es gemacht. Ich habe wohl den
Sinn, aber nicht die Ausübung, mit der Zeit denk ich auch noch diese
zu erlangen und Dir Freude mit zu machen, dann wollen wir mehr
darüber sprechen. (Steig 2:91)

The tension between musical sensibility (Sinn) and practice (Ausübung) caused a great deal of frustration, and she compared herself to
a child struggling to learn. Music continued to both "torture" and
"delight" her (sie quält und ergözt mich und fängt immer wieder von
vorne an) (Steig 2:305). While studying under Winter, she felt "like a
child on a harness led by a dumb nanny" (wie ein Kind am
Gängelbande einer etwas dummen Amme) (*Andacht* 130). Confident
in her musical insight ("much deeper than one would believe" [eine
weit tiefere Einsicht, als man glauben dürfte]), Brentano-von Arnim
was disappointed that things that "every choirboy knew" presented
her with difficulties (Steig 2:385). "I firmly believe that music could
become my daily occupation, but more difficulties appear each day;
for example, I have a true inclination to the most profound thoughts,
but my technical ability does not match up to my imagination, which
remains unfulfilled in consequence," wrote Bettina at a high point of
her musical studies in 1810. (Ich glaub gewiß, daß die Musik mir zum
Tagewerk werden könnte, doch stellen sich täglich mehr Schwierig-
keiten ein, z.B. hab ich eine wahre Neigung zu den schwersten
Gedanken, und meine Kenntniß reicht meiner Phantasie das Wasser
nicht, also daß diese verdursten muß) (Steig 2:381). Although she
worked diligently and had daily music instruction, she still felt she
was only better at "discovering the great path to the goal instead of
actually reaching it" (den großen Weg zum Ziel entdecken, statt es
selber zu erreichen) (Steig 2:381).

Brentano-von Arnim's view of the tension between genius and *Generalbaß*, "Sinn" and "Ausübung," "Phantasie" and "Kenntniß," was
influenced by her first-hand encounter with artistic genius. In the case
of her friend Peter Lindpaintner, Brentano-von Arnim began to see
knowledge that education brings as potentially harmful to natural genius.[13] Brentano-von Arnim met Lindpaintner, also a music student, at
the end of her stay in Munich, and saw aspects of herself in this young
man who had attempted various compositional forms, "however

without great technical skill" (jedoch ohne große Kenntniß) (Steig 2:
358). Her disillusionment with Winter's instruction colors her story of
Lindpaintner: "Since they too quickly assumed that he only lacked
technical skill, to form a perfect genius of him, he was taken from his
room in Augsburg, where his muse had so often bent over him, and was
set beside the old monster [Winter] in the noisy world of Munich" (Da
man nur allzuschnell einsah, daß ihm nur Kenntniß fehle, um ein
vollkommnes Genie aus ihm zu bilden, so wurde er aus seiner
Augsburger Kammer, wo sich ihm seine Muse so oft geneigt hatte, in
die lärmende Münchner Welt an des alten Ungheurs [Winter's] Seite
gesetzt) (Steig 2:358). "In this innocent soul" wrote Brentano-von
Arnim, referring to Lindpaintner but implying an application to herself, "dwells a large portion of art" (In diesem unschuldigen Gemüth
ein großer Theil der Kunst wohnt) (Steig 2:258).

Half a year later, in the spring of 1810, Brentano-von Arnim was
deeply impressed by her meeting with Beethoven in Vienna. She described him as an awe-inspiring figure, though he lived in a messy
apartment isolated from civilization, and was further cut off by his
deafness. To the surprise of those who knew him, Beethoven spent
hours in her company. He played and sang for her, dedicated his setting
of Goethe's "Neue Liebe, Neues Leben" to her, and made her promise
to write. Brentano-von Arnim saw in Beethoven the ideal of the impas-
sioned artist, one unafraid of breaking established rules of tonality.[14]

In her later literary works, Brentano-von Arnim revised letters to
Goethe (*Goethes Briefwechsel mit einem Kinde*), to her friend Karoline von Günderrode (*Die Günderode*), and to her brother (*Clemens
Brentanos Frühlingskranz*), reevaluating her years of music study and
thus bringing the tension between genius and *Generalbaß* to a kind of
resolution. While actual letters of the time show that Brentano-von
Arnim was frustrated with her slow progress in learning *Generalbaß*,
in the epistolary novels she belittled the rules as "empty eggshells"
(leeren Eierschallen) (Weimar 1:185), and expressed anger not present in the original correspondences: "I am also exasperated with
thoroughbass. I would like to blast this fraternity of tonalities into the
air" (Am Generalbaß hab ich auch meinen Ärger. Ich möchte diese
Gevatterschaft von Tonarten in die Luft sprengen) (Frankfurt 1:115).
Her teacher "crucifies" her with *Generalbaß* lessons and Achim von
Arnim's poems become "martyrs" (Frankfurt 1:668). While showing
the harmful effect of musical rules in the novels, Brentano-von Arnim
emphasizes her natural relation to the spiritual power of music: "I can

invent a melody more easily than analyze it in terms of its origin. With music, everything may be grasped more deeply by introspection than by following the law; this law is so narrow that the musical spirit overflows it at every instant" (Ich kann leichter eine Melodie erfinden als sie in ihre Ursprünglichkeit auflösen. Innerlich ist alles tiefer zu fassen in der Musik als sich ans Gesetz zu halten; dies Gesetz ist so eng, daß der musikalische Geist jeden Augenblick es überschwemmt) (Frankfurt 1:114). Rather than mastering the music, she wished to be mastered by it.

> I have no desire to become a master, I wish to allow myself to be mastered by these floods of music, which may be of no value to other ears, it doesn't matter, they converse with me and speak full chords of life to me, which I recognize as uniting me with nature.

> ich mag nicht Meister werden, ich will mich bemeistern lassen von diesen Musikfluten, von denen ich nicht weiß, ob sie Wert haben können für ein ander Ohr, das schadet nicht, sie reden mit mir und sagen mir volle Lebensakkorde, die ich erkenne als eins mich machend mit der Natur. (Frankfurt 1:482–83)

In these passages and many others, Brentano-von Arnim implies that in her innocent creativity, despite her lack of technical skill (perhaps even *because* of it), she was such a channel.

The process of reinterpreting her years of music studies and the value of her musical talents gave Brentano-von Arnim the self-confidence to publish seven songs, most of which were composed in those early years. The Hungarian composer and virtuoso pianist Franz Liszt (1811–1186) also supported her at this time with his friendship and encouragement. Despite their difference in age (at fifty-seven, Brentano-von Arnim was a generation older), Liszt claimed to be drawn to her by "the magnetic force of our two natures" (la force magnétique de nos deux natures) and praised her first epistolary novel, *Goethes Briefwechsel mit einem Kinde*, as "transfigured music" (*verklärte* Musik) (Schnapp-Berlin 720). Writing to Liszt in 1842, the year of the Spontini songbook publication, Brentano-von Arnim declares her indifference to the pedantic correctness of musical lawmakers while asserting the supremacy of her musical sense. What others might see as harmonic mistakes (such as false fifths), Brentano-von Arnim justifies as the stuttering conversations of her young soul in love with music.

I have kept my word to Spontini, by having seven songs engraved, together with their completely obstinate accompaniments. . . . As for the musical turnings, the craggy, uneven path of this product, I could not decide, even for the sakes of the foolish bigwigs who make laws governing an art which is much too powerful for their pedantic ears, to give up a single false fifth. How I explored the instrument as a child, my heart pounding, seeking to satisfy the rhythm imprinted deep within me! How many thousand times I repeated with rapture these tones that pleased only me, in whose place I never found any others, but only these, although they played for me such beautiful harmonic progressions! Therefore everything had to remain as the true, original, stuttering conversation of my soul newly in love with music; and I could not bear that my bass—which dances with quick leaps and bounds around the melody like a deer, often chimes in and echoes more clearly in its feelings what the melody is unable to express—that they master its willful turning and spinning.

An Spontini hab ich mein Wort gehalten, indem ich sieben Lieder, mit samt ihren ganz eigensinnigen Akkompagnements ihm zugeeignet, habe stechen lassen. . . . Was nun die musikalischen Wendungen, Klippenvollen Fehltrittswege dieses Produkts betrifft, so konnte ich mich nicht entschließen, auch nur, um der närrischen Perücken willen, die Gesetze machen über eine Kunst, welche viel zu gewaltig ist für pedantische Ohren, eine einzige falsche Quinte aufzuheben. Wie hab ich als Kind mit klopfendem Herzen auf dem Instrument herumgesucht, um dem tief in mich geprägten Rhythmus zu genügen. Wie viel tausendmal wiederholte ich mit Entzücken diese mir allein wolhgefälligen Töne, an deren Stelle ich nie irgendandre gerecht fand, als nur diese allein, wenn man mir auch noch so schöne Harmoniengänge vorspielte! Drum mußte alles so bleiben, wie die wirklich originalen, erste Liebe stotternden Unterhaltung meiner Seele mit der Musik gewesen sind; und ich hab nicht gelitten, daß man meinen Baß, der wie ein Reh oft die Melodie mit raschen Sätzen und Sprüngen umtanzt, oft hineinklingt und deutlicher in seiner Empfindung widerhallt, was die Melodie nicht vermag: daß man sein eigensinniges Wenden und Drehen meistere. (La Mara 125–26)

The review of the *Liederbuch* that appeared in the *Allgemeine musikalische Zeitung* (8 February 1843) underscores the unconventionality of these songs which do not seem to have developed in the direction of current taste, "but rather from a particular direction, unconcerned with current taste" (sondern aus einem eigenenen, um die Richtung des Zeitgeschmacks unbekümmerten Bedürfnisse). It points to a "certain dilettante naivete" (gewisse dilettantische Naivetät) and to originality, but also to a lack of skill that seems to fit with Brentano-von Arnim's self-perception (103–104).

Visions and Revisions

An examination of four characteristic songs shows how Brentano-von Arnim conceived the poem in relation to the music, and various ways the songs were revised for publication. Both published and manuscript versions exist for each, making them interesting case studies in Brentano-von Arnim's compositional process. Her setting of "Vom Nachen getragen" has been praised by critics as one of her most successful songs. A second Achim von Arnim setting, "Romanze," became her first published song and shows her careful mirroring of the poem's form and use of countermelodies. Although Brentano-von Arnim was inspired to set many passages from Faust, only one such song is extant, a good example of her declamatory songwriting. Finally, a setting that Brentano-von Arnim wrote to the text of Amalie von Helvig (an interesting collaboration) shows her later folk song style.

When "Vom Nachen getragen" was published as number seven in the Spontini songbook (1842), the reviewer wrote that this song was the most pleasing of the group, "since it most nearly approaches the completeness necessary in the music world, most nearly presents a whole" (da es sich einer immer in der Musikwelt nöthigen Abgeschlossenheit am Meisten nähert, am Meisten ein Ganzes vorstellt) (AMZ 104). In the published edition, the work appears as a duet, but it is evident from the two existing manuscripts that Brentano-von Arnim first conceived it as a solo. MS 30 contains a complete version of the song that is probably the earlier of the two manuscripts. On page nine of Brentano-von Arnim's music sketchbook (MS 9B), she wrote the last half of the song in an almost identical form; but here a second voice was penciled in, perhaps by Brentano-von Arnim herself, to transform the solo into a duet.

The song typifies the best of Brentano-von Arnim's early compositional style. The text is from Achim von Arnim's dramatic verse novel *Ariel* (published in 1804), and Brentano-von Arnim probably first set the words to music in 1805 at Achim's suggestion. Her setting has a gentle rocking quality to it that aptly portrays the sea

Example 2a. "Vom Nachen getragen . . . , " transcription of melody measures 9–12.

Example 2b. "Vom Nachen getragen . . . ," transcription of melody, first version, measures 47–48, MS 30.

and boat imagery. With a lilting rhythm (Example 2a), Brentano-von Arnim captures the sound of swelling waves while retaining the accents of the spoken words.

An eight-measure piano introduction establishes the key and mood of the piece, similar to the introduction for another *Ariel* setting, "Abendstille," (MS 9B 10). The accompaniment provides a simple background for the melody, typical of Brentano-von Arnim's early writing, with half-note octaves in the left hand and broken chords in the right. Also typical is the continuation of an established accompaniment pattern up to the end of the piece. The song is in a through-composed form; although there are five verses, the same melody is not repeated, but the middle part of the song builds to a climax on repeated, high pitches. A return to a hint of the opening melody near the end of the piece (measures 41–44) provides a satisfying sense of closure and unity. In the version of the song found in MS 30 (see Example 2e), Brentano-von Arnim apparently changed her mind about the ending. At first, she kept the same rhythmic pattern for the final phrase of the poem (Example 2b).

Then, to add a greater sense of finality to the closing of the piece, she augmented the rhythm of the last word (Example 2c).

Apparently, after rethinking of the meaning of the words, she crossed out the measures she had written, and slowed the pace of the entire phrase (Example 2d).

Example 2c. "Vom Nachen
getragen . . . ," transcription
of melody, revised version,
measure 48, MS 30.

Example 2d. "Vom Nachen getragen . . . ," transcription of melody,
final version, measures 47–50, MS 30.

The other manuscript version of the song (MS 9B 9) retains the
final revision above, but the melody is slightly altered for measures
35–39 and a second voice provides a countermelody throughout the
fragment.

The changes that were made to produce the published Spontini version of the song are more substantial, and Brentano-von Arnim may
have received assistance. The newspaper reviewer may not be far from
the mark when he writes, "The piano accompaniment is constructed
insightfully, and we might well presume the hand of an experienced
musician, such as dilettantes like to trust before appearing publicly"
(Die Clavierbegleitung ist einsichtig gemacht, und wir dürften hier
wohl die ordnende Hand eines Musik-erfahrenen, wie sich Dilettanten
gern vor ihrem öffentlichen Auftreten einem solchen anvertrauen,
voraussetzen) (*AMZ* 104). The changes, however, do not disturb the
original character of Brentano-von Arnim's setting. The published
version retains the same introduction, tonality, and melody, the accompaniment still provides a textured background, but beginning with the
second verse, the accompaniment figures become progressively more
complex. The rolled chords over triplets suggesting the "feathers of

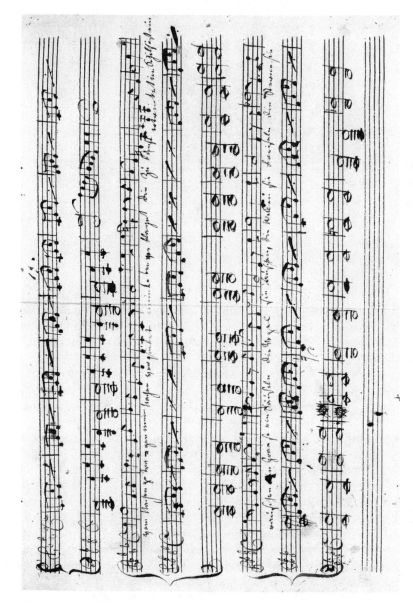

Example 2e. "Vom Nachen getragen . . ." The Dannie and Hettie HEINEMAN Collection in the Pierpont Morgan Library, New York. *Heineman* MS 30.

Example 2e, continued.

foam" (Schaumes Gefieder) in the final verse also seem inconsistent with Brentano-von Arnim's other manuscript compositions.

Brentano-von Arnim's first published song, a setting of Achim von Arnim's "Romanze," is interesting not only for its musical qualities but also for the story surrounding its origins. She composed the song a year before their marriage while Achim was in Berlin and she was living in Landshut and writing music with the help of Bihler. On February 14, 1810, Achim sent Bettina fourteen poems from his novel *Armut, Reichtum, Schuld und Buße der Gräfin Dolores*, saying he would like to publish something of hers along with the novel (Steig 2:374). His tone is less pedantic than when he had written to her regarding the *Wünderhorn* settings, and now his aesthetic ideals correspond closely to her own. The setting need not be elaborate, but should be readily singable, he wrote: "naturally, it should not be written for a special artistry or practice or natural condition of the voice, but rather come easily to anyone's voice" (es müßte natürlich nicht für eine besondre Künstlichkeit oder Uebung oder Naturbeschaffenheit der Kehle komponirt sein, sondern jedem in der Kehle liegen) (Steig 2:374). He encouraged her not to compose a song simply to please him, but only "if it so urges to come out of you, that you cannot resist" (wenn es sich so aus Dir hervordrängt, daß Du es nicht lassen kannst) (Steig 2:379).

Bettina was immediately inspired to compose the poems, or Lieder, as she enthusiastically replied: "Dear Arnim! This morning at 11 o'clock I received your letter, and already two poems are set to music that only need to be corrected and copied over" (Lieber Arnim! Heute Morgen um 11 Uhr erhielt ich Deinen Brief, und schon sind zwei Lieder in Musik gesetzt, die nur noch der Correctur und des Reinschreibens bedürfen) (Steig 2:381–382). As Achim had suggested, Bettina aimed for simplicity that matched the words and for ease of performance. Her setting of one poem was extremely simple, and required only a singer who understood the poetry; she rejected another because it was not accessible enough, but "would need to be heightened by harmonies that do not come easily to the voice and hands, but rather must be brought forth through technical skill" (müßte durch Harmonien gesteigert werden, die einem nicht so grad in die Hände und Kehle kommen, sondern durch Kenntniß müßten hervorgebracht werden) (Steig 2:382). Pleased with her settings, Achim wrote back, "You dear little angel, how can I thank you enough for your melodies!" (Du liebes Engelskind, wie dank ich Dir genug für Deine Melodieen!) (Steig 2:388). He declared of the "Ro-

Table 4. Skeletal Structural Analysis of "Romanze"

Poem

line#	1	2	3	4	5	6	7	8	9	10	11	12
rhyme	a	b	a	b	a	b	a	b	c	d	c	d

Song

phrase	A	B/A1	B1/A	B/A1	B1/C	/D	/A2	B1/
Meas.#	1	5	9	13	17	20	23	

manze," "That one I will certainly put in my book with B.B. above it" (Jenes werde ich meinem Buche gewiß beifügen und B.B. darauf setzen) (Steig 2:388). It must have been primarily Bettina's decision to use the pseudonym "Beans Beor," since all of the other contributions, including that of Louise Reichardt, were acknowledged with the full name of the composer.[15] Brentano-von Arnim believed she was already making a daring step forward by publishing her first song, so a thin veil of anonymity—many could certainly surmise the song's source—offered some security.

While the rhythm and melody of Brentano-von Arnim's "Vom Nachen getragen" setting correspond well to the poem, her ballad setting of the "Romanze," or "Der Kaiser ging vertrieben," from *Gräfin Dolores* is particularly well-suited to the mood and form of the poem. In trying to capture the poignancy of the text, Brentano-von Arnim chose what she called a "Turkish March" (minor key and duple meter): "First of all, Turkish music has something very poignant, and a melody becomes especially sorrowful when it is contradicted by its meter" (Einmal hat die türkische Musik etwas sehr herzrührendes, und besonders wird eine Melodie traurig, wenn sie durch ihre Taktart widersprochen wird) (Steig 2:382). In other words, the sorrow expressed in the text becomes heightened by the juxtaposition of a minor key (f) with a lively march tempo. Brentano-von Arnim also gave specific instructions to ensure that this effect would come across to the audience: "The Emperor's march must be sung firmly, not too loud" (Der Marsch von Kaiser muß fest, nicht zu laut gesungen werden) (Steig 2:385). The song echoes the form of the poem, each musical phrase changing with each new rhyme (Table 4).

Example 3a. "Romanze," *Grafin Dolores* 3, transcription of measures 1–4.

The poem's alternating rhymes—all a and c lines are feminine, b and d are masculine—are reflected in the rhythm of the music. With the repetition of the same rhymes for the second four lines, Brentano-von Arnim repeats the same music. When the rhyme scheme changes (line 9), Brentano-von Arnim writes melodic material based on the opening, but passes through diminished seventh harmonies before returning to familiar material in the tonic of f minor (measure 23). The section from measures 17–23 is further contrasted because Brentano-von Arnim temporarily suspends the established regularity of four-bar phrases. Short piano interludes between phrases echo the four beats just played (represented by a slash / in the table above). Thus, while A is two measures long, B is only one measure, but the motif is repeated in the piano for the one-measure interlude (Example 3a).

The interludes provide a recurring motif suggestive of a drumbeat. Brentano-von Arnim joked that her Turkish march could be made into a Prussian one for the soldiers in Berlin, and that the interludes would give them time to breathe while singing and marching (Steig 2:382). A complete—and for Brentano-von Arnim, unusually clean—manuscript of the song (Example 3b) allows comparison with the published version (Example 3c).

Again, the published version of the piece contains variations that were probably the work of an editor.[16] Among the more noticeable changes are a revised text and the use of a repeat sign after the first eight measures.[17] Two other changes are more significant: the published version of the last measure, with a i-v7-i6 cadence, caused by a slight variation in the bass line, does not give sense of completion created by the i-v7-i cadence of Brentano-von Arnim's original (see

Example 3b. "Der Kaiser ging vertrieben . . ." ["Romanze"]. The Dannie and Hettie HEINEMAN Collection in the Pierpont Morgan Library, New York. *Heineman* MS 30.

Examples 3d and 3e); and the *Adagio* tempo marking suggests a tempo slower that what Brentano-von Arnim had desired.

A third song, this one from Goethe's *Faust* and also published in the Spontini songbook, provides an example of Brentano-von Arnim's dramatic, declamatory style of composition that contrasts with the simpler folk song style of many of her songs. This song is the only one to have been recorded commercially.[18] Brentano-von Arnim chose an

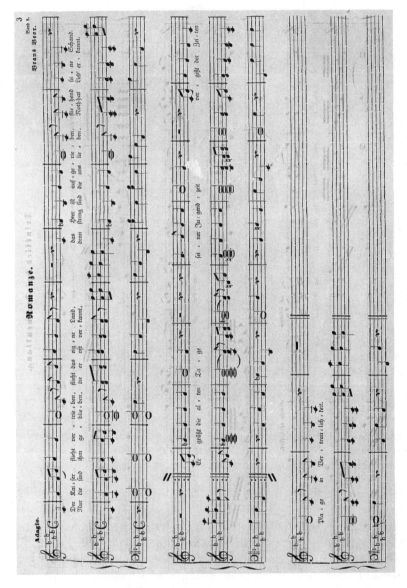

Example 3c. "Romanze," *Gräfin Dolores* 3, Staatsbibliothek Preußischer Kulturbesitz, Berlin.

Example 3d. "Der Kaiser ging vertrieben . . ." ["Romanze"], measures 25–26. The Dannie and Hettie HEINEMAN Collection in the Pierpont Morgan Library, New York. *Heineman* MS 30.

Example 3e. "Romanze," measures 24–26, *Gräfin Dolores* 3, Staatsbibliothek Preußischer Kulturbesitz, Berlin.

emotionally charged passage—the garden scene in which Faust passionately declares his love for Gretchen. This particular passage is an unusual choice, since the only other known setting is in Robert Schumann's *Faustszenen* (Moser 151). On the other hand, Brentano-von Arnim often selected passages from Goethe's poetry that express strong emotion, as this one does; her manuscripts contain sketches to such poems as "Rastlose Liebe," "Mailied," "Glückliche Fahrt," and "Herbstgefühl." Although no autograph manuscript exists for this song, a transcription is found in Maximiliane Brentano's notebook with "Von Bettina v. Arnim" inscribed at the top (Example 4).[19] The composition may date from the period between 1808 and 1810, when

Brentano-von Arnim's letters mention other *Faust* settings and an ambitious plan to compose an overture to the work.

Brentano-von Arnim captures a sense of Faust's earnest restlessness, comparable to her own, in this setting marked *Agitato ma non troppo*. Short vocal phrases interrupted by rests suggest his breathlessness, with strong accents, dotted rhythms, and wide interval leaps adding to the effect. In the accompaniment, staccato eighth notes contribute to the unsettled mood. A contrasting section begins in measure six with a sudden modulation from the opening key of D major to its parallel key, D minor, and a legato accompaniment figure. Brentano-von Arnim builds the tension harmonically through motion to the dominant, and melodically through the rising vocal line, to climax on the word "fühlen" (to feel) with an expressive, falling interval (minor sixth). This climax is echoed by the final climax on the words "kein Ende" (no end), for which Brentano-von Arnim employs the same descending interval. The pianissimo repetition of the words "kein Ende" with a falling third, suggests the sigh and perpetual longing of love.

Brentano-von Arnim's published setting of Amalie von Helvig's "Weihe an Hellas," noteworthy as her only collaboration with a woman poet, provides a final example.[20] It shows her mature style of folk song composition and demonstrates her later tendency to employ music (as she also did literature and visual art) for a political and social cause. Helvig, the Weimar poet whose literary pursuits were encouraged by Goethe and Schiller, became a close associate of Brentano-von Arnim after 1816.[21] Some of Brentano-von Arnim's comments to Helvig reveal changing sensibilities. In the spring of 1818, she used the metaphor "Lebensmelodien" (Life-melodies) to describe the everyday household events (Bissing 393). In the same year, Brentano-von Arnim declared that "Life, truth, beauty and poetry are the four pillars which support our temple, which cannot be taken from us; we want to live in this temple forever and make those who enter our friends" (Leben, Wahrheit, Schönheit, Poesie sind die vier Säulen, die unsern Tempel stützen, die man uns nicht rauben kann; wir wollen fort und fort in diesem Tempel wohnen und die da eintreten zu unsern Freunden machen) (Bissing 399). This statement—contrasted with her assertion in 1808 that music, nature, Goethe, and Achim von Arnim were the pillars of her inner temple (Steig 2:76)—shows how Brentano-von Arnim's self-image evolved. She no longer saw Goethe and Achim von Arnim as essential sustainers, but looked to people like

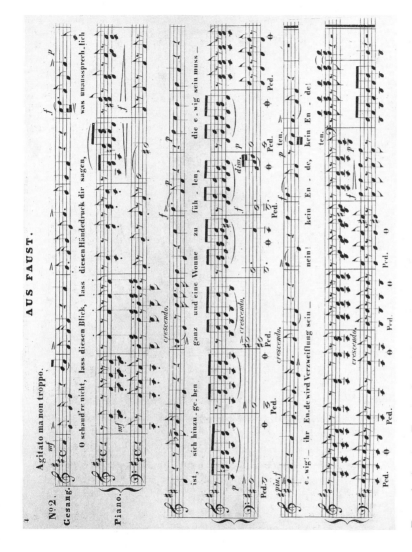

Example 4. "Aus Faust," Spontini songbook No. 2, Staatsbibliothek Preußischer Kulturbesitz, Berlin.

Helvig for friendship and mutual support. Helvig wrote a collection of poems to raise support and publicly demonstrate her sympathy for the Greeks in their fight for independence against Turkey. The proceeds of the volume, published as *Gedichte zum Besten der unglücklichen Greise, Wittwen, und Waisen in Griechenland* (1826), were donated to Greek widows and orphans. Since Helvig's husband did not share her sympathy for the Greeks or agree with the ideological viewpoint of the poems, Brentano-von Arnim's settings are not only a political statement, but also a gesture of personal support for her friend. Brentano-von Arnim's sketches to three poems were probably made after the poems were in print although they could have been done earlier, since her texts contain some variations.

The song "Weihe an Hellas" is in a simple folk song style like Brentano-von Arnim's early *Ariel* and *Wunderhorn* settings, but bears signs of a more mature approach. Two short sketches are found in Brentano-von Arnim's music notebook (34 and 69) (Example 5a), but the song in its entirety is known only as it was published in Bissing's biography of Helvig (1889).[22] The melody has a light, lilting quality with its predominance of skipping eighth-notes, often two notes per syllable.

Both sketches show that Brentano-von Arnim composed the song as a melody harmonized by at least two other voices. The sketch on page 69 is in E-flat major with two treble voices in thirds (Example 5b).

The sketch on page 34 (in a 4/4 meter) shows the melody in the treble supported by two bass countermelodies (Example 5c). This sketch is particularly interesting because it gives evidence of her skill at composing counterpoint, and because there is no trace of this bass movement in the published song. The first three lines of manuscript correspond to measures 7–10, although Brentano-von Arnim penciled in only the words "mit dem Ernste." The fourth line appears to be a countermelody for the final two measures (11 and 12), but Brentano-von Arnim neglected to write in the bass clef sign and note stems, and incorrectly placed one barline.

No Longer Forgotten

The list of great musicians and artists who recognized Brentano-von Arnim's special gifts is long. Beethoven and Liszt led the way, but

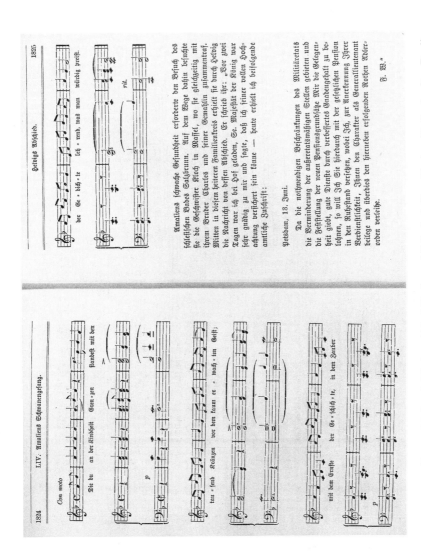

Example 5a. "Weihe an Hellas," Bissing 446–447, Staatsbibliothek Preußischer Kulturbesitz, Berlin.

Amaliens schwache Gesundheit erforderte den Besuch des schlesischen Bades Salzbrunn. Auf dem Wege dahin besuchte sie die Geschwister Koch in Kassel, wo sie gleichzeitig mit ihrem Bruder Charles und seiner Gemahlin zusammentraf. Mitten in diesem heiteren Familienkreis erhielt sie durch Helvig die Nachricht von dessen Abschied. Er schrieb ihr: „Vor zwei Tagen war ich bei Hof geladen, Se. Majestät der König war sehr gnädig zu mir und sagte, daß ich seiner vollen Hochachtung versichert sein könne — heute erhielt ich beifolgende amtliche Zuschrift:

Potsdam, 13. Juni.

Da die nothwendigen Beschränkungen des Militäretats die Verminderung der außeretatsmäßigen Stellen geboten und die Feststellung der neuen Pensionsgrundsätze Mir die Gelegenheit giebt, gute Dienste durch verbessertes Gnadengehalt zu belohnen, so will Ich Sie hierdurch mit der gesetzlichen Pension in den Ruhestand versetzen, wobei Ich, zur Anerkennung Ihrer Verdienstlichkeit, Ihnen den Charakter als Generallieutenant beilege und überdies den hierneben erfolgenden Rothen Adlerorden verleihe.

F. W."

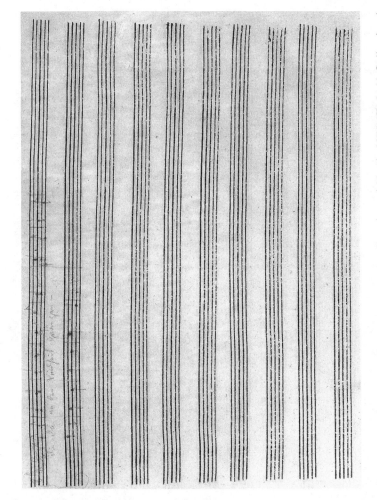

Example 5b. "Weihe an Hellas" sketch. The Dannie and Hettie HEINEMAN Collection in the Pierpont Morgan Library, New York. *Heineman* MS 9B 69.

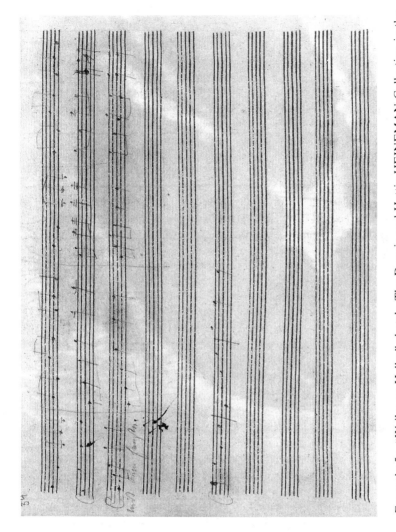

Example 5c. "Weihe an Hellas" sketch. The Dannie and Hettie HEINEMAN Collection in the Pierpont Morgan Library, New York. *Heineman* MS 9B 34.

Silhouette by Bettina: Hunting Scenes. (From: Fritz Böttger, *Bettina von Arnim. Ein Leben zwischen Tag und Traum.* Berlin, Verlag der Nation, 1986. Stiftung Weimarer Klassik.)

others followed. Robert Schumann dedicated his five piano pieces based on poems of Hölderlin to her; Johannes Brahms, as well, honored Brentano-von Arnim by dedicating the six songs of his Opus 3 to her; and up to the close of her life a number of other artists and musicians visited her at her Berlin salon.

Today, however, many people know Brentano-von Arnim's compositions only from the Oehlke edition of her collected works, published sixty years after her death (4:253–307). The ten songs found there have been so heavily edited by Max Friedlaender that the originality and vitality of her compositional style appears radically altered. Friedlaender found the accompaniments "so naive, that it was necessary to reshape them completely" (so naiv, daß es nötig war, sie vollständig zu gestalten) (4:257), and it is only his assessment of Brentano-von Arnim's style that is known. Unfortunately, his versions take little consideration of the composer's intentions and the musical sense suggested by her manuscripts.

Although Bettina Brentano-von Arnim's music has been revised to

Silhouette by Bettina. (From: Fritz Böttger, *Bettina von Arnim. Ein Leben zwischen Tag und Traum*. Berlin, Verlag der Nation, 1986. Stiftung Weimarer Klassik.)

suit changing tastes or has been forgotten in library archives, it is gradually being reconsidered. The revival of interest in Brentano-von Arnim generated by the observance of her 200th birthday anniversary, has brought renewed scholarly evaluations of her life and works. The exhibition "Herzhaft in die Dornen der Zeit greifen," which was on display in five West German cities (1985–1986), incorporated a section on Brentano-von Arnim's music (see Renate Moering's commentary in the catalog 178–201), and there are also plans to publish the music with a new German edition of her collected works.[23] The lecture-recital format has proven effective in disseminating Brentano-von Arnim's music to a lay audience. A program of lectures and music in Kronberg, West Germany, in 1986 was probably the first time in nearly two centuries that Brentano-von Arnim's songs were heard publicly.[24] Since then, two lecture recitals have taken place in the United States, both presenting newly-discovered compositions for the first time.[25]

As Brentano-von Arnim had wished as a young woman, music was her companion until the end of her life. Maximiliane von Arnim recounted that her mother, even in old age and ill health, enjoyed the sounds of a Beethoven quartet floating into her darkened room as she reminisced about the days she had known him (Werner 219). With the discovery of Brentano-von Arnim's music manuscripts and with greater understanding of her person and character, it may soon be possible for contemporary artists and lovers of music to hear not only the sounds of Beethoven, but also to hear the music of this complicated and energetic composer and to sense the spirit that inspired her.

Notes

1. The pseudonym, based on her initials B.B. translates "blessing I am blessed" and derives from Achim von Arnim's pseudonym "Amans Amor," or "loving I am loved."
2. Karl Ernst Henrici proposed this hypothesis in his description of the manuscripts for the auction of the von Arnim estate in 1929 (see Henrici 1). It was at this auction that Dannie Heineman purchased the manu-

scripts and brought them to the United States. They were donated to the Pierpont Morgan Library in 1977.

3. For a detailed analysis of the notebook and its contents, see my article "Bettines Kompositionen: Zu einem Notenheft der Sammlung Heineman," *Internationales Jahrbuch der Bettina-von-Arnim Gesellschaft* 3 (1989):193–208 ("Kompositionen"). Seven pages from the notebook, including previously unpublished, completed settings of Achim von Arnim's poems, are reproduced with this article.

4. See Moering, "Bettines Liedvertonungen" 190–91.

5. See "Kompositionen" for a detailed review of each page's contents (204–05).

6. The three songs transcribed by the virtuoso violinist and composer Joseph Joachim (1831–1907) (to poems of Goethe, Achim von Arnim, and St. John of the Cross) are housed in the Freies Deutsches Hochstift in Frankfurt (Hs 15711). Maximiliane Brentano, Brentano-von Arnim's niece, also transcribed the Goethe and St. John settings—with different accompaniments—as well as another Achim von Arnim setting into her music notebook (Frankfurt, privately owned). Finally, the published Clemens Brentano setting also exists as a nineteenth-century transcription (see Table 1).

7. See Eva Weissweiler, *Komponistinnen aus 500 Jahren: Eine Kultur- und Wirkungsgeschichte in Biographien und Werkbeispielen* (Frankfurt: Fischer, 1981).

8. See Marcia Citron's insightful article, "Women and the Lied, 1775–1850," *Women Making Music: The Western Art Tradition 1150–1950* (Urbana: U of Illinois P, 1986) 224–48.

9. The life of Fanny Mendelssohn Hensel, who was strictly forbidden to publish, provides an extreme example. See Weissweiler *Komponistinnen* and *Fanny Mendelssohn: Ein Portrait in Briefen* (Frankfurt: Ullstein, 1985).

10. Spontini (1774–1851), *Erster Kapellmeister and General-Musikdirector* under Friedrich Wilhelm III in Berlin, was facing criminal charges of disloyalty under Friedrich Wilhelm IV that Brentano-von Arnim found petty and absurd. The songbook dedication was an open gesture of moral support for the Italian opera composer. Though eventually pardoned, Spontini was socially ostracized and left Berlin.

11. Also called *bezifferten Baß* (in English thoroughbass or figured bass), the term refers to the specific practice, begun in the seventeenth century, of "realizing" and accompanying harmony from a *continuo* line, with shorthand "figures." In the nineteenth century, this practice died out, and thoroughbass came to mean the science of harmony in the broader sense in which Brentano-von Arnim uses the term. See Peter Williams's entries for *Generalbaß* and thoroughbass in *The New Grove Dictionary of Music and Musicians*, Ed. Stanley Sadie, (London: Macmillan, 1980).

12. The ten sacred songs found in Ms. 30 of the Heineman Collection represent the type such pupils would have sung, and very likely date from Brentano-von Arnim's years in Fritzlar. These one- and two-part unaccompanied hymns have Latin and German texts, such as "Stabat mater dolorosa" and "O Maria voll der Gnaden." The authorship of the songs is uncertain, however, since the writing is in various hands.

13. Peter Joseph Lindpaintner (1791–1856) became director of the *Stuttgarter Hofkapelle* in 1819.

14. Accounts of her meeting with Beethoven are found in letters to Goethe of 25 December 1810 and 11 May 1811 (Köln 5:102–103, 105–106) and to Fürst von Pückler-Muskau of March 1832 (5:207–209). Her reinterpretation appears in *Goethes Briefwechsel mit einem Kinde* on pages 343–349. See also Romain Rolland, *Goethe and Beethoven*.

15. In letters of February 1808, Brentano-von Arnim also appears reluctant to publish under her own name (Steig 2:90-91).

16. Achim von Arnim wrote that Friedrich Reichardt would oversee the music publication, so the changes may well be his (Steig 2:389).

17. While Bettina transcribed the version of the poem Achim first sent her (found on Steig 2:377) in her manuscript, the song is printed with a later but very similar version of the text. Brentano-von Arnim wrote out the repetition to accommodate the earlier text, which had an added beat in line eight ("Fest ist der Liebe Band"). Achim later corrected this line to "Noth hat Lieb' erkannt" (compare MS 30 measures 14–15 with published version).

18. Dietrich Fischer-Dieskau recorded "Aus Faust" on the album entitled *Frühe Goethe-Lieder* (Archiv 2533.149, 1973), but unfortunately he used the version edited by Friedlaender, with an accompaniment composed by Joseph Joachim.

19. Beginning about half way through the piece, the accompaniment patterns in Maximiliane Brentano's transcription and the published version do not match. Otherwise, the settings are essentially the same.

20. Brentano-von Arnim composed music to the "Suleika" of Marianne von Willemer (Friedlaender no. 10), but at the time, understood the poem to be Goethe's work.

21. See Henriette von Bissing's *Das Leben der Dichterin Amalie von Helvig geb. Freiin von Imhoff* (Berlin: Hertz, 1889).

22. Bissing reports that the composition was given her by Gisela Grimm, Brentano-von Arnim's youngest daughter (444).

23. With the rapidly changing scene in Germany, the future of editions currently in press is not known.

24. The evening was entitled "Ein Abend zu Goethes Geburtstag: Musik von und für Bettine von Arnim" and featured lectures by Renate Moering and Gerhard Schroth (6 August 1986). A private performance was sponsored the previous year by Clara von Arnim (the widow of

Bettina von Arnim's great grandson Friedmund) in honor of Brentano-von Arnim's 200th birthday on 4 April.

25. Brentano-von Arnim's songs were presented at a lecture recital entitled "Bettine von Arnim Liederabend" on 10 April 1987 at the University of Georgia (Athens) with the sponsorship of the Goethe Institute Atlanta. A similar program, entitled "Bettina von Arnim: A Woman and Her Songs" was held at Indiana University in Bloomington (25 April 1989).

Works Cited

MUSIC SOURCES

Manuscripts

Arnim, Bettina von. Autograph music compositions ms. Heinemann Coll MS Goethe-Bettine 30. The Pierpont Morgan Library, New York. N. pag., n.d.

———. Autograph Notebook ms. Heineman Coll MS 9B. The Pierpont Morgan Library, New York. 136 pages, n.d.

———. Songbook "Dedié à Spontini Directeur général de la Musique et premier maître de chapelle de S.M. le Roi de Prusse. etc. etc." Copyist's transcription ms. Heineman Coll MS 29 (Goethe). The Pierpont Morgan Library, New York. N. pag., n.d.

———. Three compositions ms. Transcription of Joseph Joachim. Hs 15711. Freies Deutsches Hochstift, Frankfurt. N. pag., n.d.

———. Three compositions ms. Transcriptions in notebook of Maximiliane Brentano. Private collection of Bernt Ture von zur Mühlen, Frankfurt. N. pag., n.d.

Published Music

Arnim, Bettina von. "Bettina von Arnims Kompositionen" [Ten songs]. Ed. Max Friedlaender. in Vol. 4 of Bettina von Arnims Sämtliche Werke. Ed. Waldemar Oehlke. 7 vols. Berlin: Mayer & Müller, 1905. 261–306.

———. "Dedié à Spontini, Directeur général de la musique et premier maître de chapelle de S.M. le Roi de Prusse. etc. etc." Leipzig: Breitkopf & Härtel, [1842]. N. pag.

———. "Lied beim Scharpiezupfen." Clemens Brentano, *Viktoria und ihre Geschwister, mit fliegenden Fahnen und brennender Lunte*. Berlin: Maurer, 1817.

———. "Lied des Schülers" in Vol. 1 of Ludwig Achim von Arnim. *Sämmtliche Werke*. Ed. Wilhelm Grimm. 11 vols. Berlin: Veit, 1839–1840. 145.

———. "Romanze," "Musikbeilage" in Vol. 8 of Ludwig Achim von Arnim. *Sämmtliche Werke*. Ed. Wilhelm Grimm. 11 vols. Berlin: Veit, 1839–1840. 3.

———. "Weihe an Hellas" in Bissing, Henriette von. *Das Leben der Dichterin Amalie von Helvig geb. Freiin von Imhoff*. Berlin: n.p., 1889. 446–447.

BETTINA BRENTANO-VON ARNIM'S LITERARY WORKS AND LETTERS

Arnim, Bettina von. *Die Andacht zum Menschenbild: Unbekannte Briefe von Bettine Brentano*. Ed. Wilhelm Schellberg and Friedrich Fuchs. 1942. Bern: Lang, 1970.

———. *Werke*. Ed. Heinz Härtl. 2 Vols. Weimar: Aufbau, 1986. *Goethes Briefwechsel mit einem Kinde*. 1:5–573. (Quoted as Weimar.)

———. *Werke und Briefe*. Eds. Gustav Konrad (1–4) and Joachim Müller (5). 5 vols. Frechen and Köln: Bartman, 1958–1963. (Quoted as Köln.)

———. *Werke und Briefe*. Eds. Walter Schmitz and Sibylle von Steinsdorff. 3 vols. Frankfurt: Klassiker Verlag, 1986. *Clemens Brentano's Frühlingskranz*. Ed. Walter Schmitz. 1:9–294; *Die Günderode*. Ed. Walter Schmitz. 1:295–746.

Steig, Reinhold, and Hermann Grimm, eds. *Achim von Arnim und die ihm nahe standen*. 3 vols. 1913. Bern: Lang, 1970.

ADDITIONAL SOURCES

Betz, Otto and Veronika Straub, eds. *Bettine und Arnim: Briefe der Freundschaft und Liebe*. 2 vols. Frankfurt: Knecht, 1986–1987.

Bihler, Anton. "Beethoven und 'das Kind.' " *Die Gartenlaube* 20 (1870): 314–315.

Bissing, Henriette von. *Das Leben der Dichterin Amalie von Helvig geb. Freiin von Imhoff.* Berlin: n.p., 1889.

Citron, Marcia J. "Women and the Lied, 1775–1850." *Women Making Music: The Western Art Tradition 1150–1950.* Urbana: University of Illinois Press, 1986. 224–248.

Helwig, Amalie von [sic.]. *Gedichte zum Besten der unglücklichen Greise, Wittwen, und Waisen in Griechenland.* Berlin: Krause, 1826.

Henrici, Karl Ernst, ed. *Bettine von Arnim: Literarisches und Politisches aus Ihrem handschriftlichen Nachlaß, darunter Goethes Briefwechsel mit einem Kinde.* Auction Catalog 148. Berlin: n.p., 1929.

Hirsch, Helmut. *Bettine von Arnim.* Reinbek bei Hamburg: Rowohlt, 1987.

La Mara [Maria Lipsius]. *Liszt und die Frauen.* Leipzig: Breitkopf & Härtel, 1911.

Milch, Werner. *Die Junge Bettine: 1785–1811.* Ed. Peter Küpper. Heidelberg: Stiehm, 1968.

Moering, Renate. "Bettines Liedvertonungen." *Herzhaft in die Dornen der Zeit greifen. . . . Bettina von Arnim exhibition catalog. Freies Deutsches Hochstift—Frankfurter Goethe-Museum.* Stuttgart: Cantz, 1985. 178–201.

———. *Die offene Romanform von Arnims 'Gräfin Dolores'.* Frankfurter Beiträge zur Germanistik 16. Heidelberg: Winter 1978.

Moser, Hans Joachim. *Goethe und die Musik.* Leipzig: Peters, 1949.

Schnapp-Berlin, Friedrich. "Unbekannte Briefe Franz Liszts." *Die Musik* 18 (1926) 717–732.

Weissweiler, Eva. *Komponistinnen aus 500 Jahren: Eine Kultur- und Wirkungs-geschichte in Biographien und Werkbeispielen.* Frankfurt: Fischer, 1981.

Werner, Johannes. *Maxe von Arnim: Tochter Bettinas / Gräfin von Oriola 1818–1894.* Leipzig: Koehler & Amelang, 1937.

Willison, Ann. "Bettines Kompositionen: Zu einem Notenheft der Sammlung Heineman." *Internationales Jahrbuch der Bettina-von-Arnim Gesellschaft* 3(1989): 183–208.

V

Defying the Canon

The Reception of Bettina Brentano-von Arnim as Author and Historical Figure

Marjanne Goozé

Ten years ago, anyone interested in finding out about the life and works of Bettina Brentano-von Arnim, would have had to find a good research library. Her collected works were not in print and there were few biographies generally available. Except for brief periods this situation prevailed since her death in 1859. Now a glance at the current *German Books in Print* (Verzeichnis lieferbarer Bücher) or the card catalogue of a research library will prove that things have changed. The many new books and editions available reveal a reassessment of Bettina Brentano-von Arnim's place in German literary and social history. The question is, however, just what is it that these works are reassessing? Ten years ago, a researcher had to be persistent indeed to uncover the many books, articles, and dissertations about Brentano-von Arnim; today the newer works provide bibliographies. Yet when reading some of the newer writings on Brentano-von Arnim, it is apparent that many critics are grappling with the same issues that their predecessors addressed. Practically all critics speak to the following pivotal issues raised in Bettina Brentano-von Arnim's writings: the relationship between form and subjectivity, life and art,

Bettina Brentano-von Arnim (1859). (Stiftung Weimarer Klassik.)

politics and idealism, and feminism and "the feminine." Many scholars and biographers pose these questions and answer them as if for
the first time. Perhaps this is because for most people discovering
Bettina Brentano-von Arnim for themselves has been a private and
personal adventure. Her works have not been part of the academic
literary canon, selections from her writings were not included in text-

book anthologies, and she was mentioned in literary histories only briefly and, usually disparagingly, in connection to Goethe.

Yet there is a tradition of Bettina Brentano-von Arnim scholarship, even if it is hard to find and much of it would not generally be considered scholarly by today's standards. The popular presentation of Brentano-von Arnim as a historical personality has gone hand-in-hand with the discovery of new materials and literary analyses. Studies about her life and her works are not divisible into minute categories. As in her books, discussions of life and art are inextricably intertwined. Until quite recently, critics rarely referred directly to earlier studies in their own interpretations. There have been very few *Forschungsberichte* (reports on the state of the research), and these have overwhelmingly concentrated on her first book, *Goethe's Correspondence with a Child* (Goethes Briefwechsel mit einem Kinde).[1]

In this essay, I will attempt to trace the tradition of scholarship by focusing on four pivotal issues addressed by most critics. First, the questions regarding the form of the books has resulted in a major controversy as to whether or not the books are literature. Second, in responding to the first question, Brentano-von Arnim's subjectivity has become a focal point for older scholars in determining the reliability and authenticity of her autobiographical writings, while for recent scholars the modernist and postmodernist concern with subjectivity evidences itself in the analyis of her work. Third, often arising from the discussion of Bettina Brentano-von Arnim's subjectivity are aesthetic and political questions regarding her femininity and feminism and the ways in which they inform her writing. In general, nineteenth-century scholars are interested in the way in which Brentano-von Arnim's writings both do and do not represent a traditionally "feminine" discourse and personality, and twentieth-century critics seek in the same writings the evidence of a feminist literary aesthetic and the beginnings of feminist politics. Fourth, since the early twentieth century there has been an increasing focus on Bettina Brentano-von Arnim's political activities. In addition, most of the newer criticism discusses the readability of Brentano-von Arnim's works in the late twentieth century.

This overview refers to almost all the literature on Bettina Brentano-von Arnim. I will begin by examining the history of the publication of her works. This is necessary because many of her editors were also her most important critics. Also, the reader will understand from the outset how difficult and challenging the task for researchers has been. They have often had to contend with inaccurate and badly edited works, if they were available at all. Dissertations are also discussed in detail since they are rarely considered. This essay, however, is not intended to replace the books, articles, essays, and dissertations discussed. Instead, I hope to demonstrate that there is a tradition of Bettina Brentano-von Arnim scholarship and that many of the pieces about her are worth finding on dusty shelves and reading. At the end, the most recent works are presented. It is to be hoped that, unlike many of their predecessors, these works will be given consideration in future studies, so that a true reassessment of her life and works can take place.

Collected Works and Individual Editions

In 1853 at the age of fifty-eight Bettina Brentano-von Arnim published her own collected works in eleven volumes. A second edition appeared in 1857.[2] She did not organize her collection chronologically, starting with the first book she wrote, *Goethes Briefwechsel mit einem Kinde*. Instead, she assembled her collection so that the four works in epistolary form could be read as a kind of autobiography of her life. She began her collection with *The Spring Wreath* (Clemens Brentanos Frühlingskranz), because the correspondence recalled in it deals with an earlier part of her life than any of the others. The politically oriented conversational novels[3] follow the epistolary in her self-published collected works. She was making the statement through this reordering of her books that she wanted to distinguish between the epistolary and dialogue forms, and that she intended the epistolary books to be read in the reverse order in which she first published them. Therefore, in her collection, *Goethes Briefwechsel mit einem Kinde* is not found at the beginning, but forms the center of her works and is placed within the context of her other writings.

Bettina Brentano-von Arnim's first major published work was *Goethes Briefwechsel mit einem Kinde*. It is the book for which she is most well-known and has been the most widely read and the most often published of her books. The book was first published in 1835 in three volumes. The first two volumes were based upon her correspondence with Goethe and his mother, while the third, the so-called "Diary of Love" (Tagebuch der Liebe), was written in diary form. Following its publication in Germany, Bettina Brentano-von Arnim then spent several years translating it into English. *Goethe's Correspondence with a Child* was published in 1837–1838.

Her second book, *Günderode* (Die Günderode), appeared in 1840. She had introduced her readers to Karoline von Günderrode in the first part of *Goethes Briefwechsel* where she included a long fictitious letter to Frau Rat Goethe in which she told the story of their friendship and of Günderrode's suicide.[4] Both *Goethes Briefwechsel* and *Die Günderode* contain some political reflections but they primarily serve as portrayals of her youth.

Bettina von Arnim's third book was very different from the first two. Rather than reflecting upon the relationships of her youth, *The King's Book* (Dies Buch gehört dem König), published in 1843, speaks directly to issues of the day. Much of the book is in dialogue form. The characters of Frau Rat Goethe, the Mayor of Frankfurt, and a Lutheran minister discuss issues of personal, political, and religious freedom. Included at the end is a sample of some of the reports Brentano-von Arnim had collected on the living conditions of poor and destitute weavers. The title of the book reflects its direct appeal to King Friedrich Wilhelm IV of Prussia to institute reforms.

She returned to her autobiographical project in 1844 with her third epistolary book, *The Spring Wreath* (Clemens Brentanos Frühlingskranz aus Jugendbriefen von ihm geflochten, wie er selbst schriftlich verlangte). Due to the political uproar following the *Königsbuch* (The King's Book) and the dedication here to Prince Waldemar, this book was banned for a short time. The implication in the title that her brother Clemens Brentano wanted her to write this book is ironic since he had strongly objected to her publication of *Goethes Briefwechsel*. Clemens Brentano had died, however, in 1842.

Bettina Brentano-von Arnim's fifth book is in epistolary form, but unlike the previous three epistolary books, in it she does not reflect on her youth. *Ilius Pamphilius und die Ambrosia* is based on her correspondence with Philipp Nathusius (he is Ilius Pamphilius and she is Ambrosia). They corresponded from 1835 to his engagement in 1839. It is the least revised and embellished of all the correspondence books, and the original letters were probably written with future publication in mind. Published in 1848, just before the uprisings of that year, the book found little response.

Bettina Brentano-von Arnim's sixth and last book was the second volume of the *The King's Book—Conversations with Demons* (Königsbuch—Gespräche mit Dämonen). After the events of the 1848

Revolution, Brentano-von Arnim had to recognize that her dream of an enlightened constitutional monarchy would never be realized by Friedrich Wilhelm IV. She continued to work on the book after 1848 and published it in 1852. No copies were sold.

Although individual volumes appeared from time to time after her death in 1859, no new edition of her collected works was published for almost seventy years for several reasons, the least of these being lack of interest. Possibly the major hindrance deterring publication of the collected works were the wishes of the Arnim family, many of whom were embarrassed by Bettina Brentano-von Arnim's books, particularly by the politically oriented conversational novels. Waldemar Oehlke, who had written his dissertation on Brentano-von Arnim, began in 1920 to publish a seven-volume collection, which was completed in 1922. Oehlke did not limit himself to letters and works the author herself published. He included some of her fairy tales and poems, as well as some highly edited versions of her musical compositions. Oehlke was interested in comparing her published works with the original materials. In this collection, titled *Bettina von Arnims Sämtliche Werke*, he published her original correspondence with Goethe and his mother, as well as other letters.[5]

Gustav Konrad published the third set of collected works, *Bettina von Arnim. Werke und Briefe*, in five volumes from 1959 to 1961. The first volume appeared on the 100th anniversary of Brentano-von Arnim's death. The fifth volume contains her letters and was edited by Joachim Müller. Konrad and Müller included additional materials discovered since the Oehlke edition was published. Their notes and commentaries on the text are more extensive than Oehlke's. Konrad does, however, make use of Oehlke's evaluative lists, indicating which of the letters in the books are the same as the original letters, interpolated with new material, or completely new. He referred to earlier editions of Bettina Brentano-von Arnim's works and was aware of contributions made by scholars. His extensive citations from the contemporary reviews of her books are most useful in assessing their reception during her lifetime. Yet despite these additions and improvements, the edition does not approach present standards for historical-critical editions.

The widespread interest in the 1970s and 1980s in German women authors and in Bettina Brentano-von Arnim in particular is a result of the women's movement. Researchers and scholars have finally begun to take her work seriously, rather than seeing her merely as a wild child of the Romantic era who was acquainted with practically all the famous men of her day. Before unification, two new editions were under way; one in the Federal Republic and one in the German Democratic Republic (GDR).[6] While these new editions were intended to present readers with well-edited versions of her books, neither was to be a complete collection of her letters, books, and political writings.

The West German edition, *Bettine von Arnim. Werke und Briefe*, published by the Deutscher Klassiker Verlag, is to be a three-volume set.[7] Edited by Walter Schmitz and Sibylle von Steinsdorff, the collection is structured like all the previous collected editions: the first book is the *Frühlingskranz*, then follow *Die Günderode* and *Goethes Briefwechsel*. The political writings are to be placed in the last volume. The Schmitz-Steinsdorff project plans to omit *Ilius Pamphilius and Ambrosia* (Ilius Pamphilius und die Ambrosia) and will include the *Poor Book* (Armenbuch) which has been discovered since the Konrad edition. The editors have provided extensive biographical and textual notes. Over one-third of the first volume is devoted to notes and commentaries. Embedded in the notes are many of her original letters.

The East German edition had promised to be more complete: five volumes were planned. As with the Klassiker Verlag edition, the first volume appeared in 1986, one year after the celebrations in East and West Germany of Brentano-von Arnim's 200th birthday.[8] But unlike all previous editions, *Bettina von Arnim. Werke*, edited by Heinz Härtl and published by Aufbau Verlag, should present the texts closely following the order in which they were written. The *Königsbücher* are to appear together with her shorter political writings. A whole volume is to be devoted to the *Armenbuch*. The editor plans to include *Ilius Pamphilius* and her shorter literary compositions. There are extensive commentaries and notes. Since this edition promises to include all of Bettina Brentano-von Arnim's published works and her political writings, if not her letters, when completed it will be a reliable source for scholars and general readers alike.

Most readers of Bettina Brentano-von Arnim, however, are not scholars and are not interested in investing in expensive annotated editions of her works. Individual editions have appeared from time to time, and most of these have been of *Goethes Briefwechsel*. The fourth edition of *Goethes Briefwechsel mit einem Kinde* (1881)—the first not published by Arnim herself—was edited by her son-in-law

Hermann Grimm. This was followed by editions by Jonas Fränkel in 1906 and a Reclam edition edited by Franz Brümmer in 1910. Heinz Amelung provided individual editions of several works, and his *Goethes Briefwechsel* came out in 1914. After the Oehlke edition appeared, individual editions of her most famous book continued to be published. An important change, however, was the appearance of shortened, condensed versions by Otto Heuschele and Alfred Kantorowicz. The latter of these continues even today to be republished.[9] Kantorowicz even changed the title to *Du wunderliches Kind . . . Bettina und Goethe*.[10] This tendency to reissue older editions is regrettable. In 1984 and 1985 Insel Verlag published *Goethes Briefwechsel* using Oehlke's edition of the text.

This same pattern is also evident in the publication history of her other books. *Die Günderode* was issued under two different editors by Insel Verlag in 1904, 1914, and 1925 (Mallon 148). Not until very recently has it received much attention. Christa Wolf's interest in Romantic women writers, and especially in Karoline von Günderrode, prompted her to write a new essay and make some corrections to the Amelung edition. Although not exactly a new edition, the publication in 1982 of *Die Günderode* under the auspices of one of the most important and respected contemporary writers in the German language did much to encourage both scholars and the general public to read Bettina Brentano-von Arnim's writings. That same year, Elisabeth Bronfen supervised the publication of the Konrad version of *Die Günderode* for Matthes & Seitz.

Interest in Clemens Brentano has been the primary motivation for the individual copies of *Clemens Brentanos Frühlingskranz*. Heinz Amelung, himself a Brentano scholar, issued the book in 1909 (Mallon 150). Wulf Segebrecht also approaches the work from his perspective as a Brentano scholar in his 1967 edition. New editions have appeared recently in both East and West Germany. The edition published in the GDR was edited with an extensive commentary by Heinz Härtl and appeared in 1985 in paperback by Reclam (Leipzig). The Insel Verlag that year also brought out an edition with a new essay by Hartwig Schultz, but the text itself was taken from the old Amelung edition.

Her political works have received even less attention. In 1982, however, a paperbound edition appeared of *Dies Buch gehört dem König* which also included a brief section from *Gespräche mit Dämonen*. It was edited by Ilse Staff who also wrote an informative essay. With Werner Vordtriede's discovery of Brentano-von Arnim's drafts for her book on the poor, another text was added to the repertoire of individual works—the *Armenbuch*.[11]

There have been only three brief periods of heightened interest in Bettina Brentano-von Arnim's works since her death in 1859. The first occurred in the 1910s and early 1920s and was probably a result of the first women's movement. The renewed interest in the 1950s accompanied the discoveries of her political writings and activities in the GDR and the 100th anniversary of her death. This period, however, produced very few readily available individual editions of her works. Only since the early 1980s have these begun to appear. At the present, most of her books are in print in the West in popular editions and new, more scholarly editions are under way.

These individual editions, however, have not satisfied the desire of a wider audience to read something by Bettina Brentano-von Arnim in order to learn about her life. All of her published works are quite long and do not lend themselves easily to casual reading. This market demand has been met in two ways. The first response has been to publish her shorter works such as the *Armenbuch* and the *Märchen* (Fairy Tales), written with her daughters. Konrad, for example, published a separate volume of her fairy tales. Two editions of her novella-length *Märchen*, written with her daughter Gisela, have recently been issued. *The Life of the High Countess Gritta von Rats-at-home-with-us* (Das Leben der Hochgräfin Gritta von Rattenzuhausbeiuns) is an interesting text in its own right, but because of its narrative form and Gisela's co-authorship, it does not give the reader a sense of Brentano-von Arnim's epistolary and conversational styles found in the longer books.

The second solution has even greater shortcomings. There seems to be no end to the small volumes of excerpts that appear on the market. Some of these editions are quite well done, whereas others leave much to be desired either because of numerous biographical errors, text selection, or outrageous editing and arrangement. These books of excerpts usually try to provide an overview of Brentano-von Arnim's life through the selections. In order to meet this goal, editors have often overlooked the absolutely essential difference between actual letters she wrote as a young woman and the much later published works. Even when originals were available, they often chose to quote from the works. This approach led to grave misreadings and misinterpretations. Many of the new collections share this problem, which could be solved by viewing the books as a kind of personal narrative rather than as historical documents, and by making distinctions where necessary between passages that are close to known originals and those that are known to have been written much later.

One of the first postwar collections was edited in 1953 by Willi Reich and called *Lebensspiel*. It avoids most of the pitfalls of other collections by organizing the material chronologically and presenting many original letters. On the other hand, some of the newer books, such as the 1987 *Meine Seele ist eine leidenschaftliche Tänzerin*, succumb to all the dangers. The excerpts are really only snippets of texts and are organized in groups of romantically idyllic thematic categories.

Dieter Kühn's collection, *Aus meinem Leben*, is embedded in his biographical narrative. It represents all that is wrong with this kind of endeavor to present her to the general reading public. There are chronological errors which could have been avoided by consulting many of the available chronologies (*Zeittafeln*). In order to set her texts off from his narrative, her texts are printed in the old gothic typeface. This prettifying of the text only makes her work seem less accessible to the interested reader. Kühn's biographical presentation ignores her life after her marriage to Achim von Arnim in 1811. The excerpts, which are all taken from the epistolary books, are not used as examples of her literary accomplishment, but as documentary support for Kühn's narrative. Another work in the same vein is Frederik Hetmann's *Bettina und Achim: Die Geschichte einer Liebe*. The book is written like a novel, including dialogue. Hetmann asserts that he has taken all the quotes from original sources.

An example of a more readable book of excerpts is the Reclam publication, *Bettina von Arnim: Ein Lesebuch*. The editors, Christa Bürger and Birgitt Diefenbach, do not attempt to use the books as documents, and substantial selections are presented from all of the books except *Ilius Pamphilius*. The *Lesebuch* also includes passages from the *Armenbuch* and the complete text of one of the *Märchen*. However, Bürger and Diefenbach only include Bettina's letters from the epistolary books, so that one only hears her half of the dialogue. No letters by the correspondents the books are named for—Clemens Brentano, Karoline von Günderrode, and Goethe—are printed. Their explanatory notes and introductions to the sections, as well as Bürger's concluding essay, "The Hunger for the Self" (Der Hunger nach dem Ich) are provocative and informative.

Two volumes of excerpts have been published in the GDR: the

first, *Bettine*, edited by Gisela Kähler in 1952, contains a good introductory biography of Bettina Brentano-von Arnim; and the second is a new collection, *Die Sehnsucht hat allemal Recht*, edited by Gerhard Wolf and also published in the West.[12]

Manuscripts and Letters

In addition to the letters available in the Oehlke and Konrad editions of the collected works, many letters and texts have been published independently. Some of these older letter editions are all that we now have, since many of the original manuscripts have been lost. In 1929 the Arnim family, in need of funds, put all of her manuscripts in their possession up for auction. Turning down an offer from the Prussian government to purchase all the papers, the family auctioned each item separately, and thereby scattered her manuscripts to the four winds. The detailed Henrici auction catalogues (*Bettine von Arnim: Literarisches und Politisches aus ihrem Nachlass*), are an invaluable resource in assessing the extent of her papers. They contain quotations from some no longer extant writings. Known manuscripts are located primarily at the *Freies Deutsches Hochstift* in Frankfurt am Main, the *Goethe-Schiller Archiv* in Weimar, in the Varnhagen collection in the Jagiellonski University library in Cracow, and at the Pierpont Morgan Library in New York in the Heineman collection.

The first original letter collections published were Bettina Brentano-von Arnim's correspondence with Goethe and his mother Frau Rat. Shortly after *Goethes Briefwechsel mit einem Kinde* appeared, questions were raised regarding the authenticity of the letters. Goethe scholars were particularly intent on showing how she distorted her relationship with Goethe in the book and on proving which letters were really written by Goethe (see Gervinius). Since she also used embellished and fictional letters as evidence that she inspired some of his works, Goethe scholars needed to concentrate on her letters too. In 1879 Gustav von Loeper edited a collection of letters published as: *Briefe Goethes an Sophie von La Roche und Bettina Brentano nebst dichterischen Beilagen*. He saw his book as a contribution to the body of Goethe's works. Fritz Bergemann, on the other hand, was interested in both Bettina Brentano-von Arnim and Goethe. In 1927 he published the complete extant correspondence between them based on the Reinhold Steig's manuscript preparation. Steig died before his project could be published. Bergemann not only published the letters, but wrote a book-length preface which may be read as an insightful biographical analysis of Bettina Brentano-von Arnim's life during her correspondence with Goethe.

For a long time the only researcher allowed access by the Arnim family to Bettina's manuscripts was Reinhold Steig. His major contribution to Bettina Brentano-von Arnim research is the three-volume collection of letters: *Achim von Arnim und die ihm nahe standen* published in 1913. The first volume presents the correspondence between Achim von Arnim and Clemens Brentano, the second the Achim and Bettina letters up to their marriage, and the third his letters with Jakob and Wilhelm Grimm. Bettina is the subject of some of the letters in the first and third volumes, so the whole collection is an asset to Bettina Brentano-von Arnim scholars. A new edition of Bettina's and Achim's letters has recently appeared under the inappropriate title: *Bettine und Arnim.*[13] The editors note that Steig's edition was quite reliable, except for a few paraphases and deletions he made and new materials subsequently discovered (2:21). Neither collection, however, contains the bulk of her correspondence with Achim, since that occurred during their marriage. These letters were published fifty years later by Werner Vordtriede and Rudolf A. Schröder in a two-volume set: *Achim und Bettina in ihren Briefen.*

The other significant correspondence with family members are her letters to her brother-in-law Savigny, who married her older sister Gunda. She was very close to the Savigny household and for a time lived with her sister and brother-in-law. Savigny often acted as her surrogate father (her parents died when she was young and she was officially the responsibility of her half-brother). Schellberg and Fuchs published this correspondence and related documents in *Die Andacht zum Menschenbild* in 1942. They were primarily Clemens Brentano scholars and three years before had published a similar collection of his letters. It is believed that her correspondence with her brother Clemens no longer exists. In the former German Democratic Republic, Heinz Härtl also published Savigny's letters to Bettina Brentano-von Arnim.

Most of her correspondences with friends have been published only in the last thirty years. The most notable older publication was edited by Ludmilla Assing who had some of the letters from Karl August Varnhagen von Ense's extensive holdings printed. We now know that there were more materials in his possession. Another older collection covers her correspondence with Fürst Pückler-Muskau. The new correspondences often tell us about her relationship with much less well-known figures. Werner Vordtriede, for example, in publishing her correspondence with Julius Döring, uncovered not only a new relationship, but helped to explain her original plan for *Ilius Pamphilius und die Ambrosia* which was at first to include her letters to several young men. One of these was Julius Döring. In the end, Brentano-von Arnim selected only one correspondent, Philipp Nathusius. Sibylle von Steinsdorff also revealed new aspects of Brentano-von Arnim's life in Munich and Landshut when she published her correspondence with Max Prokop von Freyberg.

Bettina Brentano-von Arnim's political activities are most clearly reflected in her letters. Early scholars such as Ludwig Geiger often had difficulty obtaining documents. He was continually denied access to her papers by the Arnim family primarily because he was a Jew. Geiger, however, was not easily dissuaded and published several pieces on Brentano-von Arnim, including studies of her political interests. His most important contribution is the 1902 publication of her letters to King Friedrich Wilhelm IV. Kurt Gassen later concentrated on her relationship with Rudolf Baier. Most recently, Hartwig Schultz has used her correspondence with Jakob and Wilhelm Grimm to shed new light on her efforts to get them appointed to the new university in Berlin after they lost their jobs in Göttingen. The Grimms were part of the so-called "Göttingen Seven" who had refused to sign a pledge that went against the Hessian constitution. As a consequence, they lost their jobs. This correspondence reveals the political side of both Arnim and the Grimms.

The most significant work on Bettina Brentano-von Arnim's political activities was done in the German Democratic Republic. After the Second World War many of her political papers were found in the attic of the Arnim estate in Wiepersdorf. These had not been sold in the 1929 auction, there being at that time little interest in this aspect of her life. These papers were brought to the Goethe-Schiller Archiv in Weimar. In the 1950s Gertrud Meyer-Hepner published several articles on the holdings. Like Vordtriede, she also discovered another book that Brentano-von Arnim herself planned to publish, the *Magistratsprozess* (Magistrat's Trial).[14] Most recently, a new group of her later letters appeared in *Sinn und Form*, as "Briefe und Konzepte 1837 bis 1846."

Several trends are apparent from this overview of the history of the

publication of Bettina Brentano-von Arnim's books, letters, and
other texts. There are, first of all, clearly two presentations of her
works to be found: the scholarly and the popular. This determination
can usually be made without difficulty by judging the kind of audience
the editor had in mind. Quality and unreliable editions may be found
in both categories. Books, such as the *Armenbuch* which is available
in both kinds of editions with the same editor, are to be welcomed.
The introductions and afterwords written by editors form the basis for
the critical evaluation of her works. As we shall see, her editors are
some of her most important critics.[15] The notoriety of Brentano-von
Arnim has encouraged the production of scholarly editions and studies. It can also be observed, secondly, that the publication of her
original correspondences is, in general, a response to the challenge of
the epistolary books since they are based upon many of these earlier
letters. Thirdly, there was also a difference in approach between researchers in the Federal Republic and those in the German Democratic Republic; editors from the Federal Republic placed her autobiographical epistolary books in the forefront, whereas in the German
Democratic Republic her political writings and books were the most
valued. And finally, the modern women's movement in Western Europe and America has led to an interest in her friendships and relationships with other women, and with Karoline von Günderrode in
particular. Women writers in the German Democratic Republic have
also shown an interest in Bettina Brentano-von Arnim's relationships
with other women.

Brentano-von Arnim's Reception by her Contemporaries and by *Junges Deutschland* Writers

While in her published works Brentano-von Arnim mainly focuses on
her relationships with renown men, contemporary accounts by female
friends and acquaintances reveal that Bettina Brentano-von Arnim
had some women friends. This aspect of her life has often been overlooked by critics because of their often salacious interest in her relationship with Goethe and their desire to see her as an exception to the
norms set for women's behavior. An exchange of letters between Bettina and Achim in 1827, in which he encouraged her to find some

girlfriends with whom she could share her household complaints and her rejection of his suggestion, has been seen as proof that she neither had nor wanted female friends (*Achim und Bettina* 2: 679–691). What Bettina was rejecting was not female friendship, but the type of friendship Achim had in mind. Her friendship with Karoline von Günderrode had taught Bettina Brentano-von Arnim to demand intellectual as well as moral support from her friends. Her relationship with Rahel Varnhagen, although often torn by jealousies and misunderstandings, was in the end marked by mutual care and respect. During her marriage she found in the writer Amalie von Helvig both a friend and artistic collaborator. Bissing documents their friendship and work together in her biography of Helvig. Malla Montgomery-Silferstolpe recalls her acquaintance with Brentano-von Arnim in the mid-1820s in her travel memoir, *Das romantische Deutschland*. Brentano-von Arnim could also be supportive of other women artists, as her correspondence with Pauline Steinhäuser demonstrates. And from her daughter Maxe's recollections (edited by Johannes Werner), we get a glimpse of her private life after the death of her husband and of her close relationship with her three daughters.

Her life and writings inspired other women to take a more active role in literary and political life. Fanny Lewald admired Bettina Brentano-von Arnim's work. Lewald married Adolf Stahr who supported many of Brentano-von Arnim's political efforts. In her autobiography Malwida von Meysenbug remembers how reading Brentano-von Arnim's and Rahel Varnhagen's writings influenced her own development (48). In America she found admirers in Margaret Fuller, who wrote reviews of her books for *The Dial* and began a translation of *Die Günderode*, and among the American Transcendentalists, particularly Emerson and Louisa May Alcott.[16]

Memoirs by male friends and acquaintances also provide information. An imporatant source of information about her later life are Karl August Varnhagen von Ense's extensive diaries. Because of Brentano-von Arnim's large family and numerous acquaintances who were themselves figures of note, it is virtually impossible here to list all the relevant sources that contain comments on various periods of her long life.

Immediately following the publication of *Goethes Briefwechsel*, Bettina Brentano-von Arnim became the subject of books, articles and reviews. The responses to *Dies Buch gehört dem König* were especially important, because in the extensive passages cited her ideas reached a wider readership. The effectiveness of these books was such that, although Brentano-von Arnim's book was not censored because it was more than 320 pages long, shorter excerpts were. One of these banned books was Adolf Stahr's *Bettina und ihr Königsbuch*. Stahr recognized that the historical setting of the book was merely a cover for the discussion of current issues. He observed that: "it is not Bettina from Frankfurt on the Main, it is Bettina from Berlin on the Spree whose enthusiastic speeches we are listening to here" (es ist nicht Bettina von Frankfurt am Main, es ist Bettina von Berlin an der Spree, deren begeisterten Reden wir hier belauschen) (7). A second book appeared which managed to escape the censor by pretending to be a denunciation of the *Königsbuch*. The book was published anonymously as *Ruchlosigkeit der Schrift: "Dies Buch gehört dem König"—Ein unterthäniger Fingerzeig gewagt von Lebrecht Fromm*. The writer plays devil's advocate while quoting long passages from the *Königsbuch* and in responding to Stahr. After 1848 her political works received little attention, and other writers interested in political and social issues still saw her as the wild romantic child of *Goethes Briefwechsel*.

Yet even in this role, Bettina Brentano-von Arnim influenced Young German (Junges Deutschland) writers and historians. Karl Gutzkow, Theodor Mundt, Heinrich Laube, and Ludwig Börne all commented on her works. For Young German writers, Bettina Brentano-von Arnim and Rahel Varnhagen seemed to symbolize their "emancipatory" feminine ideals. Often Charlotte Stieglitz was also considered.[17] Wulf Wülfing has examined their responses in detail and very accurately points out how later critics have greatly overestimated the liberalism of these authors' views towards women and women's rights. These writers tended to see Varnhagen and Brentano-von Arnim as competitors. The competition was played out in the pages of Rahel Varnhagen's posthumously published letters and diaries and in *Goethes Briefwechsel*. Neither were seen as authors in their own right. The goal of the competition was to explain Goethe to a somewhat hostile audience. While Bettina Brentano-von Arnim supposedly appealed to the emotions, Rahel Varnhagen approached Goethe with her intellect.[18] Ironically, critics such as Mundt found Brentano-von Arnim far more likeable than Goethe, who was taken to task for his coldness towards her (Mundt 317). Börne noted that, "Bettina is not Goethe's angel, she is his avenging fury" (Bettina ist nicht Goethes Engel, sie ist seine Rachefurie) (cited in Drewitz, *Bettine*, 166). They coined phrases that are now deeply embedded in Bettina Brentano-von Arnim criticism. When for example Mundt called her "the sibyl of the romantic literary epoch" (die Sibylle der romantischen Literaturepoche), he determined the direction of much of the subsequent criticism that would insist on viewing her as an untamed romantic personality, rather than as a serious author (317).

The Portrayal of Bettina Brentano-von Arnim in Literary Histories and Biographical Portraits

Bettina Brentano-von Arnim was usually portrayed in literary histories and reference works more as a romantic personality than as a writer. When recognized, her writing was seen as representative of the "eternal feminine." Loeper's description of her life and work for the *Allgemeine Deutsche Biographie*, emphasizes her "feminine" qualities: "Her character as a writer is also feminine" (Weiblich ist auch ihr schriftstellerischer Charakter) (2: 580). While the historical details are correct, his interpretation of them reflects his desire to place all her activities, including her political endeavors, within the boundaries of the stereotypically feminine. These critics all point out how Brentano-von Arnim's actions and writings were dictated more by her feelings than by logic. It is difficult to dismiss these observations as merely Victorian or sexist since in many ways the observations themselves are correct; the conclusions drawn from them are nevertheless highly problematic. Gutzkow asserted: "Since woman's mind can never be creative, her highest accomplishment can never be more than an unbelievable heightening of receptivity" (Da der Geist der Frauen nie schöpferisch wird, so kann ihre höchste Bildung immer nur eine unglaubliche Steigerung der Empfänglichkeit sein) (*Werke* Pt. 8: 104). Following comments like this one, later critics also portrayed Bettina Brentano-von Arnim as a personality whose sole concern and motivation in life was the love of men. Paul Kluckhohn echoes this belief in his sketch for the *Neue Deutsche Biographie*: "Bettina's artistic talent was extraordinarily diverse, manifesting itself on the whole more in receptivity and dilettantism than creativity" (Bettinas künstlerische Begabung war außerordentlich vielseitig, im ganzen mehr aufnehmend und dilettantisch sich betätigend als schöpferisch) (1: 370).

Her writing was not taken seriously and she was seen as a dilettante partly because critics did not know what to make of her epistolary books. Were they really letters? How much was documentary and how much was fiction? Every writer on her life and works has had to answer these questions. As we shall observe, how they chose to describe her books indicates to what degree they respected her talent and autonomy as a writer. In general, she receives the greatest consideration from those who also value her political views.

Literary historians who included Bettina Brentano-von Arnim in their surveys faced the problem of categorizing her works in various ways. In 1856 Julian Schmidt took a position that many others would later also assume. He declared that while Brentano-von Arnim herself was "poetic" ("dichterisch"), *Goethes Briefwechsel* was not a work of art. "These letters are not a work of art" (Ein Kunstwerk sind diese Briefe nicht), because a work of art has to free itself from subjectivity (126–127). Her subjectivity was itself artistic and romantic, but the works she produced were not. This attitude is commensurate with the cult of personality surrounding Bettina Brentano-von Arnim: literary historians saw her more as a poetic subject than a producer of art. Even evaluated within the context of other famous women, her erratic nature was emphasized. In his *Geschichte der deutschen Frauenwelt*, Scherr insists on her eternal childlike nature. She is not seen as a model for others; instead she is "half Ariel, half Puck" (halb Ariel, halb Puck) (2: 293–294). Heinrich Spiero in his 1913 history of literature by women takes the same position as Schmidt: "Bettina did not create a completely accomplished work of art . . . and yet each of her authorial remarks about her life is art" (Ein völlig vollendetes Kunstwerk hat Bettina . . . nicht geschaffen, und dennoch ist jede ihrer schriftstellerischen Lebensäußerungen Kunst) (12). Treitschke summarizes both the Gutzkow and the Schmidt positions. His assessment is example of the condescending stance towards her writing often assumed by Goethe scholars.

> Bettina's strength lay where the genius of women always lies, in the power of understanding and reception; she knew that and always remained the ivy that climbs up the strong tree trunk. She never presumed to do men's work; she never claimed that her later writing was an independent creation, but instead that it arose either from her perceptive memory or from the charitable human kindness of a pure heart.

Bettinas Stärke lag wo das Genie der Weiber immer liegt, in der Kraft des Verstehens und Empfangens; sie wußte das und blieb immer der Efeu, der sich an festen Stamme emporrankt. Männerarbeit zu tun hat sie sich nie erdreistet; was sie später schrieb erhob nicht den Anspruch für eine selbständige Schöpfung zu gelten, sondern entsprang entweder der verständnisvollen Erinnerung oder der werktätigen Menschenliebe eines reichen Herzens. (160)

By relegating her work to the feminine realm, male critics avoided the problem of categorization. Consideration of her works as literary texts would have required challenging male-defined genre categories. It was altogether easier to romanticize the author's personality than to address the issues raised by her books. It is ironic that a woman critic, Ricarda Huch, is the first to question Bettina Brentano-von Arnim's feminine receptivity. Huch found very little to like in Brentano-von Arnim precisely because she felt this was lacking: "As receptivity is the essentially feminine in people, a woman lacking in this quality will always give the impression of not being feminine" (Da die Rezeptivität das wesentlich Weibliche im Menschen ist, wird eine Frau, der diese Eigenschaft mangelt, immer den Eindruck des Unweiblichen machen) (519).

Newer literary histories present a more balanced view. I have chosen two examples: one West and one East German. Werner Kohlschmidt describes Bettina Brentano-von Arnim in the Reclam *Geschichte der deutschen Literatur* as both a personality and an author. He includes in his personality summary all the typical Brentano-von Arnim descriptors: "from childhood on, mercurial, a mixture of goblin and elf." (von Kind an quecksilbrig, Mischung von Kobold und Elfe) (3: 344). But Kohlschmidt, unlike many of his critical predecessors, sees in her youthful nonconformity and subjectivity the origins of a productive originality: "This productivity is for the most part as carelessly subjective (partly also deliberately original) as herself" (Diese Produktivität ist größtenteils so unbekümmert subjektiv [teilweise auch gewollt originell] wie ihre Person) (3: 344). He also recognizes the genre problems inherent in the epistolary books. Kohlschmidt warns that they should not be used as historical documentation; he coins a unique genre for them—"documentary letter book" (dokument-arische[s] Briefbuch) (3:344–345). The East German literary historians in *Geschichte der deutschen Literatur* are less concerned with her personality. They focus on her political and social engagement. Their primary interest lies in depicting Brentano-von Arnim's development from a romantic idealist to a political activist (8:268).

Bettina Brentano-von Arnim never had a significant place in the histories of German literature written for students and scholars, and her works were never a part of the literary "canon." As a personality, however, she continually received attention in less scholarly books. From the turn of the century, one can find numerous volumes of biographical portraits of famous women. Bettina Brentano-von Arnim is usually included in these. Most of these books are clearly aimed at a wider, less educated reading public and at female readers in particular. As with the editions of her works, the popular portraits run the gamut from the excellent to the dreadful.[19]

The first such book with a biographical sketch of Bettina Brentano-von Arnim was written by Arnold Schloenbach and published in 1856 while Brentano-von Arnim was still alive. Unlike literary historians such as Schmidt, he takes a more balanced, if somewhat contradictory view of her life. He insists on her childlike nature while at the same time praising her work with the poor. August Sauer's series of *Frauenbilder* also portrays her as a naive child whose writing is motivated solely by her love (94). In a series of biographies aimed at a female audience, Lina Morgenstern idealizes Brentano-von Arnim's marriage. Her piece on the author is generally a mass of wrong information, and yet she devotes considerable space to Brentano-von Arnim's relationship with the Grimms and to her political activities.

In 1912 Paul Kühn published a book called *Die Frauen um Goethe. Weimarer Interieurs.* The linen cover was decorated with blue hearts. He focuses exclusively on Bettina Brentano-von Arnim's relationship with Goethe. Yet despite appearances, Kühn recognized two important points that have only recently become widely accepted. He realized that Brentano-von Arnim's description of herself as a child and that her identification with the Psyche figure of her Goethe monument were deliberate idealizations of her youth (406). Kühn also praised her use of the letter form and noted how it was for her the most natural and genial mode of expression which in her hands became a "a perfected work of art" (vollendet[e] Kunstform) (406–407). Hans Kern's collection of short pieces continues in this vein.

Not all books of this type were written by men. Several were written by women. These books attempt to redress the neglect of women writers by male literary critics and historians Margarete

Susman's small volume of essays (published in 1929) provides much more than simple biographical sketches. In Susman's essay on Bettina Brentano-von Arnim, she deals directly with the issues of form and subjectivity. Susman is critical of Brentano-von Arnim's inability to logically formulate her philosophy or to achieve the objectivity necessary to present her work in a traditional literary form (117–119). What redeems the author in Susman's eyes is her mastery of language, her style: "Even if this work does have something hybrid about it, the style of the language raises it to pure literature" (Mag diese Dichtung an sich etwas Zwitterhaftes haben—der Sprachstil erhebt sie zur reinen Dichtung) (110). Susman accepts the term "epistolary novels" (Briefromane) for the books, because they are "romantic works about ideas which order themselves around a central person" (romantische Ideendichtungen, die sich um ein persönliches Zentrum anordnen) (109). Anna Siemsen states that her purpose in publishing her collection is to show how in the past individual women also struggled to develop their talents (7). In keeping with this goal, she begins her discussion of Bettina Brentano-von Arnim's work with *Die Günderode* rather than *Goethes Briefwechsel*. Ingeborg Drewitz, who wrote a long biography on Brentano-von Arnim, also published a series of portraits of Berliner salon women. While not strictly a portrait book, she organizes her chapters around specific women.

The consciousness-raising of the late 1960s and early 1970s did not stop the publication of such portrait books by unenlightened male authors; indeed it is likely that the growing women's movement enabled the publication of their works. Simply the title of Ludwig Barring's collection is a sufficient clue to his attitude—*Geist und Herz. Große Frauen in ihrer Zeit* (Mind and Soul. Great Women in their Time). Contemporary portrait books are usually published as local or popular history. Gustav Sichelschmidt's piece on Brentano-von Arnim in his collection on *Große Berlinerinnen* is quite good; it is accurate and he does not overly romanticize her life. On the other hand, Ohff's 1979 essay on Brentano-von Arnim as a political figure is full of errors. These brief pieces on her deal with the same issues of personality, artistry, and genre that are confronted in larger and more scholarly studies. They are important because these histories and collections have been the most accessible to an audience interested in learning something about the life and works of Bettina Brentano-von Arnim.

Critical Reception: 1880–1922

Until the second half of the twentieth century, it is often difficult to differentiate between critical and popular studies. Except for dissertations and the writings by the editors of her letters and books, few books and critical essays appeared devoted exclusively to Bettina Brentano-von Arnim. Most critics approached her work from their vantage point as Goethe, Brentano, or Achim von Arnim scholars.

The editors of the individual editions of *Goethes Briefwechsel* published at the turn of the century all deal with the elements of fantasy and reality in her writing style. Hermann Grimm emphasizes Brentano-von Arnim's writing process. His eyewitness account proves that she worked hard to create the illusion of hastily written letters: "She unceasingly rewrote what she did not like until it had the lightness of style as if it had just been hastily written down that way" (Sie schrieb unaufhörlich wieder ab, was ihr nicht gefiel, bis es die Leichtigkeit des Stiles empfing, als sei es flüchtig nur so hingeschrieben worden) (ix). Franz Brümmer stresses her mix of "Truth and Poetry" (Wahrheit und Dichtung)—a reversal of Goethe's title for his own autobiography, *Poetry and Truth* [*Dichtung und Wahrheit*] (12). Jonas Fränkel's interpretation is slightly psychological. He believes that the truth behind her fantasy lies in her desire "arbitrarily to suspend reality and to experience illusions" (die Wirklichkeit nach Willkür aufzuheben und Illusionen zu erleben) (viii).

Comparisons with Goethe's *Poetry and Truth* (Dichtung und Wahrheit) permeate the critical literature. While Goethe's poetical rendition of his life was regarded as the ideal model for autobiography, Bettina Brentano-von Arnim's efforts were generally viewed much more skeptically. A significant exception to this trend is Moritz Carrière's examination of all her books. Referring to her Goethe book, he noted: "Thus arose from actual reality an artistic work, truth and poetry, just as Goethe with the same intention named his own life story" (So entstand aus der thatsächlichen Wirklichkeit ein künstlerisches Werk, Wahrheit und Dichtung, wie Goethe selbst seine Lebensbeschreibung im ähnlichen Sinne genannt hat) (235).

In an article on Bettina Brentano-von Arnim, Reinhold Steig further elaborates on her selection of the epistolary form for her works. He sees her choice as a natural, since not only Goethe, but also her grandmother Sophie La Roche, Clemens Brentano, and her husband had written epistolary novels (263). Another editor of a letter collection, Ludwig Geiger, contributed to our understanding of Brentano-von Arnim's emendations to her original Goethe correspondence in his article discussing her passages on the Tyrolean War. Conrad Alberti (a pseudonym for Adelung) is thoroughly confused by Brentano-von Arnim's epistolary books. In his study, written in honor of her 100th birthday, he tries several terms, none of which seem to satisfy him. His main dilemma is the absence of plot and character development demanded by the modern novel, and he sees the epistolary novel as an archaic form (60). Alberti has little to say about the political books, because he does not believe that women can or should express political opinions (100). Luise Zurlinden, on the other hand, examines the philosophical influences on Bettina Brentano-von Arnim. Zurlinden undertakes a scholarly identification of the Platonic ideas she finds in Brentano-von Arnim's books. The fact that she deems the author worthy of this kind of comparative study is in itself a comment on her high estimation of Brentano-von Arnim.

Waldemar Oehlke was the first to undertake an academic study of Bettina Brentano-von Arnim's epistolary books. His positivistic study appeared in 1905. Using biographical information and other sources such as weather reports, Oehlke attempted to distinguish letter by letter exactly what Brentano-von Arnim had altered from her original correspondence. He is most successful with the Goethe book, since it could be compared directly with the actual letters. He also attempts a style analysis. Even though his methods seem outdated from our perspective, Oehlke's book remains an important source because he is the first critic to take Bettina Brentano-von Arnim's work as an author seriously. Oehlke wrote prefaces to each of the volumes of the collected works he edited. A long introductory essay, "Bettinas Leben und Persönlichkeit" opens the first volume. In this essay he answers the question: Why read Bettina Brentano-von Arnim's works? He believes that the issues raised regarding the original letters have been answered and that now we should ask, "if her writings by themselves do not have something to say to us in two connections: as works of art and as documents with a surprisingly modern world view which in almost every aspect, especially in the last works, touch on the thoughts and struggles of our own times" (ob ihre Schriften uns nicht durch sich selbst etwas zu sagen haben in doppelter Beziehung: als Kunstwerke und als Dokumente einer überraschend modernen Weltanschauung, die fast auf jeder Seite, zumal der letzten Werke, an die Gedanken und Kämpfe unserer Tage rührt) (iv). Oehlke, however, does not want

Brentano-von Arnim's works read as *littérature engagée*, noting that "Bettina is likewise no friend of revolutionary movements" (Bettine ist auch keine Freundin revolutionärer Bewegungen) (lxii). One of the reasons for this is that he interprets all her works as expressions of her specific subjectivity: "All of Bettina's works are only reflections of her own character" (Alle Werke Bettinas sind nur Spiegelungen ihres eigenen Wesens) (liv). In the end, Oehlke never completely resolved the conflict between a reading of the books as literature *and* as document; in his conclusion he takes a stand somewhere between "Poetry" (Dichtung) and "Truth" (Wahrheit).

Wilhelm Frels has no difficulty in making this determination in his monograph, *Bettina von Arnims Königsbuch*: "*The King's Book* is to be evaluated neither as a literary nor as a philosophical book; the ideas, events and presentiments of the times are reflected in the amusing sketches of a strong, often stubborn personality" (Das Königsbuch ist weder als literarisches noch als philosophisches, sondern als Zeitbuch zu werten; die Ideen, Geschehnisse und Ahnungen der Zeit spiegeln sich in den lustigen Zeichnungen einer starken, oft eigenwilligen Persönlichkeit) (35). For him, there is then no question of literary value. Frels is also critical of her politics; he finds her lacking in sophistication. In spite of his dismissal of the book's literary value, Frels devotes the third chapter to structural and stylistic analysis, titling it, "Literary Accoutrement and Style of *The King's Book*" (Literarische Einkleidung und Stil des Königsbuchs). Even if one sets out to discount the literary issues, they seem unavoidable when dealing with Bettina Brentano-von Arnim's work.

Critical Reception: 1923–1945

The issues of form and content continue to dominate the critical literature during this period. A body of criticism begins to take shape, but the discussion takes place almost exclusively in dissertations written by women. Male critics express interest in her only because of her relationship with Goethe. Paul Beyer describes again the specific changes she made to her original correspondence with Goethe. His examination goes farther than Oehlke's in analyzing specific changes as to their literary effect. He is in no doubt as to her abilities as an author. From the perspective of the 1920s, Bettina Brentano-von Arnim's place within the history of Romanticism is secure. Some authors, however, do not see her association with the ideals of this era as admirable. Heinz Strobl, for example, views the formlessness of her books as "the pinnacle of Romantic literature" (der Gipfel der romantischen Literatur) (40). Furthermore, he reduces her subjectivity to mere egotism (51).

The nascent women's movement of the 1920s encouraged a whole generation of women to pursue an education. In historical and literary studies they searched for feminist models and precursors. Irmgard Tanneberger puts Bettina Brentano-von Arnim's life in a feminist context in her study of Romantic women. She explains that although Brentano-von Arnim very rarely commented on the situation of women in her works, Bettina Brentano-von Arnim's life itself is an assertion of her views. Tanneberger recognizes how Brentano-von Arnim's insistence on her own unique individuality prevented her from feeling solidarity with other women (79). Brentano-von Arnim can serve as a model of public activity, Tanneberger believes (82). Helene Stöcker, who wanted to write her dissertation on Bettina Brentano-von Arnim but was not permitted to, published an article in a women's journal. She also sees Brentano-von Arnim as a model. Stöcker states, "that she was the first modern woman in Germany" (daß sie der erste moderne weibliche Mensch in Deutschland war) (100). Stöcker, unlike Tanneberger, tempers her opinion of Bettina Brentano-von Arnim's literary abilities: "Thus she would have indeed become one of the greatest women writers of all time if she had possessed just one thing: the secret of form" (So wäre sie in der Tat eine der größten Dichterinnen aller Zeiten geworden, wenn sie noch eins besessen hätte: das Geheimnis der Form) (102).

In the 1930s dissertations by women on Bettina Brentano-von Arnim began to appear. Each scholar takes up the issues of form and subjectivity. What is new are their often feminist approaches to these topics and an investigation of what might be called Bettina Brentano-von Arnim's philosophy. The focus by earlier male editors and critics on the philological problems surrounding the correspondence books and the original letters, and on biographical details, never led to substantive analyses of the content of the books. In many of the dissertations attempts are made, with varying degrees of success, to begin the process of interpretation. Selma Steinmetz enunciates this in the title of her 1931 dissertation: "Bettina Brentano: Persönlichkeit, Künstlertum und Gedankenwelt." The addition of the third term (her ideas) is significant. Steinmetz begins her analysis by setting aside the question of form. She declares the books unique to German literature: "they are in their content and their form completely original, not to be categorized within a specific literary genre" (sie sind nach ihrem Gehalt und ihrer Form durchaus originell, einer bestimmten Literaturgattung nicht einzuordnen) (2–3). They are neither "Poetry" (Dichtung) nor "Truth" (Wahrheit) and are not comparable with Goethe's autobiography (3). While these declarations do not provide a solution to the problem, by setting the issue aside Steinmetz leaves herself free to discuss the content of the books and Brentano-von Arnim's view of the world. The quality of the interpretations is uneven, but their mere presence is of major significance. Steinmetz also portrays Brentano-von Arnim as a foremother of the women's movement: "The development of the women's movement is already clearly recognizable here" (Die Entwicklung der Frauenbewegung ist hier schon deutlich zu erkennen) (72–73).

Hilde Wyss's excellent 1935 contribution to Bettina Brentano-von Arnim scholarship, "Bettina von Arnims Stellung zwischen der Romantik und dem Jungen Deutschland," confronts the image of the author as a romantic child. In Wyss's opinion, she was not herself so much an actor on the political stage as she was a motivator of men. She was not a pragmatic politician, but a political idealist (8). Brentano-von Arnim was influenced in her romantic view of the state by Novalis, Friedrich Schlegel, and Adam Müller. In her expression of these ideals as well as her actions on behalf of the poor and the accused Mieroslawski and Kinkel, she moves beyond romantic theories to demanding real changes (49). But Wyss criticizes Brentano-von Arnim's failure to develop a coherent political program. Like Stöcker and Steinmetz, Wyss defends Brentano-von Arnim's lack of expressed enthusiasm for the women's movement: "She never spoke of women's emancipation in general, although she has always advocated independence for women" (Sie sprach nie von Frauenemanzipation im allgemeinen, obschon sie immer für die Selbständigkeit der Frau eingetreten ist) (76). Wyss's study is the last for quite a while explictly to speak of the women's movement.

The remaining studies to be discussed in this section were all completed under the specter of National Socialism.[20] They are less global in scope than earlier studies. Elfriede Bansa wrote her 1938 dissertation on "Bettina von Arnims Verhältnis zur Kunst." She examines all of Brentano-von Arnim's artistic endeavors: music, drawing, painting, monument design, and of course her literary works, including the

Märchen. Bansa also elucidates Brentano-von Arnim's opinions on others' artistic works. In addition, she emphasizes the role that music played in the development of Bettina Brentano-von Arnim's writing style (31–44). Although Bansa is impressed by Brentano-von Arnim's artistry, she observes: "But she never fully succeeded in giving the stories of her fantasies a tangible form in a complete work of art" (aber es gelang ihr nie völlig, den Geschichten ihrer Phantasien greifbare Gestalt zu geben in einem geschlossenen Kunstwerk) (11).

In "Bettinas Weltbild" Gertrud Grambow attempts to outline Brentano-von Arnim's philosophy. She begins by addressing the question of form; "but it cannot be overlooked that Bettina's epistolary novels as well are not only memoirs but are also consciously constructed literary works" (aber es darf doch nicht übersehen werden, daß auch Bettinas Briefromane nicht nur Lebenserinnerungen, sondern bewußt gestaltete Dichtungen sind) (6). Grambow also recognized that Brentano-von Arnim created a character for herself in the epistolary books who should not be mistaken for the author (5–6). She expresses regret, however, that Brentano-von Arnim never clearly formulated her "Weltanschauung" (8). Bettina Brentano-von Arnim's philosophy is completely detached from active politics here. Grambow goes on to trace Brentano-von Arnim's use of terms such as "spirit," "genius," and "nature" (Geist, Genius, Natur) to describe her admiration of patriarchs. Grambow's analyses are of very uneven quality.

Two dissertations by men concentrate on *Goethes Briefwechsel* and on Goethe's mother. Hans Hajek's "Die Mythisierung der Frau Rath durch Bettina Brentano" manages to talk about *Dies Buch gehört dem König* without detailing Brentano-von Arnim's politics. He merely attributes Frau Rat's statements to Bettina Brentano-von Arnim, which is hardly surprising since she is the author (93). His project is fundamentally philological: he separates the historical Frau Rat Goethe from Brentano-von Arnim's portrayal of her. Karl Walde also begins his dissertation, "Goethes Briefwechsel mit einem Kinde und seine Beurteilung in der Literaturgeschichte," with a comparison of the book with the actual correspondence. His dissertation is the first to trace the history of one book's reception.

It is difficult to categorize Ina Seidel's book, *Bettina*. Published in 1944, her narrative reflects the influence of National Socialist rhetoric, but not so very much its ideas. Seidel's interpretation of Bettina Brentano-von Arnim's life is relatively balanced. Her biography sets out to trace the process of Brentano-von Arnim's "self-discovery"

(Selbstentdeckung) (27). Seidel does not ignore the effect Brentano-
von Arnim's marriage and the birth of seven children had on this
process. She calls the epistolary books "literature of high rank" (Dichtung vom Range) (46).

The critical reception from 1923 to 1945 was marked by several
new developments. Substantial dissertations were written on Bettina
Brentano-von Arnim, establishing a history of scholarly criticism.
Some of these studies are clearly feminist in approach, while others
indicate a retreat from the political. And many begin the essential
task of more closely interpreting her epistolary books.

Critical and Popular Reception: 1945–1970

During this period there is a profusion of critical studies, dissertations, and biographies. Gustav Konrad's edition was published, in the
GDR Meyer-Hepner completed her investigation of some of Bettina
Brentano-von Arnim's political writings, Vordtriede published several articles and editions, and Ingeborg Drewitz wrote her landmark
biography. But in spite of the wide variety of publications, Brentano-
von Arnim remained in the popular mind an interesting historical
personality. Her writings did not penetrate the literary canon. Feminist interpretations are hardly to be found until the re-emergence of
the women's movement at the beginning of the 1970s. Solely for
purposes of discussion, the material on Bettina Brentano-von Arnim
written during this period can be divided into several groups each to
be discussed separately: the West German critical editions and literature, the discoveries in the GDR, and popular portrayals.

After the war, a new series of dissertations by women appeared.
Hilde Beck's continues the trend of focusing on one aspect of Bettina
Brentano-von Arnim's work. In "Die Bedeutung der Natur in dem
Lebensgefühl der Bettina von Arnim," Beck traces Brentano-von
Arnim's philosophy of nature and the spirit, stressing the importance
of the organic in her writing and even in her political activities (6). For
Beck, every idea and concept in Brentano-von Arnim's life and works
is organic: "Nature, and above all the organic realm, is the foundation
of her being, the point of departure of her thought, the element for
Bettina and the sphere which assumes the broadest place in her
thoughts and feelings" (Die Natur, vor allem der vegetative Bereich,
ist der Grund ihres Seins, der Ausgangspunkt ihres Denkens, das Ele-

ment für Bettina und die Sphäre, die den breitesten Raum in ihrem Denken und Fühlen einnimmt) (30). The fragmentary character of her works lies, according to Beck, "in her roots in the organic realm" (an ihrer Verwurzelung im vegetativen Bereich) (114). Like Zurlinden, Beck also sees evidence of Neoplatonism in Brentano-von Arnim's philosophy (64–65). Helge Nyssen, on the other hand, observes that Brentano-von Arnim uses the terms "nature," "spirit," and "God" (Natur, Geist, Gott) as symbols for a basic life-giving principle. Nyssen is the first to interpret the *Königsbücher* in detail and to assert that Bettina Brentano-von Arnim did have a consistent revolutionary politics: "Without committing herself to a program or thoroughly developing one of her own, she remains almost unwaveringly true to her oppositional-revolutionary stance" (Ohne auf ein Programm zu schwören oder ein—durchgehendes eigenes zu entwickeln, bleibt sie doch immer ihrer oppositionell—revolutionären Grundhaltung und damit aller Sprunghaftigkeit zum Trotz fast einer einheitlichen Linie treu) (141). She also points out the importance of the dialogue form for Brentano-von Arnim (169). In an article written about the same time, Helge Pross distinguishes between Brentano-von Arnim's revolutionary social ideas about the poor and her political ideas which she feels are not revolutionary (100).

Anneliese Hopfe and Maria Zimmermann address in their dissertations the essential question of the form of the works. Hopfe's existentialist approach to Bettina Brentano-von Arnim's understanding of the creative process requires her first to examine Brentano-von Arnim's own sense of self. She notes: "The areas of her 'creative understanding' as they manifest themselves in her work are based in self-understanding and self-encounter" (Die Bereiche ihres 'schöpferischen Verstehens', wie sie sich in ihrem Werk manifestieren, sind im Selbstverstehen und um Selbstbegegnen gegründet) (32–33). Hopfe then analyzes Bettina Brentano-von Arnim's relationship to other artists such as Hölderlin and Goethe. Although she demonstrates Brentano-von Arnim's strong feelings for poetry and music, Hopfe denies Bettina Brentano-von Arnim her own identity as a writer: "She never feels herself to be a poetic writer" (Sie fühlt sich niemals als Dichterin) (105). Hopfe bases this on Brentano-von Arnim's own repeated reluctance to name and categorize her own works. By refusing to speak directly about the works as literature, Brentano-von Arnim contributed to the subsequent negative evaluation of the literary value her work. At the end of her study, Hopfe

answers the question regarding the nature of her works in the negative: "But are Bettina's works literary? Are her books 'works of
art'? One cannot answer this question in the affirmative. Bettina
was prohetically talented and poetically inclined. These elements
went into her work. But they were not raised to the level of pure
'genre' " (Aber hat Bettinas Werk mit Dichtung zu tun? Sind ihre
Bücher 'Kunstwerke'? Man wird diese Frage nicht bejahen dürfen.
Bettina war seherisch begabt und poetisch veranlagt. Diese Ele-
mente sind ihrem Werk eingegangen. Aber sie sind nicht zur reinen
'Gattung' erhoben worden] (225).

Maria Zimmermann reaches the same conclusion; Bettina
Brentano-von Arnim had a genial originality which was a product of
" 'innate poetry' " (angeborner Poesie), but this was never formed
into "literature" (Dichtung) (85). This conclusion is quite baffling,
when one considers that Zimmermann called her dissertation: "Bettina von Arnim als Dichterin." Even though she does not consider the
dialogue and letter books to be literature, Zimmermann acknowledges
the importance these forms had for Brentano-von Arnim, enabling her
to express herself through dialogue with another person (12).

Gustav Konrad published Bettina Brentano-von Arnim's collected
works, and in his essays on each of the books, he places each work
within its historical and biographical context and presents an overview of the reception, emphasizing reviews by her contemporaries.
Konrad does not provide interpretations, but he does express his
opinion. He calls *Clemens Brentanos Frühlingskranz* a "memory
book" (Erinnerungsbuch), because Arnim added to the letters what
she remembered about her brother. For this reason, Konrad believes
it is irrelevant that she altered the original correspondence (1:538). In
writing about *Die Günderode*, he directly confronts the issue of
genre:

> *Günderode* is neither a biography nor a novel in letters, even though
> this term has established itself since Oehlke's dissertation. The book is
> poetry and truth, a portrayal transformed through poetry and born in
> her spirit. What applies to the *Spring Wreath* and to *Goethe's Corre-*
> *spondence with a Child* applies to *Günderode*—that this book is any-
> thing but a historical source. The three books containing the story of
> her childhood and youth are true but not real.
>
> *Die Günderode* ist weder eine Biographie noch ein Roman in Briefen,
> wenn auch dieser terminus seit Oehlkes Dissertation sich eingebürgert

hat. Das Buch ist Dichtung und Wahrheit, eine durch die Dichtung verklärte und aus ihrem Geist geborene Schilderung. Wie für den *Frühlingskranz* und *Goethes Briefwechsel mit einem Kinde* gilt auch für *Die Günderode*, daß dies Buch alles andere ist als eine historische Quelle. Die drei Bücher der Geschichte der Kindheit und Jugend Bettinens sind wahr, aber nicht wirklich. (1:557)

These sentiments are repeated in his comments on *Goethes Briefwechsel*: "The criticism quickly determined that this was no authentic correspondence but literature" (Die Kritik hat bald festgestellt, daß hier kein authentischer Briefwechsel vorlag, sondern Dichtung) (2:719). *Ilius Pamphilius und die Ambrosia* differs from the other epistolary books because it was written with future publication in mind and because in it she is sharing the wisdom of her vast experience with a younger correspondent (2:746). Konrad prefers the epistolary books to the *Königsbücher*. He finds her politics difficult to define; they are neither completely romantic nor socialist (3:450). These works are not to be understood from the perspective of their political expression or content. "That leads either to exaggerations and historical misunderstanding or to a neglect of form" (Das führt entweder zu Übertreibungen und geschichtlichem Mißverstehen oder zu einer Vernachlässigung der Form) (3:489).

Konrad's general good opinion of Brentano-von Arnim's writings extends even to her *Gritta* fairy tale. In it he sees the mastery of the narrative form not found in her epistolary books (*Märchen* 224). In an article for Benno von Wiese's *Deutsche Dichter der Romantik*, Konrad summarizes his views on Bettina Brentano-von Arnim as an author: he does not think that the epistolary books should be read either as literary memoirs or as autobiography. Instead, they portray through both their form and content the world and society, and the culture and spirit of the time (312-313). As "Poetry and Truth" (Dichtung und Wahrheit) her books are literary works, but not in the traditional sense that the author is assumed to be detached from the work (311).

Werner Vordtriede has contributed to Bettina Brentano-von Arnim scholarship by publishing previously unavailable texts by her. In his publication of the Döring correspondence, the Teplitz manuscripts, and the *Armenbuch*, and in an article on her English translation of *Goethes Briefwechsel*, Vordtriede adds to the body of Brentano-von Arnim's literary works. He calls the Döring correspondence a "romantic novel" (Liebesroman) (479) and insists, "that here one is encountering literature, a work by Bettina" (daß man hier eine Dichtung vor sich hat, ein Werk Bettinas) (482). Vordtriede contends that the erotic scene portrayed in the Teplitz fragments was probably intended as a part of *Goethes Briefwechsel*, but was not included by Bettina Brentano-von Arnim.[21] In his opinion, the *Armenbuch* is clearly in the same class as the *Königsbücher* (1962 ed. 418). Vordtriede even asserts in his article that her English translation be treated as an independent work (271–272). Based on Vordtriede's article, a long study was done by Collins and Shelley on the reception of Bettina Brentano-von Arnim in England and America.

In 1968 a biography of Bettina Brentano-von Arnim's youth was published. Written by Werner Milch in the late 1930s and intended as the first part of a complete biography, the book was never finished. Peter Küpper edited and published the manuscript.[22] Milch provides important insights into Brentano-von Arnim's early development. However, his findings were somewhat outdated in several respects by the time they were published. Although Milch is correct in recognizing the autobiographical structure of the epistolary books, he uses this to justify quoting from them as if they were historical documents (69). Milch also criticizes those who see Brentano-von Arnim as an emancipated woman or as a political activist (47).

Criticism in the German Democratic Republic has centered on Bettina Brentano-von Arnim's political activities. As early as 1949, Jürgen Kuczynski published Brentano-von Arnim's texts relating to the Polish independence movement. Lore Mallachow's short popular biography, published in 1952, distances itself from the tradition of Goethe-dominated portraits by lamenting: "It is Bettina's tragedy that she is always drawn by Goethe's star and all light pales next to him" (Es ist Bettinas Tragik, daß sie immer wieder vom Gestirn Goethes angezogen wird und alles Licht neben ihm verblaßt) (12). Mallachow divides Brentano-von Arnim's works into "epistolary novels" (Briefromane) and "political writings" (politische Schriften) (46). She emphasizes Brentano-von Arnim's political and social endeavors. Gisela Kähler, who edited an anthology of Brentano-von Arnim's writings for popular consumption, provides a very good short biography. It is broader in scope than the more scholarly criticism of the German Democratic Republic. In her view, the epistolary books are neither a chronicle or a history but are "confession and knowledge" (Bekenntnisse und Erkenntnisse) Brentano-von Arnim shared in dialogue with those close to her (38). A book by Karl-Heinz Hahn, *Bettina von Arnim in ihrem Verhältnis zu Staat und Politik*, introduces new letters and emphasizes Bettina Brentano-von Arnim's historical importance. Her social activities are not to be viewed as naive or as stereotypically feminine charity work but as conscious humanistic and political action (46). In 1965 Ursula Püschel devoted her dissertation to "Bettina von Arnims politische Schriften." She also wrote a short piece on the *Magistratsprozess*.

Gertrud Meyer-Hepner published articles, letters, and the texts of the *Magistratsprozess*. She views Brentano-von Arnim as a unique personality, whose ideas and style can only be termed "Bettinaish," (Bettinaisch) belonging neither to Romanticism nor to Young Germany (Junges Deutschland) (28–29). Even in the texts of the *Magistratsprozess*, Brentano-von Arnim's language is "literary" (dichterisch) (28). Meyer-Hepner separates the form of Brentano-von Arnim's writing from the context in her article, "Das Bettina von Arnim Archiv:" "Bettina is only romantic in form. The content of her works goes beyond the social situation of her days, pointing far ahead past the ideology and political will of her time and beyond its possibilities" (Bettina ist nur der Form nach romantisch. Der Inhalt ihrer Werke geht vom gesellschaftlichen Sein ihrer Tage zukunftsweisend weit über die Ideologie und den politischen Willen ihrer Zeit und über deren Möglichkeiten hinaus) (594). Yet she is not indifferent to the issue of form. In another article, a reply to an essay by Schoof, she insists that each of the letter books was published as a "work of art" (Kunstwerk) ("Kritik" 236). Meyer-Hepner also criticizes the West German response to the 100th anniversary of Bettina Brentano-von Arnim's death in an article comparing the related publications in East and West Germany.

In the Federal Republic of Germany the popular response by male and some female critics still focused on her relationship with Goethe and repeated the clichés depicting her as goblin, child, and sibyl (Kobold, Kind, Sybille). In a 1949 biography, Heinrich Lilienfein underscores all the stereotypical images. He belittles her political efforts when he notes: "A political dilettante—that was Bettina too" (Eine Dilettantin der Politik—das war auch Bettina) (163). Another popular biography, by Carmen Kahn-Wallerstein, reflects the feminine ideals of the 1950s. She interprets Brentano-von Arnim's life in terms of her love relationships with men—particularly Goethe and her husband. A third popular biography, this one by Hans von

Arnim, contains no new insights. He asserts that Brentano-von Arnim remained in her actions, stubbornness, "and was also in her boundless devotion a child, and remained one her whole life long" (und dann in ihrer grenzenlosen Hingabe ein Kind, und sie ist es ihr Leben lang geblieben) (40). He also maintains: "She has little understanding of politics" (Für Politik hat sie wenig Sinn) (46). Wulf Segebrecht, in the afterword to his edition of the *Frühlingskranz*, combines an analysis of Bettina Brentano-von Arnim's sense of self with her choice of form. He does not believe that the artistic qualities of the letters stand in opposition to an expression of the truth in them (261). He places Brentano-von Arnim's epistolary book in its own special genre category: "The result of her work is neither a documentary work nor an epistolary novel nor a narrative in letters; it is a book in a literary genre which does not exist outside of Bettina's work" (Das Ergebnis ihrer Arbeit ist weder ein Dokumentarwerk noch ein Briefroman oder eine Brieferzählung; es ist das Buch einer literarischen Gattung, die es außerhalb des Werkes der Bettina nicht gibt) (270). Segebrecht treats the book as a literary work.

The appearance in 1969 of Ingeborg Drewitz's biography, *Bettine von Arnim. Romantik—Revolution—Utopie* marks the most significant turning point in the development of Brentano-von Arnim criticism. Reaching both an academic and a popular audience, her biography set a new standard for Bettina Brentano-von Arnim criticism.[23] Hers is the first biography to incorporate the materials and findings of the postwar letter collections and editions. Following its publication, articles and books on von Brentano-von Arnim that contain significant biographical errors, ignore her political activities, or overlook the difference between the original letters and documents and the published works can only be attributed to incompetent and negligent scholarship. Drewitz divides Brentano-von Arnim's life into halves. The first half of her life is dominated by her lack of independence as she fulfills her roles as family member, wife, and mother. The second half of her life began after Achim von Arnim's death; Drewitz calls this second phase "her own life" (ihr eigenes Leben), because finally she was able to develop her potential (7). Drewitz's observations are somewhat psychological in tone as she traces Brentano-von Arnim's development from dependence on male figures and self-doubt to independence. Although she does not discuss at length the literary issue of form, Drewitz makes a crucial statement regarding the original correspondence: "Her family always viewed her letters as literature"

(Die Familie hat ihre Briefe ja schon immer als Literatur begriffen) (151). Brentano-von Arnim herself did not acknowledge the letter form as a literary mode of expression until she began to publish the correspondences (33–34), but that does not mean that even the original letters may not have literary value. Drewitz devotes a substantial portion of the book to Bettina Brentano-von Arnim's political books and activities. After finding herself through her work on the first epistolary books, Brentano-von Arnim is then able to turn outward. Drewitz concludes with the assertion that love was the motivating force in Bettina Brentano-von Arnim's life: "These two extreme experiences encompass Bettina's life: the fulfillment in love of the ego and the desire for love by those who are in need" (Diese beiden extremen Erfahrungen, die Vollendung des Ich in der Liebe und das Verlangen derer, die in Not sind, nach der Liebe, umspannen Bettines Leben) (287).

The Rediscovery of Bettina von Arnim: 1970–1988

The student movement of the late 1960s and early 1970s and the women's movement demanded a fresh look at the literary canon and historical figures in both Europe and America. Critics begin to reinterpret Bettina Brentano-von Arnim's childlike image and to stress her intellectual and political development. Sibylle von Steinsdorff, who published Brentano-von Arnim's correspondence with Max Prokop in 1972, asserts that as early as 1810 she was consciously playing the role of a child: "The childlike, however, has already become a role for Bettina, a consciously chosen form of existence" (Das Kindliche ist jedoch für Bettine schon jetzt zur Rolle geworden, zur bewußt gesuchten Daseinsform) (36). The correspondence with Prokop revealed Brentano-von Arnim's exposure to contemporary religious philosophies during her stay in Munich and Landshut. These later influenced her relationship with Schleiermacher and her social consciousness. Moltmann-Wendel claims that later in Brentano-von Arnim's life: "The religion of being oneself has become the religion of a socially critical conscience" (Die Religion des Selbstseins ist zur Religion des sozialkritischen Gewissens geworden) (414).

Two very different biographies by Reuschle and Dischner were published in 1977. Neither compares in scope and accuracy with the biography by Drewitz, but both are, although in different ways, competent introductions to Bettina Brentano-von Arnim's life and works. Reuschle's book, *An der Grenze einer neuen Welt. Bettina von Arnims Botschaft vom freien Geist*, is very much in the style of the biographies from the late 1940s and 1950s. She only departs from these older books in her interpretation of the prime motivating force in Brentano-von Arnim's life. Instead of attributing all of her work to love, Reuschle identifies Brentano-von Arnim's spirituality. Although Reuschle's book provides few remarkable insights, she does not have any doubts as to the literary value of both the original letters and the epistolary books: "The letter as well as the correspondence was a legitimate art form" (Der Brief und ebenso der Briefwechsel als Kunstform war legitim) (183). The *Königsbuch* lacks, in her view, a clear plan or system: "they are simply essays in dialogue form loosely connected to one another" (es sind lediglich lose aneinander gefügte Essays in Gesprächsform) (230). The reader senses in Reuschle's narration a lack of overtly expressed enthusiasm for her topic.

Gisela Dischner's book, on the other hand, is a product of enthusiasm and is quite provocative in its theses. *Bettina von Arnim. Eine weibliche Sozialbiographie aus dem neunzehnten Jahrhundert* is one of the most widely read of the paperback biographies. It is a mixture of comment and excerpts from the published works and the documents. Dischner is inconsistent in her use of terms. On the title page, she notes that the excerpts will be taken "from the epistolary novels and documents" (aus Briefromanen und Dokumenten), and yet her first excerpts from Bettina von Arnim are taken from the *Königsbuch*. The biographical time-line [*Zeittafel*] and the bibliography are not error free. But in spite of its technical faults, Dischner makes an important contribution to Brentano-von Arnim scholarship in several respects. First, even though Dischner rather uncritically portrays Brentano-von Arnim from a feminist perspective as an emancipated woman, she sets a precedent for dealing with this issue. She boldly claims about Brentano-von Arnim: "She apparently did not feel oppressed as a woman unlike other women of the Romantic era" (Sie fühlte sich offensichtlich als Frau nicht unterdrückt, im Unterschied zu anderen Romantikerinnen) (11). Anyone who has read Bettina Brentano-von Arnim's letters to her husband knows that this was not the case. Second, she identifies "Romantic sociability" (romantische Geselligkeit) as the basis for Brentano-von Arnim's use of epistolary and dialogue forms. Like Rahel Varnhagen, Bettina Brentano-von Arnim had the courage "to view her letters as an art form, as a literary realization of romantic sociability" (ihre Briefe als Kunstform zu betrachten, als schriftliche Realisation romantischer Geselligkeit) (13). Also, in her very idealized depiction of the *Geselligkeit* of the Romantic salon, Dischner increases awareness of Brentano-von Arnim's own salon, even though she mistakenly places it far too early in her life. And finally, Dischner virtually ignores Bettina Brentano-von Arnim's relationship with Goethe and focuses on her friendship with Karoline von Günderrode. The accentuation of this female friendship over the relationship to Goethe has become a salient element in much of the recent criticism by women.

Christa Wolf's essays on Bettina Brentano-von Arnim and Karoline von Günderrode, her editions of Günderrode's works and *Die Günderode*, and her book, *No Place on Earth* (Kein Ort. Nirgends) all appeared in 1979.[24] Her writings had an enormous influence, increasing the popular and the scholarly interest in nineteenth-century women writers in both East and West Germany. Her work has placed Brentano-von Arnim's relationship with Günderrode in the forefront of scholarly interest, displacing Goethe, and dramatically boosted the interest in Günderrode's own life and works.

Wolf's essay on Bettina Brentano-von Arnim, written in the form of a letter to a friend, addresses the issues of form and subjectivity from the outset. The essay is titled: "Your Next Life Begins Today: A Letter about Bettine" (Nun ja! Das nächste Leben geht aber heute an. Ein Brief über die Bettine) (See the reprint of Wolf's essay in this volume). Wolf distinguishes three periods in Brentano-von Arnim's life: her childhood and youth until her marriage in 1811, the years of her marriage from 1811 to 1831, and the years in which she published her books and was politically active—her "third life" (drittes Leben) (291).

In Bettina Brentano-von Arnim's epistolary books she is able to create her own image (289). Brentano-von Arnim later used this self-created childlike image as a protective device in order to say what she pleased—"because only a child is allowed to say: the emperor is naked" (weil nur einem Kinde zu sagen erlaubt ist: Der Kaiser ist nackt) (286). The protection, however, also kept her from being taken seriously. "In grave times it can protect one not to be taken completely seriously" (In ernsten Zeiten kann es ein Schutz sein, nicht ganz ernstgenommen zu werden), Wolf observes regarding Brentano-von Arnim's political role.

In this essay, Wolf places *Die Günderode* within the context of

Brentano-von Arnim's political efforts, which began in earnest just after she completed this book. In Wolf's view, *Die Günderode* represents the attempt of two women to develop in opposition to the prevailing bourgeois conventions. Put simply, the book offers a feminist alternative: "An alternative, indeed. Conceived of and offered at a time when the weak were set irrevocably on exploiting nature, on inverting means and ends, and on surpressing each and every 'feminine' element in the new civilization" (Eine Alternative, ja. Gedacht und angeboten zu einer Zeit, da die Weichen gerade unwiderruflich auf Ausbeutung der Natur, auf die Verkehrung von Mittel und Zweck und auf die Unterdrückung eines jeden 'weiblichen' Elements in der neuen Zivilisation gestellt waren) (314). Wolf could just as well be making this comment about her own time, and in a sense here, she is. The problem, as she sees it, lies in the form and tone of Brentano-von Arnim's expression of her alternative. Wolf observes in her essayistic letter that when she reads these texts she is "more doubtful than confident, that the reader, the female reader of today who is used to thinking prosaically and matter-of-factly will be able to tolerate at all this dithyrambic language, this often gushy tone, and these excesses" (zweifelnd ehe denn zuversichtlich, daß der Leser, die Leserin von heute, gewöhnt, nüchtern und sachbezogen zu denken, diese dithyrambische Sprache, diesen oft schwärmerischen Ton, diese Ausschweifungen überhaupt ertragen werden) (309).[25] And yet Wolf had to have some hope or she would not have put out the edition under her name.

For Wolf, the structure of the book reveals Bettina Brentano-von Arnim's direct response to a literary aesthetic that was inextricably bound to a repressive social structure (316). Only Brentano-von Arnim's unique epistolary form of "letter-book" (Brief-Buch) is capable of adequately expressing her experience (310). The connection made here between form and experience is not entirely new to Bettina Brentano-von Arnim criticism, but stated as it is here in a feminist context and in the light of the theories of the contemporary women's movement, the observation assumes new connotations.

Gertrud Mander's 1982 short biography also addresses the linkage of form and subjectivity, but with different results. Mander posits a different motivating factor behind Bettina von Arnim's creativity: "In reality Bettina was an author whose creativity came from her eros and not from human kindness" (In Wirklichkeit war Bettina eine Autorin, die aus dem Eros und nicht aus der Menschenliebe heraus schöpferisch wurde) (128). While Mander is indeed correct in recognizing how Brentano-von Arnim eroticizes all her relationships with men (41), her thesis cannot explain either *Die Günderode* or the dialogue books. She does not see how Brentano-von Arnim's eroticized relationships could be a positive force. Instead, Mander interprets Bettina Brentano-von Arnim's erotically-charged language in psychological terms as an abnormal fixation. Brentano-von Arnim's erotic musings are excentricities, "which betray abnormal psychic structures which express themselves in all her writings, even in the political ones, as a fantastically excessive need to idolize, as a fixation on idealized objects" (die doch abnormale seelische Strukturen verraten, was sich in all ihren Schriften—auch den politischen—als ein phantastisch übersteigertes Anbetungsbedürfnis äußert, eine Fixierung auf idealisierte Objekte) (139).

A much more sophisticated portrayal of Bettina Brentano-von Arnim using psychoanalytic methods is the article by Friedrich Kittler, "Writing into the Wind, Bettina." Using Lacanian psychoanalytic theories, Kittler recognizes a plurality of female selves in Bettina von Arnim (37). He does not focus on her subjectivity, because "the only escape from becoming a subject, or rather, from becoming subjugated, is to write into the wind" (42). Kittler sees her writing as motivated by desire. In Lacanian terms, desire is a disruptive force in organized, repressed, bourgeois society. The attempt to fit her works into established literary categories is a ruse "of the universal conspiracy for the misconstruing of desire" (64). Kittler also discusses Bettina von Arnim in his article, "Autorschaft und Liebe," where he interprets her love for Goethe as love for the embodiment of authorship (160).

During the first half of the 1980s, studies by male critics appeared on various aspects of Bettina Brentano-von Arnim's life and on her relationships with men who were either not included in her books or who played only marginal roles in them. In addition, her influence on other writers was also explored. For example, David Bellos examined the connection between "Balzac and Goethe's Bettina." Ralph-Rainer Wuthenow wrote an article on the image of Hölderlin in *Die Günderode*.[26] In the Hölderlin passages, Brentano-von Arnim presents her philosophy of the musicality of language. Beethoven is discussed in *Goethes Briefwechsel* and *Ilius Pamphilius*. Brentano-von Arnim has been included in two studies on music and literature. One was written by an East German, Johannes Mittenzwei, and one by a West German, Roman Nahrebecky.

Other critics, such as Helmut Kühn and Manfred Schlösser in their article for the catalogue to the 1981 "Prussia Exibition" (Preußen-Ausstellung), prefer to focus on her political relationships and activities.[27] Most recently, this approach to Bettina Brentano-von Arnim's life and works is dominant in both East and West German studies, but is less so in those written in the United States. In her introduction to *Dies Buch gehört dem König*, Ilse Staff places the work within the history of the times and sees the work as a relevant response. She portrays Brentano-von Arnim as a Young German (Junges Deutschland) writer (52–53). Hartwig Schultz, who edited her correspondence with the Grimms, also views Brentano-von Arnim in historical terms. Unlike Staff, he believes that Brentano-von Arnim effortlessly bridged the romantic and restoration periods (16).

In 1980, influenced by Christa Wolf, Ursula Püschel again turned her attention to Bettina von Arnim in her essay collection, *Mit allen Sinnen. Frauen in der Literatur*. In an article taken from her dissertation, Püschel defends her feminist approach by placing women's emancipation in the context of the critique of bourgeois culture (50–51). She quite accurately points out how Brentano-von Arnim was accused of being both feminine and unfeminine, and how both of these are negative labels:

> Thought and action based on feeling without the control of the intellect which is therefore not political—this is the basis for the German literary establishment's qualification of Bettina von Arnim's work as *feminine*. The same reactionary impetus characterized her during her lifetime as *unfeminine*.

> Gefühlsmäßiges Denken und Handeln ohne Kontrolle durch den Verstand, das daher nicht politisch ist—das gehört zum Fundus germanistischer Qualifizierungen des Schaffens der Bettina von Arnim mit dem Prädikat *weiblich*. Der gleiche reaktionäre Impetus charakterisierte sie bei Lebzeiten als *unweiblich*. (70)

Five years later another article by Püschel appeared discussing Bettina Brentano-von Arnim's friendship with Max Prokop and her decision to marry Achim.

The response in 1985 to Bettina Brentano-von Arnim's 200th birthday may indicate that Brentano-von Arnim has finally been accepted as a significant author by mainstream literary critics. The Freies Deutsches Hochstift in Frankfurt, in conjunction with the Goethe-

Museum in Düsseldorf, mounted an exhibition on Bettina Brentano-von Arnim. The catalogue to the exhibition, *Herzhaft in die Dornen der Zeit greifen* . . . *Bettine von Arnim 1785–1859*, edited by Christoph Perels, contains an overview of her life and work, as well as seven essays by different authors on a wide range of topics. Heinz Rölleke investigates Brentano-von Arnim's contributions to *Des Knaben Wunderhorn* and other related projects involving her brother, Achim von Arnim, and the Grimms. He also discusses the *Märchen* she wrote with her daughters (225–231). Konrad Feilchenfeldt examines Brentano-von Arnim's relationships with Rahel and Karl August Varnhagen. He outlines the reception of these women by Young German [Junges Deutschland] writers, Brentano-von Arnim's often turbulent friendship with Rahel Varnhagen, and he notes the importance of Karl August to her later life. Feilchenfeldt believes that Brentano-von Arnim learned how to edit her correspondence from Rahel and Karl August von Varnhagen's edition of Rahel's letters and diaries (241). Sibylle von Steinsdorff contributed a piece on Bettina Brentano-von Arnim and Goethe. Her views are significant because she is the editor of the volume containing *Goethes Briefwechsel mit einem Kinde* in the Klassiker Verlag edition. Steinsdorff underscores the importance of viewing Brentano-von Arnim's original correspondences—her letters to Max Prokop von Freyberg, Pückler, Döring, Nathusius, and Goethe—as "epistolary *novels*" (Brief*romane*) (247). In her examination of the importance Pückler-Muskau had for Brentano-von Arnim, Enid Gajek also focuses on the letter form. She notes that Pückler's own success in publishing his letters inspired Bettina Brentano-von Arnim (255). Hartwig Schultz again concentrates on the hiring of the brothers Grimm at the university in Berlin. Wolfgang Frühwald's essay on her *Armenbuch* and the Silesian weavers assesses Brentano-von Arnim's contribution to the public awareness at the time: "Her literary merit lies in having given the poetics of sympathy of her time an eminently practical component" (Ihr literarisches Verdienst aber liegt darin, daß sie der Mitleidspoetik der Zeit eine eminent lebenspraktische Komponente gegeben hat) (277). The final essay, written by the catalogue editor Christoph Perels, enumerates how Bettina Brentano-von Arnim has herself become a literary figure in the works of twentieth-century authors such as Rilke, Hesse, Günter Eich, Peter Huchel, and Sarah Kirsch.[28]

That same year several articles on Brentano-von Arnim also

appeared, and new editions of *Goethes Briefwechsel* and the *Frühlingskranz* were published (in the Federal Republic and the German Democratic Republic). Increased recognition, however, did not always result in new views of her work. In a second essay, Wolfgang Frühwald discusses Brentano-von Arnim's epistolary books. He maintains the old opinion that while Bettina Brentano-von Arnim was herself poetic, her works are not literature.

> In Bettina's work, which is basically written speech, that is, in a work which is not polished and aesthetically constructed but rather one which, as a work in letters, unified the genial wit of Romanticism with the carefree style of the Biedermeier era, the aesthetic component is not literature but an element of a decidedly poetic life.

> In Bettines im Grunde schriftlich gesprochenem Werk, das heißt in einem Werk, das nicht gefeilt und ästhetisch konstituiert ist, sondern das als ein Briefwerk den genialischen Witz der Romantik mit der stilistischen Sorglosigkeit der Biedermeierzeit vereinte, ist auch die ästhetische Komponente nicht Literatur, sondern Element eines poetisch bestimmten Lebens. (215)

It seems ironic that this statement appeared in the 1985 *Jahrbuch des Freien Deutschen Hochstifts*, the same year that this same group sponsored the exhibition and a reassessment of Bettina Brentano-von Arnim's place in history. Charlotte Craig's use of *Goethes Briefwechsel* as historical document and her uncritical use of terms such as "the Eternal Feminine," is also disheartening. Gert Mattenklott's contribution to a volume on women writers, "Romantische Frauenkultur. Bettina von Arnim zum Beispiel," does not go much beyond the recognition of women's letter writing as a viable autobiographical form for women. Two articles containing new materials on Arnim and Schleiermacher, and on Prinz Lichnowsky, were also published in 1985 (see Patsch and Behrens, respectively).

The editors of the two *Frühlingskranz* editions, Hartwig Schultz and Heinz Härtl, each contributed an afterword. They both put the book in the context of its time. Schultz, however, concentrates on the biographical aspects more than Härtl. He calls for a reading of the *Frühlingskranz* as the first part of her autobiography (344). He correctly identifies the erotic component of Bettina's correspondence with her brother Clemens (348–349). Through her relationships here and in the other two autobiographical epistolary books, the reader can observe the "developmental and educational story of a self-emancipating romantic woman writer" (Entwicklungs und Bildungsge-schichte einer sich—emanzipierenden romantischen Schriftstellerin) (345). Although he acknowledges Brentano-von Arnim's literary accomplishment and the uniqueness of the form she selected, Schultz repeatedly uses the term "popular" (volkstümlich) to describe her metaphors, humor, and political strength. Although he does not intend this to be a pejorative term, in his insistence that "an elevated style is not intended" (ein hoher Stil nicht intendiert ist), one can detect a certain reluctance on his part to equate her works with other Romantic works written in a "higher" style (356). Härtl is much less equivocal in his analysis: "She was not inclined in the slightest in her epistolary novels to reconstruct an authentic, detailed depiction of her past, but one instead which would be illuminated in the light of contemporary problems. The 'Frühlingskranz' is not to be read as a source of information but as a work of art" (Es lag ihr nicht das geringste daran, in ihren Briefromanen ein authentisch-detailgetreues Bild der Vergangenheit zu rekonstruieren, sondern eins, das sich im Licht der aktuellen Probleme erhellte. Der 'Frühlingskranz' ist nicht als Quelle zu lesen, sondern als Kunstwerk) (288). Härtl elaborates on this statement in comparing her "technique of amalgamating Truth and Poetry" (Wahrheit und Dichtung amalgamierende Technik) with the "Historical School" (Historische[n] Schule) of the first half of the nineteenth century for whom history was to be interpreted in the light of present events (288–289). Härtl also outlines the history of the banning of the book.

Besides the new edition, the most recent comprehensive work on Bettina Brentano-von Arnim to appear in the German Democratic Republic is Fritz Böttger's comprehensive biography. Unfortunately, as is the case with all the long biographies, he does not list sources for his quotations. His history of her life is full of psychological insights. For example, he recognizes that the much talked of love that dominated her life before her marriage to Achim was both a defense against marriage and a part of her identity: "At that time love was for Bettina an inner, purely subjective experience which in no way obligated her; it was a self-confirmation and allowed her to avoid any real experience of love" (Liebe war zu jener Zeit für Bettina eine innerliche, rein subjektive Erfahrung, die sie in keiner Weise verpflichtete, ihr eine Selbstbestätigung war und doch ermöglichte, wirklicher Liebeserfahrung aus dem Wege zu gehen) (81). He addresses Brentano-von Arnim's omnipresent eroticism with the same acumen, stating that she was "a panerotic being who hardly distinguished between the different kinds of affection, so that child-like, sisterly, comradely, motherly or impulsive attachments, friend-ships and sympathies all resembled love" (ein panerotisches Wesen, das zwischen den verschiedenen Arten ihrer Zuneigung wenig unter-schied, bei der kindliche, geschwisterliche, kameradschaftliche, müt-terliche oder triebmäßige Zärtlichkeiten, Freundschaften und Sym-pathien alle der Liebe glichen) (115). In describing the form of *Goethes Briefwechsel*, Böttger suggests that Brentano-von Arnim intended to write the kind of "legend of the artist" (Künstler-legende) other Romantics wrote (214). He compares her epistolary books to the contemporary novels by Gutzkow and Mundt and as-serts that, in keeping with that period's tendency to formlessness, her work "asserts itself even today as literary and alive in the power of her language and the poetry of her style" (behauptet sich . . . durch ihre Sprachkraft und die Poesie ihrer Schreibweise bis auf den heutigen Tag als dichterisch und lebendig) (222). Of course, Böttger puts Bettina Brentano-von Arnim's life and works in their historical, social, and, importantly, economic context. He does an excellent job describing her politics and introduces new details. He achieves a remarkable balance between her political books and activities and her early life and the epistolary books.

It seems that with few exceptions the most insightful and penetrat-ing work on Bettina Brentano-von Arnim has been done by women or in the German Democratic Republic. The years from 1984 to 1988 were enormously productive for Brentano-von Arnim scholars. Three essays are of note.

First, Roswitha Burwick's essay on *Die Günderode* (published in the United States) elaborates on the distinction between Brentano-von Arnim as author and character. This separation of writer from character also takes place in the original correspondence. In addition, Brentano-von Arnim is also the editor of the epistolary books (63–65). Burwick, however, is critical of what she calls Brentano-von Arnim's narcissism.

Second, Frederiksen and Shafi also examine *Die Günderode* in their article. They undertake to interprete the book "as a female utopia" (als weibliche Utopie). The work in both its form and content presents a social alternative:

It [the text] is to be read as an historical message in that it describes an alternative conception of society, which contains the vision of a fundamentally changed community. This epistolary novel comprises at the same time concrete utopian practice, for in their friendship Bettine and Karoline realize the ideals which they themselves had proposed. They achieve in their relationship for example a kind of communication free of domination, which combines intellectual exchange with intense emotional devotion.

Er [der Text] ist als historische Botschaft zu lesen, indem er einen gesellschaftlichen Gegenentwurf beschreibt, der die Vision einer grundlegend veränderten Gemeinschaft enthält. Dieser Briefroman umfaßt zugleich gelebte, utopische Praxis, denn in ihrer Freundschaft verwirklichen Bettine und Karoline die von ihnen geforderten Ideale. Sie erreichen beispielsweise in ihrer Beziehung eine herrschaftsfreie Kommunikation, die intellektuellen Austausch mit intensiver emotionaler Hingabe verbindet. (56)

Frederiksen and Shafi emphasize the important role that dialogue plays in the development of Brentano-von Arnim's and Günderrode's utopian alternative. In their analysis, they also refer to contemporary feminist theory and in particular the writings of the French author Hélène Cixous. This new development in Brentano-von Arnim scholarship is, in my view, the only way to extricate Bettina Brentano-von Arnim criticism from the male-defined genre categories which have proved so detrimental to an appreciation of her work.

Third, the essay by Christa Bürger accompanying her collection, *Bettina von Arnim. Ein Lesebuch*, is both penetrating and problematic. She approaches Brentano-von Arnim with the question of Brentano-von Arnim's self-definition. She bases her analysis almost exclusively on theories by Habermas rather than on contemporary feminist theory. Even so, her ideas on Brentano-von Arnim's subjectivity are worth considering. Bürger calls the books "novels of relationship" (Beziehungsromane), but believes they fail because Bettina Brentano-von Arnim's correspondents remain passive (324).

Contemporary feminist studies of Brentano-von Arnim were first published by *Germanistinnen* working in the United States (and this includes Burwick, Frederiksen, and Shafi). Their works, some written in English, have not received enough attention in either West or East Germany. Five new major studies of Bettina Brentano-von Arnim are feminist in approach. Only one was written in West Germany; the

others are American dissertations, or books based on American dissertations. Edith Waldstein and Konstanze Bäumer revised their 1983
dissertations and published them as books. Bäumer's book on von
Arnim and Goethe represents such a substantial revision that it is
really a different and separate study. Waldstein's book suffers from the
five-year delay in publication, since it is not a substantial revision of the
dissertation. Goozé and French have not published revised versions of
their 1984 and 1986 dissertations. Weißenborn's study has appeared in
the Lang series of *Hochschulschriften*.

Waldstein, in her book, *Bettine von Arnim and the Politics of Romantic Conversation*, begins with Dischner's assertion that both the
epistolary and dialogue books were influenced by the culture of "romantic sociability" (romantische Geselligkeit).[29] She summarizes her
thesis in her conclusion:

> A major portion of von Arnim's cultural life, her novels and also her
> political thought embraced three of the primary concepts of romantic
> philosophy: the organic, *Poesie* and *Geselligkeit*. In her interpretation
> of the romantic world view, all three concepts are determined by total
> communication—a free and equal exchange of experience. (94)

Waldstein tries to link both sets of books to the dialogue of the Romantic salon. Her thesis is quite thought-provoking, and I believe works
excellently as a basis for interpreting the dialogue books. However, she
never mentions the ordinary linguistic distinction between actual
speech and written representations of speech regularly employed in
epistolary correspondence and philosophical dialogues. She also does
not account for the publication of at least the first epistolary book
before Brentano-von Arnim herself had a salon, although she attended
others' salons. Waldstein's analysis of Brentano-von Arnim's political
books and activities is very good. As it is currently the only monograph
in English on Brentano-von Arnim, it is regrettable that she did not
provide translations for the quotations.

Konstanze Bäumer and Birgit Weißenborn each interpret Bettina
Brentano-von Arnim's relationship with Goethe. Even though both
take on the same topic, the books are quite different. Bäumer's interpretation is clear and insightful, and relies upon contemporary feminist theory. Weißenborn attempts to write a biography of Brentano-
von Arnim's youth, as well as analyze *Goethes Briefwechsel*. Her
biography relies extensively on Bergemann, and thereby merely re-

peats what is available in many other places. While Weißenborn's review of Brentano-von Arnim's reception by Young German (Junges Deutschland) writers and by her editors is excellent, she does not devote enough attention to her own views. In her overview of the criticism, Weißenborn observes the repetition of the questions about the truth and fictionality of Brentano-von Arnim's work. Weißenborn does not, however, respond by rejecting this sort of philological hairsplitting, but instead wants to overlook the whole issue as a literary question: "The question therefore should not be whether true or false, not for what noble or unnoble reasons it may be false, but rather: when written, in what intellectual context, under which historical circumstances and with what particular intention?" (Die Frage sollte also nicht sein, echt oder falsch, nicht aus welchem edlen oder unedlen Grunde falsch, sondern: wann entstanden, in welchem geistigen Zusammenhang, unter welchen historischen Begdingtheiten und mit welcher jeweiligen Zielsetzung) (135). Weißenborn prefers to view *Goethes Briefwechsel* more as a historical document that is biographical in essence than as a literary work.

Bäumer also makes the crucial distinction between the original correspondence and *Goethes Briefwechsel*, but she focuses on the book, rather than on Brentano-von Arnim's youth. This is the first study actually to analyze the text in depth. In her title, *"Bettine, Psyche, Mignon." Bettina von Arnim und Goethe*, Bäumer uses the two spellings of Brentano-von Arnim's first name to separate the author Bettina from the character Bettine. She also examines Brentano-von Arnim's portrayal of herself as Psyche in her design and description of her Goethe monument, and her identification with Goethe's Mignon character. In addition to Psyche and Mignon, Bäumer also discusses Brentano-von Arnim's treatment of Christiane von Goethe and Jews in *Goethes Briefwechsel*, here comparing the book to the original correspondence. She also outlines the influence the original letters had on some of Goethe's works, as well as Brentano-von Arnim's use of Goethe texts in her book.

By concentrating on one book, Bäumer is able to approach *Goethes Briefwechsel* from a more traditional standpoint, handling it from the outset as a work of art. She therefore begins her study with a review of the research. Bäumer's overview particularly accents the newer studies, including the American dissertations. She then proceeds to trace the history of the writing of the work (Entstehungsgeschichte), explaining the roles played by Pückler-Muskau and Schleiermacher. Her study is the first to really illuminate how Brentano-von Arnim used symbols, interwove motifs, and created a complex literary work.

The dissertations by Marjanne Goozé and Lorely French analyze Brentano-von Arnim's use of the epistolary form. In "Bettine von Arnim, the Writer," Goozé establishes the interconnections between Brentano-von Arnim's actual letter writing and her use of multi-perspectival forms in her epistolary and dialogue books. Goozé asserts that both the original letters and the books can be read and interpreted as literature, and that neither conform to established genre traditions. She situates these books "on the margins of fictionality" (202). In comparing some original letters with the published works, she high-lights the intertextuality of all of Brentano-von Arnim's writings. Analysis of the letters is significant because, "The letters themselves are emblematic of the later works, mixing poetic, philosophical, reli-gious, narrative, and what might be termed informational discourses" (353). Relying on feminist and French psychoanalytic theories, she explores how for Bettina Brentano-von Arnim the language of the letter and the letter itself have the power to engender the presence of the absent correspondent. Goozé also briefly discusses the multipers-pectival structure of Brentano-von Arnim's political writings. She con-cludes in her dissertation that Brentano-von Arnim depended on the presence of the other in her texts to express herself. The chronological approach taken in the dissertation traces the author's development as a writer. Goozé, like Wolf, divides Brentano-von Arnim's life into three stages. However, she also stresses how Bettine was active—at least as a letter-writer—throughout her life.

Goozé's 1987 article, "Desire and Presence: Bettine von Arnim's Erotic Fantasy Letter to Goethe," provides a detailed interpretation of the process of engendering the absent correspondent. Her close read-ing of one letter serves as an example of the kind of detailed literary analysis of both Brentano-von Arnim's original letters and published books that is now beginning to be done. Goozé also demonstrates how it is possible still to take a feminist perspective while acknowledging Brentano-von Arnim's strong attachment to Goethe. In another arti-cle, "'Ja ja, ich bet' ihn an': Nineteenth-Century Women and Goethe," written on Rahel Varnhagen and Bettina Brentano-von Arnim, Goozé describes how Brentano-von Arnim's devotion to Goethe encouraged her intellectual and literary development.

Lorely French's study, "Bettine von Arnim: Toward a Women's

Epistolary Aesthetics and Poetics," is also feminist in approach, takes the newer criticism into account, and focuses on Brentano-von Arnim's epistolarity. French tests the feminist hypothesis that women's letters differ from men's by comparing views on the letter writing of Romantic women and Romantic men and by examining their letters. The first half of her dissertation is devoted to a history of epistolary aesthetics and poetics. Her work is both a contribution to Brentano-von Arnim studies, and most importantly, to anyone working on women's (or men's) letter writing. She concludes that by the early nineteenth-century the importance of letter-writing for men had declined in favor of objective narrative (131–132). But for women of the late eighteenth and early nineteenth centuries, letter writing remained an important and for many the only, form of self-expression. French aligns herself with those who contend that the letters themselves may be literature (133), and notes how Bettina Brentano-von Arnim "recognized in letter-writing an aesthetic mode of expression" (284). In her analysis of Brentano-von Arnim, French shows how her writings exemplify a feminist epistolary aesthetics and poetics, and how they challenge the partriarchal order. French does not attempt to force Brentano-von Arnim to fit into a twentieth-century feminist mold; instead she opens the definition to include Brentano-von Arnim's work within a feminist framework.

> But if we define a feminist work as something that challenges the existing patriarchal order and develops subversive strategies to overcome that order then Bettine's works qualify as such according to subsequent groups of self-acclaimed feminists. Bettine's means of expression entailed a continual defining and redefining of herself and her socialization. For her, self-actualization was necessary before self-assertion. (466)

French continually emphasizes how Bettina Brentano-von Arnim used the writing process as a means of self-evaluation and self-realization. She declines, however, to call the books autobiography, wishing instead to highlight the different narrative qualities of the epistolary form (196–198). It is understandable that French does not want to have Brentano-von Arnim's works subsumed under the more general category of autobiography, particularly because French has such a conservative definition of it. As she sees it, autobiography takes as its normative model works such as Goethe's *Poetry and Truth* (Dichtung und Wahrheit). French's specific interpretations of the epistolary works are cogent and well thought out.

In addition to these books and dissertations, Katherine Goodman's book on nineteenth-century German women's autobiography, *Dis/Closures*, devotes one chapter to Rahel Varnhagen and Bettina von Arnim. Goodman's definition of autobiography begins where French's leaves off. Goodman coins the term "epistolary autobiography," a term that is inclusive rather than exclusive in scope: "epistolary autobiography not only implicitly challenges these genre distinctions, it can also radically challenge philosophical assumptions upon which the very idea of autobiography has been based: the superior truth of a unifying perspective and the very notion of what it means to be an individual" (76). In her book, she makes a critical connection between identity and the form of personal expression chosen by women. For Goodman, Bettina Brentano-von Arnim's epistolary books "can only be properly assessed when viewed as radical autobiography" (91). Goodman realizes that Brentano-von Arnim's tendency to absorb her correspondents is not due to crass egotism, but to the interpersonal nature of women's selves.

She asserts that Brentano-von Arnim's "all-encompassing personality can only be grasped if it is seen in its complexity and generosity" (93). In her conclusion, Goodman expresses the opinion that epistolary autobiography is the form best suited to the expression of eighteenth- and nineteenth-century women's lives. This book not only makes an important contribution to the study of German women's autobiography, but to general theory as well.

It would be nice to end this review of the reception by pointing to an unbroken positive trend in the depth and quality of Brentano-von Arnim scholarship. There is, however, no definitive point in time or one work that marks the beginning of a new era in Bettina Brentano-von Arnim scholarship. Many pieces being published could have been written forty years ago, whereas others appear to belong to this new era, and most criticism falls somewhere in between.

The Rowohlt biography by Helmut Hirsch falls in the middle ground in critical perspective. In May 1987, Bettina Brentano-von Arnim was awarded a place in the series of Rowohlt "Bildmonographien." This biography is an interesting combination of scholarly research and popular rhetoric. Hirsch includes new material on Brentano-von Arnim and provides excellent information on her political activities. His popularizing rhetoric, however, is a bit demeaning to his subject. His chapter on her relationship with Achim von Arnim, titled "The Devoted Wife" (Das treue Weib), focuses more on Achim than on Bettina. The major problem with the book is that, as a historian, he sees Brentano-von Arnim primarily as a historical figure rather than as an artist. In the next to last chapter, "Artist among Artists" (Künstlerin unter Künstlern), Hirsch describes everything except her epistolary books—her music, sculpture, drawing, *Märchen*, and even the translation of *Goethes Briefwechsel*. He never discusses her books individually and seems less comfortable describing her personal relationships than her political activities. Hirsch never explicitly takes up the issue of literary valuation; his major statement of this question is: "Bettina is extremely subjective in her attempt to produce world literature" (Extrem subjektiv ist Bettine in ihrem Bestreben, Weltliteratur hervorzubringen) (113–114). Hirsch also does not review the previous literature on Brentano-von Arnim, but in his conclusion, he points out how a dissertation by Marie-Claire Hoock-Demarle and the new editions will "set the standards for Bettina's rebirth" (Maßstäbe setzen für Bettines Wiedergeburt) (131). The call for her rebirth is unfortunately not new, and in making the call Hirsch overlooks the many fine studies that have appeared since the early twentieth century in East and West Germany. Bettina Brentano-von Arnim does not need to be reborn from the head of the Zeus. Instead, her own works and the long tradition of scholarship devoted to her life and works need to be fully acknowledged.

Marie-Claire Hoock-Demarle wrote her dissertation and several articles on Bettina von Arnim as well as a book on the women of the *Goethezeit*. In her article, "Frau und Stadt," which appeared in a short book of talks published by the Karl-Marx-Haus in Trier, Hoock-Demarle focuses on Brentano-von Arnim's geographical roots in Berlin and Frankfurt. Hoock-Demarle stresses von Brentano-von Arnim's role as a social witness of her times (44). She defines Bettina Brentano-von Arnim's portrayal of nature as " 'cityfied' " (stadtgeprägt), making a brief but convincing argument that counters Hilde Beck's position (48). Her second article, "Bettinas Umgang mit Außenseitern," is more indicative of Hoock-Demarle's general opinion of Brentano-von Arnim. She explores her attraction to Beethoven and Hölderlin; her work for the Greeks, the poor, and other causes; and her public advocacy for the Jews. Hoock-Demarle attributes Brentano-von Arnim's commitment to her own inner struggles, asking: "Or is it not so that her marked preference for unusual cases and people corresponds to an inner search, a search for what is genuinely human in a time of increasing degradation, exploitation and injustice" (Oder ist es nicht so, daß ihre ausgeprägte Vorliebe für ausgefallene Fälle und Menschen einer inneren Suche entspricht, der Suche nach echten Menschen in einer Zeit der zunehmenden Herabwürdigung, der Ausbeutung und des Unrechts) (84). Brentano-von Arnim's overt advocacy for Jews as a group, as well as her often biased treatment of individuals, is perceptively enunciated here. Hoock-Demarle deals with Brentano-von Arnim primarily as a historical figure and does not discuss in these articles her books as literary production.

Two other talks were published with Hoock-Demarle's in the small volume, *Bettine von Arnim. Romantik und Sozialismus (1831–1859)*: one is by Hartwig Schultz and the other by Heinz Härtl. Härtl's is based on his afterword to his edition of *Clemens Brentanos Frühlingskranz*. While Schultz's recalls his other essays relating to the Brothers Grimm and Brentano-von Arnim, in this piece, he provides a most cogent and succinct definition of Brentano-von Arnim as a politician.

> She is in my view a born member of the non-parliamentary opposition. She had a deep repugnance for all organizations, for all established systems, even for philosophical and socio-political theories and principles. Her initiatives always derived from personal experiences and individual human lives. The purpose and intent of these initiatives coincided only temporarily with those of the increasingly visible the political parties in Prussia.

> Sie ist nach meiner Auffassung die geborene außerparlamentarische Oppositionelle. Alle Organisationen, alle festgefügten Systeme, auch philosophische, gesellschaftspolitische Theorien und Prinzipien waren ihr zutiefst verhaßt. Ihre Initiativen gingen stets von persönlichen Erfahrungen und menschlichen Einzelschicksalen aus und deckten sich in ihrer Begründung und Ausrichtung jeweils nur vorübergehend mit den Parteigruppen, wie sie damals in Preußen immer deutlicher in Erscheinung traten. (24)

This small collection of essays reflects the current interest in Brentano-von Arnim's political and social activities.

The latest developments in Bettina Brentano-von Arnim research to be considered here are the establishment of the Bettina-von-Arnim-Gesellschaft and the *Internationales Jahrbuch* published by the society, and the new editions being published in East and West Germany.

The society was founded in 1985 by the staff of the Bettina-von-Arnim-Oberschule in West Berlin. The first yearbook, published in 1987, is part academic journal and part school yearbook. The second volume contains more articles and less school news. The yearbooks are also a valuable source of information on Brentano-von Arnim scholarship, including reviews of articles and books. The *Jahrbuch* includes essays by well-known Bettina Brentano-von Arnim scholars, as well as work by lesser known critics. The quality of the contributions varies widely, from highly scholarly pieces to cliché-ridden effusings.

The first volume of the Jahrbuch contains fine articles by Helmut Hirsch, Konstanze Bäumer, and Wolfgang Bunzel. Hirsch's essay examines "Jüdische Aspekte im Leben und Werk Bettine von Arnims" (Jewish Aspects in the Life and Work of Bettina von Arnim). Hirsch makes a clear distinction between Brentano-von Arnim's idealized depictions of Jews in her books and her actual dealings with Jews. Konstanze Bäumer, who in her book on Brentano-von Arnim had also addressed the author's relationships with Jews, here briefly outlines her reception by Berliners.

The Bunzel essay, " 'Phantasie ist die freie Kunst der Wahrheit.' Bettine von Arnims poetisches Verfahren in 'Goethes Briefwechsel mit einem Kinde,' " emphasizes Brentano-von Arnim's literary accomplishments rather than her historical or political importance. Bunzel's close analysis of one book has as its goal: "to highlight the fictional character of her novels" (den fiktionalen Charakter ihrer Romane sichtbar zu machen) (7). He analyses the narrative strategy of both her original letters and *Goethes Briefwechsel* and identifies a process of double narration which serves her two purposes.

> One of its tasks is to make visible the reality behind the facade of fiction. It could therefore seem as though the demasking of deception in favor of an unvarnished representation of reality were the primary narrative principle in the 'Correspondence.' But in this we have grasped only one of the components of her poetic method in the Goethe book. Complementary to this is the recognizable intention in the poetry to break up and expand the rigid boundaries of the real. Bettina refuses to acknowledge the reality principle without reservation.
>
> Ihre Aufgabe ist es unter anderem, die Realität hinter der Fassade der Fiktion sichtbar werden zu lassen. Es könnte daher scheinen, die

Demaskierung der Täuschung zugunsten einer ungeschminkten Dar-
stellung der Wirklichkeit sei oberstes Erzählprinzip im 'Brief-wechsel.'
Doch damit haben wir nur eine Komponente des poetischen Verfahrens im Goethebuch erfaßt. Komplementär dazu verhält sich die
erkennbare Absicht, in der Poesie die starren Grenzen des Faktischen
aufzubrechen und zu erweitern. Bettine weigert sich, das Realität-
sprinzip vorbehaltlos anzuerkennen. (17)

The second volume of the *Jahrbuch* appeared in 1988. Part of this
issue was dedicated to Helmut Hirsch and his life's work, so there are
fewer articles on Bettina Brentano-von Arnim than there were in the
first volume. Also included is an essay on Robert Blum, in keeping
with the policy of the journal to publish material about Bettina
Brentano-von Arnim's contemporaries. In this volume we can see the
two continuing trends in Brentano-von Arnim research. Taken together they contribute to a balanced view of her life and work. Interest
in her as a political activist predominates in the first trend. The second
trend is marked by a serious literary interest that is producing close
readings of her works. While Heinz Monz traces "Bettine von Arnim
und Karl Marx in Bad Kreuznach" and Hoock-Demarle looks at
Brentano-von Arnim and social outsiders, the long article by Ursula
Liebertz-Grün undertakes a structural analysis of *Clemens Brentanos
Frühlingskranz*.

Liebertz-Grün identifies the major motifs and structures in the
Frühlingskranz. She treats the book as if it had a conventional plot
structure. Through her analysis she seems to construct a plot out of the
fine threads Arnim provides. Liebertz-Grün divides the work into ten
groups of letters; each of these is a variation on the main theme of the
work: "the ideal of harmonious personal development" (das Ideal der
harmonischen Bildung) (96). The structural outline proceeds along
musical lines—the harmonic progression in the work is accomplished
through the development of theme and variation. The *Frühlingskranz*
is handled by Liebertz-Grün almost exclusively as a fictional work.
Bettina and Clemens are therefore treated as main characters. Only at
the end of her article does Liebertz-Grün try to address the autobiographical nature of the epistolary books while at the same time under-
scoring their literary value.

Bettina von Arnim was a learned poet who understood how to play
sovereignly with the varieties of texts, techniques and topoi of the liter-

ary tradition. . . . Her texts are a strictly ordered chaos . . . . Her works have autobiographical character because she is convinced that the artist must reinvent himself true to his fantasy and not according to factuality.

Bettina von Arnim war eine gelehrte Poetin, die mit den Textsorten, Techniken und Topoi der literarischen Tradition souverän zu spielen verstand. . . . Ihre Texte sind ein streng geordnetes Chaos . . . Ihre Werke haben autobiographischen Charakter, weil sie der Überzeugung ist, daß der Künstler sich phantasiegetreu, nicht faktizitätsgetreu wieder erzeugen müsse. (132)

She concludes her article by taking a feminist position regarding Brentano-von Arnim's refusal either to meet nineteenth-century standards for feminine behavior or to proscribe other rules for women (1132-1133). On the issue of canonization, Liebertz-Grün places Brentano-von Arnim's works within a body of world literature today's readers may find difficult but should still read (133). The following article in the *Jahrbuch*, written by Ute Schikorra, stands in contrast to Liebertz-Grün's. Although Schickorra tries to take a feminist position in portraying Brentano-von Arnim's view of love, her effort is unsuccessful because she only discusses Goethe and Günderrode, and because she never differentiates between love and friendship.

The publication in East and West Germany of new critical editions of Bettina Brentano-von Arnim's books seems to be evidence of a positive reassessment of her work.

To date, only the first volume in the West German series and two in the East German series have appeared. The edition published by Klassiker Verlag and edited by Walter Schmitz and Sibylle von Steinsdorff (volume one) uses Brentano-von Arnim's own ordering of the collected works, beginning with the *Frühlingskranz* and *Die Günderode*. Schmitz's "Commentary" to this volume is vast. He surveys the history of her family, concentrating on the eras covered by the books and the periods in which she wrote them, and discusses her music, philosophical influences, politics, and poetics and methodology. Schmitz sees the correspondence books as a means of self-representation for Brentano-von Arnim (885). The unique character of her work is a result of her personality: "Originality is for B.[ettina] an existential as well as an aesthetic necessity, therefore she will neither submit herself to any model nor mold herself to any expectation"

(Originalität ist für B.[ettina] eine existentielle wie eine ästhetische
Notwendigkeit, deshalb will sie sich keinem Vorbild unterwerfen und
keinen Erwartungen fügen) (887). Schmitz tries to skirt the question
of genre, referring to the epistolary books as "letter art" (Briefkunst),
and thereby placing them more within the letter-writing than the
novel tradition (884). On the other hand, Schmitz acknowledges that
most of Brentano-von Arnim's texts—books and letters—were conceived of as works of art, (980–981). Schmitz concludes: "Her biography is Bettina's major work. She did not concentrate coincidentally on
the publication of the products of her life" (Ihre Biographie ist
Bettines Hauptwerk. She hat sich nicht zufällig auf die Herausgabe
von Lebenserzeugnissen konzentriert) (980). After making this observation, Schmitz then reflects upon the role his own commentary plays
in the reading of her work. He shies away from the role of arbitrator
between her autobiography and historical fact. He envisions his role
as one of facilitator, helping to make Brentano-von Arnim's world
come alive for today's reader (980).

Heinz Härtl's approach to Bettina von Arnim's writings is similar to
Schmitz's. Härtl edited the first volume of the GDR edition. This
edition, if continued as planned, is designed to present Brentano-von
Arnim's works in the order they were written. The first volume contains *Goethes Briefwechsel mit einem Kinde*, the second *Die Günderode* and the *Frühlingskranz*. Härtl differs, however, in his emphasis
on the context of Brentano-von Arnim's relationships, particularly
hers to Goethe: "Even with all its individual characteristics, Bettina's
relationship to Goethe was a group experience which was partly inspired by the Heidelberg Romantics with the intention of being written
down, indeed of being published" (Bei allen individuellen Besonder-
heiten war Bettinas Beziehung zu Goethe ein Gruppenerlebnis, das
von den Heidelberger Romantikern teilweise inspiriert und zur
schriftlichen Fixierung, ja Veröffentlichung vorgesehen wurde) (637).
He seems to overly depersonalize and—contextualize Brentano-von
Arnim's relationship with Goethe. Härtl stresses either her idealized
portrayal or the family context over the actual relationship. He also
recognizes, however, the distinction in the books between Bettina as
author and as character. The notes and commentaries guide the reader
in determining the extent of Brentano-von Arnim's revisions, additions, and excisions. Härtl also provides a history of the contemporary
reception of the book. Unlike Schmitz, he never reflects on the pur-

pose of his notes, nor does he directly take up the question of literary valuation. But in his role as editor, he is clearly an advocate for wider scholarly recognition of her life and work. Both Schmitz and Härtl provide adequate bibliographic information, but because their notes were compiled at the same time as many new studies, they are not entirely up-to-date.

Bürger's Reclam anthology, Hirsch's Rowohlt biography, the new editions, and even the *Jahrbuch* appear to represent the institutionalization of Bettina Brentano-von Arnim scholarship. The prestigious publishers of the new collected editions and articles by recognized scholars all point to this. It remains to be questioned what the ramifications may be from a feminist perspective of the acceptance of Brentano-von Arnim and her writings by the academic literary world. In many cases, the old clichés are merely repeated and no reassessment of her works has taken place, but other critics clearly make substantial contributions. The exhibition catalogue as well as the many essays that appeared surrounding her 200th birthday confirm an increased interest in Bettina Brentano-von Arnim's life and works by male scholars, and this is to be welcomed. However, as long as critics—both male and female—more often than not ignore the significant contributions made to the research by women from Fanny Lewald to Lorely French, their role in the reception of Bettina Brentano-von Arnim should be cautiously assessed. Only when critics consider the complete tradition of Brentano-von Arnim scholarship can there be a real reassessment of her place in both literary history and the history of European women. As we have seen in this review of the reception of Bettina Brentano-von Arnim as writer and historical figure, this reasessment is already under way.

Notes

This chapter is dedicated to Konstanze Bäumer in fond remembrance of our time in California, working on our Bettina Brentano-von Arnim dissertations.

I would like to thank the Humanities Center at the University of Georgia for granting me a fellowship which enabled the completion of this work.

1. The original German titles of Brentano-von Arnim's major works will be given in translation only the first time they are mentioned. Titles of other works by her are given first in English and then in German. The titles of secondary works written in German have as a rule not been translated. In some cases, if the title is given to illustrate a particular point, then a translation is provided following the original. I have translated all the German quotations into English. The following is a list of Brentano-von Arnim's major works with English translations of the titles:

    Goethes Briefwechsel mit einem Kinde (Goethe's Correspondence with a Child); *Die Günderode* (Günderode); *Clemens Brentanos Frühlingskranz* (The Spring Wreath); *Ilius Pamphilius und die Ambrosia* (Ilius Pamphilius and Ambrosia); *Dies Buch gehört dem König* (The King's Book); *Gespräche mit Dämonen* (Conversations with Demons); *Armenbuch* (Poor Book).

2. The first collected edition was partially made up of unsold copies of individual editions so that the volumes were of varying size. The second, "Neue Ausgabe," had a uniform appearance and was ten rather than eleven volumes. *The King's Book* was not divided into two volumes here. Otto Mallon's article contains valuable (if not always totally accurate) information on older volumes and editions.

3. Edith Waldstein has coined this term for the books written primarily in dialogue form.

4. Bettina Brentano-von Arnim spelled the name of her friend Günderrode with only one "r," but the family name has been consistently spelled with two. Contemporary scholarship has adopted the historically correct spelling of the name Günderrode.

5. Contemporary scholars still differ in regards to the spelling of Brentano-von Arnim's first name. Brentano-von Arnim's own preferred spelling of her first name was "Bettine." Older editions and articles most often use the standard spelling of the name, "Bettina." Citations which use this form have not been changed.

6. It now appears that the volumes still in preparation in both the Klassiker and Aufbau editions, and which would have contained many of the same works, will be published jointly by the editors. One hopes that a combined effort by these scholars will result in an edition that becomes the standard for all Bettina von Arnim scholars for many years to come.

7. At present only the first volume containing *Clemens Brentanos Frühlingskranz* and *Die Günderode* was available for review.

8. The first volume contains *Goethes Briefwechsel mit einem Kinde*, and the

second volume *Die Günderode* and the *Frühlingskranz*. The scholarly apparatus in the second volume is as extensive and as thorough as that found in the first.

9. It last appeared in 1982.

10. Birgit Weißenborn discusses each of these editions and their editors' views in detail (125–135). Also see Walde.

11. Vordtriede originally published his findings in more scholarly form in 1962 in the *Jahrbuch des Freien Deutschen Hochstifts*.

12. Three volumes of letters by women of the period that include Bettina Brentano-von Arnim are also worthy of mention, because they contain a representative sample of her letters. They are: *Frauenbriefe der Romantik*, edited by Katja Behrens, and Haberland's and Pehnt's *Frauen der Goethezeit*. The first volume of a GDR collection, edited by Fritz Böttger, *Frauen im Aufbruch*, also contains selections from von Arnim's writings.

13. Bettina Brentano-von Arnim, like many other women writers and figures of her day who were known only by their first names, is commonly referred to as "Bettina." In fact, the *Allgemeine Deutsche Biographie* lists her alphabetically under no surname, but the article on Bettina Brentano-von Arnim is located under the heading "Bettina." This use of the familiar first name as a reference to an author generally is inappropriate. Some writers may choose to refer to her as "Bettina" in order to emphasize the fact that her surname changed when she married and that women do not have surnames in the way that men do. Also, it can be confusing to refer to her sometimes as Brentano and at others as Arnim, depending on whether her life before or after her marriage is being discussed. The use of "Bettine" here puts her on an unequal footing, even though her name comes first.

14. Meyer-Hepner notes this in her introduction. She based her conclusion on the way the papers were arranged and the pages numbered, as well as on the letters themselves (*Magistratsprozess* 1).

15. As the overview of the criticism will proceed more or less chronologically, editor's evaluations and interpretations will be included along with the discussion of other critics' books and articles.

16. Emerson briefly corresponded with Gisela von Arnim just after her mother's death. Crawford and Vogel examine the influence of German Romanticism on the American transcendentalists.

17. Numerous essays by Young German (Junges Deutschland) writers and their historians have similar titles. Gutzkow wrote several of these, as well as Karl Rosenkranz and Georg Brandes. Rosenkranz's title is representative: "Rahel, Bettina und Charlotte Stieglitz." See also the articles by Wülfing and Tatlock.

18. For a discussion of the significance Goethe had in both women's develop-

ment, see my essay: " 'Ja ja, ich bet' ihn an: Nineteenth-Century Women and Goethe."

19. I have chosen to distinguish between popular and scholarly biographies and articles. Some of the criteria for this evaluation are: authors' statements regarding their intended audience; journal, series, or publisher for the book or article; and the existence or non-existence of scholarly apparatus, such as footnotes, bibliographies, and indexes. Since much Brentano-von Arnim literature falls into the popular category, and some of this material provides valuable information, it should not be ignored.

20. Wyss's dissertation was published in 1935 in Bern. Karl Walde's 1942 Swiss dissertation is so completely non-controversial and apolitical that it is disturbing.

21. See also Faber du Faur.

22. Küpper also wrote an article on the investigation surrounding the rumors during the Third Reich that the Brentanos were Jewish.

23. Drewitz first published her biography with Diederichs in 1969. A paperback edition appeared later in the series of "Heyne Biographien." Paperback and hardback editions of the text have the same pagination. Subsequent editions have updated bibliographies. Drewitz did not footnote the texts she quoted in the biography, but she did provide an extensive bibliography which is an excellent source of information. A short biographical essay on Brentano-von Arnim was translated and appeared in *New German Critique* in 1982.

24. The essays first appeared in the editions she edited. They were reprinted the following year in *Lesen und Schreiben. Neue Sammlung.* Quotes from the essays are taken from this book. The essay on Brentano-von Arnim is the last in this book and is dated December 1979.

25. Christa Bürger believes that this question has been answered negatively (5). She introduces her collection of excerpts with this opinion as a justification to her audience for not reading the texts in their entirety.

26. This topic is also discussed in Adolf Beck's 1964 article on Christoph Theodor Schwab.

27. The picture on the cover of the book is a painting by J. C. Arnold, "Quartettabend bei Bettina von Arnim in Berlin." On the one hand the editor is emphasizing Bettina Brentano-von Arnim's importance to the artistic life of Berlin, but on the other, the painting does not demonstrate her political influence.

28. A new book by Dieter Kühn, *Bettines letzte Liebschaften*, portrays his idea of her relationships with Pückler and Franz Liszt.

29. My discussion of the books by Waldstein, Bäumer, and Hirsch were taken in part from my four book reviews published in *South Atlantic Review*, *German Quarterly*, and *German Studies Review*.

Works Cited

BETTINA BRENTANO-VON ARNIM'S COLLECTED WORKS

Sämtliche Werke. Ed. Waldemar Oehlke. 7 vols. Berlin: Propyläen-Verlag, 1920.

Werke. Ed. Heinz Härtl. 5 vols. Berlin and Weimar: Aufbau Verlag, 1986–.

Werke und Briefe. 5 vols. Eds. Gustav Konrad (1–4) and Joachim Müller (5). Frechen and Köln: Bartmann, 1958–1963.

Werke und Briefe. Eds. Walter Schmitz and Sibylle von Steinsdorff. 3 vols. Frankfurt am Main: Deutscher Klassiker Verlag, 1986–.

INDIVIDUAL EDITIONS AND SELECTIONS

Aus meinem Leben. Ed. Dieter Kühn. Frankfurt am Main: Insel, 1982.

"Bettina von Arnim." Ed. Katja Behrens. *Frauenbriefe der Romantik.* Frankfurt am Main: Insel, 1981. 61–163.

Bettina von Arnims Armenbuch. Ed. Werner Vordtriede. Frankfurt am Main: Insel, 1969, 1981.

"Bettina von Arnims Armenbuch." Ed. Werner Vordtriede. *Jahrbuch des Freien Deutschen Hochstifts* (1962). 379–518.

Bettine. Eine Auswahl aus den Schriften und Briefen der Bettina von Arnim-Brentano. Ed. Gisela Kähler. Berlin: Verlag der Nation, 1952.

Dies Buch gehört dem König. Ed. Ilse Staff. Frankfurt am Main: Insel, 1982.

Clemens Brentanos Frühlingskranz. Ed. Wulf Segebrecht. München: Winkler, 1967.

Clemens Brentanos Frühlingskranz aus Jugendbriefen von ihm geflochten, wie er selbst schriftlich verlangte. Ed. Heinz Härtl. Leipzig: Reclam, 1985.

Clemens Brentanos Frühlingskranz. Afterword, Hartwig Schultz. Frankfurt am Main: Insel, 1985.

"Du wunderliches Kind . . . Bettine und Goethe. Ed. Alfred Kantorowicz. Berlin, Stuttgart: Pontes-Verlag, 1949.

Goethes Briefwechsel mit einem Kinde. Ed. Hermann Grimm. Stuttgart and Berlin: Cotta, 1881.

Goethes Briefwechsel mit einem Kinde. Ed. Franz Brümmer. Leipzig: Reclam, 1890.

Goethes Briefwechsel mit einem Kinde. Ed. Jonas Fränkel. Jena: Diedrichs, 1906.

Goethes Briefwechsel mit einem Kinde. Ed. Heinz Amelung. Berlin, Leipzig, Wien, Stuttgart, 1914.

Goethes Briefwechsel mit einem Kinde. Ed. Otto Heuschele. Stuttgart, 1947.

Goethes Briefwechsel mit einem Kinde. Ed. Waldemar Oehlke. Frankfurt am Main: Insel, 1984.

Die Günderode. Ed. and Essay, Christa Wolf. Frankfurt am Main: Insel, 1982.

Die Günderode. Ed. Elisabeth Bronfen. München: Matthes & Seitz, 1982.

Lebensspiel. Ed. Willi Reich. Zürich: Manesse, 1953.

Ein Lesebuch. Eds. Christa Bürger and Birgitt Diefenbach. Stuttgart: Reclam, 1987.

Der Magistratsprozess der Bettina von Arnim. Ed. Gertrud Meyer-Hepner. Weimar: Arion Verlag, 1960.

Märchen der Bettine, Armgart und Gisela von Arnim. Ed. Gustav Konrad. Frechen: Bartmann, 1965.

Meine Seele ist eine leidenschaftliche Tänzerin". Ed. Otto Betz. 3rd ed. Freiburg: Herder Bücherei, 1987.

Die Sehnsucht hat allemal Recht. Gedichte, Prosa, Briefe. Ed. Gerhard Wolf. (Märkischer Dichtergarten). Frankfurt: Fischer Taschenbuch, 1985.

Arnim, Bettina von, and Gisela von Arnim. *Das Leben der Hochgräfin Gritta von Rattenzuhausbeiuns.* Olten und Freiburg im Breisgau: Walter-Verlag, 1980.

———. *Das Leben der Hochgräfin Gritta von Rattenzuhausbeiuns.* Ed. Shawn Jarvis. Frankfurt am Main: Insel, 1986.

LETTER COLLECTIONS AND MISCELLANEOUS WRITINGS

Achim von Arnim und die ihm nahe standen. Ed. Reinhold Steig. 3 vols. Stuttgart and Berlin: Cotta, 1913.

Die Andacht zum Menschenbild. Unbekannte Briefe von Bettine Brentano. Ed. Wilhelm Schellberg and Friedrich Fuchs. 1942; rpt. Bern: Lang, 1970.

"Bettina und Goethe in Teplitz." Ed. Werner Vordtriede. *Jahrbuch des freien deutschen Hochstifts* (1964): 343–365.

Bettina von Arnim und die Polen. Intro. Jürgen Kuczynski, Afterword Ruth Krenn. Berlin: Aufbau, 1949.

Bettine von Arnim: Literarisches und Politisches aus ihrem Nachlass. Ed. Karl Ernst Henrici. Berlin: 1929, Auction Catalogue 148.

Bettine von Arnim: II. Handschriftlicher Nachlaß der Bettine von Arnim: Dritter und Letzter Teil. Ed. Karl Ernst Henrici. Berlin: 1929, Auction Catalogue 155.

"Briefe und Konzepte 1837 bis 1846." *Sinn und Form* 40, 4 (1988): 694–710.

"Briefe und Konzepte aus den Jahren 1849–1852." Ed. Gertrud Meyer-Hepner. Sinn und Form 5 (1953), Heft 1, 38–64; Heft 3/4, 27–58.

Arnim, Bettina von, and Achim von Arnim. *Achim und Bettina in ihren Briefen.* 2 vols. Eds. Werner Vordtriede and Rudolf Alexander Schröder. (Suhrkamp, 1961) Frankfurt am Main: Insel, 1981.

———. *Bettine und Arnim. Briefe der Freundschaft und Liebe.* Ed. Otto Betz und Veronika Straub. 2 vols. Frankfurt am Main: Josef Knecht, 1986–1987.

Arnim, Bettina von, and Armgart and Gisela von Arnim. *Märchen.* Ed. Gustav Konrad. Frechen: Bartmann, 1965.

Arnim, Bettina von, and Rudolf Baier. *Unveröffentlichte Briefe und Tagebuchaufzeichnungen.* Ed. Kurt Gassen. Greifswald: Bamberg, 1937.

Arnim, Bettina von, and Julius Döring. "Bettina von Arnims Briefe an Julius Döring." Ed. Werner Vordtriede. *Jahrbuch des freien deutschen Hochstifts* (1963): 341–488.

Arnim, Bettina von, and Max Prokop von Freyberg. *Der Briefwechsel zwischen Bettine Brentano und Max Prokop von Freyberg.* Ed. Sibylle von Steinsdorff. Berlin, New York: De Gruyter, 1972.

Arnim, Bettina von, and Friedrich Wilhelm IV. *Ungedruckte Briefe und Aktenstücke.* Ed. Ludwig Geiger. Frankfurt am Main: Kütten & Loening, 1902.

Arnim, Bettina von, and J. W. von Goethe. *Bettinas Leben und Briefwechsel mit Goethe.* Ed. Fritz Bergemann. Leipzig: Insel, 1927.

Arnim, Bettina von, and Jakob and Wilhelm Grimm. *Der Briefwechsel Bettine von Arnims mit den Brüdern Grimm. 1838–1841.* Ed. Hartwig Schultz. Frankfurt am Main: Insel, 1985.

Arnim, Bettina von, and Hermann Fürst Pückler-Muskau. "Pückler und Bettina von Arnim." *Frauenbriefe von und an Hermann Fürsten Pückler-Muskau.* Ed. Heinrich Conrad. München and Leipzig: Georg Müller, 1912. 1–218.

Arnim, Bettina von, and Friedrich Carl von Savigny. "Briefe Friedrich Carl von Savignys an Bettina Brentano." Ed. Heinz Härtl. *Wissenschaftliche Zeitschrift der Universität Halle* 28 (1979): 105–128.

Arnim, Bettine von, and Pauline Steinhäuser. "Bettina von Arnim und ihr Briefwechsel mit Pauline Steinhäuser." Ed. Karl Obser. *Neue Heidelberger Jahrbücher* 12 (1903): 85–137.

Goethe, Johann Wolfgang von. *Briefe Goethes an Sophie von La Roche und Bettina Brentano nebst dichterischen Beilagen.* Ed. G. von Loeper. Berlin: Wilhelm Hertz, 1879.

Varnhagen von Ense, Karl August. *Aus dem Nachlaß Varnhagen's von Ense.*
Briefe von Stägemann, Metternich, Heine und Bettina von Arnim, nebst
Briefen, Anmerkungen und Notizen von Varnhagen von Ense. Ed. Ludmilla
Assing. Leipzig: F. A. Brockhaus, 1865.

LITERATURE ON
BETTINA BRENTANO-VON ARNIM

Alberti, Conrad (pseudonym for Adelung). *Bettina von Arnim (1785–1859).*
Ein Erinnerungsblatt zu ihrem hundertsten Geburtstag. Leipzig: Otto
Wigand, 1885.
Arnim, Hans von. *Bettina von Arnim.* Berliner Reminiszenzen 2. Berlin:
Haude & Spenersche Verlagsbuchhandlung, 1963.
Bansa, Elfriede. *Bettina von Arnims Verhältnis zur Kunst.* Diss.,Frankfurt
am Main. Würzburg: Karl J. Triltsch, 1938.
Barring, Ludwig. *Geist und Herz. Große Frauen in ihrer Zeit.* Bayreuth:
Loewes, 1971.
Bäumer, Konstanze. *"Bettine, Psyche, Mignon": Bettina von Arnim und Goe-*
the. Stuttgart: Akademischer Verlag. Stuttgarter Arbeiten zur German-
istik 139. 1986.
———. "Die Rezeption Bettina von Arnims in der Berliner Kultur—und
Literaturgeschichte." *Internationales Jahrbuch der Bettina-von-Arnim Ge-*
sellschaft 1 (1987): 39–51.
Beck, Adolf. "Christoph Theodor Schwab über Bettina von Arnim. Ein
briefliches Porträt 1849/1850. Zugleich ein Beitrag zur Geschichte der
Wirkung Hölderlins." *Jahrbuch des Freien Deutschen Hochstifts* (1964):
366–378.
Beck, Hilde. "Die Bedeutung der Natur in dem Lebensgefühl der Bettina
von Arnim." Diss. Frankfurt am Main, 1950.
Behrens, Jürgen. "Bettine von Arnim und Felix Prinz Lichnowsky: Eine
Episode." *Archiv für Frankfurts Geschichte und Kunst* 59 (1985): 327–
446.
Bellos, David. "Balzac and Goethe's Bettina." *Proceedings of the IXth Con-*
gress of the International Comparative Literature Association. Innsbruck
Institut für Sprachwissenschaft der Universität Innsbruck, 1980. 359–364.
Beyer, Paul. "Bettinas Arbeit an 'Goethes Briefwechsel mit einem Kinde.' "
Von deutscher Sprache und Art. Beiträge zur Geschichte der neuren
deutschen Sprache, zur Sprachkunst, Sprachpflege und zur Volkskunde.
Ed. Max Preitz. Frankfurt am Main: Diesterweg, 1925. 65–82.

Bissing, Henriette von. *Das Leben der Dichterin Amalie von Helvig, geb. Freiin von Imhoff.* Berlin: Wilhelm Hertz, 1889.

Böttger, Fritz. *Bettina von Arnim. Ein Leben zwischen Tag und Traum.* Berlin: Verlag der Nation, 1986.

Brandes, Georg. "Rahel, Bettina, Charlotte Stieglitz." *Main Currents in Ninteenth Century Literature.* Vol. 6. New York: MacMillan, 1905. 277–304.

Brentano, Clemens. *Das Unsterbliche Leben. Unbekannte Briefe von Clemens Brentano.* Ed. Wilhelm Schellberg and Friedrich Fuchs. Jena: Diederichs, 1939.

Bunzel, Wolfgang. " 'Phantasie ist die freie Kunst der Wahrheit.' Bettine von Arnims poetisches Verfahren in 'Goethes Briefwechsel mit einem Kinde.' " *Internationales Jahrbuch der Bettina-von-Arnim Gesellschaft* 1 (1987): 7–28.

Bürger, Christa. "Der Hunger nach dem Ich." *Bettina von Arnim. Ein Lesebuch.* Eds. Christa Bürger and Birgitt Diefenbach. Stuttgart: Reclam, 1987. 317–347.

Burwick, Roswitha. "Bettina von Arnims 'Die Günderode.' Zum Selbstverständinis der Frau in der Romantik." *Kontroversen, alte und neue. Akten des VII. Internationalen Germanisten-Kongresses, Göttigen, 1985.* Ed. Inge Stephan and Carl Pietzcker. Vol. 6. Tübingen Niemeyer, 1986. 62–67.

Carrière, Moritz. "Bettina von Arnim." *Lebensbilder.* Vol. 12. *Gesammelte Werke.* Leipzig: Brockhaus, 1890.

Collins, Hildegard P. and Philip A. Shelley. "The Reception in England and America of Bettina von Arnim's *Goethe's Correspondence with a Child.*" *Anglo-German and American-German Crosscurrents.* Ed. Philip Shelley and Arthur Lewis. Vol. 2. Chapel Hill: University of North Carolina Press, 1962. 97–174.

Craig, Charlotte M. "Heritage and Elective Affinity: Bettina Arnim's Surrogate Mother and The Eternal Feminine." *Germanic Notes* 16 (1985): 54–57.

Crawford, Mary Caroline. *Goethe and His Women Friends.* (Boston, 1911). New York: Haskell House, 1973.

Dischner, Gisela. *Bettina von Arnim: Eine weibliche Sozialbiographie aus dem 19. Jahrhundert.* Berlin: Klaus Wagenbach, 1977.

Drewitz, Ingeborg. *Berliner Salons. Gesellschaft und Literatur zwischen Aufklärung und Industriezeitalter.* Berliner Reminszenzen 7. 2nd ed. Berlin: Haude & Spener, 1979.

———. *Bettina von Arnim. Romantik, Revolution, Utopie.* Düsseldorf: Köln: Diederichs, 1969. Paperback: Heyne, 1978.

———. "Bettine von Arnim—A Portrait." *New German Critique* 27 (1982): 115–122.

Düsterlho, Christa von. " 'Bettina von Arnim'. Liebe—Leistung—Leben."
    Internationales Jahrbuch der Bettina-von-Arnim Gesellschaft 1 (1987): 53–
    57.
Emerson, Ralph Waldo and Herman Grimm. *Correspondence Between
    Ralph Waldo Emerson and Herman Grimm.* Ed. F. W. Holls. Boston:
    Houghton Mifflin, 1903.
Faber du Faur, Curt von. "Bettina von Arnim. Ein neuer Fund." *PMLA* 75
    (1960): 216–230.
Feilchenfeldt, Konrad. "Bettine, Rahel und Varhnagen. *Herzhaft in die
    Dornen der Zeit greifen . . . Bettine von Arnim 1785–1859.* Ed. Christoph
    Perels. Frankfurt am Main: Freies Deutsches Hochstift, 1985. 233–243.
Frederiksen, Elke, and Monika Shafi. " 'Sich im Unbekannten suchen
    gehen': Bettina von Arnim's 'Die Günderode' als weibliche Utopie."
    *Kontroversen, alte und neue. Akten des VII. Internationalen Germanisten-
    Kongresses, Göttingen, 1985.* Vol. 6. *Frauensprache—Frauenliteratur?* Ed.
    Inge Stephan and Carl Pietzcker. Tübingen: Niemeyer, 1986. 54–61.
Frels, Wilhelm. *Bettina von Arnims Königsbuch. Ein Beitrag zur Geschichte
    ihres Lebens und ihrer Zeit.* Schwerin: Schmidt, 1912.
French, Lorely. "Bettine von Arnim: Toward a Women's Epistolary Aesthet-
    ics and Poetics." Diss. University of California, Los Angeles, 1986.
Fromm, Lebrecht (pseudonym). *Ruchlosigkeit der Schrift: "Dies Buch gehört
    dem König"—Ein unterthänger Fingerzeig gewagt von Lebrecht Fromm.*
    (1844). Zwickau: Ullmann, 1926.
Frühwald, Wolfgang. " 'Mephisto in Weiblicher Verkleidung'. Das Werk
    Bettine von Arnims im Spannungsfeld von Romantik und sozialer Re-
    form." *Jahrbuch des freien Deutschen Hochstifts* 1985. 202–222.
———. "Die Not der schlesischen Weber. Zu Bettine von Arnims *Armen-
    buch* 1844." *Herzhaft in die Dornen der Zeit greifen . . . Bettine von
    Arnim 1785-1859.* Ed. Christoph Perels. Frankfurt am Main: Freies
    Deutsches Hochstift, 1985. 269–280.
Gajek, Enid Margarete. "Die Bedeutung des Fürsten Hermann Pückler für
    Bettine." *Herzhaft in die Dornen der Zeit greifen . . . Bettine von Arnim
    1785-1859.* Ed. Christoph Perels. Frankfurt am Main: Freies Deutsches
    Hochstift, 1985. 253–260.
Geiger, Ludwig. "Bettina von Arnim: Mitarbeiterin an einem historischen
    Werke." *Euphorion* 9 (1902). 122–130.
———. "Bettina von Arnim: Mitarbeiterin an einem historischen Werke."
    Euphorion 9 (1902): 122–130.
Gervinius, G. G. *Ueber den Göthischen Briefwechsel.* Leipzig: Friedrich
    Engelmann, 1836.
Geschichte der deutschen Literatur von den Anfängen bis zur Gegenwart. Eds.
    Hans-Günther Thalheim, et. al. 12 vols. Berlin: Volk und Wissen, 1975.
Goodman, Katherine. *Dis/Closures: Women's Autobiography in Germany*

Between 1790 and 1914. New York University Ottendorfer Series (NF) 24. New York, Bern: Lang, 1986.

Goozé, Marjanne E. "Bettine von Arnim, the Writer." Diss. University of California, Berkeley, 1984.

———. "Desire and Presence: Bettine von Arnim's Erotic Fantasy Letter to Goethe." *Michigan Germanic Studies* 13 (Spring, 1987): 41–57.

———. " 'Ja ja, ich bet' ihn an': Nineteenth-Century Women and Goethe." *The Age of Goethe Today: Critical Reexamination and Literary Reflection*. Eds. Gertrud B. Pickar and Sabine Cramer. München: Fink, 1990. 39–49.

Grambow, Gertrud. "Bettinas Weltbild." Diss. Berlin, 1941.

Günderrode, Karoline von. *Der Schatten eines Traumes. Gedichte, Prosa, Briefe, Zeugnisse von Zeitgenossen*. Ed. and Intro. Christa Wolf. Darmstadt and Neuwied: Luchterhand, 1979.

Gutzkow, Karl. "Rahel, Bettina, Charlotte Stieglitz." *Gesammelte Werke*. Vol. 3. Leipzig: Bibliographisches Institut, 1911. 98–112.

———. *Werke*. Ed. Reinhold Gensel. 7 vols. 15 parts. 1912. Hildesheim: Olms, 1974.

Haberland, Helga, and Wolfgang Pehnt, eds. *Frauen der Goethezeit. In Briefen, Dokumenten und Bildern von der Gottschedin bis zu Bettina von Arnim. Eine Anthologie*. Stuttgart: Reclam, 1960.

Hajek, Hans. "Die Mystifizierung der Frau Rat durch Bettina Brentano." Diss. Wien, 1937. Hahn, Karl-Heinz. *Bettina von Arnim in ihrem Verhältnis zu Staat und Politik*. Weimar: Böhlau, 1959.

Hahn, Barbara. "Rahel Levin Varnhagen und Bettine von Arnim: Briefe, Bücher, Biographien." *Frauen—Literatur—Politik*. Ed. A. Pelz, M. Schuller, I. Stephan. Berlin: Argument Verlag, 1988.

Härtl, Heinz. "Bettina von Arnim. Romantikerin und Demokratin: Eine Annäherung." *Bettine von Arnim. Romantik und Sozialismus (1831–1859)*. Schriften aus dem Karl-Marx-Haus 35. Trier: Karl-Marx-Haus, 1987. 27–41.

Herzhaft in die Dornen der Zeit greifen . . . Bettine von Arnim 1785–1859. Ed. Christoph Perels. Frankfurt am Main: Freies Deutsches Hochstift, 1985.

Hetmann, Frederik. *Bettina und Achim: Die Geschichte einer Liebe*. Weinheim und Basel: Beltz, 1983.

Hirsch, Helmut. *Bettine von Arnim*. Reinbek bei Hamburg, 1987.

———. "Jüdische Aspekte im Leben und Werk Bettine von Arnims." *Internationales Jahrbuch der Bettina-von-Arnim Gesellschaft* 1 (1987): 61–75.

Hoock-Demarle, Marie-Claire. "Bettina Brentano-von Arnim 1785–1859. La mise en oeuvre d'une vie." Diss. University of Paris. 3 vols. 1985.

———. "Bettinas Umgang mit Außenseitern." *Internationales Jahrbuch der Bettina-von-Arnim Gesellschaft* 2 (1988): 76–91

———. *La femme au temps de Goethe*. Paris: Stock/Laurence Pernoud, 1987.

————. "Frau und Stadt: Erlebnis und Erfahrungen der Bettina Brentano-von Arnim. *Bettine von Arnim. Romantik und Sozialismus (1831–1859.* Schriften aus dem Karl-Marx-Haus 35. Trier: Karl-Marx-Haus, 1987. 41–57.

Hopfe, Anneliese. "Formen und Bereiche schöpferischen Verstehens bei Bettina von Arnim." Diss. München, 1953.

Huch, Ricarda. *Die Romantik.* 2 vols. Leipzig: Haessel, 1912.

Internationales Jahrbuch des Bettina-von-Arnim-Gesellschaft. Ed. Dr. Uwe Lemm. Berlin: FSP-Fotosatz GmbH.

Kahn-Wallerstein, Carmen. *Bettine. Die Geschichte eines ungestümen Herzens.* Bern: Francke, 1952.

Kern, Hans. *Vom Genius der Liebe. Frauenschicksale der Romantik.* Leipzig: Reclam, 1939.

Kittler, Friedrich. "Autorschaft und Liebe." *Austreibung des Geistes aus den Geisteswissenschaften: Programme des Poststrukturalismus.* Paderborn and München: Schöningh, 1980. 142–173.

————. "Writing into the Wind, Bettina." Trans. Marilyn Wyatt. *Glyph* 7 (1980): 32–69.

Kluckhohn, Paul. "Bettina von Arnim." *Neue Deutsche Biographie.* 1: 369–371.

Kohlschmidt, Werner. *Geschichte der deutschen Literatur von den Anfängen bis zur Gegenwart.* 5 vols. Stuttgart: Reclam, 1974.

Konrad, Gustav. "Bettina von Arnim." *Deutsche Dichter der Romantik.* Ed. Benno von Wiese. München: E. Schmidt, 1971. 310–340.

Kühn, Dieter. *Bettines letzte Liebschaften.* Frankfurt am Main: Insel, 1986.

Kühn, Helmut and Manfred Schlösser. "Bettina von Arnim: Ein Brief." *Preußen Dein Spree-Athen. Beiträge zu Literatur, Theater und Musik in Berlin.* Ed. Helmut Kühn. Reinbek bei Hamburg: Rowohlt, 1981. 98–108.

Kühn, Paul. *Die Frauen um Goethe. Weimarer Intierieurs.* Leipzig: Klinkhardt & Biermann, 1912.

Küpper, Peter. "Bettina Brentano—1936." *Euphorion* 61 (1967): 175–186.

Lewald, Fanny. *Fanny Lewald. Gefühltes und Gedachtes (1838–1888).* Ed. Ludwig Geiger. Dresden and Leipzig: Heinrich Minden, 1900.

Liebertz-Grün, Ursula. "Glanz und Elend der Romantik. Bettina von Arnim: 'Clemens Brentano's [sic] Frühlingskranz.' " *Internationales Jahrbuch der Bettina-von-Arnim Gesellschaft* 2, 1988. 95–134.

Liebertz-Grün, Ursula. *Ordnung im Chaos. Studien zur Poetik der Bettine Brentano-von Arnim.* Heidelberg: Carl Winter, 1989.

Lilienfein, Heinrich. *Bettina: Dichtung und Wahrheit ihres Lebens.* München: F. Bruckmann, 1949.

Loeper, G. "Bettina." *Allgemeine Deutsche Biographie.* 2: 578–582.

Mallachow, Lore. *Bettina.* Berlin: Das Neue Berlin, 1952.

Mallon, Otto. "Bettina-Bibliographie." *Imprimatur, ein Jahrbuch für Bücherfreunde* 4 (1933): 141–156.

Mander, Gertrud. *Bettina von Arnim.* Preußische Köpfe 11. Berlin: Stapp, 1982.

Mattenklott, Gert. "Romantische Frauenkultur. Bettina von Arnim zum Beispiel." *Frauen-Literatur-Geschichte: schreibende Frauen vom Mittelalter bis zur Gegenwart.* Ed. Hiltrud Gnüg and Renate Möhrmann. Stuttgart: Metzler, 1985. 123–143.

Meyer-Hepner, Gertrud. "Bettina in Ost und West." *Neue Deutsche Literatur*, 7, 1 (1959): 152–154.

———. "Richtigstellende Kritik zu einem Bettina Aufsatz." *Goethe* 22 (1960): 236–239.

———. "Das Bettina von Arnim-Archiv." *Sinn und Form* 6 (1954): 594–611.

———. "Neues über Bettina." *Neue Deutsche Literatur*, 7 1 (1959): 148–151.

Meysenbug, Malwida von. *Memoiren einer Idealistin und ihr Nachtrag: Der Lebensabend einer Idealistin.* Stuttgart: Deutsche Verlags-Anstalt, 1927.

Milch, Werner. *Die junge Bettine.* Heidelberg: Stiehm, 1968.

Mittenzwei, Johannes. *Das Musikalische in der Literatur.* Halle: VEB Sprache und Literatur, 1962.

Moltmann-Wendel, Elisabeth. "Bettina von Arnim und Schleiermacher." *Evangelische Theologie* 31 (1971): 395–414.

Montgomery-Silfverstolpe, Malla. *Das romantische Deutschland: Reisejournal einer Schwedin (1825–1826).* Leipzig: Albert Bonnier, 1912.

Monz, Heinz. "Bettine von Arnim und Karl Marx in Bad Kreuznach." *Internationales Jahrbuch der Bettina-von-Arnim Gesellschaft* 2, 1988. 143–157.

Morgenstern, Lina. *Die Frauen des 19. Jahrhunderts. Biographische und culturhistorische Zeit- und Charaktergemälde.* 2 vols. Berlin: Verlag der deutschen Hausfrauenzeitung, 1888.

Mundt, Theodor. *Geschichte der Literatur der Gegenwart.* Berlin, 1842.

Nahrebecky, Roman. *Wackenroder, Tieck, E.T.A. Hoffmann, Bettina von Arnim: Ihre Beziehung zur Musik und zum musikalischen Erlebnis.* Studien zur Germanistik, Anglistik und Komparatistik 86. Bonn: Bouvier, 1979.

Nill, Peggy. "Schreib Dir's ins Herz." *Internationales Jahrbuch der Bettina-von-Arnim Gesellschaft* 1 (1987): 29–37.

Nyssen, Helge. "Zur Soziologie der Romantik und des vormarxistischen Sozialismus in Deutschland. Bettina von Arnims soziale Ideen." Diss. Heidelberg, 1950.

Oehlke, Waldemar. *Bettina von Arnims Briefromane.* Palaestra 41. Berlin: Mayer & Müller, 1905.

Ohff, Heinz. "Bettina von Arnim oder Das Genie als Hofnarr." *Auch sie waren Preußen. 15 Lebensbilder.* Berlin: Safari-Verlag, 1979. 87–100.

Patsch, Herrmann. " 'Ob ich dich liebe, weiß ich nicht.' Goethe und ein

Wechselgedicht zwischen Bettina von Arnim und Friedrich Schleiermacher." *Zeitschrift für deutsche Philologie* 104 (1985): 542–554.

Perels, Christoph. "Bettines Gegenwärtigkeit in der Poesie des 20. Jahrhunderts." *Herzhaft in die Dornen der Zeit greifen . . . Bettine von Arnim
1785-1859.* Frankfurt am Main: Freies Deutsches Hochstift, 1985. 281–294.

Pross, Helge. "A Romantic Socialist in Prussia." *German Quarterly* 27
(1954): 91–103.

Püschel, Ursula. "Bettina von Arnims politische Schriften." Diss. Berlin
(Humboldt), 1965.

———. "Bettinas Zorn." *Neue Deutsche Literatur* 10 (1962): 151–53.

———. "Vor dem großen Kompromiß." *Neue Deutsche Literatur* 33,4
(1985): 107–121.

———. "Weibliches und Unweibliches der Bettina von Arnim." *Mit allen
Sinnen: Frauen in der Literatur, Essays.* Halle-Leipzig: Mitteldeutscher
Verlag, 1980. 48–82.

Reuschle, Frieda M. *An der Grenze einer neuen Welt: Bettina von Arnims
Botschaft vom freien Geist.* Stuttgart: Urachhaus, 1977.

Röllecke, Heinz. "Bettines Märchen." *Herzhaft in die Dornen der Zeit
greifen . . . Bettine von Arnim 1785–1859.* Ed. Christoph Perels. Frankfurt am Main: Freies Deutsches Hochstift, 1985. 225–232.

Rosenkranz, Karl. "Rahel, Bettina und Charlotte Stieglitz. 1837." *Neue
Studien.* Vol. 2. Leipzig: Roschny, 1875. 102–123.

Sauer, August. *Frauenbilder aus der Blütezeit der deutschen Literatur.* Leipzig:
Adolf Titze, 1885.

Scherr, Johannes. *Geschichte der deutschen Frauenwelt.* 3 vols. Leipzig: Otto
Vigand, 1879.

Schikorra, Ute. " 'Es gibt nichts wie die Liebe': Zum Liebesverständnis
Bettina von Arnims." *Internationales Jahrbuch der Bettina-von-Arnim
Gesellschaft* 2, 1988. 135–142.

Schloenbach, Arnold. *Zwölf Frauenbilder aus der Goethe-Schiller-Epoche.*
Hannover: Carl Rümpler, 1856.

Schmidt, Julian. *Geschichte der deutschen Literatur im neunzehnten Jahrhundert.* Leipzig: Herbig, 1856.

Schoof, Wilhelm. "Goethe und Bettina Brentano. Zu Bettinas 100. Todestag
am 20. Januar 1959. *Goethe* 20 (1958): 213–224.

Schultz, Hartwig. "Bettines Auseinandersetzung mit Friedrich Karl von
Savigny um die Einstellung der Brüder Grimm in Berlin." *Herzhaft in die
Dornen der Zeit greifen . . . Bettine von Arnim 1785–1859.* Ed. Christoph
Perels. Frankfurt am Main: Freies Deutsches Hochstift, 1985. 261–268.

———. "Bettine von Arnims Weg zur politischen Schriftstellerin: ihr Kampf
für die Brüder Grimm." *Bettine von Arnim. Romantik und Sozialismus
(1831–1859.* Schriften aus dem Karl-Marx-Haus 35. Trier: Karl-Marx-
Haus, 1987. 11–26.

Seidel, Ina. *Bettina*. Stuttgart: Cotta, 1944.

Sichelschmidt, Gustav. *Große Berlinerinnen. Sechzehn biographische Porträts*. Berlin: Rembrandt Verlag, 1972.

Siemsen, Anna. *Der Weg ins Freie*. Frankfurt am Main: Büchergilde Gutenberg, 1950.

Spiero, Heinrich. *Geschichte der deutschen Frauendichtung seit 1800*. Leipzig: B. G. Teubner, 1913.

Stahr, Adolf. *Bettina und ihr Königsbuch*. Hamburg, 1844.

Steig, Reinhold. "Bettina." *Deutsche Rundschau* 72 (1892): 262–274.

Steinmetz, Selma. "Bettina Brentano: Persönlichkeit, Künstlertum und Gedankenwelt." Diss. Wien, 1931.

Steinsdorff, Sibylle von. "Bettine und Goethe." *Herzhaft in die Dornen der Zeit greifen . . . Bettine von Arnim 1785–1859*. Ed. Christoph Perels. Frankfurt am Main: Freies Deutsches Hochstift, 1985. 244–252.

Stöcker, Helene. "Bettine von Arnim." *Die neue Generation*, 25 (1929): 99–105.

Strobl, Karl. *Bettina von Arnim*. Bielefeld and Leipzig: Velhagen & Klasing, 1926.

Susman, Margarete. *Frauen der Romantik*. 3rd ed. (1929). Köln: Metzler, 1960.

Tanneberger, Irmgard. *Die Frauen der Romantik und das soziale Problem*. Oldenburg: Schulzesche Hofbuchdruckerei und Verlagsbuchhandlung, 1928.

Tatlock, Lynne. "The Young Germans in Praise of Famous Women: Ambivalent Advocates." *German Life and Letters* 39 (1986): 193–209.

Treitschke, Heinrich von. *Geschichte der deutschen Literatur von Friedrich dem Grossen bis zur Märzrevolution*. Berlin-Grunewald: H. Klemm, 1927.

Varnhagen von Ense, Karl August. *Tagebücher*. 15 vols. Leipzig: Brockhaus, 1861.

Vogel, Stanley M. *German Literary Influences on the American Transcendentalists*. New Haven: Yale University Press, 1955.

Vordtriede, Werner. "Bettinas englisches Wagnis." *Euphorion* 51 (1957): 271–294.

Walde, Karl J. *Goethes Briefwechsel mit einem Kinde und seine Beurteilung in der Literaturgeschichte*. Diss. Freiburg (Schweiz) 1942. Freiburg: Aarau, 1942.

Weißenborn, Birgit. *Bettina von Arnim und Goethe: Topographie einer Beziehung als Beispiel weiblicher Emanzipation zu Beginn des 19. Jahrhunderts*. Europäische Hochschulschriften, Reihe I, 1004. Frankfurt am Main, Bern, Lang, 1987.

Waldstein, Edith. *Bettine von Arnim and the Politics of Romantic Conversation*. (Studies in German Literature, Linguistics, and Culture, 33.) Columbia, SC: Camden House, 1988.

Werner, Johannes. *Maxe von Arnim: Tochter Bettinas/Gräfin von Oriola 1818–1894. Ein Lebens und Zeitbild aus alten Quellen geschöpft.* Leipzig: Koehler & Amelang, 1937.

Wolf, Christa. "Der Schatten eines Traumes: Karoline von Günderrode—ein Entwurf." *Der Schatten eines Traumes.* Darmstadt and Neuwied: Luchterhand, 1979. 5–65. Also in *Lesen und Schreiben: Neue Sammlung,* 225–283.

———. *Kein Ort. Nirgends.* Darmstadt: Luchterhand, 1979.

———. "Nun ja! Das nächste Leben geht aber heute an. Ein Brief über die Bettine." *Lesen und Schreiben: Neue Sammlung Essays, Aufsätze, Reden.* Darmstadt and Neuwied: Luchterhand, 1980. 284–318.

Wülfing, Wulf. "Zur Mythisierung der Frau im Jungen Deutschland." *Zeitschrift für deutsche Philologie* 99 (1980): 559–581.

Wuthenow, Ralph-Rainer. "Das Hölderlin-Bild im Briefroman 'Die Günderode.' " *Homburg vor der Höhe in der deutschen Geistesgeschichte: Studien zum Freundeskreis von Hegel und Hölderlin.* Eds. Ch. Jamme and Otto Pöggeler. Deutscher Idealismus: Philosophie und Wirkungsgeschichte in Quellen und Studi en 4. Stuttgart: Klett-Cotta, 1981. 318–330.

Wyss, Hilde. *Bettina von Arnims Stellung zwischen der Romantik und dem Jungen Deutschland.* Diss., Bern. Bern and Leipzig: Max Drechsel, 1935.

Zimmermann, Maria. *Bettina von Arnim als Dichterin.* Diss., Basel. Lörrach: Schahl, 1958.

Zurlinden, Luise. *Gedanken Platons in der deutschen Romantik.* Leipzig: H. Hassel Verlag, 1910.

LIST OF CONTRIBUTORS

CLAIRE BALDWIN is assistant professor in Germanic Languages and Literatures at Washington University in St. Louis. She received her Ph.D. in Germanic Languages and Literatures from Yale University in 1992. She has worked on contemporary German Jewish literature and on eighteenth century topics. Her current book project, *Novel Poetics*, addresses narrative strategy and gender in eighteenth century German novels.

BIRGIT EBERT is adjunct assistant professor of German at Jacksonville University and University of North Florida, Jacksonville, Florida. She received her Ph.D. from the University of Maryland in 1994. Publications include: "Johanna Schopenhauer, 1766–1838" (1994) (with Elke Frederiksen); entries on Jutta Heinrich, Elisabeth Plessen and Margot Schröder in *Women Writers of Germany, Austria and Switzerland* (1989); "Leichte Mädchen, hohe Herren und energische Frauen" (1981) (with Mechthild Deutelmoser).

ELKE P. FREDERIKSEN is professor at the University of Maryland/College Park. She received her Ph.D. from the University of Colorado in Boulder in 1973. She has published *Die Frauenfrage in Deutschland 1865–1915* and a book on Austrian writer Franz Grillparzer. She has also edited *Women Writers of Germany, Austria, and Switzerland*, and a book on Luise Rinser is forthcoming. Her numerous articles focus on individual authors in nineteenth and twentieth century German literature (e.g., Johanna Schopenhauer, Bettina von Arnim, Rahel

Varnhagen, Heinrich Heine, Annette von Droste-Hülshoff, Verena Stefan, Luise Rinser), and on German women's social and literary history.

LORELY FRENCH is associate professor of German and Chair of the Foreign Languages Department at Pacific University. She received her Ph.D. from the University of California, Los Angeles in 1986. Her publications include articles on women's epistolary aesthetics and poetics, poetry in women's letters, Louise Aston and George Sand, Dorothea Schlegel, and feminist pedagogy in the foreign language classroom. She has just finished a manuscript on German women as letter-writers from 1750 to 1850.

KATHERINE R. GOODMAN is associate professor of German at Brown University. She received her Ph.D. from the University of Wisconsin. She is the author of *Dis/Closures. Women's Autobiography in Germany 1790–1914* (1986), several articles on German women's autobiography, including two on the epistolary autobiographies of Stägemann and von der Recke. She has also written on the letters and on the reception of Rahel Varnhagen in Germany, on Ellen Key, and on other women authors writing in Germany in the eighteenth and nineteenth centuries. With Edith Waldstein she co-edited *In the Shadow of Olympus. Women Authors in Germany 1790–1810* (1990).

MARJANNE E. GOOZÉ is associate professor of German and Affiliated Faculty in Women's Studies at the University of Georgia. She received her Ph.D. in German literature from the University of California, Berkeley. She has published on German women writers of the 18th–20th centuries, as well as on Kafka and Hölderlin. She has also published "The Definitions of Self and Form in Feminist Autobiography Theory." Currently, she is co-editing an anthology of essays, *International Women's Writing: New Landscapes of Identity.*

HEINZ HÄRTL is a researcher at the Stiftung Weimarer Klassik in Weimar, Germany. In 1971, he received his Ph.D. at the Martin Luther University in Halle. Since 1980 he has been working as a researcher in Weimar. His studies focus on German literary history from the Enlightenment to the *Vormärz,* especially on the later works of Goethe, the *Jena and Heidelberg Romantik,* the reception of literature of the

Goethe period and the relation of Romantic authors to the Jewish question. He is the editor of two volumes of Bettina von Arnim's works, which include *Goethes Briefwechsel mit einem Kinde, Die Günderode,* and *Clemens Brentanos Frühlingskranz.*

DOROTHEE EINSTEIN KRAHN (trans.) was born in Germany and fled to England from the Nazis after the Kristallnacht in 1938. With the help of a scholarship she studied at the University of London and holds two bachelors degrees from there. Her masters (in pure mathematics) and Ph. D. (in measurement and statistics in education) are both from the University of Maryland. After her retirement from the U.S. Government, she returned to her old love for the humanities and did some writing both in English and in German. Her translation of Lou Andreas-Salomé's two novellas "Fenitschka" and "Deviations" (Eine Ausschweifung) was published by the University Press of America in 1990.

PATRICK MCGRATH (trans.) was a Ph.D. candidate at the University of Maryland when he died of AIDS-related complications in 1993. He was co-author of an article published in 1994, "Representing Homo-sexuality: Winckelmann and the Aesthetics of Friendship."

MONIKA SHAFI is associate professor of German at the University of Delaware. She received her Ph.D. From the University of Maryland in 1986. She is the author of *Utopische Entwürfe in der Literatur von Frauen* (1990) and has published articles on Gertrud Kolmar, Annette von Droste-Hülshoff, and other women writers. She is currently working on a monograph on the Jewish poet Gertrud Kolmar.

PATRICIA ANNE SIMPSON is assistant professor in the Department of Germanic Languages and Literatures at the University of Michigan, Ann Arbor. She received her Ph.D. from Yale University. Her recent publications include " 'Wo die Ironie erscheint': Tieck als Herausgeber in den 'Jahrbücher'–Rezensionen," "Entropie, Ästhetik und Ethik im Prenzlauer Berg," and "Orchids and the Mother Tongue: Telling Turkish-German Stories." She currently is conducting research on the politics of popular culture in the former GDR.

ANN WILLISON is a Ph.D. candidate in Comparative Literature at Indiana University. Currently she is based at the University of Bonn, where she teaches English and works in the Office of International Affairs. At the "Bettine Colloquium" in Bad Homburg (1988) she presented a paper entitled "Bettines Kompositionen: Zu einem Notenheft der Sammlung Heineman," which was published in the *International Yearbook* of the Bettina von Arnim Society (1989). In 1990, the Society awarded her a research prize in recognition of her pioneering work in the area of Brentano-von Arnim's compositions.

CHRISTA WOLF is one of the best known and most successful German writers today, and one of the few German-speaking authors whose works have been translated into English. She was born in Landsberg (now in Poland) and resettled in Mecklenburg in 1945. Wolf studied German literature in Jena and Leipzig and has worked in editing and publishing, has been an independent writer, and was visiting professor in Frankfurt/Main (1982) and in Zürich (1987). Wolf has lectured in the United states on several occasions and spent 1992–93 in California on a grant from the Getty Foundation. She has received numerous prestigious literary prizes including the Heinrich-Mann-Preis (1963), the Theodor-Fontane-Preis (1972), the Georg-Büchner-Preis (1980), the Geschwister-Scholl-Preis (1987). Christa Wolf is best known for her books *Nachdenken über Christa T.*, 1968 (*The Quest for Christa T.*); *Kindheitsmuster*, 1976 (*Patterns of Childhood*); and *Kassandra*, 1983 (*Cassandra*).

INDEX

(Biographical information is given only for historical persons.)

Books in the Kritik series

Walter Benjamin: An Intellectual Biography, by Bernd Witte, trans. by James Rolleston, 1991

The Violent Eye: Ernst Junger's Visions and Revisions on the European Right, by Marcus Paul Bullock, 1991

Fatherland: Novalis, Freud, and the Discipline of Romance, by Kenneth S. Calhoon, 1992

Metaphors of Knowledge: Language and Thought in Mauthner's Critique, by Elizabeth Bredeck, 1992

Laocoon's Body and the Aesthetics of Pain: Winckelmann, Lessing, Herder, Moritz, Goethe, by Simon Richter, 1992

The Critical Turn: Studies in Kant, Herder, Wittgenstein, and Contemporary Theory, by Michael Morton, 1993

Reading After Foucault: Institutions, Disciplines, and Technologies of Self in Germany, 1750–1830, edited by Robert S. Leventhal, 1994

Bettina Brentano-von Arnim: Gender and Politics, edited by Elke P. Frederiksen and Katherine R. Goodman, 1995